Let's Keep in Touch

Follow Us

Visit US at

www.learnpersianonline.com

Call

1-469-230-3605

Online

 www.facebook.com/PersiaClubCo

www.twitter.com/PersiaClub

 www.instagram.com/LearnPersianOnline

Online Persian Lessons Via Skype

It's easy! Here's how it works.

1- Request a FREE introductory session.

2- Meet a Persian tutor online via Skype.

3- Start speaking Real Persian in Minutes.

Send Email to: **info@LearnPersianOnline.com**

Or Call: **+1-469-230-3605**

www.learnpersianonline.com

... So Much More Online!

- **FREE Farsi lessons**

- **More Farsi learning books!**

- **Online Farsi – English Dictionary**

- **Online Farsi Tutors**

Looking for an Online Farsi Tutor?

Call us at: 001-469-230-3605

Send email to: Info@learnpersianonline.com

Persian - English Dictionary

فارسی – انگلیسی

By

Reza Nazari
&
Jalal Daie

The Most Trusted Persian - English Dictionary

All inquiries should be addressed to:

info@learnpersianonline.com

www.learnpersianonline.com

ISBN-13: 978-1547026050

ISBN-10: 1547026057

Published by: Learn Persian Online Website

www.learnpersianonline.com

About Learn Persian Online Website

The *"Learn Persian Online Website"* was founded on the belief that everyone interested in Persian language should have the opportunity to learn it!

Established in 2012, the *"Learn Persian Online Website"* creates international opportunities for all people interested in Persian language and culture and builds trust between them. We believe in this cultural relations!

If you want to learn more about Persian, this beautiful language and culture, *"Learn Persian Online Website"* is your best starting point. Our highly qualified Persian experts can help you connect to Persian culture and gain confidence you need to communicate effectively in Persian.

Over the past few years, our professional instructors, unique online resources and publications have helped thousands of Persian learners and students improve their language skills. As a result, these students have gained their goals faster. We love celebrating those victories with our students.

Please view our website at:

www.learnpersianonline.com

About the Author

Reza Nazari is a Persian author. He has published more than 50 Persian learning books including:

- Learn To Speak Persian Fast series,

- Farsi Grammar in Use series,

- Persia Club Dictionary Farsi – English,

- Essential Farsi Idioms,

- Farsi Verbs Dictionary

- Read and Write Persian Language in 7 Days

- Laugh and Learn Farsi: Mulla Nasreddin Tales For Intermediate to Advanced Persian Learners

- Top 50 Persian Poems of All Time

- Farsi Reading: Improve your reading skill and discover the art, culture and history of Iran

- and many more ...

Reza is also a professional Farsi teacher. Over the past eight years, his online Persian lessons have helped thousands of Persian learners and students around the world improve their language skills effectively.

To participate in online Persian classes or ask questions about learning Persian, you can contact Reza via email at: reza@learnpersianonline.com or his Skype ID: rezanazari1

Find Reza's professional profile at:
http://www.learnpersianonline.com/farsi-tutor-reza

Guide to the use of the Dictionary

This dictionary was prepared for English people interested in Persian language. It is dedicated to the Iranian history, culture, and mythology. With a stunningly array of more than 12,000 entries on words, phrases, names, titles, events, and places, it is an invaluable work of reference. And with a comprehensive review of words, it is guaranteed to intrigue, inform, and delight lovers of the Iranian literature, poetry, and culture.

The *Persian - English Dictionary* is intended to serve as a guidebook on the meanings of all words you are most likely to read, hear, and use. The authors attempted to include all the vocabulary you are likely to need. However, no single dictionary contains all words used in a language. New words are always being added to the continually changing language.

The main form of each word given in the dictionary is the accepted Iranian standard spelling. Although there is usually one way that most words can be spelled, sometimes other spellings are also acceptable. However, the spelling given as the headword is the most that most people use.

Finding words in the dictionary

The words that are listed alphabetically in the dictionary are called entry words. The entry word, which is printed in heavy blue type, is the first part of the entry block. An entry block consists of the entry word, its pronunciation, its type (noun, adjective, verb, adverb, pronoun and preposition) and the meanings. It may be long, with many different meanings, or short, with only one meaning.

Words may play different roles in different sentences, however, the most popular one is chosen as the type of the words.

In principle, entries are presented in the singular, except when usage indicates that the plural form is preferred. The plurals of most nouns are formed by adding ها, ان or ات. These kinds of plural are not shown in the dictionary. Some popular irregular and difficult plural forms are shown as headwords, e.g. احوال. Verbs are shown in infinitive format.

The entries, whether they are composed of single or multiple words, are arranged in absolute alphabetical order.

Pronunciation

The regular letters used for written Persian stand for some different sounds. It is usually difficult to tell how a word is pronounced just by looking at how it is spelled. Therefore, it is useful to show the pronunciation of each word separately, using a system of symbols in which each symbol stands for one sound only. After each headword in this dictionary, the word is given again within two slashes to show its pronunciation.

This dictionary uses a simple spelling system to show how entries are pronounced, using the symbols listed below. Sometimes some words have the same spelling and the same pronunciation, yet they have different meanings. If two or more identical headwords are pronounced identically, only the first has a pronunciation given.

Symbol	Example	Symbol	Example
a	hat /hat	m	move /muv
â	cut / cât	n	need /nid
ay	time /tâym	o	gorgeous /gorjes
ch	church /cherch	ô	coat/ côt
d	dog /dâg	u	mood /mud
e	men /men	p	park /pârk
ey	name /neym	r	rise /rais
f	free /fri	s	seven /seven
g	get /get	sh	nation /neishen
h	his /hiz	t	train /treyn
i	feet /fit	v	vary /vari
iyu	cute /kiyut	y	yet /yet
j	jeans /jinz	z	zipper /zipper
k	key /ki	zh	measure /mezher/
kh	loch /lâkh	'	تعظیم/ ta'zim
l	loss /lâs		

Persian Alphabet

The Persian alphabet (الفبای فارسی) consists 32 letters, most of which have two forms, short and full. It is a writing style based on the Arabic script. The Persian script is entirely written cursively. That is, the majority of letters in a word connect to each other. Some of the letters are similar in shape but differ in the place and number of dots. Some others have the same sound but different shape.

Following is a table showing the Persian alphabet and how it is pronounced in English. There are also some examples of how those letters would sound if you place them in a word.

Row	Letters	Persian Alphabet Pronunciation	الفبای فارسی Sample	Pronunciation	Meaning
1.	ا – آ	alef	آب	āb	water
2.	بـ – ب	be	بابا	bābā	father
3.	پـ – پ	pe	پاپ	pāp	the pope
4.	تـ – ت	te	تاب	tāb	swing
5.	ثـ – ث	se	أثاث	asās	furniture
6.	جـ – ج	jim	تاج	tāj	crown
7.	چـ – چ	che	چای	chāi	tea
8.	حـ – ح	he	حَج	haj	pilgrimage
9.	خـ – خ	khe	خانه	khāneh	home
10.	د	dāl	دَرد	dard	pain
11.	ذ	zāl	جَذب	jazb	absorption
12.	ر	re	دَر	dar	door
13.	ز	ze	میز	miz	table
14.	ژ	zhe	ژاپُن	zhāpon	japan
15.	سـ – س	sin	أُستاد	ostād	professor
16.	شـ – ش	shin	دانشجو	dāneshjoo	student
17.	صـ – ص	sād	صَد	sad	hundred
18.	ضـ – ض	zād	وُضو	vozu	ablution

	Persian Alphabet		اَلفبای فارسی		
Row	Letters	Pronunciation	Sample	Pronunciation	Meaning
19.	ط	tā	طَناب	tanāb	rope
20.	ظ	zā	ظُهر	zohr	noon
21.	عـ – ع	eyn	عَدَد	adad	number
22.	غـ – غ	gheyn	شُغل	shoghl	job
23.	فـ – ف	fe	دَفتَر	daftar	notebook
24.	قـ – ق	ghāf	قَهوه	ghahveh	coffee
25.	کـ – ک	kāf	کتاب	ketāb	book
26.	گـ – گ	gāf	دانشگاه	dāneshgāh	university
27.	لـ – ل	lâm	کلاس	kelās	classroom
28.	مـ – م	mim	مات	māt	blur
29.	نـ – ن	nun	نان	nān	bread
30.	و	vāv	وان	vān	bath
31.	هـ ـه ه	he	ماه	māh	moon
32.	یـ – ی	ye	نیم	nim	half

آ – ۱

alef /â, a , e, o/ ▶ first letter of the Persian alphabet

آب

/âb/ ▶ noun
water

آب انبار

/âb anbâr/ ▶ noun
reservoir

آب آوردن (چشم)

/âb âvardan (cheshm)/ ▶ verb
cataract

آب بند

/âb band/ ▶ noun
dam - dyke

آب بندی کردن

/âb bandi kardan/ ▶ verb
caulk

آب بینی

/âbe bini/ ▶ noun
snot - snivel

آب پاش

/âbpâsh/ ▶ noun
pot - sprinkler

آب پاشی کردن

/âbpâshi kardan/ ▶ verb
sprinkle

آب چیزی را گرفتن

/âbe chizi ra gereftan/ ▶ verb
dehydrate

آب دادن

/âb dâdan/ ▶ verb
water - drench

آب دهان

/âbe dahân/ ▶ noun
spittle - spit

آب دهان پرتاب کردن

/âbe dahân partâb kardan/ ▶ verb
spit

آب رفتگی

/âb raftegi/ ▶ noun
shrinkage

آب زلال

/âbe zolâl/ ▶ noun
lymph

آب شور

/âbe shur/ ▶ noun
brine

آب کردن

/âb kardan/ ▶ verb
dissolve

آب گرم کن
/âbgarmkon/ ▶ noun
kettle

آپز کردن
/âbpaz kardan/ ▶ verb
scald

آب مروارید
/âbmorvârid/ ▶ noun
pearl

آبتنی
/âbtani/ ▶ noun
bathe

آب معدنی
/âb madani/ ▶ noun
spa - mineral

آبتنی کردن
/âbtani kardan/ ▶ verb
bath

آب میوه
/âbmive/ ▶ noun
juice

آبجو
/âbjo/ ▶ noun
hop

آب نبات
/âbnabât/ ▶ noun
drop - gumdrop - candy - barleysugar

آبجوساز
/âbjosâz/ ▶ noun
brewer

آب نمک
/âbnamak/ ▶ noun
saltwater - souse - brine

آبجوسازی
/âbjosâzi/ ▶ noun
brewery

آب و هواشناسی
/âbohavâshenâsi/ ▶ noun
climatology

آبخوری
/âbkhori/ ▶ noun
mug

آب وهوا
/âbohavâ/ ▶ noun
weather - climate

آبدار
/âbdâr/ ▶ adjective
succulent - juicy - aqueous

آبادسازی
/âbâdsâzi/ ▶ noun
reclamation

آبدارخانه
/âbdârkhâne/ ▶ noun
pantry

آبراه

/âbrâh/ ▶ noun
canal

آبی

/âbi/ ▶ adjective
blue - watery

آبروریزی

/âbrurizi/ ▶ noun
dishonor

آبی تیره

/âbiye tire/ ▶ adjective
sloe

آبرومند

/âbrumand/ ▶ adjective
honorable - respectful - respectable

آبیاری کردن

/âbyari kardan/ ▶ verb
irrigate

آبزی

/âbzi/ ▶ noun
aquatic

آپارتمان

/âparteman/ ▶ noun
suite - apartment

آبستن

/âbestan/ ▶ noun
pergnant - impregnant

آتش افروز

/âtash afruzi/ ▶ adjective
tinder - incendiary

آبشار

/âbshâr/ ▶ noun
fall - waterfall

آتش بازی

/âtash bazi/ ▶ noun
squib - pyrotechnic - bonfire

آبکی

/âbaki/ ▶ adjective
soupy - watery

آتش زدن

/âtash zadan/ ▶ verb
fire - alight - burn - ignite

آبگوشت

/âbgusht/ ▶ noun
soup - broth - bouillon - cullis - gravy

آتش زنه

/âtashzane/ ▶ noun
punk - silex - light

آبگیر

آتش گرفتن

/âtash gereftan/ ▶ verb
light - inflame - ignite - spunk

/âbgir/ ▶ noun
sluice - basin - pool

آتشفشان
/âtashfeshan/ ▶ noun
geyser- volkano

آخرت
/âkherat/ ▶ noun
hereafter - future

آتشین
/âtashin/ ▶ adjective
empyreal - igneous

آخرین
/âkharin/ ▶ noun
last

آتشی مزاج
/âtashimezâj/ ▶ adjective
passionate - irascible

آخور
/âkhor/ ▶ noun
stall - crib - bin - manger

آثار ادبی
/âsâre adabi/ ▶ noun
literary works

آداب
/âdâb/ ▶ noun
ceremonial - rite

آجر
/âjor/ ▶ noun
brick

آداب نماز
/âdâbe namâz/ ▶ noun
liturgy

آجودان
/âjudan/ ▶ noun
adjutant

آدم
/âdam/ ▶ noun
person - human

آجیل
/âjil/ ▶ noun
nut

آدم برفی
/âdam barfi/ ▶ noun
snowman

آچار
/âchâr/ ▶ noun
spanner - wrench

آدمخوار
/âdamkhâr/ ▶ noun
cannibal

آخر
/âkhar/ ▶ noun
end - finale - ultimate

آدمک
/âdamak/ ▶ noun
caricature - robot

آدمک سرخرمن
/âdamake sare kharman/ ▶ noun
scarecrow

آدمکش
/âdamkoshk/ ▶ noun
assassin

آذرخش
/âzarakhsh/ ▶ noun
lightning - levin

آذوقه
/âzughe/ ▶ noun
supply - provender

آذوقه رساندن
/azughe resândan/ ▶ verb
cater

آراستن
/ârâstan/ ▶ verb
attire - arrange

آراسته
/ârâste/ ▶ adjective
decorous - brisk

آرام کردن
/ârâm kardan/ ▶ verb
calm

آرامش
/ârâmesh/ ▶ noun
calmness - peace

آرامش دادن
/ârâmesh dâdan/ ▶ verb
hush

آرامگاه
/ârâmgâh/ ▶ noun
cemetery

آرایش
/ârâyesh/ ▶ noun
polish - attire - garnish - decor

آرایش دادن
/ârâyesh dâdan/ ▶ verb
decorate - garnish - beautify - adorn

آرد
/ârd/ ▶ noun
flour

آرد کردن
/ârd kardan/ ▶ verb
pound - flour

آرزو کردن
/ârezu kardan/ ▶ verb
aspire - desire - wish

آرزومند
/ârezumand/ ▶ adjective
wistful - desirous - avid - ambitious

آرمان
/ârmân/ ▶ noun
ideal

آرمان گرا
/ârmângarâ/ ► adjective
idealistic

آزادمنش
/âzâdmanesh/ ► adjective
tolerant

آرمانی
/ârmâni/ ► noun
idealistic

آزاده
/âzâdeh/ ► adjective
noble - catholic - liberal

آرمیدن
/âramidan/ ► verb
rest - repose

آزادی
/âzâdi/ ► noun
liberty - freedom

آرنج
/âranj/ ► noun
elbow

آزادی خواه
/âzâdi khâh/ ► adjective
liberal

آره
/are/ ► noun
yes

آزادی عمل
/âzâdiye amal/ ► noun
scope - latitude

آرواره
/ârvâreh/ ► noun
jaw - mandible

آزار
/âzâr/ ► noun
trouble - annoyance - hurt

آروغ
/ârugh/ ► noun
burp - belch

آزاردادن
/âzâr dâdan/ ► verb
trouble - tantalize - excruciate

آزاد
/âzâd/ ► noun
Free - gratis - exempt

آزارنده
/âzârdahandeh/ ► adjective
irritant

آزاد کردن
/âzâd kardan/ ► verb
ease - release - free - liberate - unwrap

آزردگی
/âzordegi/ ► noun
irritation - annoyance

آزردن
/âzordan/ ▶ verb
annoy - aggrieve - hurt

آزمند
/âzmand/ ▶ adjective
greedy - covetous - cormorant - avid - avaricious

آزرده
/âzorde/ ▶ adjective
irksome - indignant

آزمندی
/âzmandi/ ▶ noun
avidity

آزرده کردن
/âzorde kardan/ ▶ verb
chagrin

آزمودن
/âzmudan/ ▶ verb
examination - test

آزمایش
/âzmayesh/ ▶ noun
test - try - examination

آزمون
/âzmun/ ▶ noun
test - examination

آزمایش کردن
/âzmayesh kardan/ ▶ verb
experiment - gauge - quiz

آژیر
/âzhir/ ▶ noun
siren

آزمایش مجدد
/âzmayeshe mojadad/ ▶ noun
retrial

آسان گیر
/âsângir/ ▶ adjective
permissive - lenient - easygoing

آزمایشگاه
/âzmayeshgâh/ ▶ noun
laboratory

آسانسور
/âsânsor/ ▶ noun
elevator

آسایش
/âsâyesh/ ▶ adjective
welfare - comfort - rest

آزمایشی
/âzmayeshi/ ▶ noun
tentative - experimental - pilot

آسایش خاطر
/âsâyeshe khâter/ ▶ adjective
security - relief

آسایشگاه
/âsâyeshgâh/ ▶ noun
sanatorium - nest

آسوده
/âsude/ ▶ adjective
tranquil - calm

آسپرین
/âsperin/ ▶ noun
aspirin

آسیاب
/âsiyab/ ▶ noun
mill

آستانه
/âstâne/ ▶ adjective
threshold

آسیابان
/âsiyâbân/ ▶ noun
miller

آستین
/âstin/ ▶ noun
sleeve

آسیایی
/âsiyayi/ ▶ noun
Asian

آسفالت
/âsfâlt/ ▶ noun
asphalt

آسیب
/âsib/ ▶ noun
damage - hurt - harm - injury

آسمان
/âsemân/ ▶ noun
sky - heaven

آسیب زدن
/âsib zadan/ ▶ verb
hurt - harm

آسمان غرش
/âsemân ghoresh/ ▶ noun
thunder

آشامیدن
/âshamidan/ ▶ verb
drink - swig

آسمانی
/âsemâni/ ▶ noun
skiey - ethereal - heavenly

آسودگی
/âsudegi/ ▶ noun
convenience - ease - relief - comfort -
leisure

آشپز
/âshpaz/ ▶ noun
cook

آشکارا
/âshekârâ/ ▶ adverb
clearly

آشپزخانه
/âshpazkhâneh/ ▶ noun
kitchen

آشکارسازی
/âshkâr sâzi/ ▶ noun
showing - revelation

آشپزی
/âshpazi/ ▶ noun
cookery

آشنا
/âshenâ/ ▶ noun
familiar - acquaintance

آشتی
/âshti/ ▶ noun
reconciliation - peace

آشنا شدن
/âshenâ shodan/ ▶ verb
accustom

آشتی دادن
/âshti dâdan/ ▶ verb
conciliate - reconcile

آشنا کردن
/âshenâ kardan/ ▶ verb
introduce - affiliate

آشتی ناپذیر
/âshti nâpazir/ ▶ noun
irreconcilable

آشنایان
/âshenâyân/ ▶ noun
acquaintance

آشفتگی
/âshoftegi/ ▶ noun
disorder - chaos

آشنایی
/âshenâyi/ ▶ noun
acquaintance

آشفتن
/âshoftan/ ▶ verb
disturb - agitate

آشفته
/âshofte/ ▶ adjective
messy - phrenetic - turbulent

آشوب
/âshub/ ▶ noun
turbulence - tumult - convulsion - riot

آشکار شدن
/âshekâr shodan/ ▶ verb
reveal - unfold - peep

آشیان گرفتن
/âshiyân gereftan/ ▶ verb
nestle - nest

آشیانه

/âshiyâneh/ ► noun
nest

آفتاب

/âftâb/ ► noun
sun

آشیانه هواپیما

/âshiyâneh havâpeimâ/ ► noun
hangar

آفتاب زدگی

/âftâb zadegi/ ► noun
sunburn

آغاز تاریخ

/âghaze târikh/ ► noun
era

آفتابه

/âftâbe/ ► noun
pitcher

آغاز شدن

/âghâz shodan/ ► verb
begin

آفتابی

/âftâbi/ ► adjective
shiny - sunny - bright

آغاز کردن

/âghâz kardan/ ► verb
initial - begin - commence

آفریدگار

/âfaridegâr/ ► noun
creator

آغشتن

/âgheshtan/ ► verb
saturate - smear - imbue

آفریده

/âfaride/ ► noun
creature

آغل

/âghol/ ► noun
corral - pound - pen

آفریقا

/âfrighâ/ ► noun
Africa

آغوش

/âghush/ ► noun
lap - heart - breast

آفریقایی

/âfrighâyi/ ► noun
african

آفت

/âfat/ ► noun
pestilence - pest

آفرین

/âfarin/ ► adjective
hurrah - bravo

آفرینش
/âfarinesh/ ▶ noun
creation

آگهی دادن
/âgahi dâdan/ ▶ verb
announce - advertise

آقا
/âghâ/ ▶ noun
sir - gentleman

آگهی فوت
/âgahi fôt/ ▶ noun
necrology

آکادمی
/âkademi/ ▶ noun
academy

آلایش
/âlâyesh/ ▶ noun
stain

آکسفورد
/âksford/ ▶ noun
oxford

آلت
/âlat/ ▶ noun
tool - organ - instrumental - instrument

آگاه
/âgâh/ ▶ adjective
conscious - cognizant - aware

آلت تناسلی زن
/âlate tanâsoliye zan/ ▶ noun
gash

آگاه کردن
/âgâh kardan/ ▶ verb
acquaint - inform - warn

آلت تناسلی مرد
/âlate tanâsoliye mard/ ▶ noun
phallus

آگاهانیدن
/âgâhânidan/ ▶ verb
advise

آلت دست
/âlate dast/ ▶ adjective
tool - stooge

آگاهی
/âgâhi/ ▶ noun
knowledge - acquaintance - intelligence

آلمان
/âlmân/ ▶ noun
Germany

آگهی
/âgahi/ ▶ noun
notice - advertisement

آلمانی
/âlmâni/ ▶ noun

German

آلوچه
/âluche/ ► noun
sloe

آلودن
/âludan/ ► verb
pollute - smear

آلوده
/âlude/ ► adjective
spotty - unclean

آلوده کردن
/âlude kardan/ ► verb
infect - muck - mess

آلوده کننده
/âlude konande/ ► adjective
pollutant

آماتور
/âmâtor/ ► noun
unprofessional - amateur

آمادگی
/âmâdegi/ ► noun
readiness - preparation

آماده
/âmâde/ ► adjective
ready - beforehand - apt - able - present
provided

آماده بودن
/âmâde budan/ ► verb
ready

آماده جنگ
/âmâdeye jang/ ► adjective
warlike

آماده ساختن
/âmâde sâkhtan/ ► verb
prepare

آماده شدن
/âmâde shodan/ ► verb
prepare

آمار
/âmâr/ ► noun
statistics

آمارگر
/âmârgar/ ► noun
statistician

آماری
/âmâri/ ► noun
statistic

آماس معده
/âmâse me'de/ ► noun
gastritis

آمبولانس
/âmbolâns/ ► noun
ambulance

آمپول زدن
/âmpul zadan/ ► verb
shoot

آموزش و پرورش
/âmush va parvaresh/ ▶ noun
education and development

آمد و شد
/âmado shod/ ▶ noun
traffic

آموزشکده
/âmuzeshkade/ ▶ noun
juniorcollege

آمدن
/âmadan/ ▶ verb
come

آموزشگاه
/âmuzeshgâh/ ▶ noun
academy - school

آمدن و رفتن
/âmadan va raftan/ ▶ verb
belabor

آموزشی
/âmuzeshi/ ▶ noun
didactic

آمرزش
/âmorzesh/ ▶ noun
remission - pardon

آموزگار
/âmuzegâr/ ▶ noun
teacher - instructor

آمرزیدن
/âmorzidan/ ▶ verb
absolve - remit - forgive

آموزنده
/âmuzande/ ▶ adjective
instructive - informative

آمریکا
/âmrikâ/ ▶ noun
America

آمیختن
/âmikhtan/ ▶ verb
compound - mix

آمریکایی
/âmrikâyi/ ▶ noun
American

آمیزش
/âmizesh/ ▶ noun
mixture

آموختن
/âmukhtan/ ▶ verb
teach

آن
/ân/ ▶ pronoun
that -moment - it

آموزش
/âmuzesh/ ▶ noun
instruction - training

آناليز

/ânâliz/ ▶ noun
analysis

آنتن

/ânten/ ▶ noun
antenna

آنجا

/ânjâ/ ▶ adverb
there

آنچه

/ânche/ ▶ pronoun
whatever - what

آنزیم

/ânzim/ ▶ noun
enzyme

آنگاه

/ângah/ ▶ adverb
then

آنها

/ânhâ/ ▶ pronoun
those - they

آنی

/âni/ ▶ noun
memnetary - immediate

آه کشیدن

/âh keshidan/ ▶ verb
sigh

آهار

/âhâr/ ▶ noun
starch - souse

آهسته

/âheste/ ▶ adjective
slow

آهسته زدن

/âheste zadan/ ▶ verb
dab

آهسته کردن

/âheste kardan/ ▶ verb
slacken - decelerate

آهک

/âhak/ ▶ noun
lime

آهن

/âhan/ ▶ noun
iron

آهن آلات

/âhan âlât/ ▶ noun
ironwork - ironware

آهن ربا

/âhanrobâ/ ▶ noun
magnet

آهنگ

/âhang/ ▶ noun
music - intonation

آهنگر
/âhangar/ ▶ noun
smithy - blacksmith

آواره بودن
/âvâre budan/ ▶ verb
wander

آهنگری
/âhangari/ ▶ noun
smithy

آواز
/âvâz/ ▶ noun
song - sing

آهنین
/âhanin/ ▶ adjective
steely

آوازه
/âvâze/ ▶ noun
fame - reputation - renown - hearsay

آهو
/âhu/ ▶ noun
defect - asthma

آوردن
/âvardan/ ▶ verb
bring

آوا
/âvâ/ ▶ noun
sound - phone

آوریل
/âvril/ ▶ noun
April

آوار
/âvâr/ ▶ noun
collapse - debris

آووکادو
/âvokâdo/ ▶ noun
avocado

آوارگی
/âvâregi/ ▶ noun
tramp

آویختن
/âvikhtan/ ▶ verb
hangout - hang

آواره
/âvâre/ ▶ adjective
adrift - immigrant

آویخته
/âvikhte/ ▶ adjective
pendant - hung - underhung - dropper

آواره بودن
/âvâre budan/ ▶ verb
tramp

آویز
/âviz/ ▶ noun
earring - lobe

آویزان

/âvizân/ ► adjective
suspension - dangle

آینده نگری

/âyandenegari/ ► noun
providence

آویزان بودن

/âvizân budan/ ► verb
overhang - dangle

آیین

/âyin/ ► noun
ethic - religion - ordinance - order

آویزان کردن

/âvizân kardan/ ► verb
hang - dangle

آیین تشریفات

/âyine tashrifât/ ► noun
solemnity

آویزانی

/âvizâni/ ► noun
suspension - suspense

آیین دادرسی

/âyine dâdrasi/ ► noun
procedure

آویزه

/âvizeh/ ► noun
lug - appendix - pendant

آیین دینی

/âyine dini/ ► noun
sacrament - cult

آیا

/âyâ/ ► adverb
whether - if

آیین عشای ربانی

/âyine ashâye rabâni/ ► noun
communion

آیت

/âyat/ ► noun
sign

آیین نامه

/âyin nâme/ ► noun
bylaw - regulation

آینده

/âyande/ ► noun
future

آیین و مراسم

/âyin va marâsem/ ► noun
order

آینده نگر

/âyandenegar/ ► adjective
provident

آیینه

/âyine/ ► noun
mirror

ائتلاف کردن
/e'telâf/ ▶ verb
pool - coalesce

ابدیت
/abadiyat/ ▶ noun
immortality - eternity

ائتلافی
/e'telâfi/ ▶ noun
federal

ابر
/abr/ ▶ noun
cloud

ابتدا
/ebtedâ/ ▶ noun
outset - start

ابراز داشتن
/ebrâz dâshtan/ ▶ verb
evince

ابتذال
/ebtezâl/ ▶ noun
truism - triviality - platitude

ابراز شادی
/ebrâze shâdi/ ▶ noun
merriment

ابتکار
/ebtekâr/ ▶ noun
initiative - shebang

ابردار کردن
/abrdâr kardan/ ▶ verb
overcast

ابد
/abad/ ▶ noun
lifetime - perpetuity

ابرمرد
/abarmard/ ▶ noun
superman

ابدا
/abadan/ ▶ adverb
never - whatsoever

ابرو
/abru/ ▶ noun
eyebrow

ابداع
/ebdâ'e/ ▶ noun
innovation

ابری
/abri/ ▶ noun
overcast - cloudy

ابداع کردن
/ebdâ'e kardan/ ▶ verb
innovate - mastermind

ابری بودن
/abri budan/ ▶ verb
cloudy

ابریشم
/abrisham/ ▶ noun
silk

ابلق
/ablagh/ ▶ noun
pied - piebald

ابریشمی
/abrishami/ ▶ noun
silky - silken

ابله
/ablah/ ▶ noun
silly - fool

ابزار
/abzâr/ ▶ noun
tool - gadget

ابلهانه
/ablahane/ ▶ adverb
idiotic

ابطال
/ebtâl/ ▶ noun
disproof - nullification

ابلیس
/eblis/ ▶ noun
satan

ابعاد
/ab'âd/ ▶ noun
dimensions

ابهام
/ebhâm/ ▶ noun
ambiguity - haze - obscurity

ابقا
/ebgha/ ▶ noun
retention

اپرا
/operâ/ ▶ noun
opera

ابلاغ
/eblagh/ ▶ noun
prophecy

اتاق
/otâgh/ ▶ noun
room

ابلاغ رسمی
/eblaghe rasmi/ ▶ noun
communique

اتاق جراحی
/otâghe jarâhi/ ▶ noun
surgery

ابلاغ کردن
/eblagh kardan/ ▶ verb
impart

اتاق خواب
/otâghe khâb/ ▶ noun
chamber

اتفاق
/etefâgh/ ▶ noun
accidence - occurrence - event

اتاق مطالعه
/otâghe motâle'e/ ▶ noun
study

اتفاق افتادن
/etefâgh oftâdan/ ▶ verb
occur

اتاق نشیمن
/otâghe neshiman/ ▶ noun
sittingroom

اتفاقا
/etefâghan/ ▶ adverb
perchance - peradventure - by chance

اتاقک
/otâghak/ ▶ noun
module

اتفاقی
/etefâghi/ ▶ noun
chancy - chanceful - chance

اتحاد
/etehâd/ ▶ noun
solidarity - league - band

اتکا
/etekâ/ ▶ noun
reliance

اتحادیه
/etehâdiye/ ▶ noun
league - union - confederacy

اتلاف
/etlâf/ ▶ noun
destruction - waste - wastage

اتخاذ
/etekhâz/ ▶ noun
assumption - adoption

اتلاف وقت
/etlâfe vaght/ ▶ noun
dawdle

اتخاذ کردن
/etekhâz kardan/ ▶ verb
pursue - adopt

اتم
/atom/ ▶ noun
atom

اتصال
/etesâl/ ▶ noun
junction - union - linkage - conjuncture

اتصال دادن
/etesâl dâdan/ ▶ verb
bridge - connect

اتمام

/etmâm/ ▶ noun
completion

اتمام حجت

/etmâme hojat/ ▶ noun
ultimatum

اتهام

/etehâm/ ▶ noun
denunciation - charge

اتو

/out/ ▶ noun
iron

اتو زدن

/out zadan/ ▶ verb
press - iron

اتو کردن

/out kardan/ ▶ verb
iron

اتوبان

/otobân/ ▶ noun
highway

اتوبوس

/otobus/ ▶ noun
bus

اتومبیل

/ototomobil/ ▶ noun
automobile

اتیکت

/etiket/ ▶ noun
label

اتیکت چسباندن به

/etiket chasbândan be/ ▶ verb
tag

اثاث

/asâs/ ▶ noun
furnishings

اثبات

/esbât/ ▶ noun
proof

اثبات کردن

/esbât kardan/ ▶ verb
prove - affirm

اثر

/asar/ ▶ noun
trace - impression - vestige

اثر باقی مانده

/asare baghimânde/ ▶ noun
hangover

اثر تاریخی

/asare târikhi/ ▶ noun
monument

اثر زخم

/asare zakhm/ ▶ noun
scab

اثر زخم داشتن
/asare zakhm dâshtan/ ▶ verb
scar

اجاره کردن
/ejâre kardan/ ▶ verb
rent

اثر سوختگی
/asare sukhtegi/ ▶ noun
burn

اجاره نامه
/ejârename/ ▶ noun
lease - rental

اثر گذاشتن
/asar gozâshtan/ ▶ verb
trace

اجاره نشین
/ejâreneshin/ ▶ noun
tenant

اجابت
/ejâbat/ ▶ noun
compliance

اجازه
/ejâre/ ▶ noun
authority - permit - permission

اجابت کردن
/ejâbat kardan/ ▶ verb
comply

اجازه عبور
/ejâzeye obur/ ▶ noun
passage

اجاره
/ejâre/ ▶ noun
hire - lease - rent

اجازه نامه
/ejâzename/ ▶ noun
billet - charter

اجاره ای
/ejâre'I/ ▶ noun
rental

اجاق
/ojâgh/ ▶ noun
oven

اجاره دادن
/ejâre dâdan/ ▶ verb
lease - rent

اجبار
/ejbâr/ ▶ noun
compulsion - coercion

اجاره دار
/ejâredâr/ ▶ noun
tenant - lessee

اجبارا
/ejbâran/ ▶ adverb
perforce

اجرا کردن
/ejrâ kardan/ ▶ verb
exert - execute - perform

اجباری
/ejbâri/ ▶ noun
compulsory - compulsive - mandatory

اجرای نمایش
/ejrâye namâyesh/ ▶ noun
histrionics

اجتماع کردن
/ejtemâ'e kardan/ ▶ verb
congregate

اجرایی
/ejrâyee/ ▶ noun
executive

اجتماع مردم
/ejtemâ'e mardom/ ▶ noun
parade

اجرت
/ojrat/ ▶ noun
wage - pay

اجتماعی
/ejtemâ'I/ ▶ noun
social - collective - civic

اجماع
/ejmâ'e/ ▶ noun
consensus

اجتناب
/ejtenâb/ ▶ noun
avoid

اجمال
/ejmâl/ ▶ noun
synopsis - conspectus

اجتناب کردن
/ejtenâb kardan/ ▶ verb
avoid - eschew

اجتناب ناپذیر
/ejtenâbpazir/ ▶ noun
inevitable - unavoidable

اجمالی
/ejmâli/ ▶ adjective
curt - glancing

اجداد
/ajdâd/ ▶ noun
ancestor - predecessor

اجنبی
/ajnabi/ ▶ noun
barbarian

اجرا
/ejrâ/ ▶ noun
performance - implementation

اجیر

/ajir/ ▶ noun
hireling

احترام نظامی

/ehterâme nezami/ ▶ noun
salute

اجیر کردن

/ajir kardan/ ▶ verb
wage - hire

احتکار

/ehtekâr/ ▶ noun
hoarding - hoard

احاطه

/ehâte/ ▶ noun
siege - surround

احتمال

/ehtemâl/ ▶ noun
probability - possibility – likelihood

احاطه شدن

/ehâte shodan/ ▶ verb
surround

احتمال وقوع

/ehtemâle voghu'e/ ▶ noun
odds

احتمالا

/ehtemâlan/ ▶ adverb
perhaps - maybe - presumably

احاطه کردن

/ehâte kardan/ ▶ verb
sphere - circuit - encircle

احتمالی

/ehtemâli/ ▶ noun
probable - likely

احتراق

/ehterâgh/ ▶ noun
combustion - ignition

احتیاج

/ehtiyâj/ ▶ noun
requirement - need - necessity

احتراق پذیر

/ehterâgh pazir/ ▶ adjective
combustible

احتیاط

/ehtiyât/ ▶ noun
precaution - caution

احترام

/ehterâm/ ▶ noun
respect - curtsy - respectability

احداث کردن

/ehdâs kardan/ ▶ verb
generate - establish

احترام گذاردن

/ehterâm gozâshtan/ ▶ verb
respect

احرازمالکیت

/ehrâze mâlekiyat/ ▶ noun
seisin

احساس

/ehsâs/ ▶ noun
sense - sensation

احساس غربت

/ehsâse ghorbat/ ▶ noun
nostalgia

احساس کردن

/ehsâs kardan/ ▶ verb
sense - feel - appreciate

احساسات

/ehsâsât/ ▶ noun
emotions

احساساتی

/ehsâsâti/ ▶ adjective
sensational - pathetic - passionate

احسان

/ehsân/ ▶ noun
benefit - beneficence

احسان کردن

/ehsân kardan/ ▶ verb
benefit

احشام

/ahshâm/ ▶ noun
chattels

احضار قانونی کردن

/ehzâre ghânuni kardan/ ▶ verb
summon

احضاریه

/ehzâriye/ ▶ noun
subpoena

احمق

/ahmagh/ ▶ noun
stupid - fool

احیا

/ehyâ/ ▶ noun
revival - reclamation

احیا شدن

/ehyâ shodan/ ▶ verb
revive

اخاذی کردن

/akhâzi/ ▶ verb
extortion

اخبار

/akhbâr/ ▶ noun
news - information

اختر

/akhtar/ ▶ noun
star

اختراع

/ekhterâ'e/ ▶ noun
invention - device

اختراع کردن
/ekhterâ'e kardan/ ► verb
invent

اخترشناس
/akhtarshenâsi/ ► noun
astronomer

اختصار
/ekhtesâr/ ► noun
abbreviation - brevity

اختصاری
/ekhtesâri/ ► adjective
abbreviations

اختصاص
/ekhtesâs/ ► noun
allocation

اختصاص دادن
/ekhtesâs dâdan/ ► verb
allocate - devote - dedicate

اختصاصی
/ekhtesâsi/ ► adjective
specific

اختفا
/ekhtefâ/ ► noun
secrecy

اختلاس
/ekhtelâs/ ► noun
embezzlement

اختلاس کردن
/ekhtelâs kardan/ ► verb
embezzle - defalcate

اختلاط
/ekhtelât/ ► noun
welter - integrate - mixture - mix

اختلاف
/ekhtelâf/ ► noun
difference

اختلاف پیدا کردن
/ekhtelâf peidâ kardan/ ► verb
diverge

اختلاف داشتن
/ekhtelâf dâshtan/ ► verb
differ

اختلاف عقیده
/ekhtelâfe aghide/ ► noun
dissension

اختلال روانی
/ekhtelâle ravâani/ ► noun
neurosis

اختناق
/ekhtenâgh/ ► noun
choke - asphyxia

اخم کردن
/akhm kardan/ ▶ verb
scowl - glower - pout - lower

اختیاری
/ekhtiyâri/ ▶ adjective
voluntary - free

اخمو
/akhmu/ ▶ adjective
moody

اخذ
/akhz/ ▶ noun
grasp - catch

اخیر
/akhir/ ▶ noun
recent - late - last

اخراج
/ekhrâj/ ▶ noun
dismissal

اخیرا
/akhiran/ ▶ adverb
late - new

اخراج کردن
/ekhrâj kardan/ ▶ verb
exorcize

ادا
/adâ/ ▶ noun
gesture

اخطار
/ekhtâr/ ▶ noun
alarm - notification - notice

ادا کردن
/adâ kardan/ ▶ noun
pronounce - express - discourse

اخطار کردن
/ekhtâr kardan/ ▶ verb
notify - announce

اداره
/edâre/ ▶ noun
organization - office - bureau

اخلاق
/akhlâgh/ ▶ noun
morality - moral

اداره کردن
/edâre kardan/ ▶ verb
direct - manage

اخلاقی
/akhlâghi/ ▶ adjective
moral

اداره کننده
/edâre konande/ ▶ noun
director

اخم
/akhm/ ▶ noun
scowl - glower

اداره گمرک
/edâre gomrok/ ▶ noun
custom house

ادراری
/edâri/ ▶ noun
administrative - ministerial

ادامه
/edâme/ ▶ noun
continuance

ادامه یافتن
/edâme yâftan/ ▶ verb
resume

ادب
/adab/ ▶ noun
curtsy - complaisance - gentry

ادب کردن
/adab kardan/ ▶ verb
punish

ادب و نزاکت
/adab va nezâkat/ ▶ noun
attention

ادبی
/adabi/ ▶ adjective
didactic - literary

ادبیات
/adabiyât/ ▶ noun
literature

ادرار
/edrâr/ ▶ noun
urine

ادرار کردن
/edrâr kardan/ ▶ verb
stool - urinate

ادراک
/edrâk/ ▶ noun
realization - cognition - perception - understanding

ادعا
/ede'â/ ▶ noun
claim

ادعا کردن
/ede'â/ ▶ verb
acclaim - claim

ادعای پوچ
/ede'aye puch/ ▶ noun
jactitation

ادغام
/edghâm/ ▶ noun
merger

ادغام کردن
/edghâm kardan/ ▶ verb
umlaut

ادیب
/adib/ ▶ noun
bookman - literary - scholar

اراده کردن
/erâde kardan/ ▶ verb
will

ادیبانه
/adibâne/ ▶ adverb
literary

اذن
/ezn/ ▶ noun
permission - leave

ارادی
/erâdi/ ▶ adjective
voluntary

اذیت
/azyat/ ▶ noun
tease - annoyance

اراذل
/arâzel/ ▶ noun
gangster

اذیت کردن
/azyat kardan/ ▶ verb
annoy - tease

ارباب
/arbâb/ ▶ noun
lord - boss - master

ارائه
/erâ'e/ ▶ noun
show - presentation - representation - offer

ارباب رجوع
/arbâbroju'e/ ▶ noun
client

ارتباط
/ertebât/ ▶ noun
correlation - relevance - relation - liaison

ارائه دادن
/erâ'e dâdan/ ▶ verb
offer- present

ارتجاع
/ertejâ'e/ ▶ noun
stretch - restitution

ارابه
/arâbe/ ▶ noun
wagon - cart

ارتداد
/ertedâd/ ▶ noun
apostasy - heterodoxy - heresy

اراده
/erâde/ ▶ noun
will

ارتش

/artesh/ ▶ noun
military - army

ارتشی

/arteshi/ ▶ adjective
military

ارتعاش

/erte'âsh/ ▶ noun
shake - vibration

ارتفاع

/ertefâ'e/ ▶ noun
height

ارتقا

/erteghâ/ ▶ noun
gradation - preferment

ارث

/ers/ ▶ noun
inheritance - heritage

ارث بردن

/ers bordan/ ▶ verb
inheritance

ارثیه

/ersiye/ ▶ noun
heritage

ارج

/arj/ ▶ noun
value

ارجاع کردن

/erjâ'e kardan/ ▶ verb
assign

ارجمند

/arjmand/ ▶ adjective
venerable

اردک

/ordak/ ▶ noun
duck

اردو زدن

/ordu zadan/ ▶ verb
encamp - camp

اردوگاه

/ordugâh/ ▶ noun
camp

ارزان

/arzân/ ▶ adjective
jitney - cutrate - cheap - inexpensive

ارزش

/arzesh/ ▶ noun
value

ارزیاب

/arzyâb/ ▶ noun
assessor - appraiser

ارکان
/arkân/ ▶ noun
elements

ارزیابی
/arzyâbi/ ▶ noun
assess - appraisal - evaluation

ارکستر
/orkester/ ▶ noun
band

ارسال
/ersâl/ ▶ noun
post

اروپا
/orupâ/ ▶ noun
Europe

ارسال داشتن
/ersâl dâshtan/ ▶ verb
send

اروپایی
/orupâyee/ ▶ adjective
European

ارشد
/arshad/ ▶ adjective
superior - senior

اریب
/orib/ ▶ adjective
slant - sidle - oblique - diagonal

ارشدیت
/arshadiyat/ ▶ noun
seniority - primogeniture

از ابتدا
/az ebtedâ/ ▶ adjective
uppermost

ارضا
/erzâ/ ▶ noun
satisfaction

ارضا کردن
/erzâ kardan/ ▶ verb
ingratiate

از این رو
/az in ru/ ▶ adverb
hence - since - therefore

ارضی
/arzi/ ▶ adjective
territorial

از بر خواندن
/az bar khândan/ ▶ verb
recite

ارعاب کردن
/er'âb kardan/ ▶ verb
menace

از بر کردن
/az bar kardan/ ▶ verb
memorize - con

از خواب برخاستن
/az khâb barkhâstan/ ▶ verb
rise - uprise

از بین بردن
/az bein bordan/ ▶ verb
elimination

از خواب بیدار شدن
/akh khâb bidâr shodan/ ▶ verb
rouse

از بین رفتن
/az bein raftan/ ▶ verb
waste

از خواب بیدار کردن
/az khâb bidâr kardan/ ▶ verb
wake

از جا پریدن
/az jâ paridan/ ▶ verb
jump

از خود راضی
/az khod râzi/ ▶ adjective
overbearing - cocky - smug

از جا جستن
/az jâ jastan/ ▶ verb
jump

از دست رفته
/az dast rafte/ ▶ adjective
lost

از جان گذشته
/az jân gozashte/ ▶ adjective
desperate

از جمله
/azjomle/ ▶ preposition
among

از راه خشکی
/az râhe khoshki/ ▶ adjective
overland

از چه طریق
/az che darigh/ ▶ adverb
how

از سر تا پا
/az sar tâ pâ/ ▶ adverb
cap-a-pie

از خاک در آوردن
/az khâk dar âvardan/ ▶ verb
excavate

از سر گرفتن
/az sar gereftan/ ▶ verb
resume - renovate

از خطر آگاهانیدن
/az khatar rahânidan/ ▶ verb
alarm

از مبدا
/az mabda'e/ ► preposition
the origin

از میان
/az miyâne/ ► adverb
across

از میان برداشتن
/az miyân bardâshtan/ ► verb
surmount

از میان بردن
/az miyân bordan/ ► verb
wipe - abolish

از نو
/az no/ ► adverb
anew - again - afresh

از هم باز شدن
/az ham bâz shodan/ ► verb
unbraid

از هم باز کردن
/az ham bâz kardan/ ► verb
break - untwine - unravel - unlink

از هم جدا کردن
/az ham jodâ kardan/ ► verb
scatter - split - wedge

از وسط
/az vasat/ ► preposition
through - across

از سرگیری
/az sargiri/ ► noun
resumption

از طرف
/az tarafe/ ► preposition
behalf - for - of

از طریق
/az tarighe/ ► preposition
via

از قلم انداختن
/az ghalam andâkhtan/ ► verb
slip - drop - omit

از قید رها شدن
/az gheid rahâ shodan/ ► verb
unfetter

از کار افتادگی
/az kâr oftâdegi/ ► noun
paralysis

از کار افتاده
/az kâr oftâde/ ► adjective
lameduck - obsolete

از گرسنگی مردن
/az gorosnegi mordan/ ► verb
starve

از لحاظ
/az lahâze/ ► preposition
of

از وقتی که

/az vaghtike/ ▶ adverb
since

ازهم پاشیدن

/az ham pâshidan/ ▶ verb
dissipate - disintegrate - decompose

از یاد بردن

/az yâd bordan/ ▶ verb
unlearn

اژدر

/azhdar/ ▶ noun
torpedo

ازاین جهت

/az in jahat/ ▶ adverb
hence

اژدها

/ezhdehâ/ ▶ noun
dragon

ازدحام

/ezdehâm/ ▶ noun
huddle - crowd - throng

اسارت

/esârat/ ▶ noun
bondage - captivity

ازدحام کردن

/ezdehâm kardan/ ▶ verb
throng - crowd - overcrowd

اساس

/asâs/ ▶ noun
element - root - base

ازدست دادن

/az dast dâdan/ ▶ verb
lose

اساسنامه

/asâsnâme/ ▶ noun
statute

ازدواج

/ezdevâj/ ▶ noun
marriage

اساسی

/asâsi/ ▶ adjective
vital - basic - fundametal

ازلی

/azali/ ▶ adjective
eternal

اساطیر

/asâtir/ ▶ noun
mythology

ازلیت

/azaliyat/ ▶ noun
eternity

اسب

/asb/ ▶ noun
horse

اسب چوبی
/asbe chubi/ ▶ noun
hobbyhorse

استاد
/ostâd/ ▶ noun
professor - master

اسب سوار
/asb savâr/ ▶ noun
cavalier - horseman

استادانه
/ostâdâne/ ▶ adverb
scholastic - deft - professorial

اسب سواری
/asb savâri/ ▶ noun
riding

استبداد
/estebdâd/ ▶ noun
autarchy

اسباب
/asbâb/ ▶ noun
tool – thing - material

استبدادی
/estebdâdi/ ▶ adjective
reactionary - autocratic - absolute

اسباب بازی
/asbâb bâzi/ ▶ noun
toy - plaything

استتار
/estetâr/ ▶ noun
camouflage

اسباب زحمت
/asbâbe zahmat/ ▶ adjective
encumbrance - inconvenience

استحاله
/estehâle/ ▶ noun
permutation

اسباب سفر
/asbâbe safar/ ▶ noun
caboodle

استحقاق
/estehghâgh/ ▶ noun
merit

اسبق
/asbagh/ ▶ noun
prior - predecessor

استحکام
/estehkâm/ ▶ noun
stability - rigidity - consistency

اسپانیا
/espâniyâ/ ▶ noun
spain

استحکامات
/estehkâmât/ ▶ noun
defence - defense

استخوان بندی
/ostokhânbandi/ ► noun
skeleton - anatomy - bone

استحمام
/estehmâm/ ► noun
bath

استخوانی
/ostokhâni/ ► adjective
bony

استحمام کردن
/estehmâm kardan/ ► verb
bathe

استدعا
/ested'â/ ► noun
plea - boon - entreaty

استخدام
/estekhdâm/ ► noun
recruitment

استدعا کردن
/ested'â kardan/ ► verb
entreat - beg

استخدام کردن
/estekhdâm kardan/ ► verb
employ

استدلال
/estedlâl/ ► noun
logic - reasoning - ratiocination -
thought

استخر
/estakhr/ ► noun
pool

استخر شنا
/estakhre shena/ ► noun
swimming pool

استدلال کننده
/estedlâl konande/ ► noun
proponent

استخراج
/estekhrâj/ ► noun
derivation

استدلالی
/estedlâli/ ► adjective
logical - discursive

استخراج کردن
/estekhrâj kardan/ ► verb
extract - exploit - educe

استراتژی
/esterâtezhi/ ► noun
strategy

استخوان
/ostokhân/ ► noun
bone

استراحت
/esterâhat/ ► noun
rest - relaxation

استعداد ذاتی
/este'dâde zâti/ ► noun
natural talent

استراحتگاه
/esterâhatgâh/ ► noun
retire room

استعفا
/estefâ/ ► noun
resignation

استراق سمع کردن
/esterâghe sam'e kardan/ ► verb
eavesdrop - overhear

استعفا دادن
/estefâ dâdan/ ► verb
abdicate

استرداد
/esterdâd/ ► noun
retraction - refund

استعلام
/este'lâm/ ► noun
inquiry

استشمام
/esteshmâm/ ► noun
smell

استعمار
/este'mâr/ ► noun
colonization

استشمام کردن
/esteshmâm kardan/ ► verb
inhale - sniff

استعمارطلب
/este'mârtalab/ ► adjective
imperialistic

استطاعت
/estetâ'at/ ► noun
ability

استعمال
/este'mâl/ ► noun
use - usage

استعاره
/este'âre/ ► noun
metaphor

استعمال کردن
/este'mâl kardan/ ► verb
employ - apply - handle

استعداد
/este'dâd/ ► noun
talent - aptitude

استغفار
/esteghfâr/ ► noun
retraction

استکان
/estekân/ ▶ noun
glass

استماع
/estemâ'e/ ▶ noun
listen - audition

استمرار
/estemrâr/ ▶ noun
continuity

استمهال
/estemhâl/ ▶ noun
moratorium

استنباط
/estenbât/ ▶ noun
deduction - presumption

استنباط کردن
/estenbât kardan/ ▶ verb
infer - induct - educe - deduce

استنتاج
/estentâj/ ▶ noun
deduction - inference

استنتاج کردن
/estentâj kardan/ ▶ verb
induce - evolve - conclude

استنشاق
/estenshâgh/ ▶ noun
inspiration - inhalation

استغنا
/esteghnâ/ ▶ noun
disdain

استفاده
/estefâde/ ▶ noun
benefit - beneficiary - utilization - use

استفراغ
/estefrâgh/ ▶ noun
vomiting - puke

استفراغ کردن
/estefrâgh kardan/ ▶ verb
disgorge - vomit

استفسار
/estefsâr/ ▶ noun
query

استفهام
/estefhâm/ ▶ noun
question

استقامت
/esteghâmat/ ▶ noun
perseverance

استقرار
/esteghrâr/ ▶ noun
pitch

استقلال
/esteghlâl/ ▶ noun
independence - freedom

استنطاق

/estentâgh/ ► noun
crossquestion

اسراف

/esrâf/ ► noun
profusion - improvidence - prodigality

استهزا

/estehzâ'e/ ► noun
ridicule

اسراف کردن

/esrâf kardan/ ► verb
dissipate - lavish

استهلاک

/estehlâk/ ► noun
depreciation

اسراییل

/esrâ'il/ ► noun
Israel

استوار

/ostovâr/ ► noun
stable - immovable - constant

اسطوره

/osture/ ► noun
myth

اسفنج

/esfanj/ ► noun
sponge

استوار کردن

/ostovâr kardan/ ► verb
fix - firm - stabilize

استوانه

/ostovâne/ ► noun
cannon - roller - cylinder

اسقف

/osghof/ ► noun
bishop

اسکاتلندی

/eskâtlandi/ ► adjective
Scottish

استوانه ای

/ostovâne'I/ ► adjective
cylindrical

اسکورت

/eskort/ ► noun
escort

استیضاح

/estizâh/ ► noun
interpellation

اسکیمو

/eskimu/ ► noun
eskimo

اسرارآمیز

/asrâr âmiz/ ► adjective
secret - numinous - mysterious

اسم مصدر
/esme masdar/ ► noun
gerund

اسلام
/eslâm/ ► noun
islam

اسهال
/eshâl/ ► noun
squirt

اسلامی
/eslâmi/ ► adjective
islamic

اشاره
/eshâre/ ► noun
hint - beckon - referral - gesture

اسلحه
/aslahe/ ► noun
weapon - arm

اسم
/esm/ ► noun
noun - name - title

اشاره داشتن بر
/ashâre dâshtan bar/ ► verb
imply

(Idiom: !اسمم رو عوض می کنم
I will eat my hat)

اشاره ضمنی کردن
/eshâreye zemni kardan/ ► verb
connote

اسم اشاره
/esme eshâre/ ► noun
demonstrative

اشاره مختصر
/eshâreye mokhtasar/ ► noun
cheep

اسم رمز
/esme ramz/ ► noun
password

اشاعه دادن
/eshâ'e dâdan/ ► verb
broadcast

اسم عبور
/esme obur/ ► noun
password

اشباع
/eshbâ'e/ ► noun
saturation - glut

اسم مستعار
/esme mosta'âr/ ► noun
pseudonym

اشتباه
/eshtebâh/ ► noun
mistake - error

اشغال

/eshghâl/ ▶ noun
occupation - occupancy

اشتراک

/eshterâk/ ▶ noun
share - common

اشغال کننده

/eshghâl konande/ ▶ noun
holder - occupier - occupant

اشتراک وجه

/eshterâke vajh/ ▶ noun
parallelism

اشک

/ashk/ ▶ noun
teardrop

اشتراکی

/eshterâki/ ▶ adjective
communal - collective

اشک ریختن

/ashk rikhtan/ ▶ verb
weep

اشتعال

/eshte'âl/ ▶ noun
ignition - combustion

اشکال

/eshkâl/ ▶ noun
difficulty - drawback - disadvantage

اشتغال

/eshteghâl/ ▶ noun
occupation

اصابت

/esâbat/ ▶ noun
strike - impact

اشتیاق

/eshtiyâgh/ ▶ noun
enthusiasm - appetite

اصالت

/esâlat/ ▶ noun
gentry - originality - ism

اشرافی

/ashrâfi/ ▶ adjective
patrician - plutocrat

اصرار

/esrâr/ ▶ noun
yen - tenacity - perseverance

اشعار

/ash'âr/ ▶ noun
poetry

اصرار کردن

/esrâr kardan/ ▶ verb
persist

اشعه ایکس

/asha'e iks/ ▶ noun
xray

اصل و نسب
/aslo nasab/ ▶ noun
lineage

اصرار ورزیدن
/esrâr varzidan/ ▶ verb
insist

اصلاح
/eslâh/ ▶ noun
amendment - adjustment - revision

اصطکاک
/estekâk/ ▶ noun
friction - attrition

اصلاح شدن
/eslâh shodan/ ▶ verb
repent - reclaim

اصطکاک داشتن
/estekâk dâshtan/ ▶ verb
overlap

اصلاح طلب
/eslâh talab/ ▶ adjective
reformer

اصطکاکی
/estekâki/ ▶ adjective
spirant

اصلاح کننده
/eslâh konande/ ▶ noun
corrector - corrective

اصطلاح
/estelâh/ ▶ noun
idiom - term

اصلاح ناپذیر
/eslâh nâpazir/ ▶ adjective
incorrigible

اصطلاح عامیانه
/estelâhe âmiyâneh/ ▶ noun
slang

اصلاح نژاد کردن
/eslâhe nezhâd kardan/ ▶ verb
grade

اصطلاحی
/estelâhi/ ▶ adjective
colloquial - idiomatic

اصلاح نمودن
/eslâh nemudan/ ▶ verb
revise - edit

اصغر
/asghar/ ▶ adjective
junior - minor - lesser

اصلاحات
/eslâhât/ ▶ noun
reformation - reform

اصل کلی
/asle koli/ ▶ noun
theory - generality

اصلی
/asli/ ► adjective
basic - principal - prime - primary -
main - initial - fundametal

اضافه حقوق
/ezâfe hoghugh/ ► noun
raise

اصلیت
/asliyat/ ► noun
reality - identity

اضافه کار
/ezâfe kâr/ ► noun
overtime

اصول
/osul/ ► noun
tenet - doctrine

اضافه کردن
/ezâfe kardan/ ► verb
add

اصول اخلاقی
/osule akhlâghi/ ► noun
ethic

اضافه نمودن
/ezâfe nemudan/ ► verb
add

اصولی
/osuli/ ► adjective
principles

اضداد
/azdâd/ ► noun
paradox

اصیل
/asil/ ► adjective
noble

اضطراب
/ezterâb/ ► noun
worry - anxiety

اضافه
/ezâfeh/ ► noun
excess - access - surplus

اضطراری
/ezterâri/ ► adjective
emergency

اطاعت
/etâ'at/ ► noun
submission - obedience

اضافه بار
/ezâfe bâr/ ► noun
overload

اطاعت کردن
/etâ'at kardan/ ► verb
obey

اضافه بها
/ezâfe bahâ/ ► noun
Surcharge

اطو
/otu/ ▶ noun
iron

اظهار
/ez hâr/ ▶ noun
statement - remark

اظهار داشتن
/ez hâr dâshtan/ ▶ verb
state - remark

اظهار عشق
/ez hâre eshgh/ ▶ noun
courtship

اظهارنظر
/ez hâre nazar/ ▶ noun
assessment

اعاده
/ede'â/ ▶ noun
return - rebound

اعاده حیثیت کردن
/ede'â'e heisiyat kardan/ ▶ verb
rehabilitate

اعانه
/e'âneh/ ▶ noun
benefit - subvention

اعانه دادن
/e'âneh dâdan/ ▶ verb
contribute

اطاقک
/otâghak/ ▶ noun
box - booth - cubicle

اطراف
/atrâf/ ▶ noun
around

اطفا
/etfâ'e/ ▶ noun
quench

اطلاع
/etelâ'e/ ▶ noun
notification - notice

اطلاع دادن
/etelâ'e dâdan/ ▶ verb
inform

اطلاع نامه
/etelâ'e nâme/ ▶ noun
prospectus

اطلاعات
/etelâ'ât/ ▶ noun
data - information

اطمینان
/etminân/ ▶ noun
confidence - certainty - cretain

اطمینان بخش
/etminân bakhsh/ ▶ adjective
safe - trusty

اعتقاد

/e'teghâd/ ► noun
belief - faith

اعتبار

/e'tebâr/ ► noun
reputation - reliability - credit

اعتقاد داشتن

/e'teghâd dâshtan/ ► verb
believe

اعتبار دادن

/e'tebâr dâdan/ ► verb
authenticate

اعتماد

/e'temâd/ ► noun
trust - reliance

اعتبارنامه

/e'tebârnâme/ ► noun
credential

اعتماد بنفس

/e'temâd benafs/ ► noun
self-reliance

اعتدال

/e'tedâl/ ► noun
moderation

اعتماد کردن

/e'temâd kardan/ ► verb
trust - rely

اعتراض

/e'terâz/ ► noun
protest - objection - remonstrance

اعتنا

/e'tenâ/ ► noun
heed

اعتراف

/e'terâf/ ► noun
profession

اعتیاد

/e'tiyâd/ ► noun
addiction

اعتراف کردن

/e'terâf kardan/ ► verb
acknowledge - confess

اعجاز

/e'jâz/ ► noun
miracle - marvel

اعتصاب

/e'tesâb/ ► noun
strike - sitin

اعدام

/e'dâm/ ► noun
execution

اعتصاب کردن

/e'tesâb kardan/ ► verb
strike

اعدام کردن

/e'dâm kardan/ ▶ verb
execute

اعزام کردن

/e'zâm kardan/ ▶ verb
detach

اعشاری

/a'shâri/ ▶ adjective
decimal

اعضا

/a'zâ/ ▶ noun
staff

اعطا

/e'tâ/ ▶ noun
grant

اعطا کردن

/e'tâ kardan/ ▶ verb
grant - offer

اعظم

/a'zam/ ▶ noun
major

اعلا

/a'lâ/ ▶ noun
supreme

اعلام

/e'lâm/ ▶ noun
declaration

اعلام جرم کردن

/e'lâme jorm kardan/ ▶ verb
indict

اعلام خطر

/e'lâme khatar kardan/ ▶ noun
alert

اعلامیه

/e'lâmiye/ ▶ noun
statement - manifesto - declaration

اعلان کردن

/e'lân kardan/ ▶ verb
proclaim - announce - advertise

اعلی

/a'lâ/ ▶ noun
supreme

اعمال زور

/e'mâle zur/ ▶ noun
exertion

اعمال کردن

/e'mâl kardan/ ▶ verb
apply - exert

اغتشاش

/eghteshâsh/ ▶ noun
disarray - anarchy - turbulence

اغتشاش کردن

/eghteshâsh kardan/ ▶ verb
tumult

افتتاح
/efte'tâh/ ▶ noun
opening

اغراق
/eghrâgh/ ▶ noun
exaggeration

افتتاح کردن
/efte'tâh kardan/ ▶ verb
open - inaugurate

اغراق آمیز
/eghrâgh âmiz/ ▶ adjective
exaggerated

افتخار
/eftekhâr/ ▶ noun
glory - attribute - honor

اغفال
/eghfâl/ ▶ noun
deception

افتخارآمیز
/eftekhâr âmiz/ ▶ adjective
honorific

اغفال کردن
/eghfâl kardan/ ▶ verb
entrap - deceive

افتراق
/efterâgh/ ▶ noun
segregation

اغوا
/eghvâ/ ▶ noun
seducement - temptation

افتضاح
/eftezâh/ ▶ noun
scandal

اغوا کردن
/eghvâ kardan/ ▶ verb
entice - seduce

افراشتن
/afrâshtan/ ▶ verb
elevate - fly - erect

اغواکننده
/eghvâ konande/ ▶ adjective
tempter - hustler

افراط
/efrât/ ▶ noun
indulgence - plethora

افاده
/efâde/ ▶ noun
snobbery - pride

افراطی
/efrâti/ ▶ adjective
extrimist

افتادگی
/oftâdegi/ ▶ noun
humility

افروختن

/afrukhtan/ ▶ verb
fire

افسردگی

/afsordegi/ ▶ noun
depression

افزایش

/afzâyesh/ ▶ noun
increase

افسرده

/afsorde/ ▶ adjective
depressed

افزودن

/afzudan/ ▶ verb
enhance - add - increase

افسوس

/afsus/ ▶ noun
remorse - regret - alas

افزودنی

/afzudani/ ▶ adjective
additive

افسوس خوردن

/afsus khordan/ ▶ verb
sigh - regret

افزوده شدن

/afzude shode/ ▶ verb
increase

افسون

/afsun/ ▶ noun
charm

افزونه

/afzune/ ▶ adjective
redundant

افسونگر

/afsungar/ ▶ adjective
enchanter - charmer

افسار

/afsâr/ ▶ noun
rein

افسونگری

/afsungari/ ▶ noun
sorcery - witchcraft

افسانه

/afsâne/ ▶ noun
myth - legend - fiction

افشا

/efshâ/ ▶ noun
overture

افسر

/afsar/ ▶ noun
officer

افشاندن

/afshândan/ ▶ verb
inseminate - diffuse - spray

افضل

/afzal/ ▶ noun
supreme

افطار

/eftâr/ ▶ noun
breakfast

افق

/ofogh/ ▶ noun
horizon

افقی

/ofoghi/ ▶ adjective
lateral - horizontal

افکار

/afkâr/ ▶ noun
thoughts

افلاطون

/aflâtun/ ▶ noun
plato

افلیج

/eflij/ ▶ adjective
paralytic

افول

/oful/ ▶ noun
wane

افول کردن

/oful kardan/ ▶ verb
ebb

اقاقیا

/aghâghiyâ/ ▶ noun
locust

اقامت کردن

/eghâmat kardan/ ▶ verb
remain

اقامتگاه

/eghâmatgâh/ ▶ noun
residency

اقبال

/eghbâl/ ▶ noun
fortuity - luck

اقتباس

/eghtebâs/ ▶ noun
adoption - derivation

اقتباس کردن

/eghtebâs kardan/ ▶ verb
extract - adopt

اقتدار

/eghtedâr/ ▶ noun
power

اقتصاد

/eghtesâd/ ▶ noun
economy

اقتصادی

/eghtesâdi/ ▶ adjective
economic

اکبر
/akbar/ ▶ adjective
major

اقدام
/eghdâm/ ▶ noun
action - move

اکتساب
/ektesâb/ ▶ noun
acquisition

اقرار
/eghrâr/ ▶ noun
profession

اکتسابی
/ektesâbi/ ▶ adjective
acquisitive

اقرار کردن
/eghrâr kardan/ ▶ verb
admit - confess

اکتشاف
/ekteshâf/ ▶ noun
discovery - detection

اقلیت
/aghaliyat/ ▶ noun
minority

اکثریت
/aksariyat/ ▶ noun
majority

اقلیم
/eghlim/ ▶ noun
continent - hemisphere

اقلیمی
/eghlimi/ ▶ adjective
continental

اکراه
/ekrâh/ ▶ noun
reluctance

اقناع شدن
/eghnâ'e shodan/ ▶ verb
satiate

اکسیر
/eksir/ ▶ noun
panacea

اقوام
/aghvâm/ ▶ noun
kinfolk

اکنون
/aknun/ ▶ adverb
present - now

اقیانوس
/oghyânus/ ▶ noun
ocean

اگر
/agar/ ▶ preposition
if

اگرچه

/agarche/ ▶ preposition
albeit - however - though

الحاد

/elhâd/ ▶ noun
heresy - atheism

اگو

/olgu/ ▶ noun
sewer - model

الحاق

/elhâgh/ ▶ noun
union - incorporation - interpolation

الاغ

/olâgh/ ▶ noun
donkey

الحاقی

/elhâghi/ ▶ adjective
extension - adjunct

التزام

/eltezâm/ ▶ noun
obligation

الزام

/elzâm/ ▶ noun
commitment

التزامی

/eltezâmi/ ▶ adjective
obligation

الصاق

/elsâgh/ ▶ noun
adhesion - adherence

التماس

/eltemâs/ ▶ noun
appeal

الصاق کردن

/elgâgh kardan/ ▶ verb
stick

التماس کردن

/eltemâs kardan/ ▶ verb
obtest - supplicate - solicit

الغا

/elghâ'e/ ▶ noun
revoke - revocation

التهاب

/eltehâb/ ▶ noun
tumult - boil

الغا کردن

/elghâ'e kardan/ ▶ verb
quash

التیام

/eltiyâm/ ▶ noun
redress

الفبا

/alefbâ/ ▶ noun
alphabet

الفبای نابینایان

/alefbâye nâbinâyân/ ▶ noun
braille

القا

/elghâ/ ▶ noun
inspiration - infusion

القا کردن

/elghâ kardan/ ▶ verb
inspire - infuse - induct

الک

/alak/ ▶ noun
scalp - sift

الک کردن

/alak kardan/ ▶ verb
sift - screen

الکترود

/elekterod/ ▶ noun
electrode

الکترون

/elekteron/ ▶ noun
electron

الکتریکی

/elekteriki/ ▶ noun
electric

الکل

/alekol/ ▶ noun
alcohol

الکلی

/alekoli/ ▶ adjective
alcoholic

الکی

/alaki/ ▶ adjective
spurious

الگو

/olgu/ ▶ noun
pattern - sample - standard

الگوریتم

/algoritm/ ▶ noun
algorithm

الله

/al'lâh/ ▶ noun
god

الله کلنگ

/al'lâh kolang/ ▶ noun
seesaw

الماس

/almâs/ ▶ noun
diamond

المثنی

/almosânâ/ ▶ noun
double - reduplicate

النگو

/alangu/ ▶ noun
bracelet

الهام
/elhâm/ ▶ noun
sprite - inspiration

امان
/amân/ ▶ noun
security - respite - mercy

الهه
/elâhe/ ▶ noun
goddess

امان دادن
/amân dâdan/ ▶ verb
safeconduct

الهی
/elâhi/ ▶ adjective
divine - celestial

امان نامه
/amân nâme/ ▶ noun
safeconduct

الهیات
/elâhiyât/ ▶ noun
theology - divinity

امانت
/amânat/ ▶ noun
safekeeping - trusteeship - trust

الوار
/alvâr/ ▶ noun
lumber - timber

امانت پستی
/amânate posti/ ▶ noun
parcel

الواط
/alvât/ ▶ noun
waggish

امانت دار
/amânatdâr/ ▶ adjective
trustee

الیاف
/alyâf/ ▶ noun
yarn

امانت داری
/amânatdâri/ ▶ noun
trusteeship

اما
/amâ/ ▶ preposition
however - but

امپراتور
/emperâtur/ ▶ noun
emperor

امامت
/emâmat/ ▶ noun
pontificate

امپراتوری
/emperâturi/ ▶ adjective
emperor

امت

/omat/ ► noun
nation

امتحان

/emtehân/ ► noun
examination - quiz

امتحان کردن

/emtehân kardan/ ► verb
test - examine

امتحان نشده

/emtehân nashode/ ► adjective
untried

امتحانی

/emtehâni/ ► adjective
test

امتداد

/emtedâd/ ► noun
along

امتداد یافتن

/emtedâd yâftan/ ► verb
prolong

امتناع

/emtenâ'e/ ► noun
refusal

امتناع ورزیدن

/emtenâ'e varzidan/ ► verb
balk

امتیاز

/emtiyâz/ ► noun
rate - grant

امتیاز دادن

/emtiyâz dâdan/ ► verb
handicap

امتیازی

/emtiyâzi/ ► adjective
rate

امداد

/emdâd/ ► noun
help

امر

/amr/ ► noun
order

امر کردن

/amr kardan/ ► verb
dictate - order

امر مسلم

/amre mosalam/ ► noun
certaint

امروز

/emruz/ ► noun
today

امروزه

/emruze/ ► adverb
nowadays

املا

/emlâ/ ▶ noun
spelling

امروزی

/emruzi/ ▶ adjective
modern

املاک

/amlâk/ ▶ noun
property

امری

/amri/ ▶ adjective
imperative

املایی

/emlâyi/ ▶ adjective
spelling

امریه

/amriye/ ▶ noun
order - prescription - prescript

امن

/amn/ ▶ noun
secure - safe

امشب

/emshab/ ▶ adverb
tonight

امنیت

/amniyat/ ▶ noun
safety - security

امضا

/emzâ/ ▶ noun
endorsement

اموال

/amvâl/ ▶ noun
property

امضا کردن

/emzâ kardan/ ▶ verb
signature - sign

امید

/omid/ ▶ noun
expectancy - hope

امکان

/emkân/ ▶ noun
possibility

(Idiom: **در ناامیدی بسی امید است**
Every cloud has a silver lining)

امکان پذیر

/emkân pazir/ ▶ adjective
possible

امیدوار

/omidvâr/ ▶ adjective
hopeful

امکان ناپذیر

/emkân nâpazir/ ▶ adjective
Impossible

امیدوار بودن

/omidvâr budan/ ▶ verb
hope

انبار

/anbâr/ ▶ noun
store - depository - repository

انبار کالا

/anbâre kâlâ/ ▶ noun
storehouse - storage

انبار کردن

/anbâr kardan/ ▶ verb
store

انباشتگی

/anbâshtegi/ ▶ adjective
amplitude - accumulation

انباشتن

/anbâshtan/ ▶ verb
cumulate - accumulate

انباشته

/anbâshte/ ▶ adjective
replete

انباشته کردن

/anbâshte shodan/ ▶ verb
stockpile

انبر

/anbor/ ▶ noun
pliers

انبساط

/enbesât/ ▶ noun
expansion

انبوه

/anbuh/ ▶ noun
dense - heap

انبوه مردم

/anbuhe mardom/ ▶ noun
crowd

انتحار

/entehâr/ ▶ noun
suicide

انتخاب

/entekhâb/ ▶ noun
election - select

انتخاب کردن

/entekhâb kardan/ ▶ verb
select - elect - choose

انتخابی

/entekhâbi/ ▶ adjective
selective - elective

انتزاع

/entezâ'e/ ▶ noun
secession

انتزاعی

/entezâ'I/ ▶ adjective
abstract

انتشار
/enteshâr/ ► noun
publish

انتقال برق
/enteghâle bargh/ ► noun
convection

انتصاب
/entesâb/ ► noun
appointment

انتقال دادن
/enteghâl dâdan/ ► verb
shift - transmit

انتظار
/entezâr/ ► noun
prospect

انتقام
/enteghâm/ ► noun
revenge

انتظار داشتن
/entezâr dâshtan/ ► verb
expect

انتقام جو
/enteghâmju/ ► adjective
avenger - vengeful

انتقاد
/enteghâd/ ► noun
criticism

انتقام گرفتن
/enteghâm gereftan/ ► verb
wreak

انتقاد کردن
/enteghâd kardan/ ► verb
blame - criticize

انتگرال
/antegrâl/ ► noun
integral

انتقادناپذیر
/enteghâdnâpazir/ ► adjective
unexceptionable

انتها
/entehâ/ ► noun
end

انتقادی
/enteghâdi/ ► adjective
critical

انتهایی
/entehâyi/ ► adjective
terminal

انتقال
/enteghâl/ ► noun
transfer - transmission

انجام
/anjâm/ ► noun
implementation - accomplishment

انداختن
/andâkhtan/ ► verb
drop - cast

انجام دادن
/anjâm dâdan/ ► verb
accomplish - perform

(Idiom: یک تنه انجام دادن
Go it alone)

اندازه
/andâze/ ► noun
scale - size

انجام وظیفه کردن
/anjâme vazife kardan/ ► verb
acquit

اندازه گرفتن
/andâze gereftan/ ► verb
measure - gauge

انجمن
/anjoman/ ► noun
council - congress

اندازه گیری کردن
/andâzegiri kardan/ ► verb
meter

انجیل
/enjil/ ► noun
Bible

اندام
/andâm/ ► noun
organ - body

انحراف
/enherâf/ ► noun
deviance - detour

اندرز
/andarz/ ► noun
advice

انحصار
/enhesâr/ ► noun
monopoly

اندرون
/andarun/ ► noun
seraglio

انحطاط
/enhetât/ ► noun
decline - downhill - downfall

اندک
/andak/ ► adjective
scarce - paucity - little

انحلال
/enhelâl/ ► noun
breakup

اندوختن
/andukhtan/ ► verb
store - save - accumulate

اندوه

/anduh/ ▶ noun
grief - dole - distress

انزجار

/enzejâr/ ▶ noun
phobia - disgust

اندوهگین

/anduhgin/ ▶ adjective
grieve

انزوا

/enzevâ/ ▶ noun
seclusion - retreat

اندوهگین کردن

/anduhgin kardan/ ▶ verb
grieve

انس گرفتن

/ons gereftan/ ▶ verb
accustom

اندوهناک

/anduhnâk/ ▶ adjective
sad - woeful

انسان

/ensân/ ▶ noun
man - human

اندیشمند

/andishmand/ ▶ noun
thoughtful - thinker

انسانی

/ensâni/ ▶ adjective
human

اندیشه

/andishe/ ▶ noun
thought - mentality - plan

انسجام

/ensejâm/ ▶ noun
solidarity

اندیشیدن

/andishidan/ ▶ verb
think

انسداد

/ensedâd/ ▶ noun
blockage - block

اندیکاتور

/andikâtur/ ▶ noun
indicator

انسولین

/ansolin/ ▶ noun
insulin

انرژی

/enerzhi/ ▶ noun
energy

انشا

/enshâ/ ▶ noun
essay - theme

انعطاف پذیر
/en'etâfpazir/ ► adjective
flexible

انشعاب
/enshe'âb/ ► noun
ramification - offshoot

انعقاد
/en'eghâd/ ► noun
coalescence - ratification

انشعاب یافتن
/enshe'âb yâftan/ ► verb
diverge

انعکاس
/en'ekâs/ ► noun
reaction

انصاف
/ensâf/ ► noun
justice

انعکاس صدا
/en'ekâse sedâ/ ► noun
echo

انصراف
/enserâf/ ► noun
relinquishment

انفجار
/enfejâr/ ► noun
blast - explosion

انضباط
/enzebât/ ► noun
discipline

انفجاری
/enfejâri/ ► adjective
volcanic

انطباق
/entebâgh/ ► noun
conformity

انفرادی
/enferâdi/ ► adjective
sporadic

انطباقی
/entebâghi/ ► adjective
adaptive

انفصال
/enfesâl/ ► noun
discharge - separate

انعام
/an'âm/ ► noun
tip - bonus

انفعال
/enfe'âl/ ► noun
passivity

انعطاف
/en'etâf/ ► noun
flexibility

انقباض

/enghebâz/ ▶ noun
contraction

انقراض

/engherâz/ ▶ noun
extinction

انقطاع

/enghetâ'e/ ▶ noun
discontinuity

انقلاب

/enghelâb/ ▶ noun
revolution

انقلابی

/enghelâbi/ ▶ adjective
revolutionary

انقیاد

/enghiyâd/ ▶ noun
subordination

انکار

/enkâr/ ▶ noun
denial

انکارپذیر

/enkârpazir/ ▶ adjective
retractable

انکارناپذیر

/enkârnâpazir/ ▶ adjective
irrefutable - undeniable

انگاشتن

/engâshtan/ ▶ verb
assume

انگشت

/angosht/ ▶ noun
finger

انگشت زدن

/angosht zadan/ ▶ verb
finger

انگشت نما

/angosht namâ/ ▶ adjective
egregious

انگشتر

/angoshtar/ ▶ noun
hoop - ring

انگل

/angal/ ▶ noun
parasite

انگلستان

/engelestân/ ▶ noun
england

انگلیس

/engelis/ ▶ noun
Britain

انگور

/angur/ ▶ noun
grape

اهدا
/ehdâ/ ▶ noun
grant - present

انگیزش
/angizesh/ ▶ noun
motivation

اهدا کردن
/ehdâ kardan/ ▶ verb
donate

انگیزه
/angizeh/ ▶ noun
incentive - motive

اهرم
/ahrom/ ▶ noun
lever

انگیزه اصلی
/angizeye asli/ ▶ noun
mainspring

اهریمن
/ahriman/ ▶ noun
demiurge

انهدام
/enhedâm/ ▶ noun
destruction - demolition

اهریمنی
/ahrimani/ ▶ adjective
diabolic - devilish

انواع
/anvâ'e/ ▶ noun
types

اهل
/ahl/ ▶ noun
inmate - inhabitant

اهانت
/ehânat/ ▶ noun
contempt

اهل ایران
/ahle irân/ ▶ noun
Iranian

اهانت آمیز
/ehânat âmiz/ ▶ adjective
contemptuous

اهل بیت
/ahle beit/ ▶ noun
household - inmate

اهانت کردن
/ehânat kardan/ ▶ verb
scorn

اهلی
/ahli/ ▶ adjective
tame - domestic

اهتزاز
/ehtezâz/ ▶ noun
swing - sway

اهمال

/ehmâl/ ▶ noun
negligence - neglect

اوج گرفتن

/ôj gereftan/ ▶ verb
soar

اهمیت

/ahamiyat/ ▶ noun
significance - importance

اوراق چی

/ôrâghchi/ ▶ noun
wrecker

اهمیت دادن

/ahamiyat dâdan/ ▶ verb
importance

اوراق قرضه

/ôrâghe gharze/ ▶ noun
bond

اهمیت داشتن

/ahamiyat dâshtan/ ▶ verb
important

اوراق کردن

/ôrâgh kardan/ ▶ verb
scrap

او

/u/ ▶ pronoun
she - he

اورژانس

/orzhâns/ ▶ noun
emergency

او را

/urâ/ ▶ pronoun
him - her

اورشلیم

/orshalim/ ▶ noun
Jerusalem

اوباش

/ôbâsh/ ▶ noun
gangster

اوقات تلخ

/ôghât talkh/ ▶ adjective
stuffy - indignant - angry

اوت

/ôt/ ▶ noun
August

اول

/aval/ ▶ adjective
first - initial

اوج

/ôj/ ▶ noun
climax - zenith - top

اولاد

/ôlâd/ ▶ noun
slip

اولویت
/ôlaviyat/ ▶ noun
preference

ایام
/ay'âm/ ▶ noun
time

اولی
/avali/ ▶ adjective
prior

ایتالیا
/italiyâyi/ ▶ adjective
Italy

اولین
/avalin/ ▶ adjective
initial - first

ایتالیایی
/italiyâyi/ ▶ adjective
Italian

اولیه
/avaliye/ ▶ noun
preliminary - incipient

ایجاد
/ijâd/ ▶ noun
creation

اونس
/ons/ ▶ noun
ounce

ایجاد کردن
/ijâd kardan/ ▶ verb
product - engender - create

ای
/ei/ ▶ preposition
hey

ایجاز
/ijâz/ ▶ noun
brevity

ایالات متحده
/iyâlâte motahede/ ▶ noun
United States

ایده آل
/ideâl/ ▶ adjective
ideal

ایالت
/iyâlat/ ▶ noun
state - province

ایرادگیر
/irâdgir/ ▶ adjective
prig

ایالتی
/iyâlati/ ▶ adjective
statehood - provincial

ایرانی
/irâni/ ▶ adjective
Iranian - Persian

ایضا
/izâ/ ▶ noun
ibidem - ditto

ایزد
/izad/ ▶ noun
god

ایفا
/ifâ/ ▶ noun
performance - play

ایست
/ist/ ▶ noun
stop

ایفا کردن
/ifâ kardan/ ▶ verb
perform

ایستا
/istâ/ ▶ adjective
static

ایفاکننده
/ifâ konande/ ▶ noun
performer

ایستادگی
/istâdegi/ ▶ noun
persist - resistance

ایکاش
/eikâsh/ ▶ preposition
I wish

ایستادگی کردن
/istâdegi kardan/ ▶ verb
resist - abide

ایل
/il/ ▶ noun
tribe

ایستادن
/istâdan/ ▶ verb
stand

ایمان
/imân/ ▶ noun
belief - faith

ایستگاه
/istgâh/ ▶ noun
station - stop

ایمان آوردن
/imân âvardan/ ▶ verb
believe

ایستگاه آتش نشانی
/istâhe âtashneshâni/ ▶ noun
firehouse

ایمن
/imen/ ▶ adjective
secure - safe

ایشان
/ishân/ ▶ pronoun
they

ایمنی

/imeni/ ▶ noun
safety - security

این

/in/ ▶ preposition
this

(Idiom: این به اون در
Tit for tat)

این طور

/intor/ ▶ adverb
such

این قدر

/inghadr/ ▶ adverb
so mush

اینان

/inân/ ▶ pronoun
these

اینجا

/injâ/ ▶ adverb
here

اینطور

/intor/ ▶ adverb
so - thus

اینقدر

/inghadr/ ▶ adverb
so

اینک

/inak/ ▶ adverb
now - behold

اینها

/inhâ/ ▶ pronoun
these

ب - بـ

be /be/ ▶ second letter of the Persian alphabet

با
/bâ/ ▶ preposition
with - by

با ارزش
/bâ arzesh/ ▶ adjective
valuable - noteworthy

با استعداد
/bâ este'dâd/ ▶ adjective
brilliant - clever

با استقامت
/bâ esteghâmat/ ▶ adjective
standup - staminal

با اعتبار
/bâ e'tebâr/ ▶ adjective
prestigious

با انصاف
/bâ ensâf/ ▶ adjective
fair

با اهمیت
/bâ ahamiyat/ ▶ adjective
important - main

با ایمان
/bâ imân/ ▶ adjective
believer

با این وجود
/bâ in vojud/ ▶ adverb
nonetheless

با اینحال
/bâ inhâl/ ▶ adverb
yet - nonetheless

با اینکه
/bâ inke/ ▶ adverb
despite

با پا زدن
/bâpâ zadan/ ▶ verb
kick

با چشم حقارت
/bâ chashme heghârat/ ▶ noun
askance

با حرارت
/bâ harârat/ ▶ adjective
warm - ebullient

با حرمت
/bâhormat/ ▶ adjective
deferential

با ضربه زدن
/bâzarbe zadan/ ▶ verb
quash

با حسن نیت
/bâhosne niyat/ ▶ adjective
faith

با طراوت
/bâtarâvat/ ▶ adjective
youthful

با حوصله
/bâhosele/ ▶ adjective
meek

با محبت
/bâ mohabat/ ▶ adjective
kind

با خشونت
/bâkhoshunat/ ▶ adjective
violence

با مروت
/bâmorovat/ ▶ adjective
humanize

با دقت
/bâ deghat/ ▶ adjective
careful

با ملاحظه
/bâmolâheze/ ▶ adjective
considerate - thoughtful

با دقت دیدن
/bâ deghat didan/ ▶ verb
pore

با ملایمت
/bâmolâyemat/ ▶ noun
gently

با سخاوت
/bâsekhâvat/ ▶ adjective
bounteous

با نزاکت
/bânezâkat/ ▶ adjective
tactful - polite

با سلیقه
/bâsalighe/ ▶ adjective
stylish

با وقار
/bâvaghâr/ ▶ adjective
courtly - grand

با سوادی
/bâsavâdi/ ▶ adjective
literacy

بااحتیاط
/bâ ehtiyât/ ▶ adjective
careful

با شخصیت
/bâshakhsiyat/ ▶ adjective
personable

باتقوا
/bâtaghvâ/ ► adjective
virtuous

بادب
/bâ adab/ ► adjective
polite - respectful

باتلاق
/bâtlâgh/ ► noun
swamp - bog

باب
/bâb/ ► noun
chapter - door

باج
/bâj/ ► noun
tribute - toll

باب روز
/bâbe ruz/ ► noun
chic - in - stylish

باج گیر
/bâjgir/ ► adjective
ransom

بابا
/bâbâ/ ► noun
father

باج گیری
/bâjgiri/ ► noun
levy

بابت
/bâbat/ ► noun
regard - concern - behalf

باجداری
/bâjdâri/ ► noun
tollgate

باتجربه
/bâtajrobe/ ► adjective
experienced

باجرات
/bâjor'at/ ► adjective
brave

باتدبیر
/bâtadbir/ ► adjective
prudent

باحیا
/bâhayâ/ ► adjective
modest

باتربیت
/bâtarbiyat/ ► adjective
gentle

باخبر
/bâkhabar/ ► adjective
aware - conscious - cognizant

باتری
/bâtri/ ► noun
battery

باخت
/bâkht/ ▶ noun
loss

باختر
/bâkhtar/ ▶ noun
west

باخرد
/bâkherad/ ▶ adjective
discreet

باد
/bâd/ ▶ noun
wind

(Idiom: باد آورده را باد می برد
Easy come, easy go)

بادام
/bâdâm/ ▶ noun
almond

بادبان
/bâdebân/ ▶ noun
sail

بادپا
/bâdpâ/ ▶ adjective
fleet

بادشکن
/bâdshekan/ ▶ noun
windbreaker – windbreak

بادکنک
/bâdkonak/ ▶ noun
balloon

بادگیر
/bâdgir/ ▶ noun
windward

باده
/bâdeh/ ▶ noun
wine

بادوام
/bâdavâm/ ▶ adjective
lasting - hardy

بادیه نشین
/bâdiye neshin/ ▶ adjective
nomadic

بار
/bâr/ ▶ noun
burden - cargo

بار سفر بستن
/bâre safar bastan/ ▶ verb
truss

بار کردن
/bâr kardan/ ▶ verb
pack - burden - load

باران
/bârân/ ▶ noun
rain

بارو
/bâru/ ▶ noun
rampart - fortification

باربر
/bârbar/ ▶ adjective
porter - backer

بارور
/bârvar/ ▶ adjective
prolific

باربری
/bârbari/ ▶ noun
freight - bearing

باریک
/bârik/ ▶ adjective
thin - tender - narrow

باربند
/bârband/ ▶ noun
rack

باز
/bvz/ ▶ adjective
open

باردار
/bârdâr/ ▶ adjective
pergnant

باز داشتن
/bâzdâshtan/ ▶ verb
block - impede - interdict - prevent

بارز
/bârez/ ▶ noun
obvious - manifest

باز گرداندن
/bâzgrdândan/ ▶ verb
restoration

بارش
/bâresh/ ▶ noun
downfall - rainfall - rain

بازار
/bâzâr/ ▶ noun
market

بارگاه
/bârgâh/ ▶ noun
court

بازبینی
/bâzbini/ ▶ noun
control - revision

بارندگی
/bârandegi/ ▶ noun
rainfall - rain

بازپخش
/bâzpakhsh/ ▶ noun
relay

بارها
/bârhâ/ ▶ noun
often - freuqently

بازپرداخت
/bâzpardâkht/ ▶ noun
reimbursement

بازداشتگاه
/bâzdâshtgâh/ ▶ noun
lockup

بازپرس
/bâzpors/ ▶ noun
interrogator

بازده
/bâzde/ ▶ noun
output

بازتاب
/bâztâb/ ▶ noun
reflex - reflection

بازدید
/bâzdid/ ▶ noun
visit - review

بازجویی
/bâzjuyi/ ▶ noun
inquiry

بازرسی
/bâzresi/ ▶ noun
audit - detection

بازجویی کردن
/bâzjuyi kardan/ ▶ verb
examine - assay

بازرسی کردن
/bâzresi kardan/ ▶ verb
examine - inspect

بازخرید
/bâzkharid/ ▶ noun
redemption

بازرگان
/bâzargan/ ▶ noun
trader - businessman - merchant

بازخواست
/bâzkhâst/ ▶ noun
interpellation

بازرگانی
/bâzargâni/ ▶ adjective
commercial - commerce - trade

بازدارنده
/bâdârande/ ▶ adjective
deterrent

بازشدن
/bâz shodan/ ▶ verb
unroll - unlatch

بازداشت
/bâzdâsht/ ▶ noun
stoppage - deterrence

بازگشت
/bâzgasht/ ▶ noun
return

بازی
/bâzi/ ▶ noun
game - play

بازگشتن
/bâzgashtan/ ▶ verb
comeback

بازی کردن
/bâzi kardan/ ▶ verb
play - perform

بازگفتن
/bâzgoftan/ ▶ verb
restate - repeat

بازی ورق
/bâziye varagh/ ▶ noun
playing card

بازگو
/bâzgu/ ▶ noun
repetition - repeat

بازیابی
/bâzyâbi/ ▶ noun
detection - retrieval

بازمانده
/bâzmânde/ ▶ adjective
survivor - hinder

بازیافت
/bâzyâft/ ▶ noun
recycling

بازنده
/bâzande/ ▶ adjective
loser

بازیافتن
/bâzyâftan/ ▶ verb
retrieve - resume - regain - recover

بازنشسته
/bâzneshaste/ ▶ adjective
retired

بازیچه
/bâziche/ ▶ noun
toy - plaything

بازو
/bâzu/ ▶ noun
arm

بازیکن
/bâzikon/ ▶ noun
player

بازوبند
/bâzuband/ ▶ noun
brachial - bracelet

بازیگر
/bâzigar/ ▶ noun
actor

باستان شناس
/bâstânshenâs/ ► noun
archaeologist

باطل
/bâtel/ ► adjective
invalid - inoperative - void - vain - null

باستانی
/bâstâni/ ► adjective
ancient

باطل ساختن
/bâtel sâkhtan/ ► verb
override

باستثنای
/be estesnâ'e/ ► noun
except

باطل کردن
/bâtel kardan/ ► verb
dispense - cancel - abrogate

باشتاب
/bâshetâbi/ ► adverb
summarily - apace

باطله
/bâtele/ ► adjective
useless - waste

باشرافت
/bâsherâfat/ ► adjective
truly

باطنی
/bâteni/ ► adjective
intrinsic - internal - inner

باشگاه
/bâshgâh/ ► noun
club

باعث
/bâes/ ► noun
cause

باصره
/bâsere/ ► noun
sight

باعث شدن
/bâes shodan/ ► verb
cause

باصفا
/bâsafâ/ ► adjective
pleasing

باعجله
/bâ ajale/ ► adverb
hastily

باضافه
/be'ezâfe/ ► noun
plus - beside

باعظمت
/bâ azemat/ ► adjective
majestic

باقاعده
/bâ ghâ'ede/ ▶ adjective
regular

باغ
/bâgh/ ▶ noun
garden

باقیمانده
/bâghimânde/ ▶ noun
survivor - remainder

باغبان
/bâghebân/ ▶ noun
gardener

باکره
/bâkere/ ▶ adjective
virgin

باغبانی
/bâghebâani/ ▶ noun
hush

بال
/bâl/ ▶ noun
wing

باغیرت
/bâ gheirat/ ▶ adjective
zealous

بالا
/bâlâ/ ▶ noun
upside - up

بافت
/bâft/ ▶ noun
tissue - texture

بالا آمدن
/bâlâ âmadan/ ▶ verb
rise - uprise

بافتن
/bâftan/ ▶ verb
weave

بالا آوردن
/bâlâ âvardan/ ▶ verb
nauseate - puke

بافراست
/bâ farâsat/ ▶ adjective
sage - sagacious

بالا انداختن
/bâlâ andâkhtan/ ▶ verb
toss

بافندگی
/bâfandegi/ ▶ noun
weave - texture

بالا بردن
/bâlâ bordan/ ▶ verb
upraise - uplift - upgrade - raise

بافنده
/bâfande/ ▶ noun
weaver

بالا کشیدن

/bâlâ keshidan/ ► verb
embezzle - raise

بالغ

/bâlegh/ ► adjective
adult - mature

بالابرنده

/bâlâ barande/ ► adjective
uplifter

بالکن

/bâlkon/ ► noun
balcony

بالاتر

/bâlâtar/ ► adverb
senior - superior - upper

بالن

/bâlon/ ► noun
dirigible

بالاترین

/bâlâtarin/ ► adjective
superlative - upmost

بالون

/bâlun/ ► noun
balloon

بالاتنه

/bâlâtane/ ► noun
bust

بالیدن

/bâlidan/ ► verb
glory

بالانس

/bâlâns/ ► noun
handstand

بالین

/bâlin/ ► noun
dedside

بالایی

/bâlâyi/ ► adverb
superior - over - upper

بام خانه

/bâme khâne/ ► noun
housetop

بالبداهه

/belbedâhe/ ► noun
impromptu

بامداد

/bâmdâd/ ► noun
morning

بالش

/bâlesh/ ► noun
pillow

بامزه

/bâmaze/ ► adjective
zestful – racy

بانجام رساندن
/be anjâm resândan/ ► verb
complete - accomplish

بانی
/bâni/ ► noun
bonnie - sponsor

باندازه
/be andâze/ ► adjective
enough - within

باهم
/bâham/ ► adverb
together

بانشاط
/bâneshât/ ► adjective
fresh - unwearied - vivacious

باهمدیگر
/bâhamdigar/ ► adverb
together

باهوش
/bâhush/ ► adjective
keen - clever - bright - intelligent

بانفوذ
/bânofuz/ ► adjective
influential

باوجود
/bâvojud/ ► adjective
notwithstanding - despite

بانک
/bânk/ ► noun
bank

باور
/bâvar/ ► noun
belief

بانگ
/bâng/ ► noun
cry - call

باور نکردنی
/bâvar nakardani/ ► adjective
incredible - unbelievable

بانگ زدن
/bâng zadan/ ► verb
exclaim - crow

باوفا
/bâvafâ/ ► adjective
loyal

بانو
/bânu/ ► noun
lady - gentlewoman

باید
/bâyad/ ► adverb
must - ought

بتکده

/botkade/ ► noun
pagoda

بایر

/bâyer/ ► adjective
sterile - arid

بتونه

/batune/ ► noun
putty - primer

بایست

/bâyest/ ► adverb
ought - must - shall

بجا

/bejâ/ ► adjective
proper - right

بایکوت

/bâikot/ ► adjective
boycott

بجز

/bejoz/ ► preposition
except

بایگان

/bâyegân/ ► adjective
recorder - archivist

بجز اینکه

/bejoz inke/ ► preposition
except

بایگانی

/bây'gâni/ ► noun
archive - record

بجوش آوردن

/bejush âvardan/ ► verb
stir

بایگانی راکد

/bây'ganiye râked/ ► noun
morgue

بچگانه

/bachegâne/ ► adverb
chilish - infantile

بت

/bot/ ► noun
idol

بچگی

/bachegi/ ► noun
childhood

بت پرست

/botparast/ ► adjective
idolatry

بچه

/ba'che/ ► noun
baby - kid - child

بت شکن

/botshekan/ ► adjective
iconoclast

بخت

/bakht/ ► noun
chance - luck

بختیار

/bakhtiyâr/ ► noun
auspicious - lucky

بخش

/bakhsh/ ► noun
portion - division - district

بخشاینده

/bakhshâyande/ ► adjective
clement

بخشش

/bakhshesh/ ► noun
mercy - generosity - remission

بخشنامه

/bakhshnâme/ ► noun
circular

بخشندگی

/bakhshandegi/ ► noun
munificence

بخشنده

/bakhshide/ ► adjective
donor - generous

بخشودگی

/bakhshudegi/ ► noun
clemency

بچه دزد

/ba'che dozd/ ► adjective
kinnaper

بحث

/bahs/ ► noun
agument - discussion - debate -
controversy

بحث و جدل

/bahso jadal/ ► noun
toil - polemic - disputation

بحر

/bahr/ ► noun
measure

بحران

/bohrân/ ► noun
crisis

بحرانی

/bohrâni/ ► adjective
critical - climacteric

بخار

/bokhâr/ ► noun
steam - gas - reek - haze

بخار شدن

/bokhâr shodan/ ► verb
vaporize - evaporate

بخشی
/bakhshi/ ▶ adjective
divisor - partial - sectorial - sectional

بخشیدن
/bakhshidan/ ▶ verb
bestow - donate - grant - forgive

بخشیدنی
/bakhshidani/ ▶ adjective
venial

بخصوص
/bekhosus/ ▶ adjective
particular - specific

بخیه
/bakhiye/ ▶ noun
suture - stitch

بد
/bad/ ▶ adjective
evil - dreadful - bad - ill

بدآنجا
/bedânja/ ▶ adverb
there

بداخلاق
/bad akhlâgh/ ▶ adjective
moody - immoral - licentious

بداخلاقی
/bad akhlâghi/ ▶ noun
immorality - misconduct

بداندیش
/bad andish/ ▶ adjective
malicious

بداهه
/bedâhe/ ▶ noun
offhand

بدبخت
/badbakht/ ▶ adjective
woeful - miserable - unfortunate

بدبین
/badbin/ ▶ adjective
pessimistic - pessimist

بدتر
/badtar/ ▶ adjective
worse

بدترین
/badtarin/ ▶ adjective
worst

بدجنس
/badjens/ ▶ adjective
mischievous

بدخو
/badkhu/ ▶ adjective
cranky - wicked

بدطینت

/badtinat/ ▶ adjective
vicious - malignant

بدخواه

/badkhâh/ ▶ adjective
sinister - malignant - malevolent

بدقول

/badghol/ ▶ adjective
unfaithful - unfaith

بدخیم

/badkhim/ ▶ adjective
virulent

بدکاره

/badkâre/ ▶ adjective
quean

بددهن

/bad dahan/ ▶ adjective
ribald - scurrilous

بدگو

/badgu/ ▶ adjective
vilifier

بدذات

/bad zât/ ▶ adjective
naughty - villainous - villain

بدل

/badal/ ▶ adjective
substitute - spurious

بدرد آوردن

/bedard âvardan/ ▶ verb
sprain

بدلی

/badali/ ▶ noun
spurious - imitation

بدرفتاری

/badraftâri/ ▶ noun
misuse - misdeed - misconduct

بدمزه

/badmaze/ ▶ adjective
unsavory - tasting

بدرقه

/badraghe/ ▶ noun
convoy - escort

بدن

/badan/ ▶ noun
body

بدرقه کردن

/badraghe kardan/ ▶ verb
convoy

بدنام

/badnâm/ ▶ adjective
disreputable - infamous - infamous -
unpopular

بدست آوردن

/be dast âvardan/ ▶ verb
procure - earn - obtain - gain

بدنام کردن

/badnâm kardan/ ▶ verb
blemish - malign - denigrate - defame -
calumniate

بدیع

/badi'e/ ▶ adjective
novel - original

بدنه

/badane/ ▶ noun
framework - body - shaft - trunk

بدیمن

/bad yomn/ ▶ adjective
sinister - ominous - unlucky

بدنه ساختمان

/badaneye sâkhtemân/ ▶ noun
shell

بدین وسیله

/bedinvasile/ ▶ adverb
hereto - hereby

بدنهاد

/bad nahâd/ ▶ adjective
malign - malevolent

بدینسان

/bedinsân/ ▶ adverb
thus

بدهکار

/bedehkâr/ ▶ adjective
yielder - indebted - debtor

بدیهی

/badihi/ ▶ adjective
evident - natural - obvious - inevitable -
immediacy

بدهی

/bedegi/ ▶ noun
debt - debit - liability

بدیهیات

/badihiyât/ ▶ noun
obvious

بدوش کشیدن

/bedush keshidan/ ▶ verb
horse

بذر

/bazr/ ▶ noun
seed

بدون

/bedune/ ▶ preposition
without

بذل

/bazl/ ▶ noun
giveaway - munificence

بدی

/badi/ ▶ noun
evil - vice

بذله گو

/bazegu/ ▶ adjective
humorist - joker

بذله گویی
/bazle gu'I/ ▶ noun
pleasantry

برآیند
/barâyand/ ▶ noun
consequent - resultant

بر
/bar/ ▶ preposition
upon - against - on

برابر
/barâbar/ ▶ adjective
equivalent - equal

بر باد دادن
/bar bâd dâdan/ ▶ verb
squander - misspend

برابری
/barâbari/ ▶ noun
equation - equality parallelism

بر باد رفتن
/bar bâd raftan/ ▶ verb
evaporate

برادر
/barâdar/ ▶ noun
brother

بر شمردن
/bar shemordan/ ▶ verb
enumerate - recount

برازندگی
/barâzandegi/ ▶ noun
propriety

برآشفته
/bar'âshofte/ ▶ adjective
angry - wroth

برازنده
/barâzande/ ▶ adjective
graceful

برآمدگی
/barâmadegi/ ▶ noun
bump - mound

برافراشتن
/barafshândan/ ▶ verb
raise - hoist

برآمده
/barâmade/ ▶ adjective
protuberant - bouffant

برافراشته
/barafrâshte/ ▶ adjective
elate

برآورد
/barâvord/ ▶ noun
calculation - estimate – assessment

برافروختن
/barafrukhtan/ ▶ verb
inflame - relume - overheat - kindle -
glow - provoke

براق
/barâgh/ ▶ adjective
splendid - shiny - glossy - lucid

براق کردن
/barâgh kardan/ ▶ verb
shine - polish - glaze

برانداختن
/barandâkhtan/ ▶ verb
exterminate - overthrow

برانگیختن
/barangikhtan/ ▶ verb
provoke - excite - exasperate

برانگیزاندن
/barangizândan/ ▶ verb
yerk

برای
/barâye/ ▶ preposition
sake - toward - for

برای آنکه
/barâye ânke/ ▶ preposition
that

برای اینکه
/barâye inke/ ▶ preposition
for – because

برای چه
/barâyeche/ ▶ adverb
why - wherefore

برای همیشه
/barâye hamishe/ ▶ adverb
forever

بربریت
/barbariyat/ ▶ noun
barbarism

برپا کردن
/barpâ kardan/ ▶ verb
pitch - inaugurate - establish - erect -
raise

برتر
/bartar/ ▶ adjective
premier - dominant - superior

برتر بودن
/bartar budan/ ▶ verb
outrank

برتری
/bartari/ ▶ noun
trancscendent - vantage - advantage

برتری یافتن
/bartari yâftan/ ▶ verb
transcend

برچسب
/barchasb/ ► noun
ticket - tally - label

برترین
/bartarin/ ► adjective
paramount

برچیدن
/barchidan/ ► verb
remove - liquidate

برتن کردن
/bar tan kardan/ ► verb
don

برحسب
/barchasbe/ ► noun
to - unitage - at

برج
/borj/ ► noun
tower

برحق بودن
/bar hagh budan/ ► verb
legitimacy

برج کلیسا
/borje kelisâ/ ► noun
steeple

برخاستن
/barkhâstan/ ► verb
rise - arise - uprise

برج مراقبت
/borje morâghebat/ ► noun
watchtower

برخلاف
/barkhalâfe/ ► preposition
unlike - athwart - with

برج نگهبانی
/borje negâhbani/ ► noun
watchtower

برخورد
/barkhord/ ► noun
strike - smash - encounter

برجستگی
/barjastegi/ ► noun
eminence - notability - prominence

برخورد کردن
/barkhord kardan/ ► verb
collide - osculate

برجسته
/barjaste/ ► adjective
prominent - saleint - laureate - prime

برخی
/barkhi/ ► pronoun
some

بررسی
/bar'rasi/ ► noun
scrutiny - survey

برخی از
/barkhi az/ ► pronoun
some - several

بررسی کردن
/bar'rasi kardan/ ► verb
peruse - survey - study

برد
/bord/ ► noun
win

برروی
/bar ruye/ ► preposition
on - upon

بردار
/bordâr/ ► noun
vector - resultant

برزخ
/barzakh/ ► noun
limbo - isthmus

برداشتن
/bardâshtan/ ► verb
take - pickup - remove

برش
/boresh/ ► noun
slice - slash - cut - clip - recision

بردبار
/bordbâr/ ► adjective
tolerant - patient - meek

برضد
/bar zede/ ► noun
versus - athwart - against

بردباری
/bordbâri/ ► noun
patience - spartanism - tolerance

برعکس
/bar'aks/ ► noun
viceversa - inverse

بردگی
/bardegi/ ► noun
slavery - servitude

برف
/barf/ ► noun
snow

بردن
/bordan/ ► verb
win - lead

برف پاک کن
/barf pak kon/ ► noun
wiper

برده
/barde/ ► adjective
slave

برکه
/berke/ ▶ noun
pool - lake

برفراز
/barfarâze/ ▶ noun
over - upon

برگ
/barg/ ▶ noun
card - page - leaf

برفی
/barfi/ ▶ adjective
snowy

برگ ریزان
/bargrizân/ ▶ noun
autumn

برق
/bargh/ ▶ noun
electricity

برگردان
/bargardân/ ▶ noun
turnover - revers - refrain

برق انداختن
/bargh andâkhtan/ ▶ verb
gloss

برگزیدگی
/bargozidegi/ ▶ noun
predilection

برق زدن
/bargh zadan/ ▶ verb
flash - glisten

برگزیدن
/bargozidan/ ▶ verb
elite - elect - designate - prefer

برقرار
/bargharâr/ ▶ noun
indefeasible

برگزیده
/bargozide/ ▶ adjective
selective - select - picked - favorite

برقرار کردن
/bargharâr kardan/ ▶ verb
establish - appoint - institute

برگشت
/bargasht/ ▶ noun
backstroke - revert - return

برقی
/barghi/ ▶ adjective
electric

برگشتن
/bargashtan/ ▶ verb
comeback - return

برکت
/barkat/ ▶ noun
bliss - benediction – felicity

برگه
/barge/ ▶ noun
form - paper

برلیان
/barliân/ ▶ noun
brilliant

برنا
/bornâ/ ▶ adjective
young

برنامه آموزشی
/barnâmeye âmuzeshi/ ▶ noun
curriculum

برنامه ریزی
/barnâme rizi/ ▶ noun
planning

برنامه ریزی کردن
/barnâme rizi kardan/ ▶ verb
schedule

برنامه سفر
/barnâmeye safar/ ▶ noun
itinerary

برنج
/berenj/ ▶ noun
rice

برندگی
/borandegi/ ▶ noun
Sharpness

برنده
/barande/ ▶ adjective
winner

برنزه
/boronze/ ▶ adjective
tan

برهان
/borhân/ ▶ noun
logic

برهم زدن
/bar ham zadan/ ▶ verb
disturb - disorder - disband - disarrange

برهنگی
/berehnegi/ ▶ noun
nudity

برهنه
/berehne/ ▶ adjective
naked - nude

بروز
/beruz/ ▶ noun
outbreak

برون
/borum/ ▶ noun
outside

بریان
/beryân/ ▶ adjective
barbecue

بزرگ نما	بریتانیا
/bozorg namâ/ ► adjective grandiose	/beritaniyâ/ ► noun Britain

بزرگتر	بریدگی
/bozorgtar/ ► adjective senior - elder	/boridegi/ ► noun cut

بزرگداشت	بریدن
/bozorgdâsht/ ► noun respect	/boridan/ ► verb cut - slice

بزرگراه	بز
/bozorgrâh/ ► noun superhighway - highway - freeway	/boz/ ► noun goat

بزرگوار	بزاق
/bozorgvâr/ ► adjective honorable - magnaimous	/bozâgh/ ► noun sputum - spit

بزرگی	بزدل
/bozorgi/ ► noun magnitude - dignity - eminence	/bozdel/ ► adjective timorous - coward

بزغاله	بزرخ
/bozghâle/ ► noun goat	/barzakh/ ► noun purgatory

بزم	بزرگ
/bazm/ ► noun party - banquet - shindig	/bozorg/ ► adjective great - grand - enormous - large

بزهکار	بزرگ کردن
/bezehkâr/ ► adjective criminal - guilty - sinner	/bozorg kardan/ ► verb amplify - enlarge

بستردریا

/bestare daryâ/ ▶ noun
ooze

بزودی

/bezudi/ ▶ adverb
soon - early

بستری

/betari/ ▶ noun
bedridden - confined

بس

/bas/ ▶ adverb
enough

بستن

/bastan/ ▶ verb
tighten - bind

بس بودن

/bas budan/ ▶ verb
suffice

بسته

/baste/ ▶ noun
parcel - packet - package - bundle

بساط

/basât/ ▶ noun
counter - layout - stall

بسته بند

/baste bandi/ ▶ noun
packer

بسامد

/basâmad/ ▶ noun
frequency

بستوه آوردن

/besotuh âvardan/ ▶ verb
annoy - haze - harass

بست

/bast/ ▶ noun
girth - outrigger - spanner

بسختی

/besakhti/ ▶ noun
hardly

بستانکار

/bestânkâr/ ▶ adjective
creditor

بسد

/basd/ ▶ noun
coral

بستر

/bestar/ ▶ noun
bed

بسط

/bast/ ▶ noun
extension - expansion - development –
outspread

بشریت

/bashariyat/ ▶ noun
humanity - mortality

بشقاب

/boshghâb/ ▶ noun
dish - plate - vessel

بشکه

/boshke/ ▶ noun
barrel

بصری

/basari/ ▶ adjective
visual

بصیرت

/basirat/ ▶ noun
intuition - insight

بطالت

/betâlat/ ▶ noun
vanity

بطرف

/betarafe/ ▶ noun
toward - to

بطری

/botri/ ▶ preposition
bottle

بطلان

/botlan/ ▶ noun
discomfit

بسلامتی

/besalâmati/ ▶ noun
pledge

بسنده

/basande/ ▶ adjective
enough - adequate

بسوی

/besuye/ ▶ preposition
into - at - against - toward

بسیار

/besyâr/ ▶ adjective
plenty - very - much - many

بسیارخوب

/besyâr khub/ ▶ adjective
excellent - okay

بسیط

/basit/ ▶ adjective
extensive - comprehensive

بشاش

/bashâsh/ ▶ adjective
jocund - cheerful

بشدت

/beshedat/ ▶ adverb
sorely - vengeful

بشر

/bashar/ ▶ noun
human

بطن
/batn/ ▶ noun
ventricle

بعضی
/ba'zi/ ▶ preposition
some

بطنی
/batni/ ▶ adjective
uterine - umbilical - abdominal

بعلاوه
/be'alâve/ ▶ adverb
moreover - plus - also - besides

بعد
/ba'd/ ▶ adjective
next - then

بعلت
/be'elate/ ▶ preposition
due to

بعد
/bo'd/ ▶ adjective
dimension

بعید
/baid/ ▶ adjective
unseemly - unlikely

بعدا
/ba'dan/ ▶ adverb
afterwards

بغرنج
/boghranj/ ▶ adjective
intricate - obscurant - complex

بعد از
/badaz/ ▶ adverb
since - after

بغض
/boghz/ ▶ noun
spite - hatred

بعدازظهر
/badazohr/ ▶ noun
afternoon

بغل
/baghal/ ▶ noun
bosom - armpit - sheaf

بعدها
/ba'dhâ/ ▶ adverb
thereafter

بغل کردن
/baghal kardan/ ▶ verb
embrace - hug

بعدی
/ba'di/ ▶ adjective
subsequent

بفرمایید
/befarmâyid/ ▶ verb
sit down

بقا
/baghâ/ ▶ noun
survival

بقال
/baghâl/ ▶ noun
grocer

بقالی
/baghâli/ ▶ noun
grocery

بقایا
/baghâyâ/ ▶ noun
leftover - vestige

بقچه
/boghche/ ▶ noun
pack - bundle - truss

بقدر
/beghadre/ ▶ preposition
for

بقدر کفایت
/beghadre kefâyat/ ▶ adjective
enough

بکار بردن
/bekâr bordan/ ▶ verb
exert - handle - use - apply

بکر
/bekr/ ▶ adjective
mint - original

بکلی
/bekoli/ ▶ adverb
throughout - quite

بلا
/balâ/ ▶ noun
disaster - calamity - pest - misadventure

بلااثر
/belâ asar/ ▶ adjective
null

بلااستفاده
/belâ estefâde/ ▶ adjective
useless

بلاتصدی
/belâ tasadi/ ▶ adjective
vacant

بلاتلکیفی
/belâ'taklifi/ ▶ noun
uncertainty

بلادرنگ
/belâderang/ ▶ adverb
straightaway

بلاعوض
/belâ avaz/ ▶ adjective
gratuitous

بلاهت
/belâhat/ ▶ noun
tommyrot - stupor

بلندگو
/bolandgu/ ▶ noun
loudspeaker - microphone

بلاواسطه
/belâvâsete/ ▶ adverb
immediate

بلندنظر
/bolandnazar/ ▶ adjective
catholic

بلبل
/bolbol/ ▶ noun
nightingale

بلندهمت
/bolandhemat/ ▶ adjective
chivalrous - ambitious

بلدرچین
/belderchin/ ▶ noun
quail

بلندی
/bolandi/ ▶ noun
height - lift

بلژیکی
/beljiki/ ▶ adjective
Belgian

بله
/bale/ ▶ noun
yes

بلع
/bal'e/ ▶ noun
gulp - godown

بلوا
/balva/ ▶ noun
riot - uproar - uprising

بلند
/boland/ ▶ adjective
aloud - lofty - high - vociferous

بلوار
/bolvâr/ ▶ noun
boulevard

بلند شدن
/boland shodan/ ▶ verb
rise - ascend - arise - uprear - upheave

بلوز
/boluz/ ▶ noun
jumper - blouse

بلندتر کردن
/bolantar kardan/ ▶ verb
heighten

بلوط
/balut/ ▶ noun
chestnut

بلندقد
/boland ghad/ ▶ adjective
tall

بلوغ

/bolugh/ ► noun
maturity - maturation

بلوف زدن

/belof zadan/ ► verb
puff

بم

/bam/ ► adjective
bass - grave

بمب

/bomb/ ► noun
bomb

بمثابه

/bemasâbehe/ ► adjective
tantamount

بمراتب

/bemarâteb/ ► adverb
far

بمنظور

/bemanzure/ ► preposition
sake

بموقع

/bemoghe/ ► adjective
timely - punctual - proper

بن

/bon/ ► noun
root

بن بست

/bonbast/ ► noun
deadlock

بنا

/banâ/ ► noun
mason - structure

بنابراین

/banâvarin/ ► preposition
hence - so - thus - therefore

بناچار

/benâchâr/ ► adverb
perforce

بنام

/benâm/ ► adjective
namely- famous

بنا نهادن

/banâ nahâdan/ ► verb
establish

بنای یادبود

/banâye yâdbud/ ► noun
monument

بند

/band/ ► noun
rope

بندانگشت

/bande angosht/ ► noun
knuckle - phalange

بنیاد

/bonyâd/ ▶ noun
institute - basis - base - root

بندر

/bandar/ ▶ noun
seaport - port

بنیادی

/bonyâdi/ ▶ adjective
fundametal

بندرگاه

/bandargâh/ ▶ noun
harbor - port

بنیان

/bonyân/ ▶ noun
root - basis - valence

بنده

/bande/ ▶ noun
slave - servant - vassal

بنیه

/bonye/ ▶ noun
stamina - gut

بنزین

/benzin/ ▶ noun
gasolene - gas

به

/be/ ▶ preposition
in - into - on

بنظر رسیدن

/benazar residan/ ▶ verb
sound - peer

به آسانی

/be âsâni/ ▶ adverb
easily

بنفش

/banafsh/ ▶ adjective
violet

به آنطرف

/be ântaraf/ ▶ adverb
thither

بنفع

/benaf'e/ ▶ adverb
pro

به اصطلاح

/be'estelâh/ ▶ adverb
so called

بنکدار

/bonakdâr/ ▶ noun
wholesaler

به اینجا

/be injâ/ ▶ adverb
hither

بنگاه

/bongâh/ ▶ noun
institution - institute

به بهای

/be bahâye/ ▶ preposition
for

به درازا کشیدن

/be derâzâ keshidan/ ▶ verb
last

به پشت

/be poshte/ ▶ adverb
backward

به رخ کشیدن

/be rokh keshidan/ ▶ verb
boast

به پیش

/be pishe/ ▶ adverb
onward - on

به رسمیت شناختن

/be rasmiyat shenâkhtan/ ▶ verb
recognition

به پیوست

/be peivast/ ▶ adverb
appendix

به رمز نوشتن

/be ramz neveshtan/ ▶ verb
cryptograph

به جلو

/be jelo/ ▶ adverb
forward

به عقب

/be aghab/ ▶ adverb
back - aback

به چشم

/bechashm/ ▶ adverb
well

به فرزندی پذیرفتن

/be farzandi paziroftan/ ▶ verb
affiliate - adopt

به چه کسی

/be che kasi/ ▶ preposition
whom

به قطعات تقسیم کردن

/be ghata'ât taghsim kardan/ ▶ verb
parcel

به خواست

/bekhâste/ ▶ adjective
voluntary

به میراث بردن

/be mirâs bordan/ ▶ verb
inherit

به خود پیچیدن

/be khod pischidan/ ▶ verb
agonize

به نتیجه رسیدن

/be natije residan/ ▶ verb
aim - result

به هدف خوردن

/be hadaf khordan/ ► verb
quiver

به هم ریختن

/be ham rikhtan/ ► verb
disassemble

به هم زدن

/beham zadan/ ► verb
disarrange

بها

/bahâ/ ► noun
cost - worth - price - value

بهار

/bahâr/ ► noun
spring

بهارخواب

/baharkhâb/ ► noun
terrace

بهاری

/bahâri/ ► noun
spring

بهانه

/bahâne/ ► noun
excuse

بهانه آوردن

/bahâne âvardan/ ► verb
pretext - alibi

بهانه کردن

/bahâne kardan/ ► verb
dissemble

بهانه گیر

/bahânegir/ ► adjective
pernickety

بهبود

/behbud/ ► noun
improvement

بهبود ناپذیر

/behbud nâpazir/ ► adjective
incurable - incorrigible

بهبود یافتن

/behbud yâftan/ ► verb
recover - mend - improve

بهت

/boht/ ► noun
amazement

بهت آور

/boht âvar/ ► adjective
stupendous

بهت و حیرت

/boht va heirat/ ► noun
consternation

بهتان

/bohtân/ ► noun
vilification

بهتان زدن
/bohtân zadan/ ▶ verb
vilify

بهره
/bahre/ ▶ noun
share - portion

بهتر شدن
/behtar shodan/ ▶ verb
ameliorate - improvement

بهره بردار
/bahrebardâr/ ▶ adjective
beneficiary

بهتر کردن
/behtar kardan/ ▶ verb
improve - ameliorate

بهره داشتن
/bahre dâshtan/ ▶ verb
partake

بهترین
/behtarin/ ▶ adjective
best

بهساز
/behsâz/ ▶ adjective
reformer

بهداشت
/behdâsht/ ▶ noun
hygiene

بهشت
/behesht/ ▶ noun
zion - heaven

بهداشتی
/behdâshti/ ▶ adjective
sanitary

بهشت برین
/beheshte barin/ ▶ noun
paradise

بهرام
/bahrâm/ ▶ noun
mars

بهشتی
/beheshti/ ▶ adjective
heavenly

بهرحال
/beharhâl/ ▶ adverb
however - anyway - though

بهم آمدن
/beham âmadan/ ▶ verb
match

بهرسو
/beharsu/ ▶ adverb
about

بهم آمیختن
/beham âmikhtan/ ▶ verb
fold

بهم بافتن
/beham bâftan/ ▶ verb
twine

بهم قفل کردن
/beham ghofl kardan/ ▶ verb
interlock

بهم پیوستن
/beham peivastan/ ▶ verb
incorporate - bind

بهمن
/bahman/ ▶ noun
avalanche

بهم پیوسته
/beham peivaste/ ▶ adjective
conjunct

بهنگام
/behengâm/ ▶ adjective
timely

بهم چسبیدن
/beham chasbidan/ ▶ verb
hang together

بهوش
/behush/ ▶ adjective
conscious

بهم چسبیده
/beham chasbide/ ▶ adjective
impacted

بهوش آمدن
/behush âmadan/ ▶ verb
revive - respire - recover

بهم خوردگی
/beham khordegi/ ▶ noun
turmoil - revolt - collission

بهوش آوردن
/behush âvardan/ ▶ verb
sober - resuscitate

بهم خوردن
/beham khordan/ ▶ verb
collission - collide

بهیجان آمدن
/behayejân âmadan/ ▶ verb
quake

بهم ریختگی
/beham rikhtegi/ ▶ noun
tumble

بهیچ وجه
/behichvajh/ ▶ adverb
whatsoever

بهم زدن
/beham zadan/ ▶ verb
disturb - roust - rouse

بهینه
/behine/ ▶ adjective
optimum

بو
/bu/ ► noun
scent - savor - smell

بودار
/budâr/ ► adjective
aromatic - redolent - smelly

بو کردن
/bu kardan/ ► verb
smell - respire

بودن
/budan/ ► verb
exist - stand

بوالهوس
/bolhavas/ ► adjective
whimsical - capricious

بور
/bur/ ► adjective
auburn - blond

بوته
/bute/ ► noun
bush - brushwood - herb

بوران
/burân/ ► noun
sleet - squall

بوجار
/bujâr/ ► noun
sifter

بورس
/burs/ ► noun
exchange

بوجد آوردن
/bevaj âvardan/ ► verb
rapture

بوزینه
/buzine/ ► noun
jackanapes - simian - ape - monkey

بوجود آوردن
/bevojud âvardan/ ► verb
generate

بوس
/bus/ ► noun
kiss

بوستان
/bustân/ ► noun
garden

بوحشت انداختن
/bevahshat andâkhtan/ ► verb
wolf

بوسه
/buse/ ► noun
kiss

بود
/bud/ ► verb
Was

بول

/bôl/ ► noun
urine

بوسیدن

/busidan/ ► verb
kiss

بوم

/bum/ ► noun
region - habitat

بوسیله

/bevasileye/ ► preposition
by - with

بوی تند

/buye tond/ ► adjective
tang

بوف

/buf/ ► noun
owl

بوی خوش

/buye khosh/ ► adjective
perfume

بوفه

/bufe/ ► noun
buffet

بویایی

/buyâyi/ ► noun
smell

بوق

/bugh/ ► noun
trumpet - horn

بوییدن

/buyidan/ ► verb
smell

بوق زدن

/bugh zadan/ ► verb
hoot

بی

/bi/ ► preposition
without

بوقت

/bevaght/ ► adverb
timely

بی آب

/biâdab/ ► adjective
thirsty - dry

بوقلمون

/bughalamun/ ► noun
turkey

بی آب کردن

/biadabi kardan/ ► verb
dehydrate

بوکس

/boks/ ► noun
box

بی آبرو کردن
/bi âberu kardan/ ▶ verb
defamation

بی آبرویی
/biâberuyi/ ▶ adjective
disrepute - disgrace

بی آزار
/bi âzâr/ ▶ adjective
inoffensive

بی آلایش
/bi âlâyesh/ ▶ adjective
simplex

بی اثر
/biasar/ ▶ adjective
ineffective - inactive

بی اثربودن
/biasar budan/ ▶ verb
quail

بی اثری
/biasari/ ▶ noun
inaction

بی اجر
/bi ajri/ ▶ adjective
vageless

بی احترامی
/bi ehterâmi/ ▶ noun
disrespect - disrepute

بی احترامی کردن
/bi ehterâmi kardan be/ ▶ verb
dishonor - insult

بی احتیاط
/bi ehtiyât/ ▶ adjective
incautious - imprudent - improvident -
injudicious

بی احتیاطی
/bi ehtiyâti/ ▶ noun
imprudence - improvidence

بی احساس
/bi ehsâs/ ▶ adjective
apathetic

بی اختیار
/bi ekhtiyâr/ ▶ adjective
spontaneous - involuntary

بی ادب
/biadab/ ▶ adjective
discourteous - impolite

بی ادبانه
/bi adabâne/ ▶ adverb
discourteous

بی ادبی
/bi adabi/ ▶ noun
irreverence - discourtesy

بی اعتبار
/bi etebâr/ ▶ adjective
insecure

بی ادبی کردن
/bi adabi kardan/ ▶ verb
misbehave

بی اعتقاد
/bi eteghâd/ ▶ adjective
unbelievin - unbeliever

بی ادعا
/bi ede'â/ ▶ adjective
unassuming

بی اعتنا
/bi e'tenâ/ ▶ adjective
inattentive - reckless

بی اساس
/bi asâs/ ▶ adjective
unfounded

بی اندازه
/bi andâze/ ▶ adjective
infinite - indefinite - immense -
immeasurable

بی استعداد
/bi este'dâd/ ▶ adjective
inapt - unintelligent

بی انصاف
/bi ensâf/ ▶ adjective
unjust - unfair

بی اشتها
/bi eshtehâ/ ▶ adjective
jadish

بی انصافی
/bi ensâfi/ ▶ noun
injustice - iniquity - inequity

بی اشتیاق
/bi eshtiyâgh/ ▶ adjective
lackadaisical - lukewarm

بی اهمیت
/bi ahamiyat/ ▶ adjective
negligible - unimportant

بی اصل
/bi asl/ ▶ adjective
unfounded

بی ایمان
/bi imân/ ▶ adjective
unbeliever

بی اطلاع
/bi ete'lâ/ ▶ adjective
unknowable - uninformed

بی اطلاع بودن از
/bi ete'lâ budan/ ▶ verb
misknow

بی پدر
/bipedar/ ► adjective
unfathered

بی باک
/bi bâk/ ► adjective
brave - heroic - bold

بی پرده
/biparde/ ► adjective
straightforward - frank

بی باک
/bibâk/ ► adjective
ruthless

بی پروا
/biparvâ/ ► adjective
adventurer

بی باکانه
/bi bâkâne/ ► adverb
audacious

بی پروایی
/biparvâyi/ ► noun
audacity - impetuosity

بی باکی
/bibâki/ ► noun
audacity

بی پناه
/bipanâh/ ► adjective
shelterless

بی برکت
/bibarkat/ ► adjective
meager

بی پول
/bipul/ ► adjective
broke - poor

بی بها
/bibahâ/ ► adjective
priceless

بی تاب
/bitâb/ ► adjective
impatient

بی بی
/bibi/ ► noun
queen - dame

بی تابی
/bitâbi/ ► noun
impatience

بی پایان
/bipâyân/ ► noun
eternal

بی تجربه
/bitajrobe/ ► adjective
immature - inexpert

بی پایه
/bipâye/ ► adjective
unstable – unfounded

بی جهت
/bijahat/ ▶ adjective
unduly

بی تدبیر
/bitadbir/ ▶ adjective
imprudent

بی حرکت
/biharkat/ ▶ adjective
immobile - pat

بی تربیتی
/bitarbiyati/ ▶ noun
peasantry - discourtesy

بی حرمت کردن
/bihormat kardan/ ▶ verb
desecrate - defile

بی تردید
/bitardid/ ▶ adjective
undoubtedly

بی حس
/bihes/ ▶ adjective
stolid - dead - vapid

بی تقوایی
/bitaghvâyi/ ▶ noun
impiety

بی حساب
/bihesâb/ ▶ adjective
incalculable

بی توجهی
/bitavajohi/ ▶ noun
neglect

بی ثبات
/bisobât/ ▶ adjective
unstable

بی حسی
/bihesi/ ▶ noun
apathy

بی ثباتی
/bisobâti/ ▶ noun
instability - inconsistency

بی حوصلگی
/bihoselegi/ ▶ noun
impatience

بی ثمر
/bisamar/ ▶ adjective
unprofitable - unfruitful

بی حوصله
/bihosele/ ▶ adjective
impatient

بی جا
/bijâ/ ▶ adjective
indecorous - unseasonable

بی حیا
/bihayâ/ ▶ adjective
brash – indecent

بی خرد
/bikherad/ ► adjective
brute - fool

بی دندان
/bidandân/ ► adjective
toothless

بی خردانه
/bikheradâne/ ► adverb
injudicious

بی دوام
/bidavâm/ ► adjective
brittle

بی خطر
/bikhatar/ ► adjective
safe - secure

بی دین
/bidin/ ► adjective
irreligious - ungodly

بی خواب
/bikhâb/ ► adjective
watchful

بی دینی
/bidini/ ► noun
perfidy- irriligion

بی خود
/bikhod/ ► adjective
unduly

بی راهه
/birâhe/ ► adjective
devious

بی خیال
/bikhiyâl/ ► adjective
carefree

بی ربط
/birabt/ ► adjective
irrelevant

بی خیالی
/bikhiyâli/ ► noun
abandon

بی رحم
/birahm/ ► adjective
brute - brutal

بی دقت
/bideghat/ ► adjective
careless - negligent

بی رغبتی
/bireghbati/ ► noun
distaste

بی دلیل
/bidalil/ ► adjective
unreasonable

بی رمق
/biramagh/ ► adjective
spent

بی رنگ
/birang/ ▶ adjective
colourless

بی شرف
/bisharaf/ ▶ adjective
dishonest

بی روح
/biruh/ ▶ adjective
apathetic

بی شرفی
/bisharafi/ ▶ noun
dishonor

بی ریا
/biriyâ/ ▶ adjective
sincere - heartfelt

بی شرم
/bisharm/ ▶ adjective
immodest - unabashed - brazen

بی زحمت
/bizahmat/ ▶ adjective
easy

بی شرمی
/bisharmi/ ▶ noun
brass - indecency

بی سابقه
/bisâbeghe/ ▶ adjective
unprecedented - unheard

بی شعور
/bisho'ur/ ▶ adjective
brutish

بی سرپرست
/bisarparast/ ▶ adjective
derelict

بی شکل
/bishekl/ ▶ adjective
formless

بی سروصدا
/bisarosedâ/ ▶ adjective
serene

بی شمار
/bishomâr/ ▶ adjective
innumerable - uncounted

بی سیم
/bisim/ ▶ noun
wireless

بی صبری
/bisabri/ ▶ noun
impatience

بی شباهت
/bishebâhat/ ▶ adjective
dissimilar - unlike

بی صدا
/bisedâ/ ▶ adjective
noiseless - mute

بی صداقت

/besedâghat/ ► adjective
insincere

بی عیب

/bi eib/ ► adjective
unexceptionable - perfect

بی ضرر

/bizarar/ ► adjective
harmless

بی عیبی

/bi eibi/ ► noun
integrity

بی طرف

/bitaraf/ ► adjective
neutral

بی فایدگی

/bi fâyedegi/ ► noun
drawback - disadvantage

بی عاطفه

/bi âtefe/ ► adjective
insensitive - insensate

بی فایده

/bi fâyede/ ► adjective
useless - wasteful

بی عرضه

/bi orze/ ► adjective
inept- incapable

بی فرهنگ

/bifarhang/ ► adjective
lowbrow

بی عفتی

/bi efati/ ► noun
unchastity - adultery

بی فکر

/bi fekr/ ► adjective
thoughtless - inconsiderate

بی عقل

/bi aghl/ ► adjective
insane

بی قاعده

/bi ghâ'ede/ ► adjective
promiscuous

بی علاقگی

/bi alâghegi/ ► noun
apathy - indifference

بی قرار

/bigharâr/ ► adjective
restless- fidgety

بی علاقه

/bi alâghe/ ► adjective
nonchalant - unresponsive - uninterested

بی قراری

/bigharâri/ ► noun
Disquiet

بی مانند
/bi mânand/ ► adjective
unique - unexampled

بی قیدوبند
/bigheido band/ ► adjective
unihibited - unihibit

بی مایگی
/bi mâyegi/ ► noun
superficiality

بی کاره
/bi kâre/ ► adjective
inactive

بی مبالات
/bi mobâlât/ ► adjective
perfunctory - remiss

بی کفایت
/bi kefâyat/ ► adjective
incompetent - inefficient

بی محابا
/bi mahâbâ/ ► adjective
slambang - impavid

بی کفایتی
/bi kefâyati/ ► noun
inefficiency - incompetence -
inadequacy

بی محابایی
/bimahâbâyi/ ► noun
unreserve

بی کله
/bi kale/ ► adjective
blockhead - imbecile

بی مرز
/bi marz/ ► adjective
spaceless

بی گدار
/bi godâr/ ► adjective
impassable

بی مزه
/bimaze/ ► adjective
tame - arid - vapid

بی گناه
/bi gonâh/ ► adjective
innocent

بی مسلولیت
/bi mas'uliyat/ ► adjective
unresponsive

بی لیاقتی
/bi liyâghati/ ► noun
inaptitude - inability

بی مصرف
/bi masraf/ ► adjective
useless

بی نتیجه

/bi natije/ ► adjective
resultless- ineffectual - indeterminate

بی معنی

/bimani/ ► adjective
absurd - unmeaning - nonsense

بی نزاکت

/bi nezâkat/ ► adjective
indelicate - indecorous - unceremonious
- boorish

بی مغز

/bimaghz/ ► adjective
insane - fool

بی مقدمه

/bi moghadame/ ► adjective
sudden

بی نشان

/bi neshân/ ► adjective
untitled

بی ملاحظه

/bi molâheze/ ► adjective
thoughtless - reckless

بی نظم

/binazm/ ► adjective
chaotic - amorphous

بی منطق

/bi mantegh/ ► adjective
inept

بی نظیر

/binazir/ ► adjective
unique - unexampled

بی مورد

/bi mored/ ► adjective
inappropriate - inopportune

بی نهایت

/bi nahâyat/ ► adjective
intolerable

بی موقع

/bi moghe'/ ► adjective
untimely - inopportune - unseasonable

بی نوا

/binavâ/ ► adjective
pauper

بی میل

/bi meil/ ► adjective
loathloth - resentful - reluctant -
unwilling

بی نیاز

/biniyâz/ ► adjective
needless

بی میلی

/bimeili/ ► noun
distaste - dismay - disaffection

بی هدف

/bi hadaf/ ► adjective
Causeless

بی وفا

/bi vafâ/ ► adjective
disloyal - unfaithful - unfaith

بی همتا

/bihamtâ/ ► adjective
matchless - peerless - unique

بی وفایی

/bi vafâyi/ ► noun
adultery- treason

بی همه چیز

/bi hamechiz/ ► adjective
shyster

بیاد آوردن

/beyâd âvardan/ ► verb
remind - recall

بی هنر

/bi honar/ ► adjective
inartistic

بیان

/bayân/ ► noun
statement - explanation - remark

بی هوش

/bihush/ ► adjective
comatose - unintelligent - unwitting

بیان مبهم

/bayâne mobham/ ► noun
enigma

بی هوش کردن

/bihush kardan/ ► verb
anesthetize

بیان مجدد

/bayâne mojadad/ ► noun
restatement

بی هوش کننده

/bihush konande/ ► adjective
anesthetic

بیانگر

/bayângar/ ► adjective
explanatory

بی هوشی

/bihushi/ ► noun
anesthesia - unintelligence

بیانیه

/bayâniye/ ► noun
manifesto - manifest - bulletin

بی واهمه

/bivâheme/ ► adjective
undaunted

بیباکی

/bibâki/ ► noun
temerity

بی وجدان

/bi vojdân/ ► adjective
wretch - unconscionable

بیت المقدس
/beitol moghadas/ ▶ noun
Jerusalem

بیتا
/bitâ/ ▶ adjective
unrivaled - unique

بیتابی
/bitâbi/ ▶ noun
unrest

بیجا
/bijâ/ ▶ adjective
inapt - inappropriate - improper

بیجان
/bijân/ ▶ adjective
inanimate

بیجواب
/bijavâb/ ▶ adjective
unanswerable

بیچارگی
/bichâregi/ ▶ noun
calamity - misfortune - misery

بیچاره
/bichâre/ ▶ adjective
misery - wretched - wretch

بیچاره کردن
/bichâre kardan/ ▶ verb
bust - beggar

بیحاصل
/bi hâsel/ ▶ adjective
lean - ungainly

بیحال
/bihâl/ ▶ adjective
torpid - supine - passive - lethargic - insensate

بیحال شدن
/bihâl shodan/ ▶ verb
languish

بیحرمتی
/bihormati/ ▶ noun
irreverence

بیحس
/bihes/ ▶ adjective
senseless - insensate

بیحس کردن
/bihes kardan/ ▶ verb
amortize - paralyze

بیخ
/bikh/ ▶ noun
butt

بیخبر
/bikhabar/ ▶ adjective
unaware - abrupt

(Idiom: بیخبری خوش خبری ست
No news is good news)

بیخرد

/bikherad/ ▶ adjective
unreasonable

بیداری

/bidâri/ ▶ noun
rouse - wake

بیخود

/bikhod/ ▶ adjective
gratuitous - idle

بیدرنگ

/biderang/ ▶ adjective
suddenly - outright

بید

/bid/ ▶ adjective
willow

بیدمشک

/bidmeshk/ ▶ noun
pussy

بیداد

/bidâd/ ▶ noun
injustice

بیراه

/birâh/ ▶ adjective
astray - aberrant

بیدادگر

/bidâdgar/ ▶ adjective
cruel

بیرحم

/birahm/ ▶ adjective
cruel - relentless

بیدار

/bidâr/ ▶ adjective
awake - vigilant - wakeful

بیرحمی

/birahmi/ ▶ noun
savagery - brutality

بیدار شدن

/bidâr shodan/ ▶ verb
awaken - awake

بیرق

/beiragh/ ▶ noun
flag - banner

بیدار کردن

/bidâr kardan/ ▶ verb
waken - awaken

بیرنگ

/birang/ ▶ adjective
effeminate - neutral - gray

بیدار ماندن

/bidâr mândan/ ▶ verb
awake

بیروح

/biruh/ ▶ adjective
tame - vapid - meek

بیرون

/birun/ ▶ adverb
outside - outdoors - abroad

بیرون شهر

/birune shahr/ ▶ noun
countryside

بیرون آمدن

/birun âmadan/ ▶ verb
emerge - pullout

بیرون کردن

/birun kardan/ ▶ verb
fire - evict - dispossess

بیرون آوردن

/birun âvardan/ ▶ verb
scoop - unweave

بیرونی

/biruni/ ▶ adjective
outward - external - exterior

بیرون از

/birun az/ ▶ adverb
out

بیریا

/biriyâ/ ▶ adjective
unaffected

بیرون افتادن

/birun oftâdan/ ▶ noun
loll

بیزار

/bizâr/ ▶ adjective
loathloth - averse

بیرون افکندن

/birun afkandan/ ▶ verb
jettison

بیزار بودن

/bizâr budan/ ▶ verb
dislike - hate

بیرون انداختن

/birun andâkhtan/ ▶ verb
throw

بیزار کردن

/bizâr kardan/ ▶ verb
loathe - disgust

بیرون دادن

/birun dâdan/ ▶ verb
exhale - evolve

بیزاری

/bizâri/ ▶ noun
aversion - hatred

بیرون زده

/birun zade/ ▶ adjective
saleint

بیسابقه

/bisâbeghe/ ▶ adjective
unexampled

بیستم
/bistom/ ▶ adjective
twentieth

بیش ازهمه
/bishaz hame/ ▶ adjective
most

بیستمین
/bistomin/ ▶ adjective
twentieth

بیشتر
/bishtar/ ▶ adverb
rather - further - more - major

بیشترین
/bishtarin/ ▶ adjective
most - maximum

بیسکویت
/biskuit/ ▶ noun
biscuit

بیشرم
/bisharm/ ▶ adjective
audacious

بیسواد
/bisavâd/ ▶ adjective
illiterate - unlettered

بیشرمی
/bisharmi/ ▶ noun
effrontery

بیسوادی
/bisavâdi/ ▶ noun
illiteracy

بیشعور
/bisho'ur/ ▶ adjective
insensible

بیش
/bish/ ▶ adverb
more than

بیشمار
/bishomâr/ ▶ adjective
countless - populous - myriad

بیش از اندازه
/bishaz andâze/ ▶ adjective
ample - excessive

بیشه
/bishe/ ▶ noun
brushwood - forest

بیش ازحد
/bishaz had/ ▶ adjective
inordinate

بیشین
/bishin/ ▶ adjective
maximum - majority

بیصدا
/bi sedâ/ ► adjective
silent - quiet

بیکاره
/bikâre/ ► adjective
vagabond - idler

بیضه
/beize/ ► noun
testicle

بیکاری
/bikâri/ ► noun
unemployment

بیطرفی
/bitarafi/ ► noun
neutrality - impartiality

بیگانه
/bigâne/ ► adjective
stranger - exotic

بیعانه
/bayâne/ ► noun
deposit

بیگانه پرست
/bigâne parast/ ► adjective
xenophile

بیعت
/bei'at/ ► noun
allegiance - homage

بیگانه کردن
/bigâne kardan/ ► verb
alienate - estrange - stranger

بیفما بردن
/beyaghmâ bordan/ ► verb
sack

بیگانه وار
/bigâne vâr/ ► adverb
outlandish

بیقرار بودن
/bighârâr budan/ ► verb
shuffle

بیل
/bil/ ► noun
shovel - spade

بیقراری
/bighârâri/ ► noun
unrest - malaise

بیل زدن
/bil zadan/ ► verb
hack - spade - shovel

بیکار
/bikâr/ ► adjective
unemployed

بیلچه
/bilche/ ► noun
spade - paddle

بیم

/bim/ ► noun
scare - phobia - fear

بیمزگی

/bimaze/ ► noun
vapidity - platitude

بیمناک

/bimnâk/ ► adjective
tremulous - umbrageous

بیم و وحشت

/bimo vahshat/ ► noun
alarm

بیمه

/bime/ ► noun
insurance

بیمار

/bimâr/ ► noun
sick - ill - patient

بیمه کردن

/bime kardan/ ► verb
assure - insure

بیمار روانی

/bimâre ravâni/ ► noun
psychotic - psychopath

بیمه نامه

/bime nâme/ ► noun
insurance

بیمار ساختن

/bimâr sâkhtan/ ► verb
indispose

بین فرهنگی

/beine farhangi/ ► noun
intercultural

بیمار کردن

/bimâr kardan/ ► verb
sicken

بین قاره ای

/beine ghâre'I/ ► noun
intercontinental

بیمارستان

/bimârestân/ ► noun
clinic - hospital

بینا

/binâ/ ► adjective
perspicacious

بیماری

/bimâri/ ► noun
malady

بینایی

/binâyi/ ► noun
sight - vision - perspective

بیماری روانی

/bimâre ravâni/ ► noun
Psychosis

بینوا

/benavâ/ ► adjective
poor - unblessed

بیوه

/bive/ ► adjective
lone - widow

بینوایی

/binavâyi/ ► noun
poverty

بینی

/bini/ ► noun
nose

بیهودگی

/bihudegi/ ► noun
vanity - inaction

بیهوده

/bihude/ ► adjective
unfruitful - idle - vain

بیهوده گفتن

/bihude goftan/ ► verb
rant

بیهوده گویی

/bihude guyi/ ► noun
rant

بیهوشی

/bihushi/ ► noun
anesthesia

بیوگرافی

/biogerâfi/ ► noun
biography

پ - پـ

pe /pe/ ► third letter of the Persian Alphabet

پا
/pâ/ ► noun
leg - foot

پا برجا کردن
/pâ barjâ kardan/ ► verb
fix

پا برهنه
/pâ berehne/ ► adjective
discalced - barefoot

پابرجا
/pâ barjâ/ ► adjective
stable - firm - indefeasible

پابند
/pâband/ ► adjective
shackles

پاپ
/pâp/ ► noun
Pope

پاپا
/pâpâ/ ► noun
papa - father

پات (درشطرنج)
/pât (dar shatrang)/ ► noun
stalemate

پاتوق
/pâtogh/ ► noun
discussion - resort - rendezvous

پاتولوژی
/pâtolozhi/ ► noun
pathology

پاتیل
/pâtil/ ► noun
caldron

پاچه
/pâche/ ► noun
foot - leg

پاچه شلوار
/pâcheye shalvâr/ ► noun
leg

پاداش
/pâdâsh/ ► noun
remuneration - reward

پاداش دادن
/pâdâsh dâdan/ ► verb
compensate

پادتن
/pâdtan/ ► noun
antibody

پارافین
/pârâfin/ ► noun
paraffin

پادری
/pâdari/ ► noun
mat

پاراگراف
/pârâgerâf/ ► noun
paragraph

پادزهر
/pâdzahr/ ► noun
antidote

پارامتر
/pârâmetr/ ► noun
parameter

پادشاه
/pâdeshâh/ ► noun
king - monarch

پارتی
/pârti/ ► noun
party

پادشاهی
/pâdeshâhi/ ► adjective
kingdom - sovereignty

پارچ
/pârch/ ► noun
pitcher

پادگان
/pâdegân/ ► noun
garrison - presidio

پارچه
/pârche/ ► noun
textile - cloth

پادو
/pâdo/ ► noun
page

پارچه بافی
/pârche bâfi/ ► noun
drapery

پارازیت
/pârâzit/ ► noun
noise - parasite

پارچه نخی
/pârche nakhi/ ► noun
cotton

پاراف
/pârâf/ ► noun
initial

پارسا
/pârsâ/ ► adjective
pious

پاراف کردن
/pârâf kardan/ ► verb
initial

پاره پاره کردن
/pâre pâre kardan/ ▶ verb
analyze - tatter - scalpel

پارسال
/pârsâl/ ▶ noun
last year - yesteryear

پارو
/pâru/ ▶ noun
shovel - oar

پارسایی
/pârsâyi/ ▶ noun
piety - pietism

پارو زدن
/pâru zadan/ ▶ verb
paddle - row - oar - scull

پارسنگ
/pâresang/ ▶ noun
countermeasure - counterbalance

پازدن
/pâzadan/ ▶ noun
pedal

پارک
/pârk/ ▶ noun
park

پازهر
/pâdzahr/ ▶ noun
antidote

پارگی
/pâregi/ ▶ noun
tear - rupture

پاس
/pâs/ ▶ noun
pass

پارلمان
/pârlemân/ ▶ noun
parliament

پاس دادن
/pâs dâdan/ ▶ verb
pass

پارلمانی
/pârlemâni/ ▶ adjective
parliamentary

پاساژ
/pâsâzh/ ▶ noun
passage

پاره
/pâre/ ▶ noun
fragment - bit - scrap

پاسبان
/pâsebân/ ▶ noun
guard - policeman - police

پاره آجر
/pâre âjor/ ▶ noun
brickbat - glut - rubble

پاشنه جوراب
/pâshneye jurâb/ ► noun
heel

پاسبانی کردن
/pâsebâni kardan/ ► verb
patrol

پاشیدن
/pâshidan/ ► verb
spray - pour

پاسخ
/pâsokh/ ► noun
response - respond - reply - answer

پافشاری
/pâfeshâri/ ► noun
persistence - insistence

پاسخ دادن
/pâsokh dâdan/ ► verb
answer - respond - reply

پافشاری کردن
/pâfeshâri kardan/ ► verb
insist - persist

پاسدار
/pâsdâr/ ► adjective
guardsman - guard

پاک
/pâk/ ► adjective
pure - clean

پاسدارخانه
/pâsdârkhâne/ ► noun
guardhouse

پاک زاد
/pâkzâd/ ► adjective
highborn

پاسداری
/pâsdâri/ ► noun
patrol - watch

پاک شدن
/pâk shodan/ ► verb
refine

پاسگاه
/pâsgâh/ ► noun
post

پاک کردن
/pâk kardan/ ► verb
erase - efface - wipe - wash - clean -
purify

پاسیو
/pâsiyo/ ► noun
patio

پاشنه
/pâshne/ ► noun
heel - pivot

پاک کرده
/pâk karde/ ► adjective
Picked

پاک کن

/pâk kon/ ▶ noun
wiper

پاک نشدنی

/pâk nashodani/ ▶ adjective
indelible

پاکت

/pâkat/ ▶ noun
pocket

پاکدامن

/pâkdâman/ ▶ adjective
virtuous - virgin - chaste

پاکدامنی

/pâkdâmani/ ▶ noun
purity - chastity - probity - virtue

پاکساز

/pâksâzi/ ▶ adjective
purgative

پاکی

/pâki/ ▶ noun
innocence - purity

پاکیزه

/pâkize/ ▶ adjective
tidy - clean - neat

پاگیر

/pâgir/ ▶ noun
Obstacle

پالان

/pâlân/ ▶ noun
panel

پالان زدن

/pâlân zadan/ ▶ verb
saddle

پالایش

/pâlâyesh/ ▶ noun
purge

پالایشگاه

/pâlâyeshgâh/ ▶ noun
refinery

پالتو

/pâlto/ ▶ noun
overcoat

پالودگی

/pâludegi/ ▶ noun
refinement

پالودن

/pâludan/ ▶ verb
purify - refine

پانسمان کردن

/pânsemân kardan/ ▶ verb
dress

پانسیون
/pânsiyon/ ► noun
pension

پایتخت
/pâytakht/ ► noun
capital

پای کوبیدن
/pây kubidan/ ► verb
hoof

پایدار
/pâydâr/ ► adjective
resistant - permanent

پایا
/pâpâ/ ► adjective
perennial - durable

پایدارماندن
/pâydâr mândan/ ► verb
abide

پایان
/pâyân/ ► noun
end

پایداری
/pâydâri/ ► noun
stability - permanency

پایان ناپذیر
/pâyân nâpazir/ ► adjective
interminable - inexhaustible

پایداری کردن
/pâydâri kardan/ ► verb
resist

پایان نامه
/pâyân nâme/ ► noun
thesis - dissertation

پایکوبی
/pâykubi/ ► noun
stomp

پایان یافتن
/pâyân yâftan/ ► verb
over

پایکوبی کردن
/pâykubi kardan/ ► verb
foot

پایانه
/pâyâne/ ► noun
terminus - terminal

پایگاه
/pâygâh/ ► noun
base

پایایی
/pâyâyi/ ► noun
perpetuity

پایمال کردن
/pâymâl kardan/ ► verb
override

پایمردی
/pâymardi/ ► noun
fortitude - assistance - intercession

پایین آوردن
/pâyin âvardan/ ► verb
bate - disrate

پایه
/pâye/ ► noun
base - root - pillar - basis

پایین تر
/pâyintar/ ► adjective
subordinate - beneath - lower

پایه دار
/pâye dâr/ ► adjective
leggy

پایین ترین
/pâyintarin/ ► adjective
bottommost - undermost

پایه زدن
/pâye zadan/ ► verb
truss

پایین رتبه
/pâyin rotbe/ ► adjective
inferior - minor

پاییدن
/pâyidan/ ► verb
guard- surveillance - watch

پایین رفتن
/pâyin raftan/ ► verb
comedown

پاییز
/pâyiz/ ► noun
autumn - fall

پایینی
/pâyini/ ► noun
beneath - underneath

پاییزی
/pâyizi/ ► adjective
autumnal

پتانسیل
/petansiel/ ► noun
potential

پایین
/pâyin/ ► noun
underneath - bottom - beneath

پتروشیمی
/petroshimi/ ► noun
petrochemical

پتک
/potk/ ► noun
sledge - hammer - mallet

پایین آمدن
/pâyin âmadan/ ► verb
descend- fall

پتک زدن

/potk zadan/ ► verb
sledge

پدافند

/padâfand/ ► noun
defence - defense

پتو

/patu/ ► noun
blanket

پدال

/pedâl/ ► noun
pedal

پچ پچ کردن

/pech pech kardan/ ► verb
chatter - whisper

پدر

/pedar/ ► noun
sire - father

پخت

/pokht/ ► noun
decoction

پدر یا مادر

/pedar ya mâdar/ ► noun
parent

پختن

/pokhtan/ ► verb
cook

پدرانه

/pedarâne/ ► adverb
paternal

پخته

/pokhte/ ► adjective
ripe

پدربزرگ

/pedarbozorg/ ► noun
grandpa - grandfather

پخش

/pakhsh/ ► noun
prevalence - effluence - diffusion

پدرسالار

/pedarsâlâr/ ► noun
patriarch

پخش شدن

/pakhsh shodan/ ► verb
run - pervade

پدری

/pedari/ ► adjective
patronymic - paternal

پخش کردن

/pakhsh kardan/ ► verb
strew - spread - diffuse

پدری کردن

/pedari kardan/ ► verb
father

پذیرفتنی

/paziroftani/ ► adjective
admissible - acceptable

پذیرنده

/pazirande/ ► adjective
receptive

پر

/par/ ► noun
feather

پر

/por/ ► adjective
populous - ample - full

پر آشوب

/por âshub/ ► adjective
stormy - pellmell

پر افاده

/por efâde/ ► adjective
snobbish

پر التهاب

/por eltehâb/ ► adjective
arduous

پر جمعیت

/por jamiyat/ ► adjective
populous

پر سروصدا

/por saro sedâ/ ► adjective
noisy - obstreperous

پدیدار

/padidâr/ ► adjective
visible - conspicuous

پدیدار شدن

/padidâr shodan/ ► verb
emerge

پدیداری

/padidâri/ ► noun
visibility

پدیده

/padide/ ► noun
phenomenon

پذیرا

/pazirâ/ ► adjective
receptive - acceptable

پذیرایی

/pazirâyi/ ► noun
reception

پذیرایی کردن

/pazirâyi kardan/ ► verb
lodge - entertain - welcome

پذیرش

/paziresh/ ► noun
reception - admission - acceptance

پذیرفتن

/paziroftan/ ► verb
admit - accept

پرپا

/pariyâ/ ► noun
pteropod

پر کردن

/por kardan/ ► verb
full load

پرپر زدن

/par par zadan/ ► verb
flicker

پرآب و تاب

/por âbotâb/ ► adjective
rotund - grandiose - ornate

پرپشت

/porposht/ ► adjective
steady - thick - lush - exuberant - rich

پراکندن

/parâkandan/ ► verb
transmit - scatter - cast

پرپشت شدن

/por posht shodan/ ► verb
luxuriate

پراکنده

/parâkande/ ► adjective
diffuse - outspread - sporadic - sparse

پرپشت کردن

/por posht kardan/ ► verb
thicken

پراکنده کردن

/parâkande kardan/ ► verb
intersperse - meddle - disperse - dash

پرپیچ و خم

/por picho kham/ ► noun
roundabout

پراکنش

/parâkonesh/ ► noun
transmittal

پرت

/part/ ► noun
faraway - remote

پرانتز

/parântez/ ► noun
parenthesis - bracket

پرت شدن

/part shodan/ ► verb
overshoot - cropper

پربار

/porbâr/ ► adjective
weighty

پرتاب

/partâb/ ► noun
throw - toss

پربها

/porbahâ/ ► adjective
valuable – invaluable

پرتاب شدن

/partâb shodan/ ► verb
slat - shove

پرچانگی کردن

/porchânegi kardan/ ► verb
jaw

پرتاب کردن

/partâb kardan/ ► verb
shoot - jaculate - thrust

پرچانه

/porchâne/ ► adjective
pernickety - talkative

پرتقال

/porteghâl/ ► noun
orange- Portugal

پرچم

/parcham/ ► noun
banner - flag

پرتقالی

/porteghâli/ ► adjective
Portuguese

پرچم دار

/parchamdâr/ ► adjective
ensign

پرتگاه

/partgPortugueseh/ ► noun
crag - headland - precipice - bluff

پرچین

/parchin/ ► noun
fence - hedge

پرتلاطم

/portalâtom/ ► adjective
wavy

پرچین ساختن

/pachin sâkhtan/ ► verb
hedge

پرتو

/parto/ ► noun
beam - ray - radiance

پرحادثه

/porhâdese/ ► adjective
eventful

پرحرارت

/porharârat/ ► adjective
steamy - spunky

پرتوافشان

/parto âfshân/ ► adjective
radioactive

پرحرف

/porharf/ ► adjective
talkative - chatty

پرتوافکن

/parto afkan/ ► noun
projector

پرداخت
/pardâkht/ ► noun
payoff - payment - pay

پرحرفی کردن
/porharfi/ ► verb
gash - palaver

پرداخت کردن
/pardâkht kardan/ ► verb
pay

پرخاش
/parkhâsh/ ► noun
quarrel - ruffe

پرداختن
/pardâkhtan/ ► verb
pay

پرخاش کردن
/parkhâsh kardan/ ► verb
bicker

پرداختنی
/pardâkhtani/ ► noun
solvency - due - payable

پرخاشگر
/parkhâshgar/ ► adjective
aggressor - aggressive

پردردسر
/pordardesar/ ► adjective
troublous - bothersome

پرخرج
/porkharj/ ► adjective
sumptuous - expensive

پرده
/parde/ ► noun
curtain - screen

پرخطر
/porkhatar/ ► adjective
hazardous - dngerous

پرده برداری
/pardebardâri/ ► noun
unveil

پرخور
/porkhor/ ► adjective
greedy - gobbler - voracious

پرده بکارت
/pardeye bekârat/ ► noun
hymen

پرخوری
/porkhori/ ► noun
avidity - gorge

پرده دار
/pardedâr/ ► noun
chamberlain

پرخوری کردن
/porkhori kardan/ ► verb
gorge

پرستار
/parastâr/ ► noun
nurse

پرده درب ورودی
/pardeye darbe vorudi/ ► noun
portiere

پرستاربچه
/parastâre bache/ ► noun
nanny

پرده زدن
/parde zadan/ ► verb
upholster - veil

پرستاری کردن
/parastâri kardan/ ► verb
nurse

پرده سینما
/pardeye sinamâ/ ► noun
screen

پرستش
/parastesh/ ► noun
worship

پررنگ
/por rang/ ► adjective
chromatic

پرستش کردن
/parastesh kardan/ ► verb
worship

پررو
/por ru/ ► adjective
impudent - cheeky

پرستو
/parastu/ ► noun
swallow

پرز
/porz/ ► noun
fuzz - nap

پرستیدن
/parastidan/ ► verb
worship

پرزرق و برق
/por zargho bargh/ ► adjective
splendid - gaudy - gaily

پرسش
/porsesh/ ► noun
inquiry - question - query

پرس
/peres/ ► noun
pressure

پرسش کردن
/porsesh kardan/ ► verb
question

پرس کردن
/peres kardan/ ► verb
smash

پرطاقت
/portâghat/ ► adjective
hardy - wiry - staminal

پرسشگر
/porseshgar/ ► adjective
questioner

پرفروغ
/porforugh/ ► adjective
luminary

پرسشنامه
/porseshnâme/ ► noun
questionnaire

پرفسور
/porofesor/ ► noun
professor

پرسنل
/persenel/ ► noun
personnel - staff

پرکار
/porkâr/ ► adjective
prolific - overwrought - hardworking

پرسه زدن
/parse zadan/ ► verb
ramble - scamp - prowl

پرگار
/pargâr/ ► noun
compass

پرسیدن
/porsidan/ ► verb
ask - question - query

پرمدعا
/pormoda'â/ ► adjective
pretentious

پرش
/paresh/ ► noun
startle - spout - jump - leap - bounce

پرندگان
/parandegân/ ► noun
birds

پرشکوفه
/porshokufe/ ► adjective
buddy

پرنده
/parande/ ► noun
bird

پرصدا
/porsedâ/ ► adjective
noisy - loud - vociferous

پرنشاط
/porneshât/ ► adjective
primrose

پرصلابت
/porsalâbat/ ► adjective
rocky

پرنور
/pornur/ ► adjective
shiny

پروانه
/parvâne/ ► noun
butterfly - permission - license

پرهیاهو
/por hayâhu/ ► adjective
obstreperous - loudmouthed

پروبال
/parobâl/ ► noun
plumage

پرهیجان
/por hayejân/ ► adjective
ebullient

پروردگار
/parvardegâr/ ► noun
god

پرهیز
/parhiz/ ► noun
abstinence - diet

پروردن
/parvaridan/ ► verb
raise - breed - feed - nurture

پرهیزگار
/parhizgâr/ ► adjective
pious

پرورش
/parvaresh/ ► noun
nurture - upbringing

پرهیزگاری
/parhizgâri/ ► noun
continence - piety - pietism

پرورش دادن
/parvaresh dâdan/ ► verb
develop - foster

پروا
/parvâ/ ► noun
heed - solicitude - prudence

پروژکتور
/prozhektor/ ► noun
projector

پرواز
/parvâz/ ► noun
wing - fly - flight - plane

پروژه
/prozhe/ ► noun
projection - project

پروازبلند
/parvâze boland/ ► noun
kite

پروگرام
/progrâm/ ► noun
program

پرونده
/parvande/ ► noun
case - dossier

پژمرده
/pazhmorde/ ► adjective
sear

پریدن
/pridan/ ► verb
jump - fly

پژمرده شدن
/pazhmorede shodan/ ► verb
droop - miff - languish - quail

پریشان
/parishân/ ► adjective
disheveled - disconsolate - faraway -
heartsick

پژواک
/pezhvâk/ ► noun
echo - reflection

پریشان کردن
/parishân kardan/ ► verb
oppress - confound - distract - buffalo

پژوهش
/pazhuhesh/ ► noun
research

پریشانی
/parishâni/ ► noun
bother - remorse

پژوهش کردن
/pazhuhesh kardan/ ► verb
research

پز
/poz/ ► noun
posture

پژوهشگر
/pazhuheshgar/ ► noun
researcher

پزشک
/pezeshk/ ► noun
medico - medic - physician

پژوهشنامه
/pazhuheshname/ ► noun
bulletin

پزشکی
/pezeshki/ ► adjective
medicine - medic

پس
/pas/ ► adverb
thus - so - forth - again - back

پژمردن
/pazhmordan/ ► verb
Blight

پس از
/pas az/ ► adverb
after - since

پس انداز کردن

/pasandâz kardan/ ► verb
save

پس دادن

/pas dâdan/ ► verb
giveback - repay - refund

پس دادن به

/pas dâdan be/ ► verb
repay

پس زدن

/pas zadan/ ► verb
setback - recoil - rebut - rebound

پس گردن

/pase gardan/ ► noun
scruff - nape

پس گرفتن

/pas gereftan/ ► verb
retrieve - retreat - recapture - withdraw

پس مانده

/pasmânde/ ► noun
scum - leftover - excrement - residue - remainder

پست

/past/ ► noun
ungenerous - inferior - villain- poor

پست تر

/past tar/ ► adjective
beneath - lower – less

پست سفارشی

/poste sefâreshi/ ► noun
registeredmail

پست شدن

/past shodan/ ► verb
bastardize - grovel

پست فطرت

/past fetrat/ ► adjective
rascal

پست و حقیر

/pasto haghir/ ► adjective
knave

پستان

/pestân/ ► noun
breast

پستان بند

/pestânband/ ► noun
bra

پستچی

/postchi/ ► noun
postman

پستخانه

/postkhâne/ ► noun
post

پسته

/peste/ ► noun
pistachio

پستو
/pastu/ ► noun
closet

پسربچه
/pesarbache/ ► noun
youngster - callan - lad - page - boy

پستی
/pasti/ ► adjective
postal

پسرفت
/pasraft/ ► noun
recession

پسر
/pesar/ ► noun
son - boy

پسروی
/pasravi/ ► noun
retrogradation - regress

پسر برادر
/pesare barâdar/ ► noun
nephew

پسند
/pasand/ ► noun
choice - approbation

پسر پسر
/pesare pesar/ ► noun
grandson

پسند کردن
/pasand kardan/ ► verb
approve - admire

پسر خواهر
/pesare khâhar/ ► noun
nephew

پسندیدن
/pasandidan/ ► verb
choose - allow - accept

پسر دختر
/pesare dokhtar/ ► noun
grandson

پسندیده
/pasandide/ ► adjective
honorable - admirable - acceptable -
desirable

پسر زن
/pesare zan/ ► noun
stepson

پسوند
/pasvand/ ► noun
suffix

پسر شوهر
/pesare shohar/ ► noun
stepson

پسین
/pasin/ ► adjective
subsequent - astern - hindmost

پشتگرمی
/poshtgarmi/ ▶ noun
assurance

پشت
/posht/ ▶ noun
rear - backside - backbone

پشته
/poshte/ ▶ noun
hill - heap - mound - barrow

پشت پا
/poshte pa/ ▶ noun
instep

پشتوانه
/poshtvâne/ ▶ noun
bankroll

پشت پنجره
/poshte panjare/ ▶ noun
shutter

پشتی
/poshti/ ▶ noun
pad - pillow

پشت درد
/posht dard/ ▶ noun
lumbago - backache

پشتیبان
/poshtibân/ ▶ adjective
protector - backer

پشت سر
/poshte sar/ ▶ noun
behind - back

پشتیبانی
/poshtibâni/ ▶ noun
patronage

پشت سر گذاشتن
/poshte sar gozâshtan/ ▶ verb
distance

پشکل
/peshkel/ ▶ noun
dung

پشت سرهم
/poshte sare ham/ ▶ adverb
consecutive

پشمالو
/pashmâlu/ ▶ adjective
shaggy - ulotrichous

پشت گردن
/poshte gardan/ ▶ noun
nape - cervix

پشه
/pashe/ ▶ noun
mosquito

پشتکار
/poshtekâr/ ▶ noun
perseverance

پل ساختن
/pol sakhtan/ ► verb
bridge

پل متحرک
/pole moteharek/ ► noun
drawbridge

پل هوایی
/pole havâyi/ ► noun
skyway - overpass

پلاستیک
/pelâstik/ ► noun
plastic

پلاک
/pelâk/ ► noun
plate - plaque

پلک
/pelk/ ► noun
eyelid

پلکان
/pelekân/ ► noun
step - stairway - ramp - pitch

پلنگ
/palang/ ► noun
tiger

پله
/pele/ ► noun
echelon - step - stair

پشیمان
/pashimân/ ► adjective
regretful - penitent

پشیمانی
/pashimâni/ ► noun
remorse - regret

پف
/pof/ ► noun
puff - snuff - whiff

پف کردن
/pof kardan/ ► verb
puffy - puff

پف کرده
/pof karde/ ► adjective
bouffant - bloat

پفک
/pofak/ ► noun
blowgun - puff

پک زدن
/pok zadan/ ► verb
puff

پکر
/pakar/ ► adjective
pensive - body

پل
/pol/ ► noun
Bridge

پله برقی
/pele barghi/ ► noun
escalator

پناه دادن
/panâh dâdan/ ► verb
shelter - refug

پله نردبان
/peleye nardebân/ ► noun
rung

پناهگاه
/panâhgâh/ ► noun
shelter - covert

پلید
/palid/ ► adjective
frowzy - foul

پناهندگی
/panâhandegi/ ► noun
refuge

پلیس
/polis/ ► noun
police - cop

پناهنده سیاسی
/panâhandeye siyâsi/ ► noun
refugee

پلیور
/poliver/ ► noun
sweater

پنبه
/panbe/ ► noun
cotton

پماد
/pomâd/ ► noun
ointment - pomade

پنبه دانه
/panbedâne/ ► noun
cottonseed

پناه
/panâh/ ► noun
safeguard - guard

پنبه زنی
/panbe zani/ ► noun
card

پناه بردن
/panâh bordan/ ► verb
harbor - refuge

پنج ضلعی
/panjzel'I/ ► noun
pentagon

پناه بردن به
/panâh bordan be/ ► verb
quarter

پنج قلو
/panj gholu/ ► noun
quintuplet

پنج گوشه
/panj gushe/ ► noun
pentangle - pentagon

پند
/pand/ ► noun
advice

پنجاه
/panjâh/ ► noun
fifty

پند دادن
/pand dâdan/ ► verb
advise - admonish

پنجر شدن
/panchar shodan/ ► verb
blowout

پنداشتن
/pendâshtan/ ► verb
suppose - assume - imagine

پنجره
/panjere/ ► noun
window

پنهان
/penhân/ ► adjective
hidden

پنجگانه
/panjgâne/ ► adjective
five - quintuplet

پنهان سازی
/penhân sâzi/ ► noun
hide

پنجمین
/panjomin/ ► noun
fifth

پنهان شدن
/penhânshodan/ ► verb
abscond - hide

پنجه
/panje/ ► noun
paw - fork

پنهان کردن
/penhân kardan/ ► verb
cover - mask - hide

پنچر
/panchar/ ► noun
puncture

پنهانی
/penhâni/ ► adjective
privacy - hidden

پنچر شدن
/panchar shodan/ ► verb
puncture

پنی سیلین
/penisilin/ ► noun
penicillin

پهن کردن
/pahn kardan/ ▶ verb
broaden - expand - widen

پنیر
/panir/ ▶ noun
cheese

پهنا
/pahnâ/ ▶ noun
width - breadth

پهلو
/pahlu/ ▶ noun
hand - side

پهناور
/pahnâvar/ ▶ adjective
vast - broad - wide

پهلو به پهلو
/pahlu be pahlu/ ▶ noun
collateral - abreast

پهنه
/pahne/ ▶ noun
width - poll - palm - arena

پهلو زدن
/pahlu zadan/ ▶ verb
emulate

پوچ
/puch/ ▶ adjective
empty - vain - absurd

پهلوان
/pahlavân/ ▶ noun
athlete - champion

پوچ کردن
/puch kardan/ ▶ verb
void

پهلوانی
/pahlavâni/ ▶ adjective
athletic

پود
/pud/ ▶ noun
stamen - woof

پهلوی
/pahlavi/ ▶ noun
at - by

پودر
/pudr/ ▶ noun
powder - flour

پهلویی
/pahluyi/ ▶ noun
next - lateral - immediate

پودر شدن
/pudr shodan/ ▶ verb
flour

پهن
/pahn/ ▶ adjective
wide - flat

پوزخند
/puzkhand/ ▶ noun
snicker - sneer - smirk

پوست کندن
/pust kandan/ ▶ verb
peel

پوزخند زدن
/puzkhand zadan/ ▶ verb
snicker - smirk

پوست کنده
/pust kande/ ▶ adjective
picked - aboveboard

پوزش
/puzesh/ ▶ noun
pardon - apology

پوسته
/puste/ ▶ noun
chaff - case - cortex - membrane

پوزش خواستن
/puzesh khâstan/ ▶ verb
apologize

پوسته دار
/pustedar/ ▶ adjective
rinded

پوزه
/puze/ ▶ noun
nozzle - muzzle - beak

پوسته مانند
/puste mânand/ ▶ adjective
crusty

پوست
/pust/ ▶ noun
peel - skin - shell

پوسیدن
/pusidan/ ▶ verb
putrefy - decay - corrode - rot

پوست آرایی
/pust ârâyi/ ▶ noun
taxidermy

پوسیده
/puside/ ▶ adjective
musty - frowzy - ruttish - rotten

پوست دار
/pustdâr/ ▶ adjective
husky

پوسیده شدن
/puside/ ▶ verb
spoil

پوست کن
/pustkan/ ▶ noun
skinner

پوشاک
/pushâk/ ▶ noun
weed - wear - garment - clothing

پوشال

/pushâl/ ► noun
chaff

پوشاندن

/pushândan/ ► verb
cover - shroud

پوشانیدن

/pushânidan/ ► verb
cover - wrap

پوشش

/pushesh/ ► noun
shroud - shield - camouflage

پوشه

/pushe/ ► noun
membrane - wrapper

پوشیدن

/pushidan/ ► verb
wear

پوشیده

/pushide/ ► adjective
covert - secret

پوشیده از چمن

/pushide az chaman/ ► adjective
grassy

پوشیده از چوب

/pushide az chub/ ► adjective
woody

پوشیده از یخ

/pushide az yakh/ ► adjective
icy

پوشیده شدن

/pushide shodan/ ► verb
beetle

پوک

/puk/ ► adjective
hollow

پول

/pul/ ► noun
money

پول توجیبی

/pul tu jibi/ ► noun
spending money

پول خرد

/pule khord/ ► noun
change - cash

پول دادن

/pul dâdan/ ► verb
pay

پول نقد

/pule naghd/ ► noun
cash

پولاد

/pulâd/ ► noun
steel

پولادین
/pulâdin/ ▶ adjective
steely

پوییدن
/puyidan/ ▶ verb
seek

پولدار
/puldâr/ ▶ adjective
plutocrat

پی
/pei/ ▶ noun
following

پولک
/pulak/ ▶ noun
shale

پی آمد
/pey âmad/ ▶ noun
consequence - result - outcome

پولک دار
/pulakdâr/ ▶ adjective
scaly - scaled

پی بردن
/pei bordan/ ▶ verb
discover

پولکی
/pulaki/ ▶ adjective
mercenary

پی درپی
/pei dar pei/ ▶ adjective
consecutive - incessant

پولی
/puli/ ▶ noun
monetary

پیاده
/piyâde/ ▶ adverb
pedestrian

پونز
/punez/ ▶ noun
thumbtack - tack

پیاده رو
/piyâdero/ ▶ noun
sidewalk - pavement

پویا
/puyâ/ ▶ adjective
dynamic

پیاده روی
/piyâderavi/ ▶ noun
walking

پیاده شدن
/piyâde shodan/ ▶ verb
land

پویایی
/puyâyi/ ▶ noun
mobility - dynamism

پیاده شطرنج

/piyâdeye shatranj/ ▶ noun
pawn

پیپ

/pip/ ▶ noun
pipe

پیاده کردن

/piyâde kardan/ ▶ verb
implementation

پیچ

/pich/ ▶ noun
screw - twist - twine - buckle - bolt

پیاز

/piyâz/ ▶ noun
onion

پیچ خوردگی

/pichkhordegi/ ▶ adjective
screw - twist

پیازچه

/piyâzche/ ▶ noun
onion

پیچ خوردن

/pich khordan/ ▶ verb
loop - wry - wrench

پیازگل

/piyâze gol/ ▶ noun
bulb

پیچ دار

/pichdâr/ ▶ adjective
swept

پیاله

/piyâle/ ▶ noun
cup

پیچ دار کردن

/pichdâr kardan/ ▶ verb
twist

پیام

/payâm/ ▶ noun
message

پیچ و تاب

/picho tâb/ ▶ noun
warp

پیامبر

/payâmbar/ ▶ noun
prophet

پیچ وخم

/pichokham/ ▶ noun
maze - bight

پیانو

/piyâno/ ▶ noun
piano

پیچ وخم داشتن

/pichokham dâshtan/ ▶ verb
meander

پیچاندن

/pichândan/ ▶ verb
screw - twitch - wrest

پیدا

/peidâ/ ▶ adjective
visible - apparent - transparent

پیچانده

/pichânde/ ▶ adjective
wound

پیدایش

/peidâyesh/ ▶ noun
birth - appearance - genesis

پیچانیدن

/pichânidan/ ▶ verb
trill

پیدایشی

/peidâyeshi/ ▶ noun
genetic

پیچش

/pichesh/ ▶ adjective
wrest - torsion

پیر

/pir/ ▶ adjective
old

پیچک

/pichak/ ▶ noun
scroll

پیر شدن

/pir shodan/ ▶ verb
aging

پیچیدگی

/pichidegi/ ▶ noun
compiexity - intricacy

پیراستن

/pirâstan/ ▶ verb
decorate - embellish

پیچیدن

/pichidan/ ▶ verb
twist - twinge - enwrap

پیراسته

/pirâste/ ▶ adjective
trim

پیچیده

/pichide/ ▶ adjective
intricate - indirect - obscurant

پیرامونی

/pirâmuni/ ▶ noun
peripheral

پیچیده کردن

/pichide kardan/ ▶ verb
entangle - complicate

پیراهن

/pirâhan/ ▶ noun
shirt

پیراهن پوشیدن
/pirâhan pushidan/ ► verb
dress

پیروی کردن
/peiravi kardan/ ► verb
imitate

پیرایشگر
/pirâyeshgar/ ► noun
trimmer

پیری
/piri/ ► noun
aging

پیره زن
/pirezan/ ► noun
witch

پیژامه
/pizhâme/ ► noun
pajama

پیروان
/peirovân/ ► noun
followers

پیستون
/piston/ ► verb
piston

پیروز
/piruz/ ► noun
triumphant - victorious - victor

پیش
/pish/ ► adverb
forward - forth - foreside - past

پیروز شدن
/piruz shodan/ ► verb
triumph - outfight - win

پیش آمد
/pishâmad/ ► noun
accidence

پیروزمندانه
/piruzmandâne/ ► adverb
triumph

پیش آمدن
/pish âmadan/ ► verb
protrude

پیروزی
/piruzi/ ► noun
win - conquest - victory

پیش آهنگ
/pishâhang/ ► noun
scout

پیروی
/peiravi/ ► noun
imitation - follow

پیش از
/pish az/ ► adverb
past – before

پیش درآمد
/pish darâmad/ ► noun
prologue - overture - prelude

پیش از این
/pish az in/ ► adverb
already

پیش رفتگی
/pishraftegi/ ► noun
jut - protrusion

پیش بردن
/pish bordan/ ► verb
further - hustle - advance

پیش کسوت
/pishkesvat/ ► noun
protagonist

پیش برنده
/pish barande/ ► adjective
promoter

پیش نویس
/pishnevis/ ► noun
draft - minute

پیش بینی
/pishbini/ ► noun
foresight - expectancy

پیش نیاز
/pishniyâz/ ► noun
prerequisite

پیش پا افتاده
/pishepâ oftâde/ ► adjective
ordinary - commonplace - common

پیشاپیش
/pishâpish/ ► noun
beforehand

پیش پرداخت
/pishpardâkht/ ► noun
prest - prepayment

پیشامد
/pishâmad/ ► noun
event - circumstance - occurrence -
accident

پیش پرده
/pishparde/ ► noun
curtainraiser

پیش داوری
/pishdâvari/ ► noun
prejudice

پیشامدگی
/pishâmadegi/ ► noun
prominence

پیش داوری کردن
/pishdâvari kardan/ ► verb
prejudge

پیشانی
/pishâni/ ► noun
frontal

پیشانی بند

/pishâniband/ ▶ noun
headband

پیشرو

/pishro/ ▶ adjective
forward

پیشتاز

/pishtâz/ ▶ adjective
vanguard

پیشروی

/pishravi/ ▶ noun
advance - headway - progress

پیشتر

/pishtar/ ▶ adverb
before - heretofore

پیشقدم

/pishghadam/ ▶ adjective
pioneer - van - pacemaker

پیشخدمت

/pishkhedmat/ ▶ noun
servant - bellboy

پیشقدم شدن

/pishghadam shodan/ ▶ verb
pioneer

پیشرفت

/pishraft/ ▶ noun
progress - improvement - development -
growth

پیشقدمی

/pishghadami/ ▶ noun
initiative

پیشرفت کردن

/pishraft kardan/ ▶ verb
progress - improve

پیشقراول

/pishgharâvol/ ▶ noun
vanguard

پیشرفتن

/pishraftan/ ▶ verb
proceed

پیشکش

/pishkesh/ ▶ noun
gift - offer - dedicate - present

پیشکش کردن

/pishkesh kardan/ ▶ verb
offer

پیشرفته

/pishrafte/ ▶ adjective
advanced

پیشکشی

/pishkeshi/ ▶ noun
present - gift

پیشنهاد کردن
/pishnahâd kardan/ ► verb
suggest - offer

پیشگام
/pishgâm/ ► adjective
trailblazer - van - pioneer

پیشه
/pishe/ ► noun
profession - craft - occupation - function

پیشگفتار
/pishgoftâr/ ► noun
preface - prologue

پیشه ور
/pishevar/ ► noun
tradesman

پیشگویی
/pishguyi/ ► noun
prophecy - sooth - oracle - omen -
augury - prediction

پیشه وری
/pishevari/ ► noun
trade

پیشگیری
/pishgiri/ ► noun
prevention

پیشوا
/pishvâ/ ► adjective
leader - primate

پیشگیری کردن
/pishgiri kardan/ ► verb
prevent

پیشوند
/pishvand/ ► noun
prefix

پیشگیری کننده
/pishgiri konande/ ► adjective
prophylactic

پیشی
/pishi/ ► noun
puss - kitty - antecedent

پیشنهاد
/pishnahâd/ ► noun
offer - bid - plea - purpose - proposal

پیشی جستن از
/pishi jostan/ ► verb
outstrip

پیشنهاد ازدواج کردن
/pishnahâde ezdevâj kardan/ ► verb
propose

پیشی گرفتن از
/pishi gereftan/ ► verb
outshine

پیشنهاد دادن
/pishnahâd dâdan/ ► verb
suggest- recommend

پیک
/peik/ ▶ noun
messenger - mercury

پیک نیک
/piknik/ ▶ noun
picnic

پیکار
/peikâr/ ▶ noun
toil - battle - combat

پیکان
/peikân/ ▶ noun
dart - arrow - barb

پیکر
/peikar/ ▶ noun
statue - figure - effigy - likeness

پیکره
/peikare/ ▶ noun
statue

پیگرد
/peigard/ ▶ noun
pursuit

پیگیری
/peigiri/ ▶ noun
pursuit

پیل
/pil/ ▶ noun
bishop

پیشین
/pishin/ ▶ adjective
prior - primitive - previous - former

پیشینه
/pishine/ ▶ noun
record - history - past

پیغام
/peighâm/ ▶ noun
message - errand - dispatch - word

پیغام آور
/peighâm âvar/ ▶ adjective
messenger

پیغام بر
/peighâmbar/ ▶ adjective
mercury

پیغام دادن
/peighâm dâdan/ ▶ verb
message

پیغام رسانی
/peighâmresâni/ ▶ noun
instant

پیغمبر
/peighambar/ ▶ noun
prophet

پیغمبری
/peighambari/ ▶ adjective
prophecy

پیله

/pile/ ▶ noun
cocoon

پیه

/piye/ ▶ noun
suet

پیمان

/peimân/ ▶ noun
agreement - oath

پیوست

/peivast/ ▶ noun
appendage - annex - enclosure

پیمان بستن

/peimân bastan/ ▶ verb
promise - covenant

پیوستگی

/peivastegi/ ▶ noun
juncture - unity - union - continuity

پیمان نامه

/peimân nâme/ ▶ noun
convention

پیوستن

/peivastan/ ▶ verb
join - connect

پیمانه

/peimâne/ ▶ noun
measure - bushel - gauge - yardstick

پیوسته

/peivaste/ ▶ adjective
uninterrupted - allied

پیمایش

/peimâyesh/ ▶ noun
survey - padding

پیوند

/peivand/ ▶ noun
link - union - consociation - confederacy

پیمودن

/peimudan/ ▶ verb
run - pace - mete

پیوند زدن

/peivand zadan/ ▶ verb
join - crossbreed

پینه

/pine/ ▶ noun
callus

پیوند کردن

/peivand kardan/ ▶ verb
splice

پینه دوز

/pineduz/ ▶ adjective
cobbler

ت – تـ

te /te/ ► forth letter of the Persian alphabet

تا

/tâ/ ► preposition
than - bale - until - to

تا آنجاییکه

/tâjâyike/ ► preposition
inasmuchas

تا آنکه

/tâ ânke/ ► preposition
till

تا آنوقت

/tâ ânvaght/ ► adverb
yet

تا ابد

/tâ abad/ ► adverb
forever

تا اندازه ای

/tâ ândâze'l/ ► adverb
something - somedeal

تا اینجا

/tâ injâ/ ► adverb
hitherto

تا اینکه

/tâ inke/ ► preposition
till - than - until

تا جاییکه

/tajâyike/ ► preposition
insofaras

تا حدودی

/tâhodudike/ ► adverb
somedeal

تا کردن

/tâ kardan/ ► verb
fold

تاب

/tâb/ ► noun
patience - swing - sway

تاب آوردن

/tâb âvardan/ ► verb
abide - bear - withstand

تاب برداشتن

/tâb bardâshtan/ ► verb
warp

تاب خوردگی

/tâbkhordegi/ ► noun
ruga

تابان

/tâbân/ ► adjective
shiner - brilliant - luminous

تابناک
/tâbnâk/ ▶ adjective
radiant - bright - sunny

تابانیدن
/tâbânidan/ ▶ verb
glint

تابندگی
/bâbandegi/ ▶ noun
radiance

تابحال
/tâbehâl/ ▶ adverb
hitherto

تابنده
/tâbande/ ▶ adjective
spinner - phosphorous - phosphoric

تابستان
/tâbestân/ ▶ noun
summer

تابوت
/tâbut/ ▶ noun
coffin - chest - cassette

تابش
/tâbesh/ ▶ noun
glitter - glint - brilliance - shine

تاتو
/tâto/ ▶ noun
pony

تابش دار
/tâbeshdâr/ ▶ adjective
radioactive

تاثر
/ta'asor/ ▶ noun
regret - greet

تابشی
/tâbeshi/ ▶ adjective
radial

تاثرآور
/ta'asor âvar/ ▶ adjective
pathetic - heinous

تابع
/tâbe'/ ▶ noun
ancillary - accessory - citizen - function

تاثرپذیر
/ta'asor pazir/ ▶ adjective
impressionable - passive

تابعیت
/tâbe'iyat/ ▶ noun
citizen - nationality

تاثیر
/ta'sir/ ▶ noun
influence - hank

تابلو
/tâblo/ ▶ noun
tableau - sign

تادیب

/ta'dib/ ▶ noun
discipline - correction

تاثیرپذیر

/ta'sirpazir/ ▶ adjective
impressible

تادیب کردن

/ta'dib kardan/ ▶ verb
discipline

تاج

/tâj/ ▶ noun
rostrum - crown - crest - corona

تاراج

/târâj/ ▶ noun
spoil - plunder - pillage

تاج گل

/tâjegol/ ▶ noun
wreath - garland

تارک دنیا

/târek donyâ/ ▶ adjective
hermit - monk - ascetic

تاجر

/tâjer/ ▶ noun
businessman - merchant

تارکننده

/târkonande/ ▶ adjective
dimmer

تاحدی

/tâhadi/ ▶ adverb
kind of - partly - somewhat

تارکی

/târki/ ▶ noun
vertical

تاخت کردن

/tâkht kardan/ ▶ verb
attack

تاروپود

/târopud/ ▶ noun
sinew - texture - warpandwoof

تاخت و تاز

/tâkhto tâz/ ▶ noun
ravage - raid - attack

تاری

/târi/ ▶ noun
umbrage - obscurity

تاخیر

/ta'khir/ ▶ noun
late - demur

تاریخ

/târikh/ ▶ noun
history - date - era

تاخیر کردن

/ta'khir kardan/ ▶ verb
linger - lag - delay - defer

تاریخ دان
/târikhdân/ ► noun
historian

تازه تر
/tâzetar/ ► adjective
junior

تاریخچه
/târikhche/ ► noun
record - chronicle - annals - memoir -
history

تازه کار
/tâzekar/ ► adjective
tyro - novice - ham - beginner

تاریخی
/târikhi/ ► adjective
epochal - historic

تازه کردن
/tâze kardan/ ► verb
refresh - fresh

تاریک
/târik/ ► adjective
dark - dusky

تازه نفس
/tâzenafas/ ► adjective
fresh

تاریک کردن
/târik kardan/ ► verb
gloom - overshadow - obscure - dark

تازه وارد
/tâzevâred/ ► adjective
immigrant - newcomer

تازگی
/tâzegi/ ► noun
fresshness - novelty

تازی
/tâzi/ ► noun
Arabic

تازمانی که
/tâzamânike/ ► preposition
pending

تازیانه
/tâziyâne/ ► noun
scourge - lash - rawhide - whip

تازه
/tâze/ ► adjective
recent - fresh - uptodate

تازیانه زدن
/tâziyâne zadan/ ► verb
scourge - whip

تازه به دوران رسیده
/tâze bedorân reside/ ► adjective
upstart

تازیدن
/tâzidan/ ► verb
gallop

تاسف

/ta'asof/ ▶ noun
ruth - regret

تاقچه دار کردن

/tâghchedâr kardan/ ▶ verb
shelve

تاسف آور

/ta'asof âvar/ ▶ adjective
wretched

تاکستان

/tâkestân/ ▶ noun
arbor - vineyard

تاسف خوردن

/ta'asof khordan/ ▶ verb
sorrow

تاکسی

/tâksi/ ▶ noun
taxi - cab

تاسیس کردن

/ta'sis kardan/ ▶ verb
establish - constitute - make - invent -
institute

تاکنون

/tâkonun/ ▶ adverb
yet - hitherto - heretofore

تاکید

/ta'kid/ ▶ noun
emphasis - underscore - accent - stress

تاسیسات

/ta'sisât/ ▶ noun
installation

تاکید کردن

/ta'kid kardan/ ▶ verb
stress - playup - accent - underline -
enforce

تاشو

/tâsho/ ▶ adjective
jackknife - slipper - pliant - lissome -
limber

تالاب

/tâlâb/ ▶ noun
lagoon - pond

تافی

/tâfi/ ▶ noun
caramel - butterscotch - taffy

تالار

/tâlâr/ ▶ noun
amphitheater - hall

تاقچه

/tâghche/ ▶ noun
shelf

تالم آور

/ta'alom âvar/ ▶ adjective
grievous

تاول

/tâval/ ► noun
gall - welt - blister - bleb - scorch - scald

تالیف

/ta'lif/ ► noun
essay - compilation

تاول زدن

/tâval zadan/ ► verb
scorch - breakout - blister

تالیف کردن

/ta'lif kardan/ ► verb
write - compile

تاویل

/ta'vil/ ► noun
gloss - paraphrase

تامل

/ta'amol/ ► noun
indecision

تایید

/ta'yid/ ► noun
support - endorsement - grace

تامل کردن

/ta'amol kardan/ ► verb
hesitate

تب و تاب

/tabotâb/ ► noun
flame - ardor

تامین

/ta'min/ ► noun
security - secure

تبادل

/tabâdol/ ► noun
exchange

تانک

/tânk/ ► noun
tanker - tank

تبادل کردن

/tabâdol kardan/ ► verb
interchange

تاوان

/tâvân/ ► noun
penalty - indemnity - reparation - fine

تبانی

/tabâni/ ► noun
collusion - cahoot

تاوان دادن

/tâvân dâdan/ ► verb
compensate - retaliate - remunerate -
indemnify - penalize

تباه شدن

/tabâh shodan/ ► verb
vitiate

تاوقتی که

/tâ vaghtike/ ► preposition
until

تباه کردن
/tabâh kardan/ ▶ verb
destroy - deprave - gangrene - vitiate

تباه کننده
/tabâhkonande/ ▶ adjective
corrosive

تباهی
/tabâhi/ ▶ noun
spoil - ruination - ruin - destruction -
depravity - degeneration - decay

تبخیر شدن
/tabkhir shodan/ ▶ verb
evaporate - vaporize

تبخیر کردن
/tabkhir kardan/ ▶ verb
vaporize - evaporate

تبدیل
/tabdil/ ▶ noun
reduction - commutation - conversion

تبدیل کردن
/tabdil kardan/ ▶ verb
commute - turquoise - transmute -
transform

تبر
/tabar/ ▶ noun
chopper

تبریک گفتن
/tabrik goftan/ ▶ verb
greet - congratulate

تبسم
/tabasom/ ▶ noun
smile

تبعه یک کشور
/taba'eye yek keshvar/ ▶ noun
citizen

تبعیت
/taba'iyat/ ▶ noun
allegiance - adherence

تبعید
/tab'id/ ▶ noun
proscription - expultion - exile

تبعید کردن
/tab'id kardan/ ▶ verb
deport - exile - displace - proscribe

تبعیض
/tab'iz/ ▶ noun
prejudice

تبعیض آمیز
/tab'iz âmiz/ ▶ adjective
prejudicial

تبلیغ
/tabligh/ ▶ noun
propagation - propaganda

تپلی
/topoli/ ▶ noun
squab - rondure

تبلیغ کردن
/tabligh kardan/ ▶ verb
proselyte

تپنده
/tapande/ ▶ verb
palpitant

تبلیغات
/tablighât/ ▶ noun
incantation - publicity - propaganda

تپه
/tape/ ▶ noun
mount - mound - hill - barrow

تبه کار
/tabah kâr/ ▶ adjective
wicked - untoward - villain

تثبیت کردن
/tasbit kardan/ ▶ verb
stabilize - confirm - reinstate

تبه کاری
/tabah kâri/ ▶ noun
villainy - crime

تپانچه
/tapânche/ ▶ noun
pistol

تجارت
/tejarat/ ▶ noun
commerce - trade

تپاندن
/tapândan/ ▶ verb
stuff

تجارت کردن
/tejârat kardan/ ▶ verb
merchandise - commerce

تپش
/tapesh/ ▶ noun
beat - pant - pitterpatter - tremor - throb
- pump

تجارتخانه
/tejâratkhâne/ ▶ noun
firm

تپش دل
/tapeshe del/ ▶ noun
heartbeat

تجارتی
/tejârati/ ▶ adjective
mercantile - commercial

تپل
/topol/ ▶ adjective
rotund

تجاری
/tejâri/ ▶ adjective
joinery

تجربه
/tajrobe/ ▶ noun
experiment - experience

تجانس
/tajânos/ ▶ noun
congruity - congruence

تجربه کردن
/tajrobe kardan/ ▶ verb
experiment - experience

تجاهل
/tajâhol/ ▶ noun
evasion

تجربی
/tajrobi/ ▶ adjective
experimental

تجاوز
/tajâvoz/ ▶ noun
assault - agression - overrun - offense

تجزیه
/tajziye/ ▶ noun
resolution - anatomy - analysis

تجدید
/tajdid/ ▶ noun
revival - resumption - restoration -
repetition - repeat

تجزیه پذیر
/tajziye pazir/ ▶ adjective
dissoluble

تجدید بنا
/tajdide banâ/ ▶ noun
reconstruction

تجزیه شدن
/tajziye shodan/ ▶ verb
parse - disintegrate

تجدید حیات
/tajdide hayât/ ▶ noun
resurgence - renascence - rebirth

تجزیه طلب
/tajziye talab/ ▶ adjective
secessionist

تجدید خاطره
/tajdide khâtere/ ▶ noun
recollection

تجزیه طلبی
/tajziye talabi/ ▶ noun
secessionism - secession

تجدید قوا
/tajdide ghovâ/ ▶ noun
rest - refection

تجزیه کردن
/tajziye kardan/ ▶ verb
decompose - dismember - comminute -
liberate - breakdown - analyze

تجدید نظر
/tajdide nazar/ ▶ noun
revision - revisal - review –
reconsideration

تجزیه ناپذیر
/tajziye nâpazir/ ▶ adjective
irresolvable - indissoluble

تجسس
/tajasos/ ▶ noun
search - research

تجسم
/tajasom/ ▶ noun
portrayal - incarnation - projection

تجسم روح
/tajasome ruh/ ▶ noun
ghost

تجلی
/tajali/ ▶ noun
expression - influence - phenomenon

تجلی کردن
/tajali kardan/ ▶ verb
transfigure - emanate

تجلیل
/tajlil/ ▶ noun
homage - celebration - kudos

تجلیل کردن
/tajlil kardan/ ▶ verb
exalt - ennoble - glorify - celebrate

تجلیلی
/tajlili/ ▶ adjective
honorific

تجمع
/tajamo'/ ▶ noun
aggregation

تجمل
/tajamol/ ▶ noun
pomp

تجهیز
/tajhiz/ ▶ noun
outfit

تجهیزات
/tajhizât/ ▶ noun
materiel - equipment

تجویز
/tajviz/ ▶ noun
prescription - approval

تجویز کردن
/tajviz kardan/ ▶ verb
prescribe

تحت
/that/ ▶ noun
subject - sub - under

تحت اللفظی
/tahtol'lafzi/ ▶ noun
verbatim - verbal - literal

تحدید

/tahdid/ ▶ noun
limitation - restriction

تحت تاثیر قرار دادن

/tahte ta'sir gharâr dâdan/ ▶ verb
touching

تحرک

/taharok/ ▶ noun
stimulus - bolubility - locomotion -
mobility

تحت تاثیر واقع شدن

/tahte ta'sir vâghe shodan/ ▶ verb
react

تحریر کردن

/tahrir kardan/ ▶ verb
write - redact

تحت تسلط

/tahte tasalot/ ▶ adjective
subject - under

تحریردار

/tahrirdâr/ ▶ adjective
tremulous

تحت فشار

/tahte feshâr/ ▶ adjective
impacted - beneath

تحریری

/tahriri/ ▶ adjective
scribal

تحت محاصره

/tahte mohâsere/ ▶ adjective
enclave

تحریف

/tahrif/ ▶ noun
anagram - distortion - garble -
sophistication

تحت نفوذ

/tahte nofuz/ ▶ adjective
beneath

تحریف شدن

/tahrif shodan/ ▶ verb
mutilate

تحتانی

/tahtâni/ ▶ noun
beneath

تحریف کردن

/tahrif kardan/ ▶ verb
slant - skew - garble - distort - agonize

تحجر

/tahajor/ ▶ noun
calcification

تحدب

/tahadob/ ▶ noun
bulge

تحریک

/tahrik/ ▶ noun
persuasion - boil - provacation –
stimulus

تحریک پذیر
/tahrik pazir/ ► adjective
irritable

تحصیل
/tahsil/ ► noun
study

تحریک شدن
/tahrik shodan/ ► verb
induce

تحفه
/tohfe/ ► noun
curio - rarity - trove

تحریک کردن
/tahrik kardan/ ► verb
provoke - stimulate - excite - arouse -
bestir - motivate

تحقق
/tahaghogh/ ► noun
realization

تحریم
/tahrim/ ► noun
prohibition - embargo - interdict -
boycott

تحقق یافتن
/tahaghogh yâftan/ ► verb
comeoff - realize

تحقیر
/tahghir/ ► noun
scorn - humility - disdain - contempt

تحریم کردن
/tahrim kardan/ ► verb
boycott - blackball - ban - proscribe -
prohibit

تحقیق
/tahghigh/ ► noun
research - rummage - probe - inquiry -
quest

تحسین
/tahsin/ ► noun
praise - applause

تحقیق کردن
/tahghigh kardan/ ► verb
research - investigate - interrogate -
inquire - verify

تحسین کردن
/tahsin kardan/ ► verb
applaud - admire

تحکم آمیز
/tahakom âmiz/ ► adjective
imperious

تحصن
/tahason/ ► noun
refuge

تحول

/tahavol/ ▶ noun
evolution - solstice

تحکم کردن

/tahakom kardan/ ▶ verb
domineer

تحول شدید

/tahavole shadid/ ▶ adjective
upthrow

تحلیل

/tahlil/ ▶ noun
analysis

تحویل

/tahvil/ ▶ noun
transfer - delivery

تحلیل رفتن

/tahlil raftan/ ▶ verb
atrophy

تحمل

/tahamol/ ▶ noun
tolerance - endurance

تحویل دادن

/tahvil dâdan/ ▶ verb
deliver - surrender

تحمل پذیر

/tahamol pazir/ ▶ adjective
endurable

تحویلدار

/tahvil dâr/ ▶ noun
cashier

تحمل خسارت

/tahamole khesarat/ ▶ noun
toll

تخت

/takht/ ▶ noun
sole - throne - couch

تحمل کردن

/tahamol kardan/ ▶ verb
undergo - bear - withstand - endure -
suffer - tolerate

تختان

/takhtân/ ▶ noun
terrace

تحمیل

/tahmil/ ▶ noun
tax - protrusion - incurrence - imposition
- levy

تختخواب

/takhtekhâb/ ▶ noun
bed - hay

تخته

/takhte/ ▶ noun
sheet - tablet - gob - lumber - brede -
board - plank - ledger

تحمیل کردن

/tahmil kardan/ ▶ verb
burden - inflict - impose - saddle –
protrude

(Idiom: یک تخته کسی کم بودن
Have screw loose)

تخته ای
/takhte'I/ ► adjective
tabular

تخته سنگ
/takhte sang/ ► noun
slab - crag - cliff - roach - boulder

تخته سیاه
/takhte siyâh/ ► noun
blackboard

تخته شطرنج
/takhteye shatranj/ ► noun
chessboard

تخته نرد
/takhte nard/ ► noun
backgammon

تخدیر
/takhdir/ ► noun
stupefaction

تخدیر کردن
/takhdir kardan/ ► verb
drug - dope - stupefy

تخریب
/takhrib/ ► noun
subversion - destruction - demolition

تخصص
/takhasos/ ► noun
proficiency - specialty

تخصیص
/takhsis/ ► noun
devotion - designation

تخصیص دادن
/takhsis dâdan/ ► verb
designate - consecrate - apportion - allot

تخطی از قانون
/takhati az ghânun/ ► noun
misdemeanor

تخطی کردن
/takhati kardan/ ► verb
trepass - encroach - contravene - offend
- impinge

تخفیف
/takhfif/ ► noun
slake - discount - remission - relaxation
- refraction - rebate

تخم مرغ
/tokhme morgh/ ▶ noun
egg

تخفیف دادن
/takhfif dâdan/ ▶ verb
discount - relieve

تخم مرغی شکل
/tokhmemorghi shekl/ ▶ noun
oval

تخفیف درد
/takhfife dard/ ▶ noun
analgesia

تخمدان
/tokhmdân/ ▶ noun
ovary - pod

تخفیف یافتن
/takhfif yâftan/ ▶ verb
scant - lessen

تخمک
/tokhmak/ ▶ noun
ovum

تخلف
/takhalof/ ▶ noun
transgression - delinquency - infraction

تخمیر
/takhmir/ ▶ noun
fermentation - zymosis

تخلف کردن
/takhalof kardan/ ▶ verb
infract

تخمیر شدن
/takhmir shodan/ ▶ verb
yeast

تخلیه کردن
/takhliye kardan/ ▶ verb
vacate

تخمیر کردن
/takhmir kardan/ ▶ verb
quicken

تخم
/tokhm/ ▶ noun
semen - seed - egg

تخیل
/takhayol/ ▶ noun
specter

تخم دان
/tokhm dâdan/ ▶ noun
cyst

تخیلات
/takhayolât/ ▶ noun
vagary

تخم گذاشتن
/tokhm gozâshtan/ ▶ verb
hatch

تدارک

/tadârok/ ► noun
preparation - purvey - provision

تدارک دیدن

/tadârok didan/ ► verb
supply

تدارکات

/tadârokât/ ► noun
munition

تدبیر

/tadbir/ ► noun
contrivance - contraption - plan -
machination - scheme

تدریج

/tadrij/ ► noun
gradation

تدریجی

/tadriji/ ► adjective
gradual

تدریس

/tadris/ ► noun
teaching- training

تدریس کردن

/tadris kardan/ ► verb
profess - prelect - lesson- teach

تدفین

/tadfin/ ► noun
interment

تدلیس کردن

/tadlis kardan/ ► verb
dissemble

تذکر

/tazakor/ ► noun
hint - mention - remembrance -
notification

تذکر دادن

/tazakor dâdan/ ► verb
warn - callup

تر

/tar/ ► adjective
humid - moist - rainy - wet

تر شدن

/tar shodan/ ► verb
moisten

تر کردن

/tar kardan/ ► verb
moisten - wet - dab

تر و تازه

/taro tâze/ ► adjective
pristine - green - fresh - spannew

تر و تمیز

/taro tamiz/ ► adjective
trim - trig - shipshape - prissy

ترا

/torâ/ ► noun
thee

ترابری

/tarâbari/ ► noun
transport

تراز

/tarâz/ ► noun
balance - slight

ترازو

/tarâzu/ ► noun
scale

تراس

/terâs/ ► noun
terrace

تراشه

/tarâshe/ ► noun
chip - ribbon - excelsior - splinter

تراشیدگی

/tarâshidegi/ ► noun
erasure

تراشیدن

/tarâshidan/ ► verb
scrape - trim - shave - raze - rase - carve
- expunge - excoriate - erase

تراکم

/tarâkom/ ► noun
density - congestion - congeries -
compression

تربیت

/tarbiyat/ ► noun
upbringing - pedagogy - manner - gentry
- nurture - civility - steerage

تربیتی

/tarbiyati/ ► adjective
education

ترتیب

/tartib/ ► noun
rank - configuration - setup - sequence

ترتیب دادن

/tartib dâdan/ ► verb
ordain - arrange - agree

ترتیبی

/tartibi/ ► adjective
serial - ordinal

ترجمان

/tarjomân/ ► noun
translation

ترجمه

/tarjome/ ► noun
translation

ترجیحا

/tarjihan/ ► adverb
rather

ترحم

/tarahom/ ► noun
pathos

ترحم کردن

/tarahom kardan/ ▶ verb
pity

ترد

/tord/ ▶ adjective
brittle - mealy - plucky

تردستی

/tardasti/ ▶ noun
agility - dexterity - sleight - skill -
juggle

تردید

/tardid/ ▶ noun
suspicion - skepticism - doubt

ترس

/tars/ ▶ noun
fear - horror - misgiving - awful

ترس آور

/tarsâvar/ ▶ adjective
bloodcurdling - awesome

ترساندن

/tarsândan/ ▶ verb
scare - fright - horrify - abhor

ترساننده

/tarsânande/ ▶ adjective
deterrent - scaremonger - scarer

ترسانیدن

/tarsânidan/ ▶ verb
dismay

ترسناک

/tarsnâk/ ▶ adjective
terrific - terrible - tremendous - ugsome

ترسو

/tarsu/ ▶ adjective
skittish - timid - pusillanimous - pigeon

ترسیدن

/tarsidan/ ▶ verb
quail - bash - abhor - scare

ترسیده

/tarside/ ▶ adjective
afraid

ترسیم کردن

/tarsim kardan/ ▶ verb
depict - trace - map

ترسیم نمودن

/tarsim nemudan/ ▶ verb
delineate

ترسیمی

/tarsimi/ ▶ adjective
graphic

ترش

/torsh/ ▶ adjective
sour - tart - acid - acetic

ترش بودن

/torsh budan/ ▶ verb
sour

ترش مزه

/torshmaze/ ► adjective
tart

ترشح

/tarashoh/ ► noun
discharge - sprinkle - spray - splutter -
spatter

ترشرو

/toroshru/ ► adjective
petulant - morose - moody

ترشرویی

/toroshruyi/ ► noun
scowl - sulk - lower

ترشی

/torshi/ ► noun
pickle - acidity - acerbity - souse

ترشی انداختن

/torshi andâkhtan/ ► verb
pickle

ترشیده

/torshide/ ► adjective
overripe - reechy - rank - rancid -
frowzy

ترغیب

/targhib/ ► noun
prod - persuasion

ترغیب کردن

/targhib kardan/ ► verb
persuade

ترفیع

/tarfi'/ ► noun
raise - upgrade - mount - preferment -
promotion

ترقه

/taraghe/ ► noun
cracker

ترقی

/taraghi/ ► noun
promotion - progress - boost - ascent -
lift - growth - development

ترقی خواه

/targhikhâh/ ► adjective
progressive

ترقی دادن

/taraghi dâdan/ ► verb
advance - boost - promote

ترقی کردن

/taraghi kardan/ ► verb
climb - remunerate - grow - upwell - up

ترقیق

/targhigh/ ► noun
rarefaction

ترک

/tarak/ ► noun
crack - clef - chap - renunciation -
fracture

ترک خدمت

/tarke khedmat/ ► noun
desertion

ترک خوردگی
/tarak khordegi/ ► noun
fraction

ترکه ای
/tarke'I/ ► adjective
wicker

ترک خورده
/tark khorde/ ► adjective
clef

ترکی
/torki/ ► adjective
Turkish

ترک دار
/tarkdâr/ ► adjective
rimose

ترکیب
/tarkib/ ► noun
structure - admixture - blend - physique
- mixture - compound

ترک عقیده
/tarke aghide/ ► noun
apostasy

ترکیدگی
/tarakidegi/ ► noun
bust

ترک کردن
/tark kardan/ ► verb
defect - evacuate - disuse - leave

ترکیدن
/tarakidan/ ► verb
explode - dehisce - crack - reave

ترک گفتن
/tark goftan/ ► verb
abdicate - walkouton

ترمز
/tormoz/ ► noun
brake

ترکاندن
/tarakândan/ ► verb
chap - pop - blowup - blast

ترمز کردن
/tormoz kardan/ ► verb
skid - brake

ترکش
/tarkesh/ ► noun
quiver

ترمیم
/tarmim/ ► noun
relief

ترکه
/tarke/ ► noun
rod - offshoot - wattle - wand

ترمیم کردن
/tarmim kardan/ ► verb
amend - rehabilitate – reform

تروشرویی

/toroshruyi/ ► noun
austerity - glower

تزلزل ناپذیر

/tazalzol nâpazir/ ► adjective
adamant - imperturbable

ترویج

/tarvij/ ► noun
promotion

تزویر

/tazvir/ ► noun
artifice - wile - duplicity

ترویج کردن

/tarvij kardan/ ► verb
cultivate - promulgate - promote

تزویر کردن

/tazvir kardan/ ► verb
fox

تریاک

/taryâk/ ► noun
opium

تزیین کردن

/tazyin kardan/ ► verb
decorate - prank

تز

/tez/ ► noun
dissertation

تزیینات

/tajyinât/ ► noun
decorations

تزریق

/tazrigh/ ► noun
infusion - shot - transfusion

تزیینی

/tazyini/ ► adjective
complement

تزریق خون

/tazrighe khun/ ► noun
transfusion

تساوی

/tasâvi/ ► noun
parity - par - equality

تزکیه

/tazkiye/ ► noun
refinement

تساوی حقوق

/tasâviye hoghugh/ ► noun
equity

تزلزل

/tazalzol/ ► noun
shake - insecurity

تسبیح

/tasbih/ ► noun
hallelujah - rosary

تسخیر
/taskhir/ ▶ noun
capture

تسلط
/tasalot/ ▶ noun
gripe - dominance

تسخیر کردن
/taskhir kardan/ ▶ verb
import - conquer

تسلی دادن
/tasali dâdan/ ▶ verb
solace - relieve - cherish - console

تسخیرناپذیر
/taskhir nâpazir/ ▶ adjective
unconquerable - indomitable

تسلی دهنده
/tasali dahande/ ▶ adjective
comforter

تسریع
/tasri'/ ▶ noun
speed up - expedition

تسلیت دادن
/tasliyat dâdan/ ▶ verb
console - condole

تسریع کردن
/tasri' kardan/ ▶ verb
speed - precipitate - advance - accelerate

تسلیت گفتن
/tasliyat/ ▶ verb
solace

تسطیح کردن
/tastih kardan/ ▶ verb
surface - grade

تسلیحات
/taslihât/ ▶ noun
armament - weaponry

تسکین
/taskin/ ▶ noun
solace - sedation - relief

تسلیم
/taslim/ ▶ noun
deference - resignation - rendition

تسکین دهنده
/taskin dahande/ ▶ adjective
sooth - sedate - pacifier

تسلیم شدن
/taslim shodan/ ▶ verb
surrender - succumb - submit - defer -
knuckle - obey - capitulate

تسلسل
/tasalsol/ ▶ noun
sequence - continuum - continuity

تسمه
/tasme/ ▶ noun
ribbon - hoop - halter - lash - belt – bail

تسهیم کردن
/tashim kardan/ ▶ verb
whack - portion

تسویه
/tasviye/ ▶ noun
solution - settlement - settle - adjustment

تسویه کردن
/tasviye kardan/ ▶ verb
defray - compromise - liquidate - payoff

تسویه نمودن
/tasviye nemudan/ ▶ verb
adjust

تشابه
/tashâboh/ ▶ noun
similarity - correspondence -
resemblance

تشبیه
/tashbih/ ▶ noun
metaphor - comparison - simile

تشخیص
/tashkhis/ ▶ noun
specification - recognition - denotation -
assessment

تشخیص دادن
/tashkhis/ ▶ verb
recognize - espy - distinguish - discern

تشخیص هویت دادن
/tashkhishe hoviyat dâdan/ ▶ verb
identify

تشخیصی
/tashkhishi/ ▶ adjective
diagnostic

تشدید
/tashdid/ ▶ noun
accent - intensification

تشدیدکننده
/tashdid konande/ ▶ adjective
booster

تشر زدن
/tashar zadan/ ▶ verb
browbeat

تشریح
/tashrih/ ▶ noun
description - dissection - anatomy

تشریفات
/tashrifât/ ▶ noun
ritual - ceremony - ceremonial

تشریفاتی
/tashrifâti/ ▶ adjective
ceremonial

تشریک مساعی
/tashrike masâ'I/ ▶ noun
cooperation – collaborate

تشریحی
/tashrihi/ ▶ noun
explanatory - interpretive

تشنج
/tashanoj/ ▶ noun
convulsion - fit - paroxysm

تشعشع
/tasha'sho/ ▶ noun
glare - refulgence - ray - radiance - flash

تشنگی
/teshnegi/ ▶ noun
thirst

تشک
/toshak/ ▶ noun
panel - pad - mattress

تشنه
/teshne/ ▶ adjective
thirsty

تشکر
/tashakor/ ▶ noun
thank

تشنه شدن
/teshne shodan/ ▶ verb
dry

تشکر کردن
/tashakor kardan/ ▶ verb
thank

تشویش
/tashvish/ ▶ noun
phobia - anxiety

تشکیل دادن
/tashkil dâdan/ ▶ verb
vocalize - form - constitute

تشویق و ترغیب کردن
/tashvigh va targhib kardan/ ▶ verb
exhort

تشکیل دهنده
/tashkil dahande/ ▶ adjective
constitutive - fundametal - former

تشویقی
/tashvighi/ ▶ adjective
persuasive

تشکیل شده
/tashkil shode/ ▶ adjective
formed

تصاحب کردن
/tasâhob kardan/ ▶ verb
seize

تشکیلات
/tashkilât/ ▶ noun
organization

تصادف
/tasâdof/ ▶ noun
coincidence - accidence - incidence

تصادف کردن
/tasâdof kardan/ ► verb
jar - hurtle - bop

تصادفا
/tasâdofan/ ► adverb
peradventure, chance

تصادفات
/tasâdofât/ ► noun
casualty

تصادفی
/tasâdofi/ ► adjective
random - chromatic - chancy - chanceful

تصادم
/tasâdom/ ► noun
smash - shock - collission - clash -
concussion

تصاعد
/tasâod/ ► noun
progression

تصاعدی
/tasâodi/ ► adjective
progressive

تصحیح
/tashig/ ► noun
correction - redress - rectification -
amendment

تصدی
/tasadi/ ► noun
tenure - inning - incumbency -
commission - charge

تصدیق
/tasdigh/ ► noun
ratification - admission -
acknohledgement - testimony

تصدیق کردن
/tasdigh kardan/ ► verb
justify - affirm - admit - acknowledge -
confirm - concede - certify

تصرف
/tasarof/ ► noun
seizure - tenure - occupation -
occupancy - possession

تصریح
/tasrih/ ► noun
speciosity - specification

تصریح کردن
/tasrih kardan/ ► verb
stipulate - specify - affirm - reiterate

تصفیه
/tasfiye/ ► noun
catharsis - infiltration - administration -
settlement - settle

تصفیه خانه
/tasfiye khâne/ ► noun
refinery

تصور غلط

/tasavore ghalat/ ▶ noun
misconception

تصور کردنی

/tasavor kardani/ ▶ adjective
conceivable

تصور نکردنی

/tasavor nakardani/ ▶ adjective
inconceivable

تصویب

/tasvib/ ▶ noun
sanction - resolution - approval -
approbation - passage

تصویب نامه

/tasvibnâme/ ▶ noun
decree

تصویر کردن

/tasvir kardan/ ▶ verb
figure - portrait

تصویر کشیدن

/tasvir keshidan/ ▶ verb
portray

تصویربردار

/tasvirbardâr/ ▶ noun
xerographic

تصویربرداری

/tasvirbardâri/ ▶ noun
xerography

تصفیه کننده

/tasfiye konande/ ▶ adjective
cathartic

تصمیم

/tasmim/ ▶ noun
decision - resolution - canon

تصمیم گرفتن

/tasmim gereftan/ ▶ verb
determine - decide - resolve

تصنعی

/tasano'I/ ▶ noun
sophisticated - mannered

تصنیف

/tasnif/ ▶ noun
song - sing - ballad - impromptu

تصنیف کردن

/tasnif kardan/ ▶ verb
compose - make

تصور

/tasavor/ ▶ noun
supposition - image - if - idea - picture -
vision - notion - fancy

تصور کلی

/tasavore koli/ ▶ noun
concept

تصورات

/tasavorât/ ▶ noun
Imagery

تصویری

/tasviri/ ► adjective
figurative - pictorial

تطابق

/tatâbogh/ ► noun
accordance

تضاد

/tazâd/ ► noun
confliction - conflict - opposition -
polarization - polarity

تطبیق

/tatbigh/ ► noun
adjustment

تضرع

/tazaro'/ ► noun
imprecation

تطبیق کردن

/tatbigh kardan/ ► verb
reconcile - fit - check

تضعیف روحیه کردن

/taz'ife ruhiye kardan/ ► verb
demoralize - cow

تطبیقی

/tatbighi/ ► adjective
comparative

تضعیف کردن

/taz'if kardan/ ► verb
unbrace - castrate

تطمیع

/tatmi'/ ► noun
lure - entice

تضمین

/tazmin/ ► noun
guaranty - warranty - collateral -
assurance

تطمیع کردن

/tatmi' kardan/ ► verb
bribe - allure

تضمین کردن

/tazmin kardan/ ► verb
bond - ensure - certify - warrant

تطهیر

/tathir/ ► noun
catharsis - purge

تضمین کننده

/tazmin konande/ ► adjective
voucher

تطویل

/tatvil/ ► noun
prolongation

تضییع

/taz'yi'/ ► noun
wastage

تطیر

/tathir/ ► noun
auspices

تظاهر

/tazâhor/ ▶ noun
ostentation - display - pretension -
pretense

تظاهرات

/tazâhorât/ ▶ noun
demonstration - parade

تظاهرات کردن

/tazâhorât kardan/ ▶ verb
demonstrate

تظلم

/tazalom/ ▶ noun
plaint - petition

تعادل

/ta'âdol/ ▶ noun
equilibrium - parity - par

تعارف

/ta'ârof/ ▶ noun
compliment - comity - chivalry

تعالی

/ta'âli/ ▶ noun
sublimity - ascendency - eminence

تعاون

/ta'âvon/ ▶ noun
cooperation

تعبیر

/ta'bir/ ▶ noun
comment - explanation

تعبیر کردن

/ta'bir kardan/ ▶ verb
construe - comment - phrase

تعبیه

/ta'biye/ ▶ noun
appliance - improvisation - shift

تعبیه کردن

/ta'biye kardan/ ▶ verb
workout - devise - contrive - improvise

تعجب

/ta'ajob/ ▶ noun
marvel - wonder

تعجب کردن

/ta'ajob kardan/ ▶ verb
admire - muse

تعجیل

/ta'jil/ ▶ noun
haste

تعداد

/te'dâd/ ▶ noun
some

تعدد

/ta'adod/ ▶ noun
multiplicity - plurality

تعدی

/ta'adi/ ▶ noun
oppression - abusive - inroad - infringe –
incursion

تعطیل

/ta'til/ ► noun
holiday - vacation

تعدی کردن

/ta'adi kardan/ ► verb
trepass - ingrate - oppress

تعطیل شدن

/ta'til shodan/ ► verb
closure - shut

تعدیل

/ta'dil/ ► verb
adjustment - trammel

تعطیل کردن

/ta'til kardan/ ► verb
vacate - stop - shut

تعدیل کردن

/ta'dil kardan/ ► noun
modulate - modify - moderate - adapt

تعطیل موقتی

/ta'tiliye movaghati/ ► noun
recess

تعدیل کننده

/ta'dil konande/ ► adjective
regulator

تعظیم

/ta'zim/ ► noun
bow - curtsy - obeisance

تعرض کردن

/ta'aroz kardan/ ► verb
remonstrate

تعظیم کردن

/ta'zim kardan/ ► verb
bow - bend - beck

تعریف

/ta'rif/ ► noun
compliment - explanation - description -
definition

تعفن

/ta'afon/ ► noun
putrefaction - stink - stench

تعریف کردن

/ta'rif kardan/ ► verb
unreel - praise - recount - emblazon -
define

تعقیب

/ta'ghib/ ► noun
chase-chace - pursuit

تعصب

/ta'asob/ ► noun
zealotry - zeal - prejudice -
preconception - bigotry - bias

تعقیب کردن

/ta'ghib kardan/ ► verb
pursue - follow - chase

تعمق

/ta'amogh/ ▶ noun
cud

تعمق کردن

/ta'amogh kardan/ ▶ verb
ponder - deliberate

تعمید

/ta'mid/ ▶ noun
baptism

تعمیر

/ta'mir/ ▶ noun
reparation - renovation - maintenance

تعمیر کردن

/ta'mir kardan/ ▶ verb
mend - restore - repair - remodel

تعمیرپذیر

/ta'mir pazir/ ▶ adjective
reparable

تعمیرکار

/ta'mirkâr/ ▶ noun
serviceman

تعمیرگاه

/ta'mirgâh/ ▶ noun
shootinggallery

تعمیم

/ta'mim/ ▶ noun
popularization - universalization

تعلق

/ta'alogh/ ▶ noun
dependency

تعلق داشتن

/ta'alogh dâshtan/ ▶ verb
belong

تعلل

/ta'alol/ ▶ noun
delay

تعلیق

/ta'ligh/ ▶ noun
suspension - abeyance - precipitant -
hang

تعلیم

/ta'lim/ ▶ noun
edification - training

تعلیم دادن

/ta'lim dâdan/ ▶ verb
guide - educate - teach

تعمد

/ta'amod/ ▶ noun
witting

تعمدا

/ta'amodan/ ▶ adverb
deliberate

تعمدی

/ta'amodi/ ▶ adjective
studied

تعمیم دادن

/ta'mim dâdan/ ▶ verb
generalize - distribute

تعهد

/ta'ahod/ ▶ noun
commitment - assurance - mandate

تعهد دادن

/ta'ahod dâdan/ ▶ verb
plight

تعهد کردن

/ta'ahod kardan/ ▶ verb
guarantee - underwrite - undertake

تعهد پرداخت

/ta'ahod pardâkhtan/ ▶ noun
subscription

تعویض

/ta'viz/ ▶ noun
replacement - refill - switch - substitute -
shift - turnover

تعویض کردن

/ta'viz kardan/ ▶ verb
change - shift - supplant - substitute

تعویق

/ta'vigh/ ▶ noun
procrastination - deferment

تعیین

/ta'yin/ ▶ noun
nomination - avow - appointment

تعیین قیمت

/ta'yine gheimat/ ▶ noun
appraisal

تعیین کردن

/ta'yin kardan/ ▶ verb
determine - bound - assign

تعیین کننده

/ta'yin konande/ ▶ adjective
determinant

تغذیه

/taghziye/ ▶ noun
nutrition - nurture - nourishment -
nourish - sustenance

تغذیه کردن

/taghziye kardan/ ▶ verb
feeding - pasture

تغلیظ

/taghliz/ ▶ noun
condensation - concentrate

تغیر

/taghayor/ ▶ noun
huff

تغییر

/tagh'yir/ ▶ noun
conversion - change - vicissitude -
vexation - variation

تغییر جهت دادن

/tagh'yire jahat dâdan/ ▶ verb
veer - shunt

تغییر دادن

/tagh'yir dâdan/ ▶ verb
turquoise - alter - affect - interchange -
permute - vary - modify - change

تغییر شکل

/tagh'yire shekl/ ▶ noun
transiguration - metamorphosis -
paramorphic - palingenesis - evolution

تغییر شکل دادن

/tagh'yire shekl dâdan/ ▶ verb
misshape - transform - transfigure

تغییر فاحش

/tagh'yire fâhesh/ ▶ noun
upheaval

تغییر فصل

/tagh'yire fasl/ ▶ noun
weather

تغییر فکر

/tagh'yire fekr/ ▶ noun
quirk

تغییر کردن

/tagh'yir kardan/ ▶ verb
revolve - change

تغییر مکان

/tagh'yire makân/ ▶ noun
movement - move - shift

تغییر ناگهانی

/tagh'yire nâgahâni/ ▶ noun
whim - quirk - revulsion - mutation

تغییرپذیر

/tagh'yirpazir/ ▶ adjective
convertible - changeable - plastic -
variable

تغییرپذیری

/tagh'yirpaziri/ ▶ noun
variation

تغییرجهت

/tagh'yire jahat/ ▶ noun
turquoise - shift

تغییردهنده

/tagh'yir dahande/ ▶ noun
transformer - changer

تغییرعلامت

/tagh'yire alâmat/ ▶ noun
duff

تغییرناپذیر

/tagh'yir nâpazir/ ▶ adjective
unalterable - immutable - ireversible -
inelastic

تف

/tof/ ▶ noun
sputum - spittle - spit

تف انداختن

/tof andâkhtan/ ▶ verb
spit

تفاخر کردن

/tafâkhor kardan/ ▶ verb
pride

تفاصیل

/tafâsil/ ▶ noun
detail

تفاله

/tofâle/ ▶ noun
slop - slag - scum - ross - dross - crap -
bagasse

تفاوت

/tafâvot/ ▶ noun
difference - diversity - discrepancy

تفاوت داشتن

/tafâvot dâshtan/ ▶ verb
differ

تفتیش

/taftish/ ▶ noun
detection

تفحص

/tafahos/ ▶ noun
disquisition

تفحص کردن

/tafahos kardan/ ▶ verb
hunt - dive

تفرج

/tafaroj/ ▶ noun
promenade - outing

تفرج کردن

/tafaroj kardan/ ▶ verb
promenade

تفرجگاه

/tafarojgâh/ ▶ noun
promenade

تفرقه

/tafraghe/ ▶ noun
division - sequester - schism

تفرقه انداز

/tafraghe andâz/ ▶ adjective
divisive

تفریح

/tafrih/ ▶ noun
pastime - play - recreation - gust -
diversion – jaunt

تفریح کردن
/tafrih kardan/ ▶ verb
play - game - recreate

تفکر
/tafakor/ ▶ noun
thought - cud - dump - reflection -
recollection

تفریحگاه
/tafrihgâh/ ▶ noun
playground

تفکر کردن
/tafakor kardan/ ▶ verb
ponder - meditate - imagine - chew -
contemplate - consider - speculate

تفریحی
/tafrihi/ ▶ adjective
recreation

تفکیک
/tafkik/ ▶ noun
segregation - segregate - detachment -
denotation

تفریق کردن
/tafrigh kardan/ ▶ verb
deduce

تفکیک پذیر
/tafkikpazir/ ▶ adjective
severable

تفسیر
/tafsir/ ▶ noun
commentary - explanation

تفکیک شدن
/tafkik shodan/ ▶ verb
part

تفسیر کردن
/tafsir kardan/ ▶ verb
translate - annotate - interpret - construe
- expound

تفکیک کردن
/tafkik kardan/ ▶ verb
separate - centrifuge - denote - breakup -
partition - part

تفصیل
/tafsil/ ▶ noun
gloss - circumstance - detail

تفکیک کننده
/tafkik konande/ ▶ adjective
diacritic

تفصیلی
/tafsili/ ▶ adjective
formal

تفنگ
/tofang/ ▶ noun
gun - rifle

تفنگدار

/tofangdâr/ ▶ noun
gunman

تفهیم

/tafhim/ ▶ noun
realization

تفوق

/tafavogh/ ▶ noun
supremacy - ascendency - advantage -
prevalence - predominance

تفویض

/tafviz/ ▶ noun
submission - investiture - resignation -
conferment

تق کردن

/tegh kardan/ ▶ verb
crack

تقابل

/taghâbol/ ▶ noun
contrast

تقارب

/taghârob/ ▶ noun
convergence

تقارن

/taghâron/ ▶ noun
symmetry - polarity - parallelism

تقاضا

/taghâza/ ▶ noun
request - importance - prayer - postulate
- plea - solicitation

تقاضا کردن

/taghâzâ kardan/ ▶ verb
demand - putin - sue - solicit

تقاضا کننده

/taghâzâ konande/ ▶ adjective
applicant

تقبل کردن

/taghabol kardan/ ▶ adjective
undertake - assume

تقبیح کردن

/taghbih kardan/ ▶ adjective
denounce - decry

تقدس

/taghados/ ▶ noun
sanctity - sacrosanctity - holiness -
venerability

تقدم

/taghadom/ ▶ noun
primacy - preference - lead

تقدیر

/taghdir/ ▶ noun
thank - fate - ordinance - destiny -
destination

تقدیس

/taghdis/ ► noun
edification - canonization - veneration

تقدیس کردن

/taghdis kardan/ ► verb
bless - hallow - celebrate - consecrate -
enshrine - edify

تقدیم

/taghdim/ ► noun
offer - proffer - presentation

تقریب

/taghrib/ ► noun
access

تقریبا

/taghriban/ ► adverb
almost - about

تقریبی

/taghribi/ ► adjective
approximate - proximate

تقریر

/taghrir/ ► noun
statement - emprise

تقسیم

/taghsim/ ► noun
division - cleavage

تقسیم شدن

/taghsim shodan/ ► verb
Cleave

تقسیم کننده

/taghsim konande/ ► adjective
denominator - divisive

تقصیر

/taghsir/ ► noun
offense - guilt - rap - delinquency -
crime - error

تقلا

/taghalâ/ ► noun
muss - wrestle - exertion - effort - strife
- stress - strain - slog - scramble -
scrabble

تقلا کردن

/taghalâ kardan/ ► verb
scramble - tug - slog - struggle - wrestle
- attempt - agonize - heave - labor

تقلب

/taghalob/ ► noun
slur - skulduggery - cross

تقلب کردن

/taghalob kardan/ ► verb
sharpen

تقلبی

/taghalobi/ ► adjective
unfeigned - unfathered

تقلید

/taghlid/ ► noun
fake - mimicry - mime - imitation -
burlesque

تقلیدی
/taghlidi/ ▶ adjective
imitative

تقلیل
/taghlil/ ▶ noun
depletion - cutback - diminution -
reduction

تقلیل دادن
/taghlil dâdan/ ▶ verb
lessen - weaken - cutdown - cutback

تقلیل دهنده
/taghlil dahande/ ▶ adjective
reducer

تقوا
/taghvâ/ ▶ noun
piety - pietism - virtue

تقویت
/taghviyat/ ▶ noun
support - nutrition - revival -
reinforcement - fuel - fortification

تقویت دادن
/taghviyat dâdan/ ▶ verb
strengthen

تقویت شدن
/taghviyat shodan/ ▶ verb
invigorate

تقویت کردن
/taghviyat kardan/ ▶ verb
reinforce - rally - fort - uphold -
undergird - bolster - beef - augment

تقویم
/taghvim/ ▶ noun
valuation - assessment - appraisal -
estimate - calendar

تقویم کردن
/taghvim kardan/ ▶ verb
evaluate - assess - apprise - appraise

تقیه
/taghiye/ ▶ noun
reservation

تک
/tak/ ▶ noun
solo - solitaire - singular - single -
individual - one - odd

تک خوان
/tak khân/ ▶ adjective
soloist

تک نواز
/tak navâz/ ▶ adjective
soloist

تک یاخته
/tak yâkhte/ ▶ noun
protozoan

تکاپو

/takâpu/ ► noun
search - prowl - roam

تکاپو کردن

/takâpu kardan/ ► verb
scour

تکافو

/takâfu/ ► noun
adequacy

تکان

/tekân/ ► noun
shake - movement - move - motion -
convulsion

تکان تند

/tekâne tond/ ► adjective
jerk

تکان خوردن

/tekân khordan/ ► verb
move - jolt - wag - vibrate - quake

تکان دادن

/tekân dâdan/ ► verb
impulse - hustle - move - convulse -
wiggle - wag - stir - startle - shake

تکان سر

/tekâne sar/ ► noun
nod

تکاور

/takâvar/ ► noun
commando

تکبر

/takbir/ ► noun
insolence - height - pride - arrogance -
ruffe

تکثیر

/taksir/ ► noun
propagation - reproduction

تکذیب

/takzib/ ► noun
disproof - denial - refutation - rebuttal

تکرار

/tekrâr/ ► noun
repetition - renewal - rehearsal -
recapitulation - frequency

تکرار شدن

/tekrâr shodan/ ► verb
recur

تکرار کردن

/tekrâr kardan/ ► verb
repeat - renew - reiterate - rehearse -
reduplicate

تکرار مکررات

/tekrâre mokararât/ ► noun
rehash

تکرار کننده

/tekrâr konande/ ▶ adjective
repeater

تکراری

/tekrâri/ ▶ adjective
repetitive - repetitious

تکریم

/takrim/ ▶ noun
tribute - reverence - veneration

تکریم کردن

/takrim kardan/ ▶ verb
venerate - dignify - glorify

تکفل

/takafol/ ▶ noun
sponsorship

تکفیر

/takfir/ ▶ noun
commination

تکفیر کردن

/takfir kardan/ ▶ verb
excommunicate

تکلم

/takalom/ ▶ noun
language

تکلم کردن

/takalom kardan/ ▶ verb
speak

تکلیف

/taklif/ ▶ noun
task - imposition - duty

تکمیل

/takmil/ ▶ noun
replete - compiction

تکمیل کردن

/takmil kardan/ ▶ verb
supplement - perfect - round

تکمیلی

/takmili/ ▶ adjective
supplementary

تکه

/teke/ ▶ noun
slice - bit - loaf - item - portion - morsel
- dab - fragment - whit

تکه تکه

/teke teke/ ▶ adjective
patchy - piecemeal - scrappy

تکه تکه کردن

/teke teke kardan/ ▶ verb
slab

تکه فلز

/teke felez/ ▶ noun
nugget

تکه کاغذ

/teke kâghaz/ ▶ noun
slip

تل شنی
/tele sheni/ ▶ noun
dune

تکوین
/takvin/ ▶ noun
genesis

تلاش
/talâsh/ ▶ noun
quest - muss - endeavor - effort - prowl -
scramble

تکوینی
/takvini/ ▶ adjective
genetic

تلاش کردن
/talâsh kardan/ ▶ verb
endeavor

تکیه
/tekye/ ▶ noun
stay - loll - emphasis - reliance

تلاطم
/talâtom/ ▶ noun
shock - seethe - turbulence - toss - lop -
ruffle

تکیه دادن
/tekye dâdan/ ▶ verb
rest - bolster - accent

تلاطم داشتن
/talâtom dâshtan/ ▶ verb
roll

تکیه زدن
/tekye zadan/ ▶ verb
lean

تلافی
/talâfi/ ▶ noun
incidence - amends - greet - retribution -
retort - restitution - reprisal - repay

تکیه کردن
/tekye kardan/ ▶ verb
recline - lean

تکیه گاه
/tekyegâh/ ▶ noun
base - backrest - back

تلافی کردن
/talâfi kardan/ ▶ verb
gantlet

تگرگ
/tagarg/ ▶ noun
hail

تلالو
/tala'lo/ ▶ noun
sparkle - glitter - glint

تل
/tel/ ▶ noun
plume - hill

تلفظ کردن

/talafoz kardan/ ▶ verb
enunciate - vocalize - pronounce

تلخ

/talkh/ ▶ noun
bitter - virulent

تلفن

/telefon/ ▶ noun
telephone - phone

تلخ کردن

/takh kardan/ ▶ verb
embitter

تلفن چی

/telefonchi/ ▶ noun
operator

تلخ و شیرین

/talkho shirin/ ▶ adjective
bitter and sweet

تلفن زدن

/telefon zadan/ ▶ verb
telephone - phone

تلخی

/talkhi/ ▶ noun
poignancy - virulence - gall

تلفن کردن

/telefon kardan/ ▶ verb
telephone

تلخیص

/talkhis/ ▶ noun
precis

تلفنی

/telefoni/ ▶ adjective
telephonic

تلف شدن

/talaf shodan/ ▶ verb
perish

تلفیق

/talghin/ ▶ noun
compilation - reconciliation -
incorporation - syncretism- dictation

تلف کردن

/talaf kardan/ ▶ verb
squander - lose - misspend

تلقین کردن

/talghin kardan/ ▶ verb
suggest - inculcate - insinuate -
indoctrinate

تلفات

/talafât/ ▶ noun
casualty - victim

تلفظ

/talafoz/ ▶ noun
pronunciation - accent - intonation

تلکسوپ
/teleskob/ ▶ noun
telescope

تلوتلو خوردن
/telo telo khor/ ▶ verb
tipsy

تلگراف
/telegrâf/ ▶ noun
telegraph - telegram - dispenser

تلویحا گفتن
/talvihan goftan/ ▶ verb
mince

تلگرام
/telegrâm/ ▶ noun
telegram

تلویزیون
/telvezion/ ▶ noun
television

تلمبه
/tolombe/ ▶ noun
ram - pump

تمارض کردن
/tamâroz kardan/ ▶ verb
malinger

تلمبه زدن
/tolombe zadan/ ▶ verb
pump

تماس
/tamâs/ ▶ noun
tangent - contiguity - contact - impact

تلمذ
/talamoz/ ▶ noun
pupilage

تماشا
/tamâshâ/ ▶ noun
spectacle - sight

تله
/tale/ ▶ noun
train - grin - quicksand - hook - pitfall

تماشاچی
/tamâshâchi/ ▶ noun
audience

تماشاچی بودن
/tamâshâchi budan/ ▶ verb
spectate

تله انداختن
/tale andâkhtan/ ▶ verb
entrap

تماشاخانه
/tamâshâkhâne/ ▶ noun
opera - theater

تله موش
/tale mush/ ▶ noun
rattrap

تمایل

/tamâyol/ ▶ noun
inclination - tilt - tenor - tendency

تماشایی

/tamâshâyi/ ▶ adjective
spectacular

تمبر

/tamr/ ▶ noun
stamp

تمام

/tamâm/ ▶ noun
entire - complete - full - whole - all -
through

تمثال

/temsâl/ ▶ noun
effigy - representation - image - statue

تمام شدن

/tamâm shodan/ ▶ verb
finish

تمثیل

/tamsil/ ▶ noun
parable - allegory

تمام عیار

/tamâm ayâr/ ▶ adjective
sterling - hipandthigh - perfect

تمجید

/tamjid/ ▶ noun
plaudit - stratagem

تمام کردن

/tamâm kardan/ ▶ verb
end - attain - process - integrate

تمجید کردن

/tamjid kardan/ ▶ verb
exalt - laud

تمام و کمال

/tamâmo kamâl/ ▶ adjective
thoroughgoing - consummate - wholly

تمدن

/tamadon/ ▶ noun
civilization - culture

تماما

/tamâman/ ▶ adverb
all - quite - wholly - well - stark -
throughout

تمدید

/tamdid/ ▶ noun
revival - extension

تمامیت

/tamâmiyat/ ▶ noun
totality - integrity - entirety

تمدید کردن

/tamdid kardan/ ▶ verb
extend

تمرد

/tamarod/ ► noun
contumacy - recalcitrance - rebellion

تمنا کردن

/tamanâ kardan/ ► verb
request

تمرد کردن

/tamarod kardan/ ► verb
rebel

تمهید

/tamhid/ ► noun
appliance - device - contrivance

تمرکز

/tamarkoz/ ► noun
centralization

تمهید کردن

/tamhid/ ► verb
vamp

تمرین

/tamrin/ ► noun
practise - practice - exercise - drill -
workout - rehearsal

تمول

/tamavol/ ► noun
wealth

تمرین دادن

/tamrin dâdan/ ► verb
experience - exercise

تمیز

/tamiz/ ► noun
clean - neat - dinky - dapper - prim -
pure

تمساح

/temsâh/ ► noun
alligator - crocodile

تمیز دادن

/tamiz dâdan/ ► verb
distinguish - discern

تمسخر

/tamaskhor/ ► noun
sneer - scorn - scoff - derision - irony

تمیز کننده

/tamiz kardan/ ► adjective
scourer

تمسخر کردن

/tamaskhor kardan/ ► verb
ridicule - deride - scoff

تن

/tan/ ► noun
body

تمکین

/tamkin/ ► noun
deference – stoop

تنبل

/tanbal/ ► adjective
lazy - laze - indolent - inactive - idle

تن در دادن

/tan dar dâdan/ ► verb
acquiescence - acquiesce - accede

تنبلی

/tanbali/ ► noun
indolence - inaction - sloth

تنابه

/tanâbe/ ► noun
humor

تنبلی کردن

/tanbali kardan/ ► verb
laze

تنازع

/tanâzo'/ ► noun
struggle

تنبیه

/tanbih/ ► noun
punishment

تناسب

/tanâsob/ ► noun
cooridnation - congruence - analogy -
scale - propriety - proportion

تنبیهی

/tanbihi/ ► adjective
pnitive

تناسلی

/tanâsoli/ ► noun
sexual - reproductive - genie

تند

/tond/ ► adjective
spicy - fast - wrench - keen - glassy -
rash - rapid - racy - caustic - intensive -
hot

تناقض

/tanâghoz/ ► noun
incoherence - antithesis - repugnance

تناوب

/tanâvob/ ► noun
alternation - frequency

تند راه رفتن

/tondrah raftan/ ► verb
scud

تناوبی

/tanâvobi/ ► adjective
alternative - alternating

تند رفتن

/tond raftan/ ► verb
fleet

تنباکو

/tanbâku/ ► noun
tobacco

تند شدن
/tond shodan/ ▶ verb
accelerate

تندمزاج
/tond mezâj/ ▶ adjective
hot - irritable - peevish

تند و تیز
/tondo tiz/ ▶ noun
stringent - nippy - astringent - ardent -
peppery

تندی
/tondi/ ▶ adjective
acrimony - acerbity - virulence -
violence - velocity - impetuosity -
rapidity

تندباد
/tondbâd/ ▶ noun
jetstream - hurricane - gust - gale

تندیس
/tandis/ ▶ noun
statue

تندتند حرف زدن
/tond tond harf zadan/ ▶ verb
chatter - patter

تندیس گر
/tandisgar/ ▶ adjective
sculptor

تندخو
/tondkhu/ ▶ adjective
acrid - fierce

تنزل
/tanazol/ ▶ noun
depression - depreciation - decay -
decadence - abate - setback

تندر
/tondar/ ▶ noun
thunder

تنزل دادن
/tanazol dâdan/ ▶ verb
reduce - playdown - lower

تندرست
/tandorost/ ▶ adjective
healthy - fit - well

تنزل رتبه
/tanazole rotbe/ ▶ noun
demotion

تندرستی
/tandorosti/ ▶ noun
health

تنزل قیمت
/tanazole gheimat/ ▶ noun
cutrate

تندرو
/tondro/ ▶ adjective
speedster - extrimist - fast - rapid – racer

تنزل کردن

/tanazole gheimat/ ▶ verb
fall - decline - decay

تنفیذ کردن

/tanfiz kardan/ ▶ verb
validate

تنزیل

/tanzil/ ▶ noun
interest

تنک

/tonok/ ▶ adjective
sparse

تنظیم

/tanzim/ ▶ noun
conduction - regulation - alignment -
adjustment

تنگ

/tong/ ▶ adjective
narrow - close - decanter - cruse -
disgrace - strait - shoal - scarce

تنظیم کردن

/tanzim kardan/ ▶ verb
order - regiment - redact - frame - edit -
control - modulate - adjust

تنگدست

/tangdast/ ▶ adjective
indigent - underprivileged

تنگدستی

/tangdasti/ ▶ noun
distress

تنفر

/tanafor/ ▶ noun
abhorrence - hatred - hate - distaste -
disgust

تنگراه

/tangrâh/ ▶ noun
bottleneck

تنفر شدید

/tanafore shadid/ ▶ noun
revulsion

تنگنا

/tangnâ/ ▶ noun
jaw - strait - warpath - hairbreadth

تنفرآور

/tanafor âvar/ ▶ adjective
revulsive - repulsive

تنگنظر

/tangnazar/ ▶ adjective
insular

تنفس

/tanafos/ ▶ noun
intake - respiration - recess

تنگه

/tange/ ▶ noun
strait - neck - gut - canyon – bottleneck

تنگی
/tangi/ ▶ noun
stricture - drouth

تنگی نفس
/tangiye nafas/ ▶ noun
asthma

تنه زدن
/tane zadan/ ▶ verb
shove - jostle - hunch

تنها
/tanhâ/ ▶ adjective
solitary - sole - single - alone - mere -
lonely - lone

تنها گذاشتن
/tanhâ gozashtan/ ▶ verb
strand

تنهایی
/tanhayi/ ▶ noun
privacy - solitude

تنور
/tanur/ ▶ noun
oven

(Idiom: تا تنور داغه، نان را چسباندن
Make hay while the sun shines!)

تنوع
/tanavo'/ ▶ noun
variety - potpourri - intermezzo –
diversity

تنومند
/tanumand/ ▶ adjective
sturdy - stalwart - rugged - robust -
corpulent - burly - huge

تنیدن
/tanidan/ ▶ verb
spin

تنیس
/tandis/ ▶ noun
tennis

ته
/tah/ ▶ noun
stub - extremity - heel - butt - bottom -
bed - base

ته چک
/tah chek/ ▶ noun
stub

ته ریش
/tahrish/ ▶ noun
stubble - tuft

ته کشیدن
/tah keshidan/ ▶ verb
peter

ته مانده
/tahmânde/ ▶ noun
scrap - silt - riffraff

تهاتر

/tahâtor/ ▶ noun
cambium - dicker

تهاجم

/tahâjom/ ▶ noun
incursion - invasion - inroad - agression

تهذیب

/tahzib/ ▶ noun
polish - edification - reformation -
refinement

تهمت

/tohmat/ ▶ noun
scandal - tax - slur - defamation - libel -
abusive

تهمت زدن

/tohmat zadan/ ▶ verb
accuse - mudslinger - slander - task -
scandal

تهنیت

/tahniyat/ ▶ noun
salutation

تهور

/tahavor/ ▶ noun
impetuosity - temerity

تهویه

/tahviye/ ▶ noun
ventilation

تهی

/tohi/ ▶ adjective
empty - indigent - inane - hollow - void

تهیدست

/tohidast/ ▶ adjective
unfunded - impecunious - indigent

تهیه

/tahiye/ ▶ noun
provision - procurement - preparation

تهییج

/tahyij/ ▶ noun
excitement - fry - incitement

تو

/tu/ ▶ noun
inside - thou

تو رفتن

/turaftan/ ▶ verb
enter - retract

توابع

/tavâbe'/ ▶ noun
environs

تواضع کردن

/tavâzo' kardan/ ▶ verb
condescend

توافق

/tavâfogh/ ▶ noun
agreement - adhesion - accordance -
accord - band - compromise

توافق داشتن

/tavâfogh dâshtan/ ► verb
adhere

توافقی

/tavâfoghi/ ► adjective
adaptive

توالت

/tu'âlet/ ► noun
toilet

توالی

/tavâli/ ► noun
subsequence - sequence - train - track -
progression

توان

/tavân/ ► noun
vim - vigor - valence - power - potency -
exponent

توانا

/tavânâ/ ► adjective
mighty - authoritative - able - capable

توانایی

/tavânâyi/ ► noun
strength - energy - authority - ability -
influence - potency - vim - might

توانبخشی

/tavânbakhsh/ ► noun
rehabilitation

توانگر

/tavângar/ ► adjective
wealthy - rich

توبه

/tobe/ ► noun
penitence - contrition - repentance

توبه کردن

/tobe kardan/ ► verb
repent

توبیخ

/tobikh/ ► noun
snuff - reproach - rail - vituperation

توبیخ کردن

/tobikh kardan/ ► verb
telloff - reprehend - rebuke - rail

توپ

/tup/ ► noun
ball - artillery - gun

توپ بازی

/tup bâzi/ ► noun
ball

توجه

/tavajoh/ ► noun
tendency - consideration - remark -
regard - notice - notation - heed -
attention

توجه کردن

/tavajoh kardan/ ► verb
tent - attend - assist - mark - ward

توده شدن

/tude shodan/ ► verb
drift

توجهات

/tavajohât/ ► noun
auspices

توده شن

/tudeye shen/ ► noun
sandpile

توجیه

/tojihpazir/ ► noun
justification - justification -
rationalization

تودهنی

/tudahani/ ► noun
slap

توجیه پذیر

/tojihpazir/ ► adjective
justifiable

تور

/tur/ ► noun
saveall - net - gauze

توجیه کردن

/tojih kardan/ ► verb
legtimize - vindicate - justify

تور ساختن

/tur sâkhtan/ ► verb
mesh

توجیه کننده

/tojih konande/ ► adjective
justifier

تورق

/tavarogh/ ► noun
slate

توحید

/tohid/ ► noun
theism - monotheism

تورم

/tavarom/ ► noun
inflation - protuberance - swell

توخالی

/tukhâli/ ► adjective
gash

توری

/turi/ ► noun
net - lace

توده

/tude/ ► noun
bulk - block - mass - hill - heap -
volume - riffraff - rick - gross

توس

/tus/ ► noun
birch

توسط
/tavasot/ ► noun
per - via

توسعه
/tose'e/ ► noun
extension - expansion - development -
increment

توسعه دادن
/tose'e dâdan/ ► verb
develop - expand - enlarge

توسعه یافتن
/tose' yâftan/ ► verb
developing

توسل
/tavasol/ ► noun
recourse

توشه
/tushe/ ► noun
luggage - outfit - provision

توشیح
/toshih/ ► noun
sign - signature

توصیف
/tosif/ ► noun
description

توصیف کردن
/tosif kardan/ ► verb
portray - characterize – describe

توصیفی
/tosifi/ ► adjective
descriptive

توصیه
/tosiye/ ► noun
recommendation

توصیه کردن
/tosiye kardan/ ► verb
advise

توضیح
/tozih/ ► noun
statement - gloss - comment -
explanation - paraphrase

توضیح دادن
/tozih dâdan/ ► verb
state - illustrate - explain - elucidate -
clear - clarify

توضیحات
/tozihât/ ► noun
description - preamble

توطئه
/tote'e/ ► noun
underplot - plot - conspiracy

توفان
/tufân/ ► noun
tornado - storm - squall

توفانی

/tufâni/ ▶ adjective
boisterous - stormy

تولد

/tavalod/ ▶ noun
birth

توفیق

/tofigh/ ▶ noun
success

توله

/tule/ ▶ noun
cub - whelp

توقف

/tavaghof/ ▶ noun
stop - stay - pause - close - cessation -
cease

توله سگ

/tule sag/ ▶ noun
whelp - puppy - pup

توقف کردن

/tavaghof kardan/ ▶ verb
stop - stay - stand

تولید کردن

/tolid kardan/ ▶ verb
supply - generate - inbreed - produce

توقفگاه

/tavaghofgâh/ ▶ noun
stay

تولیدکننده

/tolid konande/ ▶ adjective
productive - producer

توقیف

/tughigh/ ▶ noun
custody - constraint - durante - nab -
arrest - bail - holdup - lockup -
internment - suppression

تونل

/tunel/ ▶ noun
tunnel - tube

توهین

/tohin/ ▶ noun
insult - insolence - offense

توقیف کردن

/toghif kardan/ ▶ verb
seize - suppress - grab - detain - arrest -
apprehend

توهین آمیز

/tohin âmiz/ ▶ adjective
abusive

توکل

/tavakol/ ▶ noun
trust - reliance

توی

/tuye/ ▶ noun
within - aboard - in - into

تیره و تار

/tireotâr/ ► adjective
bleary

تیپ

/tip/ ► noun
brigade

تیز

/tiz/ ► adjective
sharp - trenchant - incisive - hot - pointy
- poignant - acute - brisk - bitter - keen

تیر

/tir/ ► noun
shot - staple - stanchion - dart - gunshot
- arrow

تیز شدن

/tiz shodan/ ► verb
sharpen - peak

تیررس

/tir'ras/ ► noun
range - gunshot

تیز کردن

/tiz kardan/ ► verb
sharpen - sharp - whet - keen - grind -
point

تیرگی

/tiregi/ ► noun
obscurity - gloom - fog - muddle - blur

تیزهوش

/tiz hush/ ► adjective
perspicacious - sitted

تیره

/tire/ ► adjective
muddy - dark - obscure - nebulous -
gloomy - thick

تیشه

/tishe/ ► noun
hatchet

تیره رنگ

/tire rang/ ► adjective
dingy - austere

تیغ

/tigh/ ► noun
thorn - bur - prick

تیره روز

/tire ruz/ ► adjective
miserable

تیغ آفتاب

/tighe âftab/ ► noun
sunrise - sunbeam - streamer

تیره کردن

/tire kardan/ ► verb
gloom - overcast - obscure - fog - dim -
dark - blur - mud - tarnish - shade

تیغه

/tighe/ ► noun
partition - bulkhead - blade - midriff -
knife - septum

تیک

/tik/ ► noun
click

تیله

/tile/ ► noun
marble - dib

تیله بازی

/tile bâzi/ ► noun
dib - marble

تیم

/tim/ ► noun
team

تیمار

/timâr/ ► noun
attendance - care

تیمار کردن

/timâr kardan/ ► verb
groom

تیمارستان

/timârestan/ ► noun
madhouse - bedlam - asylum

ث - ﺛ

se /se/ ▶ fifth letter of the Persian alphabet

ثابت
/sabet/ ▶ noun
immobile - permanent - equable - resolute - firm - standstill - staid - stable

ثابت قدم
/sâbet ghadam/ ▶ adjective
steadfast - staunchstanch - unflinching - constant - consistent - resolute

ثابت کردن
/sâbet kardan/ ▶ verb
prove - clinch - evidence - immobilize - posit

ثابت ماندن
/sâbet mândan/ ▶ verb
fix

ثالث
/sâles/ ▶ adjective
third - tertiary

ثانوی
/sânavi/ ▶ adjective
peripheral - secondary - second - sec

ثانی
/sâni/ ▶ adjective
second

ثانیه
/sâniye/ ▶ noun
second

ثبات
/sabât/ ▶ noun
constancy - grit - fortitude - poise - permanency - stability

ثبات قدم
/sabâte ghadam/ ▶ noun
loyalty - perseverance - resolution

ثبت
/sabt/ ▶ noun
notation - roll - registration - inscription

ثبت کردن
/sabt kardan/ ▶ verb
scroll - score - put - inscribe - register - record - note - docket

ثروت
/servat/ ▶ noun
treasure - worth - wealth - gold - fortune - money - mammon - possession

ثروتمند
/servatmand/ ▶ adjective
wealthy

ثلث

/sols/ ▶ adjective
third

ثمر

/samar/ ▶ noun
fruit

ثمر دادن

/samar dâdan/ ▶ verb
yield

ج - ج

jim /je/ ▶ sixth letter of the Persian alphabet

جا

/jâ/ ▶ noun
situation - site - seat - stead - station - space - emplacement - room - place - location - house

جا افتاده

/jâ oftâde/ ▶ adjective
mellow - ripe

جا انداختن

/jâ andâkhtan/ ▶ verb
set

جا زدن

/jâzadan/ ▶ verb
fake

جا کردن

/jâ kardan/ ▶ verb
fold

جا گذاشتن

/jâgozashtan/ ▶ verb
misplace

جا گرفتن

/jâgereftan/ ▶ verb
situate - hold

جابجا شدن

/jâbejâ shodan/ ▶ verb
supplant - metastasis

جابجا کردن

/jâbejâ kardan/ ▶ verb
displace - dislocate - reposit - replace - heave - unhorse

جابر

/jâber/ ▶ adjective
violent

جاخالی

/jâkhâli/ ▶ noun
dodge

جادار

/jâdâr/ ▶ adjective
commodious - roomy - roomful - large - spacious

جاده

/jâde/ ▶ noun
pathway - path - pad - line - causeway - way - turnpike - track - street

جادو

/jâdu/ ▶ noun
talisman - spell - magic - incantation - glamor - glamour - wizard - weird

جارو

/jâru/ ▶ noun
sweep

جادوگر

/jâdugar/ ▶ adjective
spellbinder - hex - powwow - mare -
wizard

جاروب

/jârub/ ▶ noun
broom

جادوگری

/jâdugari/ ▶ noun
sorcery - wizardry - witchcraft -
incantation - voodoo

جاروکش

/jârukesh/ ▶ adjective
sweeper

جادویی

/jâduyi/ ▶ adjective
wizardry - magical

جاری بودن

/jâri budan/ ▶ verb
flow

جاذب

/jâzeb/ ▶ adjective
attractive - absorbent - bibulous

جاسوس

/jâsus/ ▶ noun
spy - snoop - undercover - informer

جار

/jâr/ ▶ noun
candelabrum

جاسوس بودن

/jâsus budan/ ▶ verb
spy

جار زدن

/jâr zadan/ ▶ verb
blaze - blare - proclaim

جاسوسی

/jâsusi/ ▶ noun
intelligence - espionage

جار کشیدن

/jâr keshidan/ ▶ verb
acclaim

جاسوسی کردن

/jâsusi kardan/ ▶ verb
spy - espy - pickeer

جارچی

/jârchi/ ▶ noun
trumpeter - herald - blazer

جاکش

/jâkesh/ ▶ adjective
bawd - pimp

جالب

/jâleb/ ▶ adjective
attractive - memorable - marvelous -
yummy - spicy

جالب توجه

/jâleb tavajoh/ ▶ adjective
notable - remarkable - lively - liberal -
unco

جاليز

/jâliz/ ▶ noun
patch

جام

/jâm/ ▶ noun
cup - chalice - goblet - glass - bowl -
beaker

جامد

/jâmed/ ▶ noun
insensitive - inorganic - rigid -
exanimate

جامع

/jâme'/ ▶ noun
spacious - general - comprehensive -
catholic - universal - precise - plenary -
large

جامعه

/jâme'e/ ▶ noun
society

جامعه شناس

/jâme'e shenâs/ ▶ noun
sociologist

جامعیت

/jâme'iyat/ ▶ noun
universality - universalism

جامه

/jâme'e/ ▶ noun
suit - costume - gear - garment - raiment
- clobber - habit - apparel

جان

/jân/ ▶ noun
life - breath - spirit

جان پناه

/jânpanâh/ ▶ noun
turret - trench - shelter - parapet

جان دادن

/jân dâdan/ ▶ verb
die - enliven - act

جان سخت

/jânsakht/ ▶ adjective
diehard

جان کلام

/jâne kalâm/ ▶ noun
gist

جان کندن

/jân kandan/ ▶ verb
grub - durdge

جانبدار

/jânebdâr/ ▶ adjective
partial

جانورشناسی
/jânevarshenâsi/ ▶ noun
zoology

جانبداری
/jânebdâri/ ▶ noun
predilection

جانی
/jâni/ ▶ adjective
criminal - convict - bane

جاندار
/jândâr/ ▶ noun
animate

جاه
/jâh/ ▶ noun
dignity - eminence - pomp

جانشین
/jâneshin/ ▶ noun
substitute - vicarious - vicar - pinch -
deputy - relief

جاه طلب
/jâhtalab/ ▶ adjective
ambitious

جانشین شدن
/jâneshin shodan/ ▶ verb
inherit - surrogate - supersede

جاه طلب بودن
/jâhtalab budan/ ▶ verb
ambition

جانشین کردن
/jâneshin kardan/ ▶ verb
swap - substitute

جاه طلبی
/jâhtalabi/ ▶ noun
ambition

جانفشان
/jânfeshân/ ▶ adjective
zealot

جاهد
/jâhed/ ▶ adjective
studious

جانفشانی
/jânfeshâni/ ▶ noun
zeal

جاهل
/jâhel/ ▶ adjective
ignoramus - unwise - unknowing -
unknowable - uninformed

جانگداز
/jângodâz/ ▶ adjective
piteous

جاوید
/jâvid/ ▶ noun
eternal - immortal

جانورشناس
/jânevarshenâs/ ▶ noun
zoologist

جاویدان
/jâvidân/ ▶ noun
immortal - forever

جای مقدس
/jâye moghadas/ ▶ noun
shrine

جای پا
/jâye pâ/ ▶ noun
trace - toe - vestige - rake

جای ویژه
/jâye vizhe/ ▶ noun
booth - bench - box

جای خالی
/jâye khâli/ ▶ noun
lacuna

جایز
/jâyez/ ▶ noun
allowable

جای خلوت
/jâye khalvat/ ▶ noun
solitude

جایزه
/jâyez/ ▶ noun
testimonial - trophy - prize - premium -
bonus - award

جای دادن
/jây dâdan/ ▶ verb
place - implant

جایگاه
/jâygâh/ ▶ noun
station - seat - place - house

جای زخم
/jâye zakhm/ ▶ noun
sore

جایگاه مقدس
/jâygâhe moghadas/ ▶ noun
sanctum - sanctuary

جای شیب
/jâye shib/ ▶ noun
pitch

جایگاه ویژه
/jâygahe vizhe/ ▶ noun
stall

جای ضربت
/jâye zarbat/ ▶ noun
dent

جایگزین شدن
/jâygozin shodan/ ▶ verb
tabernacle

جای عکس
/jâye aks/ ▶ noun
album

جایگزینی
/jâygozini/ ▶ noun
situation

جبهه

/jebhe/ ► noun
deploy

جایی

/jâyi/ ► noun
someplace

جت

/jet/ ► noun
jet

جاییکه

/jâyike/ ► adverb
whither

جثه

/jose/ ► noun
bulk

جبار

/jabâr/ ► adjective
taskmaster - unmercifully - unmerciful

جد

/jad/ ► noun
progenitor - predecessor - ancestor

جبر

/jabr/ ► noun
gouge - force - algebra

جدا

/jodâ/ ► adverb
discrete - asunder - apart - another -
several - separate - segregate

جبران

/jobrân/ ► noun
amends - restitution - reprisal - relief -
rectification - recovery

جدا شدن

/jodâ shodan/ ► verb
part - dissent

جبران خسارت

/jobrâne khesârat/ ► noun
redress

جدا کردن

/jodâ kardan/ ► verb
unzip - untwist - unlink - disconnect -
detach - cutoff

جبران کردن

/jobrân kardan/ ► verb
compensate - reimburse - redress

جبران ناپذیر

/jobrân nâpazir/ ► adjective
irreparable - irrecoverable

جدار

/jedâr/ ► noun
septum - curtain - wall

جبرییل

/jebre'il/ ► noun
gabriel

جدول
/jadval/ ▶ noun
table - schedule

جدی
/jedi/ ▶ adjective
rigid - serious - sedate - stickler

جدیت
/jediyat/ ▶ noun
enthusiasm - gravity

جدید
/jadid/ ▶ noun
modern - maiden - uptodate -
unprecedented - recent - novel - new

جدیدا
/jadidan/ ▶ adverb
new

جذاب
/jazâb/ ▶ adjective
slick - dashing - cute - personable -
lovable

جذابیت
/jazâbiyat/ ▶ noun
grace - spell

جذام
/jozâm/ ▶ noun
leprosy

جداسازی
/jodâsâzi/ ▶ noun
detachment - severance - segregate

جداشدنی
/jodâ shodani/ ▶ adjective
severable - separable - detachable -
dissoluble - precipitant

جداکننده
/jodâ konande/ ▶ adjective
insulator

جداگانه
/jodâgâne/ ▶ adverb
separate - aside - antiseptic

جدال
/jedâl/ ▶ noun
controversy - battle

جدال آمیز
/jedâl âmiz/ ▶ adjective
controversial

جدال کردن
/jedâl kardan/ ▶ verb
dispute

جدانشدنی
/jodâshodani/ ▶ adjective
irresolvable - inseparable

جدایی
/jodâyi/ ▶ noun
sepration- segregation - divorce

جذب

/jazb/ ▶ noun
absorption - suction

جذب کردن

/jazb kardan/ ▶ verb
sop - sponge - magnet - imbibe - attract -
amuse - absorb

جذبه

/jazabe/ ▶ noun
rapture - appeal - magnetism

جذر

/jazr/ ▶ noun
square

جر زدن

/jer zadan/ ▶ verb
cheat

جر و بحث کردن

/jaro bahs kardan/ ▶ verb
squabble

جرات

/jor'at/ ▶ noun
courage - gut - venture - mettle - spunk -
spirit

جرات دادن

/jor'at dâdan/ ▶ verb
abet - hearten - heart

جرات کردن

/jor'at kardan/ ▶ verb
dare

جراح

/jarâh/ ▶ noun
surgeon

جراحت

/jerâhat/ ▶ noun
wound - sore - stricture

جراید

/jarâyed/ ▶ noun
press

جرثقیل

/jarsaghil/ ▶ noun
lift - derrick - crane

جرح

/jarh/ ▶ noun
mayhem

جرز

/jazr/ ▶ noun
pillar - pier

جرعه

/jor'e/ ▶ noun
sip - shot - swig - quaff - potion - gulp -
godown

جرعه جرعه نوشیدن

/jor'e jor'e nushidan/ ▶ verb
dram

جرقه

/jaraghe/ ▶ noun
arc - scintillation - sparkle - spark

جریمه کردن

/jarime kardan/ ▶ verb
fine - penalize

جرقه زدن

/jaraghe zadan/ ▶ verb
scintillate - sparkle - spark

جز

/joz/ ▶ preposition
except - but - retail - forby

جرم

/jorm/ ▶ noun
crime - guilt

جزا

/jaza/ ▶ noun
penalty

جریان

/jariyân/ ▶ noun
outflow - ooze - gush - flow - circuit -
stream

جزای کیفر

/jazaye keifar/ ▶ noun
payoff

(Idiom: در جریان گذاشتن
keep someone posted)

جزاین

/joz in/ ▶ adverb
else

جریحه

/jarihe/ ▶ noun
wound

جزاینکه

/joz inke/ ▶ adverb
unless

جریحه دار

/jarihedâr/ ▶ adjective
raw

جزر

/jazr/ ▶ noun
ebb

جریحه دار کردن

/jarihedâr kardan/ ▶ verb
hurt - harrow - raw

جزوه

/jozveh/ ▶ noun
brochure - booklet - pamphlet

جریمه

/jarime/ ▶ noun
surcharge - fine - penalty

جزیره

/jazire/ ▶ noun
isle - island

جزیی

/jozyi/ ▶ adjective
trivial - small - inconsiderable - partial -
paltry - negligible

جزییات

/joz'iyat/ ▶ noun
detail - elaboration

جسارت

/jesârat/ ▶ noun
audacity - presumption - venture -
insolence - effrontery

جسارت کردن

/jesârat kardan/ ▶ verb
obtrude

جست

/jast/ ▶ noun
leap - bounce

جست زدن

/jast zadan/ ▶ verb
vault

جست و خیز

/jasto khiz/ ▶ noun
spring - curvet - caper - bound

جستار

/jostâr/ ▶ noun
inquiry - inquest - query

جستجو

/jostoju/ ▶ noun
search - research - rummage - quest -
probe - hunt

جستجو کردن

/jostoju kardan/ ▶ verb
search - look - quest - seek - scour

جستجوگر

/jostojugar/ ▶ adjective
explorer

جستن

/jostan/ ▶ verb
scoot - jump - leap - hip

جسد

/jasad/ ▶ noun
corpse - carcase - body - bier

جسم

/jesm/ ▶ noun
substance - corpus - metal - material -
bulk - body

جسم شناور

/jesme shenâvar/ ▶ adjective
buoy - drift

جسمانی

/jesmâni/ ▶ adjective
material - physical - bodily - worldly -
carnal - corporeal - earthen

جسمی
/jesmi/ ► adjective
substantial - material - carnal - corporeal
- corporal

جسور
/jasur/ ► adjective
adventurer - bold - hardy

جشن
/jashn/ ► noun
ceremony - celebration - carnival

جشن تولد
/jashne tavalod/ ► noun
birthday

جشن عروسی
/jashne arusi/ ► noun
marriage - bridal

جعبه
/ja'be/ ► noun
box - chest - case

جعبه ابزار
/ja'beye abzâr/ ► noun
toolbox

جعل
/ja'l/ ► noun
fiction - fake

جعل کردن
/ja'l kardan/ ► verb
mint - manufacture - counterfeit -
concoct

جعلی
/ja'li/ ► adjective
spurious - counterfeit - apocryphal -
bogus - imitation

جغرافی
/joghrâfi/ ► noun
geography

جغرافی دان
/joghrâfidân/ ► adjective
geographer

جغرافیا
/joghrâfiyâ/ ► noun
geography

جفا
/jafâ/ ► noun
misbehavior

جفت
/joft/ ► noun
twin - double - couple - geminate - pair -
mate - match - peer

جفت کردن
/joft kardan/ ► verb
twin - truss - assemble - accompany -
link - husband - graft - geminate

جک زدن
/jak zadan/ ► verb
jack

جگر

/jegar/ ▶ noun
liver

جلا

/jalâ/ ▶ noun
polish - varnish - burnish - buff

جلا دادن

/jalâ dâdan/ ▶ verb
surface - japan - burnish - polish -
varnish

جلاد

/jalâd/ ▶ noun
deathsman

جلال

/jalâl/ ▶ noun
refulgence - kudos - glory - honest

جلب

/jalb/ ▶ noun
jalap - invitation

جلب رضایت کردن

/jalbe rezâyat kardan/ ▶ verb
atone

جلب کردن

/jalb kardan/ ▶ verb
solicit - catch - entice - engross - have -
attract - atone

جلد

/jeld/ ▶ noun
cover - shell - sheathe

جلد کتاب

/jelde ketâb/ ▶ noun
wrapper

جلد کردن

/jeld kardan/ ▶ verb
jacket - cover - case

جلسه

/jalase/ ▶ noun
session - seance

جلف

/jelf/ ▶ adjective
rank - racy - gaudy - tawdry - jaunty -
jackanapes - sporty

جلگه

/jolge/ ▶ noun
flat - plain

جلو

/jolo/ ▶ noun
along - ahead - beforehand - before -
forward - forth - foreside

جلو بردن

/jolo bordan/ ▶ verb
boost - advance - further

جلو رفتن

showing - seeming - display - flash -
bravery - parade - luster

/jolo raftan/ ► verb
comealong

جلوه داشتن

جلو زدن

/jelve dâshtan/ ► verb
luster

/jolo zadan/ ► verb
outgo

جلوه گر

جلوتر

/jelvegar/ ► adjective
smart

/jolotar/ ► adjective
further

جلوی

جلوتر بودن از

/joloye/ ► noun
forward - former - fore - prior

/jolotar budan az/ ► verb
precede

جلیقه

جلودار

/jelighe/ ► noun
underwaist - vest

/jolodâr/ ► adjective
front - herald - harbinger - vanguard -
van

جماع

جلوس

/jemâ'/ ► noun
copulation - coitus - coition

/jolus/ ► noun
accession

جماعت

/jamâ'at/ ► noun
passel - posse - stream - school

جلوس کردن

/jolus kardan/ ► verb
sit - agree

جمال

جلوگیری کردن

/jamâl/ ► noun
beauty

/jologiri kardan/ ► verb
arrest - prevent - intercept - keep -
rebuff

جمجمه

/jomjome/ ► noun
skull - scalp

جلوه

/jelve/ ► noun

جمع
/jam'/ ▶ noun
total - tot - tale - summation - mass -
plural - aggregate

جمله
/jomle/ ▶ noun
term - sentence - outright

جمع آوری کردن
/jam' âvari kardan/ ▶ verb
levy - muster - mass - cull - reap - rake

جمهور
/jomhur/ ▶ noun
populace

جمع بستن
/jam' bastan/ ▶ verb
tot

جمهوری
/jomhuri/ ▶ noun
republic

جمع کردن
/jam' kardan/ ▶ verb
purse - add - gather - collect

جمهوری خواه
/jomhurikhâh/ ▶ adjective
republican

جمع کل
/jam'e kol/ ▶ noun
entirety - gross

جن
/jen/ ▶ noun
sprite - spook - elf - deuce - goblin -
urchin - bogey

جمعا
/jam'an/ ▶ adverb
utter - wholly

جناب
/jenâb/ ▶ noun
excellency

جمعه
/jom'e/ ▶ noun
friday

جناح
/jenâh/ ▶ noun
shoulder - aisle - wing

جمعی
/jam'I/ ▶ adjective
plural - collective

جنایتکار
/jenâyatkâr/ ▶ adjective
jailbird - criminal

جمعیت
/jam'iyat/ ▶ noun
throng - crowd - gang - flock population

جنتلمن
/jentelman/ ► noun
gallant

جنجال
/janjâl/ ► noun
tumult - scuffle - brawl - hubbub

جنجال راه انداختن
/janjâl râh andâkhtan/ ► verb
tumult

جنجال کردن
/janjâl kardan/ ► verb
jangle

جنده
/jende/ ► adjective
hack - townswoman - trollop

جنس
/jens/ ► noun
substance - stuff - stamp - breed - brand - mettle - commodity - kind - genus - gender

جنس نر
/jense nar/ ► noun
johnny - male

جنسی
/jensi/ ► adjective
sexual - sex - kind - generic

جنایی
/jenâyi/ ► noun
criminal

جنب
/jazb/ ► noun
next - side

جنب و جوش
/jonbojush/ ► noun
motion - milling

جنباندن
/jonbândan/ ► verb
shake - rock - wigwag - waggle - wag - bestir

جنبنده
/jonbande/ ► adjective
jiggly - wobbly - wiggler

جنبه
/janbe/ ► noun
aspect - phase - leer - sight - self - prospect

جنبی
/janbi/ ► noun
next - lateral

جنبیدن
/jonbidan/ ► verb
vibrate - vacillate - move - wobble - wiggle - wag

جنگ
/jang/ ▶ noun
anthology - battle - warfare - war - scrap

جنگلی
/jangali/ ▶ adjective
sylvan - wild

جنگ افروز
/jang afruz/ ▶ adjective
warmonger

جنگی
/jangi/ ▶ adjective
military - martial - warlike

جنگ افزار
/jang afzâr/ ▶ noun
armament - arm - weaponry - weapon

جنوب
/jonub/ ▶ noun
south

جنگاور
/jangâvar/ ▶ adjective
warrior

جنوب خاوری
/jonube khâvari/ ▶ adjective
southeast

جنگجو
/jangju/ ▶ adjective
pugnacious - martial - belligerent -
bellicose - comatant - warrior

جنوب شرقی
/jonube sharghi/ ▶ adjective
southeast

جنگجویی
/jangjuyi/ ▶ noun
militancy

جنوبی
/jonubi/ ▶ adjective
southerner - southern - south

جنگل
/jangal/ ▶ noun
forest - woodland - greenwood - jungle

جنون
/jonun/ ▶ noun
insanity - psychosis

جنگل نشین
/jangalneshin/ ▶ adjective
woodman

جنی
/jeni/ ▶ adjective
hobgoblin - goblin

جنگلبان
/jangalbân/ ▶ noun
woodman

جنین
/jenin/ ▶ noun
chrysalis - germ

جهاد
/jahâd/ ► noun
jehad

جهاز
/jahâz/ ► noun
ship - system - appurtenance - apparatus
- dowry

جهالت
/jehâlat/ ► noun
ignorance - idiotism

جهان
/jahân/ ► noun
world - universe - macrocosm

جهان آفرین
/jahân âfarin/ ► adjective
demiurge

جهانگرد
/jahângard/ ► noun
tourist

جهانگردی
/jahângardi/ ► noun
tourism

جهانگردی کردن
/jahângardi kardan/ ► verb
tourist

جهانی
/jahâni/ ► adjective
universal - ecumenical - global

جهانی کردن
/jahâni kardan/ ► verb
universalize

جهت
/jahat/ ► noun
set - sake - course - vector - point - aim

جهت یابی کردن
/jahat yâbi/ ► verb
orient

جهش
/jahesh/ ► noun
jump - startle - spurt - lunge - braid -
pounce - vault

جهل
/jahl/ ► noun
ignorance

جهنده
/jahande/ ► adjective
springy - jumper - jumper - hopper

جهنم
/jahanam/ ► noun
hell - hades

جهود
/johud/ ► noun
jew

جهيزيه

/jahiziye/ ► noun
dowry

جو

/jav/ ► noun
atmosphere - barley - grain

جو دادن

/jav dâdan/ ► verb
oat

جواب

/jurâb/ ► noun
reply - rejoinder

جواب دادن

/javâb dâdan/ ► verb
answer

جواب رد

/javâbe rad/ ► noun
recalcitrance

جواب منفی

/javâbe manfi/ ► noun
nope

جوابگو

/javâbgu/ ► adjective
respondent

جواز

/javâz/ ► noun
sanction - permit - immunity - license -
pass - paper

جوان

/javân/ ► adjective
young

جوانان

/javânân/ ► noun
youth

جوانترین

/javântarin/ ► adjective
youngest

جوانمرد

/javânmard/ ► adjective
manly - chivalrous - sportsmanlike -
youth

جوانمردی

/javânmardi/ ► noun
chivalry - magnanimity

جوانه

/javâne/ ► noun
tiller - sprout - bud - offshoot - chrysalis

جوانه زدن

/javâne zadan/ ► verb
erupt - ratoon - nip - spurt - sprout - sprit
- tiller

جوانی

/javâni/ ► adjective
youth - springtime

جواهر
/javâher/ ► noun
jewel - treasure - bijou - ouch - gem

جواهرساز
/javâhersâz/ ► noun
jeweller - jeweler

جواهرفروش
/javâherforush/ ► noun
jeweller - jeweler

جواهرفروشی
/javâherforushi/ ► noun
jewelry

جواهری
/javâheri/ ► adjective
jeweler

جوجه
/juje/ ► noun
squab - chick - bird

جوجه تیغی
/jujetighi/ ► noun
urchin - hedgehog

جوجه کشی
/jujekeshi/ ► noun
incubation

جوخه
/jukhe/ ► noun
squad

جور
/jur/ ► noun
sort - brand - compatible - kind - genus -
oppression

جور بودن
/jur budan/ ► verb
comport - adhere - accordance

جور شدن
/jur shodan/ ► verb
piece - mesh

جور کردن
/jur kardan/ ► verb
sort - suit - consort - concert - assort -
accord

جوراب
/jurab/ ► noun
socks

جوراب بافی
/jurâb bâfi/ ► noun
hosiery

جوراب کوتاه
/jurâbe kutâh/ ► noun
vamp

جورواجور

/jurâjur/ ▶ noun
various

جوش

/jush/ ▶ noun
spout - simmer - gush - weld - eruption -
effervescence - boil - pimple

جوش دادن

/jush dâdan/ ▶ verb
solder - shut - weld - vulcanize

جوش زدن

/jush zadan/ ▶ verb
breakout - effervesce

جوش سرسیاه

/jushe sarsiyâh/ ▶ noun
blackhead

جوشاندن

/jushândan/ ▶ verb
seethe - bubble - boil - decoction

جوشانده

/jushânde/ ▶ adjective
sodden

جوشکار

/jushkâr/ ▶ adjective
welder

جوشکاری کردن

/jushkâri kardan/ ▶ verb
weld

جوشن

/joshan/ ▶ noun
mail - armor - armature

جوشیدن

/jushidan/ ▶ verb
seethe - gurgle - bubble - perk

جولان

/jôlân/ ▶ noun
parade

جوهر

/jôhar/ ▶ noun
ink - acid - juice

جوهری

/jôhari/ ▶ noun
inky

جوی

/juy/ ▶ noun
stream - cut - rush - gutter - atmospheric

جویدن

/javidan/ ▶ verb
munch - masticate - chew - chaw -
champ

جوینده

/javande/ ▶ adjective
hunter – acquisitive

جوییدن
/javidan/ ▶ verb
seek

جیره
/jire/ ▶ noun
stipend - allotment

جیب
/jib/ ▶ noun
tangent - purse - sinus - pocket

جیره بندی کردن
/jire bandi kardan/ ▶ verb
ration

جیره دادن
/jire dâdan/ ▶ verb
allowance

جیب بر
/jib bor/ ▶ adjective
cutpurse - dip - bung - pickpocket

جیغ
/jigh/ ▶ noun
shriek - shout - screech - scream

جیب بری کردن
/jib bori kardan/ ▶ verb
purse

جیغ زدن
/jigh zadan/ ▶ verb
scream - yelp - yaup - yawp - shout

جیب دار
/jib dâr/ ▶ adjective
pocket

جیک زدن
/jik zadan/ ▶ verb
peep

جیبی
/jibi/ ▶ adjective
pocket

جیم شدن
/jim shodan/ ▶ verb
scram - nip - guy

جیپ
/jip/ ▶ noun
jeep

جین
/jin/ ▶ noun
gin

جیر
/jir/ ▶ noun
chamoisleather

جیوه
/jive/ ▶ noun
quicksilver - mercury

چ - چ

che /che/ ▶ seventh letter of the Persian alphabet

چابک

/châbok/ ▶ adjective
swift - agile - brisk - handy

چابک دست

/châbokdast/ ▶ adjective
jimmy

چابک سوار

/châboksâvâr/ ▶ adjective
jockey

چابکی

/châboki/ ▶ noun
alacrity - agility - activity - dexterity

چاپ

/châp/ ▶ noun
stamp - edition - press - impression

چاپ کردن

/châp kardan/ ▶ verb
publish - reproduce - print

چاپ مجدد

/châpe mojadad/ ▶ noun
reissue

چاپار

/châpâr/ ▶ noun
mail - post

چاپلوس

/châplus/ ▶ adjective
bootlick - servile

چاپلوسانه

/châplusâne/ ▶ adverb
silky - greasy

چاپلوسی

/châplusi/ ▶ noun
subservience - blarney - cajole - flattery
- grease

چاپلوسی کردن

/châplusi kardan/ ▶ verb
collogue - butter - slaver

چاپی

/châyi/ ▶ noun
print - letterpress

چاپیدن

/châpidan/ ▶ verb
rob - loot - plunder - hurry - harry

چاخان

/châkhân/ ▶ noun
quack - bluff - whiff

چاخان کردن

/châkhân kardan/ ▶ verb
vapor - palaver

چادر
/châdor/ ► noun
tent - veil

چادر زدن
/châdor zadan/ ► verb
encamp

چارپایه
/chârpâye/ ► noun
stool

چاردیواری
/chârdivâri/ ► adjective
enclosure

چارقد
/chârghad/ ► noun
kerchief

چارگوش
/chârgush/ ► noun
square

چاره
/châre/ ► noun
makeshift - remedy - recourse

چاره کردن
/châre kardan/ ► verb
ameliorate

چاشنی
/châshni/ ► noun
sauce - detonator - condiment - relish -
flavor - primer

چاشنی غذا
/châshinye ghazâ/ ► noun
spice - ketchup

چاق
/châgh/ ► noun
fat - overweight - obese - pudgy - tubby

چاق شدن
/châgh shodan/ ► verb
blubber - batten - plump

چاقو
/châghu/ ► noun
knife - whittle

چاقی
/châghi/ ► adjective
overweight

چاک
/châbok/ ► noun
agile – swift

چاک خوردن
/châk khordan/ ► verb
sliver

چاکر
/châker/ ► adjective
menial

چال
/châl/ ► noun
trench - cavern

چالاک
/châlâk/ ► adjective
agile - prompt - jimmy - deft - nippy -
nimble - natty - adroit - handy

چاله
/châle/ ► noun
pit

چاله چاله
/châle châle/ ► adjective
pitted

چانه
/châne/ ► noun
chin - haggle

چانه زدن
/châne zadan/ ► verb
bargain - bargain - haggle

چاه
/châh/ ► noun
pit - shaft

چای
/châi/ ► noun
tea

چاییدن
/châyidan/ ► verb
Cool

چپ
/chap/ ► noun
squint

چپ چپ
/chap chap/ ► adjective
askew - askance - awry

چپ دست
/chap dast/ ► adjective
soiuthpaw - gauche

چپاندن
/chapândan/ ► verb
cram - jam - thrust - stuff - squeeze

چپانیدن
/chapânidan/ ► verb
frank

چپاول
/chapâvol/ ► noun
loot - plunder - raven - ransack

چپاولگر
/chapâvolgar/ ► adjective
marauder - robber

چتر
/chatr/ ► noun
umbrella

چتر نجات
/chatre nejât/ ► noun
parachute

چترباز
/chatrbâz/ ▶ noun
parachutist

چرب زبان
/charbzabân/ ▶ adjective
glib

چخماق
/chakhmâgh/ ▶ noun
hammer

چرب زبانی
/charbzabâni/ ▶ noun
lard - bolubility - unction

چرا
/cherâ/ ▶ adverb
why - wherefore

چرب زبانی کردن
/charbzabâni kardan/ ▶ verb
coax

چراغ
/cherâgh/ ▶ noun
light - lamp

چرب کننده
/charbkonande/ ▶ adjective
lubricant

چراغ خانه
/cherâghe khâne/ ▶ noun
lighthouse

چرب و نرم
/charbo narm/ ▶ adjective
sleek - voluble - unctuous

چراغ قوه
/cherâghe ghove/ ▶ noun
torch

چربی
/charbi/ ▶ noun
fat - oil - grease

چراغانی کردن
/cherâghâni kardan/ ▶ verb
illuminate

چربیدن
/charbidan/ ▶ verb
prevail - predominate

چراندن
/charândan/ ▶ verb
feed - graze - grass

چرت
/chort/ ▶ noun
snooze - slumber - nap - doze

چرب
/charb/ ▶ adjective
sebaceous - greasy - fatty - fat - oily -
unctuous

چرت زدن
/chort zadan/ ▶ verb
nap - snooze - slumber

چرت زن

/chortzan/ ▶ adjective
drowsy

چرت کوتاه

/chorte khotâh/ ▶ noun
catnap

چرخ

/charkh/ ▶ noun
loop - axle - rhomb - cart - wheel - cycle
- turquoise

چرخ دنده

/charkhe dande/ ▶ noun
sprocket - gearwheel - gear - cogwheel

چرخ زدن

/charkh zadan/ ▶ verb
eddy - gyrate - pirouette

چرخ فلک

/charkhofalak/ ▶ noun
girandole

چرخان

/charkhân/ ▶ noun
twister - rotor

چرخاندن

/charkhândan/ ▶ verb
pivot - wind - swivel - spin

چرخانیدن

/charkhânidan/ ▶ verb
whirl

چرخش

/charkhesh/ ▶ noun
turquoise - tumble - troll - evolution -
revolution - roll - gyration - whirl

چرخشی

/charkheshi/ ▶ adjective
rotatory - gyration

چرخک

/charkhak/ ▶ noun
pulley - trundle - whirligig - caster

چرخکار

/charkhkâr/ ▶ noun
machinist'smate - machinist

چرخنده

/charkhande/ ▶ adjective
revolving - rotative - rotary - whirler

چرخیدن

/charkhidan/ ▶ verb
swing - whirl - wheel - revolve

چرک

/cherk/ ▶ adjective
slag - squawk - lymph - impure - dirty -
dirt - dingy

چرک دار

/cherkdâr/ ▶ adjective
pussy

چرک شدن

/cherk shodan/ ▶ verb
soil - foul

چروکیده شدن

/chorukide shodan/ ▶ verb
wrinkle

چرکی

/cherki/ ▶ adjective
septic - pussy

چریدن

/charidan/ ▶ verb
browse - graze - grass

چرکین

/cherkin/ ▶ verb
dirty - lousy

چسب

/chasb/ ▶ noun
gum - gluten - glue - agglutinate - paste
- lime - mucilage

چرم

/charm/ ▶ noun
leather - hide

چسب زدن

/chasb zadan/ ▶ verb
gum

چرمی

/charmi/ ▶ adjective
leathery

چسباندن

/chasbândan/ ▶ verb
stick - cement - attach - agglutinate

چرند

/charand/ ▶ adjective
nonsensical - rigmarole - crap

چسبانیدن

/chasbânidan/ ▶ verb
affix

چرند گفتن

/charand goftan/ ▶ verb
twaddle

چسبدار

/chasbdâr/ ▶ adjective
adhesive

چروک شدن

/choruk/ ▶ verb
puchery - shrivel - shrink - constringe

چسبناک

/chasbnâk/ ▶ adjective
tacky - slab - string - sticky - stick -
gooey - cohesive

چروکیدن

/chorukide/ ▶ verb
crimp - wrinkle

چشم بند

/cheshmband/ ▶ noun
blind

چشم پزشک

/cheshm pezeshk/ ▶ noun
oculist

چشم پوشی

/cheshm pushi/ ▶ noun
connivance - renunciation - waiver

چشم پوشیدن

/cheshm pushidan/ ▶ verb
ignore - relinquish

چشم داشت

/cheshmdâsht/ ▶ noun
outlook

چشم دوختن

/cheshm dukhtan/ ▶ verb
gaze

چشمک

/cheshmak/ ▶ noun
twinkle - blink - wink

چشمک زن

/cheshmak zan/ ▶ adjective
blinker

چشمگیر

/cheshmgir/ ▶ adjective
saleint

چسبندگی

/chasbandegi/ ▶ noun
tenacity - stick - cohesion - adherence -
adherence

چسبنده

/chasbide/ ▶ adjective
innate - inherent - adhesive - gummy -
gooey - sticky - tenacious

چسبیدگی

/chasbidegi/ ▶ adjective
coherency - adhesion

چسبیدن

/chasbidan/ ▶ verb
cohere - cling - cleave

چشایی

/cheshâyi/ ▶ adjective
taste

چشم

/chashm/ ▶ noun
eye - sight - shiner

چشم انداز

/chashmandâz/ ▶ noun
vision - scenery - prospect - overlook -
outlook - perspective - vista - view -
landscape

چشم بستن

/cheshm bastan/ ▶ verb
blindfold

چشمه
/cheshme/ ▶ noun
fountain - well - mesh - springhead -
spring - source

چشیدن
/cheshidan/ ▶ verb
assay - palate - gust - sip - taste

چفت
/cheft/ ▶ noun
snap - hasp - lid - latch

چفت در
/chefte dar/ ▶ noun
slot

چفت زدن به
/cheft zadan be/ ▶ verb
lid

چقدر
/cheghadr/ ▶ adverb
what - any - any

چک
/chek/ ▶ noun
cheque

چکامه
/chakâme/ ▶ noun
ode - poem

چکامه سرا
/chakâme sarâ/ ▶ adjective
poet

چکانیدن
/chekânidan/ ▶ verb
trickle - drip - dribble

چکاوک
/chakâvak/ ▶ noun
warbler

چکش
/chakosh/ ▶ noun
hammer

چکش زدن
/chakosh zadan/ ▶ verb
hammer - mallet

چکه
/cheke/ ▶ noun
sprinkle - drop - drip - leakage - leak

چکیده
/chekide/ ▶ adjective
ooze - succinct - tabloid

چکیده کلام
/chekideye kalâm/ ▶ noun
resume

چکیده مطلب
/chekideye matlab/ ▶ noun
précis

چگالی
/chegâli/ ▶ noun
density

چگالی سنج
/chegâlisanj/ ► noun
aerometer

چماق
/chomâgh/ ► noun
stick - stave - cudgel - bludgeon - bat

چگونگی
/chegunegi/ ► noun
how - quality - circumstance - condition

چماق زدن
/chomâgh zadan/ ► verb
mace - cudgel

چگونه
/chegune/ ► adverb
how

چمدان
/chamedân/ ► noun
baggage - kist - suitcase

چلاق
/cholâgh/ ► adjective
cripple

چمن
/chaman/ ► noun
grass - lawn - prairie - meadow - arbor

چلاق کردن
/cholâgh kardan/ ► verb
maim

چمن زار
/chamanzâr/ ► noun
meadow

چلاندن
/chelândan/ ► verb
squeeze - wring - crush

چموش
/chamush/ ► noun
skittish - restive - cantankerous -
rowdyish - outlaw

چلچله
/chelchele/ ► noun
swallow

چنان
/chenân/ ► preposition
so

چلغوز
/chalghuz/ ► adjective
guano

چنانچه
/chenânche/ ► preposition
if - if

چلیپا
/chelipâ/ ► noun
cross

چندگانگی
/chandgânegi/ ▶ noun
plurality

چنانکه
/chenânke/ ▶ preposition
as - how

چندلا
/chandlâ/ ▶ adjective
fold - multiple

چنته
/chante/ ▶ noun
knapsack - cod - pouch - bag

چندی
/chandi/ ▶ adverb
partly - quantity - quantitative

چند
/chand/ ▶ adjective
several

چندین
/chandin/ ▶ adverb
multiple - several

چند برابر کردن
/chand barâbar kardan/ ▶ verb
manifold

چنگ
/chang/ ▶ noun
grip - grapple - clutch - claw - uncus -
sackbut

چند جانبه
/chandjânebe/ ▶ adjective
multilateral

چنگ زدن
/chang zadan/ ▶ verb
clutch - claw - grasp - grab - harp

چند صدا
/chandsedâ/ ▶ adjective
allophone

چندان
/chandân/ ▶ adverb
very - fold

چنگ نواز
/changnavâz/ ▶ adjective
harper

چندپهلو
/chand pahlu/ ▶ adjective
multilateral

چنگال
/changâl/ ▶ noun
fork

چندتا
/chandtâ/ ▶ adverb
some - various - manifold

چنگک
/changak/ ▶ noun
tach - prong - gaff - rake - uncus

چنین

/chenin/ ▶ noun
thus - so - such - likewise

چهارپا

/chehârpâ/ ▶ adjective
quadruped - beast

چه

/che/ ▶ preposition
or - whether - what - any

چهارچوب

/chehârchub/ ▶ noun
frame

چه اندازه

/che andâze/ ▶ preposition
what

چهارچوبه

/chehârchube/ ▶ noun
framework

چه خوب

/che khub/ ▶ adverb
benedicite

چهاردهم

/chehârdaham/ ▶ noun
fourteenth

چه کسی

/che kasi/ ▶ preposition
whom - who

چهارشنبه

/chehârshanbe/ ▶ noun
Wednesday

چه کسی را

/che karirâ/ ▶ preposition
whom

چهارضلعی

/chehâr zel'I/ ▶ adjective
quadrilateral

چه مقدار

/che meghdâr/ ▶ preposition
what

چهارقلو

/chehârgholu/ ▶ adjective
quadruplet

چه نوع

/che no'e/ ▶ preposition
what type

چهارگانه

/chehârgâne/ ▶ adverb
quadruplet

چه وقت

/che vaght/ ▶ preposition
when

چهارگوش

/chehârgush/ ▶ adjective
quadrilateral - quadrant - quadrangle

چهارلا

/chehârlâ/ ► adjective
uradruple

چوب پنبه

/chub panbe/ ► noun
stopper - cork

چهارنعل

/chehâr na'l/ ► noun
scamper - gallop - canter

چوب خط

/chub khat/ ► noun
score

چهچه زدن

/chah chahe zadan/ ► verb
twitter

چوب زدن

/chub zadan/ ► verb
beat - bastinado - drub - cudgel

چهره

/chehre/ ► noun
visage - face

چوبه

/chube/ ► noun
shaft

چوب

/chub/ ► noun
wood - rod

چوبه دار

/chubeye dâr/ ► noun
gibbet - gallows - tree

چوب افرا

/chube afrâ/ ► noun
maple

چوبی

/chubi/ ► adjective
woody - wooden - wood

چوب بادوام

/chube bâdavâm/ ► noun
hardwood

چوپان

/chupân/ ► noun
rancher - pastor

چوب بر

/chub bor/ ► adjective
lumberjack - logger

چوچوله

/chuchule/ ► noun
clitoris

چوب بست

/chub bast/ ► noun
scaffold - framework

چوگان

/chôgân/ ► noun
wicket - mallet - bat

چیز

/chiz/ ▶ noun

thing - stuff - article - res - nip – object

(Idiom: یک چیز تو همان مایه ها

Or something)

چون

/chon/ ▶ preposition

since - whereas - as

چونکه

/chonke/ ▶ adverb

because

چیستان

/chistân/ ▶ noun

puzzle - crux - conundrum - enigma - problem

چیدن

/chidan/ ▶ verb

arrange - pare - lop - pluck - pickup - pick - mow

(Idiom: بادمجان دور قاب چیدن

Suck up to somebody)

چین

/chin/ ▶ noun

China - fold - offset - wrinkle - crimp - crease - puchery

چین خوردگی

/chinkhordegi/ ▶ noun

wrinkle

چیدنی

/chidani/ ▶ adjective

ripe

چین خوردن

/chin khordan/ ▶ verb

shrivel

چیرگی

/chiregi/ ▶ noun

effrontery - proficiency

چین خورده

/chinkhorde/ ▶ adjective

crackly

چیره

/chire/ ▶ adjective

proficient - dominant

چین دادن

/chindâr/ ▶ verb

shirr - quill - wrinkle - corrugate

چیره دست

/chiredast/ ▶ adjective

dextrous - dexterous - adroit - master

چینی
/chini/ ▶ adjective
sinitic - chinese - china - porcelain

he /he/ ▶ eighth letter of the Persian
alphabet

حاجب
/hâjat/ ▶ noun
chamberlain - porter

حاد
/hâd/ ▶ adjective
torrid - acute - acute - hot - keen

حادثه
/hâdese/ ▶ noun
accident - accidence

حادثه تاریخی
/hâdeseye târikhi/ ▶ noun
epoch

حادثه ناگوار
/hâdeseye nâgovâr/ ▶ noun
mischance - miscarriage - misadventure

حاذق
/hâzegh/ ▶ adjective
proficient

حاشا
/hâshâ/ ▶ adverb
denial – never

حاشا کردن
/hâshâ kardan/ ▶ verb
deny

حاشیه
/hâshiye/ ▶ noun
purl - brink - brim - braid - border -
verge - margin - rand - outskirt - gloss

حاصل
/hâsel/ ▶ noun
product - harvest - upshot - resume -
resultant - result - outgrwth - outcome

حاصل جمع
/hâsele jam'/ ▶ noun
sum - total

حاصل کردن
/hâsel kardan/ ▶ verb
afford - acquire - get - generate

حاصلخیز
/hâselkhiz/ ▶ adjective
prolific - pergnant

حاصلخیزی
/hâselkhizi/ ▶ noun
productivity

حاصلضرب
/hâselzarb/ ▶ noun
product

حاضر

/hâzer/ ▶ adjective
stock - present

حافظ

/hâfez/ ▶ noun
keeper - retentive - patron

حافظه

/hâfeze/ ▶ noun
memory - retention

(Idiom: دروغگو کم حافظه است
a liar ought to have a good memory)

حاکم

/hâkem/ ▶ noun
governor

حاکم بودن

/hâkem budan/ ▶ verb
govern

حاکی

/hâki/ ▶ noun
symptomatic - symbolic - redolent -
expressive

حاکی بودن

/hâki budan/ ▶ verb
portend

حال

/hâl/ ▶ noun
health - mood - state - situation - now

حال آنکه

/hâl ânke/ ▶ preposition
while

حالا

/hâlâ/ ▶ noun
now

حالت

/hâlat/ ▶ noun
mood - temperament - situation - status -
predicament

حالت تهوع

/hâlate tahavo'/ ▶ noun
nausea - qualm

حامل

/hâmel/ ▶ adjective
carrier - conveyer - porter - bearer

حامل بودن

/hâmel budan/ ▶ verb
comport

حاملگی

/hâmelegi/ ▶ noun
pregnancy

حامله

/hâmele/ ▶ adjective
peregnant

حامله بودن

/hâmele budan/ ► verb
peregnant

حبه

/habe/ ► noun
bean - grain

حامی

/hâmi/ ► adjective
protector - sponsor - patron - partisan - advocate - actor - bulwark - booster

حبوبات

/hobubât/ ► noun
cereal - grain

حاوی

/hâvi/ ► noun
receptacle

حتما

/hatman/ ► adverb
certainly - inevitable

حایل شدن

/hâyel shodan/ ► verb
intervene - intercept

حتمی

/hatmi/ ► noun
imminent - indispensable - emergence - emergency - cocksure - cretain

حایل کردن

/hâyel kardan/ ► verb
thwart

حتی

/hatâ/ ► adverb
even

حب

/hob/ ► noun
pill - pellet

حجاب

/hejâb/ ► noun
veil

حباب

/hobâb/ ► noun
bubble - boll - blubber - blob - globe

حجاب زدن

/hejâb zadan/ ► verb
veil

حبس

/habs/ ► noun
jail - custody - durante - calaboose - imprisonment - prison

حجار

/hejâr/ ► noun
sculptor

حبس ابد

/habse abad/ ► noun
life

حجامت

/hejâmat/ ▶ noun
cup - leech

حجت

/hojat/ ▶ noun
agument

حجله

/hejle/ ▶ noun
bridechamber

حجم

/hajm/ ▶ noun
volume - bulk

حجيم

/hajim/ ▶ adjective
large - voluminous - massive

حد

/had/ ▶ noun
limit - quantity - precinct - period -
measure

حدس

/hads/ ▶ noun
guess

حدسى

/hadsi/ ▶ adjective
conjectural

حدقه

/hadghe/ ▶ noun
pupil - socket - orbit

حدود

/hodud/ ▶ noun
precinct - periphery - verge - module

حدوسط

/hadevasat/ ▶ noun
average - mediocrity - mediocre - mean
- norm

حذف

/hazf/ ▶ noun
omission - ellipse - elimination -
deletion

حذف كردن

/hazf kardan/ ▶ verb
omit - expurgate - eliminate - delete -
dele

حراج

/harâj/ ▶ noun
auction - outcry

حراج كردن

/harâj kardan/ ▶ verb
auction

حرارت

/harârat/ ▶ noun
heat - fire - ginger - warmth -
impetuosity - vehemence - ardor

حرارتى

/harârati/ ▶ adjective
thermal

حراست

/herâsat/ ▶ noun
preservation

حرف اضافه

/harfe ezâfe/ ▶ noun
preposition

حرام

/harâm/ ▶ noun
unlawful - illegal - taboo

حرف بزرگ

/harfe bozorg/ ▶ noun
capital

حرام کردن

/harâm kardan/ ▶ verb
waste

حرف بی ربط

/harfe birabt/ ▶ noun
rigmarole

حرامزاده

/harâmzâde/ ▶ adjective
spurious - whoreson - unfathered -
adulterate - bastard

حرف بی صدا

/harfe bisedâ/ ▶ noun
consonant

حربه

/harbe/ ▶ noun
weapon

حرف پوچ

/harfe puch/ ▶ noun
nonsense - moonshine

حرص

/hers/ ▶ noun
avidity - avarice - greed

حرف زدن

/harf zadan/ ▶ verb
speak - talk

حرص زدن

/hers zadan/ ▶ verb
raven

حرف شنو

/harfsheno/ ▶ adjective
obedient

حرف

/harf/ ▶ noun
say - talk - speech - letter -
blabbermouth - particle - word -
grapheme

(Idiom: یک بند حرف زدن

Keep talking)

حرف شنوی

/harfshenavi/ ▶ noun
obedience

حرف مفت

/harfe moft/ ▶ adjective
tattle - guff

حرف مفت زدن

/harfe moft zadan/ ▶ verb
prattle

حرمت

/hormat/ ▶ noun
reverence - revere - sanctity

حروف الفبا

/horufe alefbâ/ ▶ noun
script

حرف منفی

/harfe manfi/ ▶ noun
negative word - not

حرفه

/herfe/ ▶ noun
avocation - mystery - metier - profession
- vocation - career - trade - pursuit

حریص

/haris/ ▶ adjective
greedy - fierce - avid - avaricious -
hungry - vulture - voracious

حرفه ای

/herfe'I/ ▶ adjective
vocation - professional

حریص بودن

/haris budan/ ▶ verb
greed

حرکت

/harkat/ ▶ noun
movement - move - motion

حریف

/harif/ ▶ noun
foe - rival - opponent - adversary -
match

حرکت دادن

/harkat dâdan/ ▶ verb
propel - stir - rouse - move

حریق

/harigh/ ▶ noun
fire

حرکت دورانی

/harkate davarâni/ ▶ noun
evolution

حریم

/harim/ ▶ noun
sanctum

حرکتی

/harkati/ ▶ noun
dynamic

حزب

/hezb/ ▶ noun
party - sect - junta

حرم مطهر

/harame motahar/ ▶ noun
sanctuary

حزبی

/hezbi/ ▶ adjective
sectarian

حزن

/hozn/ ▶ noun
sorrow - grief - despondency

حس

/hes/ ▶ noun
sense - sensation - quale

حس ششم

/hese sheshom/ ▶ noun
sixthsense

حساب

/hesâb/ ▶ noun
score - calculation - arithmetic - account

(Idiom: حساب حساب است کاکا برادر
Business is business)

حساب بدهی

/hesâbe bedehi/ ▶ noun
debit

حساب نشده

/hesân nashode/ ▶ noun
unaccounted

حسابدار

/hesâbdâr/ ▶ noun
accountant

حسابداری

/hesâbdâri/ ▶ noun
accounting

حسابگر

/hesâbgar/ ▶ adjective
calculator - arithmetic

حسابی

/hesâbi/ ▶ adjective
smackdab - square - arithmetic

حسادت

/hesâdat/ ▶ noun
jealousy

حساس

/hasâs/ ▶ noun
sensory - sensitive - touchy - ticklish -
tender - techy - vigilant - acute - delicate

حساسیت

/hasâsiyat/ ▶ noun
sensitivity - sensibility - friction

حسن

/hosn/ ▶ noun
virtue- advantage- beauty

حسود

/hasud/ ▶ adjective
jealous - envious

حسودانه

/hasudâne/ ▶ adverb
invidious

حسی

/hesi/ ▶ adjective
sensory - sensational - intuitive

حشرات موذی

/hasharâte muzi/ ▶ noun
vermin - moth

حضرت

/hazrat/ ▶ noun
honor - holiness

حشره

/hashare/ ▶ noun
bug - insect

حضور

/hozur/ ▶ noun
attendance - presence

حشره کش

/hasharekosh/ ▶ noun
larva - insecticide

حضورذهن

/hozure zehn/ ▶ noun
immediacy

حشیش

/hashish/ ▶ noun
kef - hemp - marijuana

حظ

/haz/ ▶ noun
joy - unction

حصار

/hesâr/ ▶ noun
fence - wall - barrier - inclose - hedge -
hag

حفاری

/hafâri/ ▶ noun
dig

حصبه

/hasbe/ ▶ noun
typhoid

حفاظ

/hefâz/ ▶ noun
shield - shell - scabbard - safeguard -
hangar - awning

حصول

/hosul/ ▶ noun
recovery - reach

حفر

/hafr/ ▶ noun
dig

حصیر

/hasir/ ▶ noun
matting - mat - straw

حفر کردن

/hafr kardan/ ▶ verb
gull - grave - cave - excavate

حضار

/hozâr/ ▶ noun
audience - attendance - grandstand

حفرکننده

/hafr konande/ ▶ adjective
excavator

حفره

/hofre/ ▶ noun
hole - cavity - cavern - ditch - delve -
dale

حفره دار

/hofredâr/ ▶ adjective
pitted - alveolar

حفظ

/hefz/ ▶ noun
retinue - preservation

حفظ کردن

/hefz kardan/ ▶ verb
fence - retain - memorize - preserve -
secure - protect

حق

/hagh/ ▶ noun
title - right - due - law

حق تقدم

/haghe taghadom/ ▶ noun
priority - preferment - precedence

حقه

/hoghe/ ▶ noun
shift - trick - knack - bob - monkeyshine
- hob - intake

حقه باز

/hoghe bâz/ ▶ adjective
phony - trickster - snide - slicker

حقه بازی

/hoghe bâzi/ ▶ noun
juggle - cog - underhand - quackery -
legerdemain

حقه بازی کردن

/hoghe bâzi kardan/ ▶ verb
spoof - trick

حقوق

/hoghugh/ ▶ noun
salary - emolument - due - pension - law

حقوق بازنشستگی

/hoghughe bâzneshastegi/ ▶ noun
pension

حقوق دادن

/hoghughdân/ ▶ verb
jurist (tic) - lawyer

حقیر

/harghir/ ▶ adjective
runty - little - slight

حقیقت

/haghighat/ ▶ noun
truth - verity - principle - reality

حقیقتا

/haghighatan/ ▶ adverb
simply - indeed - verily

حقیقی

/haghighi/ ▶ adjective
fact - real - genuine - unfeigned - actual - veracious - intrinsic - true

حک

/hak/ ▶ noun
erasure

حک کردن

/hak kardan/ ▶ verb
lithograph - carve

حکاکی

/hakâki/ ▶ noun
gravure

حکاکی کردن

/hakâki kardan/ ▶ verb
scribe - engrave - inscribe

حکایت

/hekâyat/ ▶ noun
allegory - marchen - narrative - story - tale

حکم

/hokm/ ▶ noun
sentence - edict - rule - mandate - pardon - arbiter

حکم بازداشت

/hokme bâzdâsht/ ▶ noun
interdict - injunction

حکم دادگاه

/hokme dâdgâh/ ▶ noun
decision

حکم کردن

/hokm kardan/ ▶ verb
adjudicate - command - rule - decree

حکمت

/hekmat/ ▶ noun
doctrine - wisdom - motto

حکمت الهی

/hokme elâhi/ ▶ noun
theosophy - theology

حکمران

/homrân/ ▶ noun
ruler - governor

حکمرانی

/hokmrâni/ ▶ noun
reign

حکمفرما

/hokmfarmâ/ ▶ noun
dominant - rampant - predominant

حکمفرما بودن

/hokmfarmâ budan/ ▶ verb
dominate - reign

حکمفرمایی

/hokmfarmâyi/ ▶ noun
reign

حکمیت

/hakamiyat/ ▶ noun
umpire - umpirage

حکومت

/hokumat/ ▶ noun
government - reign - administration

حکیم

/hakim/ ▶ adjective
sage

حل

/hal/ ▶ noun
resolvent - resolution - solution

حل کردن

/hal kardan/ ▶ verb
workout - dissolve - solve

حلال

/halâl/ ▶ adjective
solvent - kosher - resolvent - lawful

حلال زاده

/halâlzâde/ ▶ adjective
legitimate

حلبی

/halabi/ ▶ noun
tinfoil - tin

حلزون

/halazun/ ▶ noun
mollusk

حلق

/halgh/ ▶ noun
gorge

حلق آویز

/halgh âviz/ ▶ noun
gadarene

حلقه

/halghe/ ▶ noun
loop - hoop - hank - vortex - ring - ran -
chain - earring

حلقه ای

/halghe'I/ ▶ adjective
gyrate

حلقه زدن

/halghe zadan/ ▶ verb
ring - wind - encompass - encircle

حلقه کردن

/halghe kardan/ ▶ verb
curl - fake

حلقوی

/halghavi/ ▶ adjective
convoluted

حلیم

/halim/ ▶ noun
submissive - meek

حماسه

/hamâse/ ▶ noun
saga - epopee - epic

حماسی

/hamâsi/ ► adjective
heroic - bardic - epic

حماقت

/hemâghat/ ► noun
stupidity - unreason - idiotism - idiocy

حمال

/hamâl/ ► noun
porter - backer

حمالی کردن

/hamâli kardan/ ► verb
porter

حمام

/hamâm/ ► noun
therm - washroom - bathroom

حمام گرفتن

/hamâm gereftan/ ► verb
bath

حمایت

/hemâyat/ ► noun
shelter - aid - patronage

حمایل

/hamâyel/ ► noun
baldric

حمل

/haml/ ► noun
deport - conveyance - consignment -
portage - address - shipment

حمل و نقل

/hamlonaghl/ ► noun
transport - haul

حمله

/hamle/ ► noun
offense - rush - attack - assault - access -
venue - inroad

حمله کردن

/hamle kardan/ ► verb
assail - impinge - layon - pop

حنایی

/hanâyi/ ► adjective
russet

حنجره

/hanjare/ ► noun
larynx

حواس

/havâs/ ► noun
attention

حواس پرت

/havâspart/ ► adjective
wacky

حواله

/havâle/ ► noun
order - assignment

حوری
/huri/ ▶ noun
nymph

حیاط
/hayât/ ▶ noun
quirk - compound - curtilage - court

حوزه
/hôze/ ▶ noun
district - compass - circuit - circle -
precinct - module - zone

حیثیت
/heisiyat/ ▶ noun
prestige

حوصله
/hôsele/ ▶ noun
mood

حیرانی
/heirâni/ ▶ noun
perplexity

حوض
/hôz/ ▶ noun
pool

حیرت
/heirat/ ▶ noun
surprise - consternation - wonder -
amazement - quandary

حوله
/hôle/ ▶ noun
towel

حیرت آور
/heiratâvar/ ▶ adjective
stupendous - marvelous - prodigious

حومه
/hume/ ▶ noun
vicinity - outskirt - environs

حیرت انگیز
/heiratangiz/ ▶ adjective
wonder

حومه شهر
/humeye shahr/ ▶ noun
suburbia - suburb - countryside

حیرت زا
/heiratzâ/ ▶ adjective
wondrous

حیات
/hayât/ ▶ noun
life

حیرت زدگی
/heiratzadegi/ ▶ noun
transfixion

حیاتی
/hayâti/ ▶ adjective
vital

حیطه
/hite/ ▶ noun
gamut - compass

حیف

/heif/ ▶ noun
alack

حیله

/hile/ ▶ noun
trick - guile - gimmick - gaff - deception
- deceit

حیله باز

/hilebâz/ ▶ adjective
cunning - gyp

حیله زدن

/hile zadan/ ▶ verb
trick

حیله گر

/hilegar/ ▶ adjective
crafty - captious - shrewd - shifty -
janusfaced - trepanation

حیله گری

/hilegari/ ▶ noun
quackery

حیوان

/heivân/ ▶ noun
animal

حیوانی

/heivâni/ ▶ adjective
animal - brutish - bestial

خ – خ

khe /khe/ ▶ ninth letter of the Persian alphabet

خار

/khâr/ ▶ noun
thorn - teazle - goad - burr - barb - prick

خاراندن

/khârândan/ ▶ verb
scrape

خائن

/khâen/ ▶ adjective
traitorous - traitor - treacherous - renegade - untrue

خارپشته

/khârposhte/ ▶ noun
hedge

خائنانه

/khâenâne/ ▶ adverb
treacherous - traitorous - insidious

خارج

/khârej/ ▶ noun
external - out - abroad - away

خاتم

/khâtam/ ▶ noun
cachet - signet

خارج از

/khârej az/ ▶ noun
out - off

خاتم کاری

/khâtamkâri/ ▶ noun
inlay

خارج قسمت

/khâreje ghesmat/ ▶ noun
ration - quotient

خاتمه

/khâteme/ ▶ noun
sequel - expiry - end - closure

خارج کردن

/khârej kardan/ ▶ verb
evict - emit

خاتمه دادن

/khâteme dâdan/ ▶ verb
terminate

خارجی

/khâreji/ ▶ adjective
strange - external - outsider

خادم

/khâdem/ ▶ adjective
servant

خاردار

/khârdâr/ ▶ adjective
barbed - picked - thorny

خارش

/khâresh/ ▶ noun
itch - scabies

خاطر

/khâter/ ▶ noun
attention - remembrance - sake

خارش کردن

/khâresh kardan/ ▶ verb
itch

خاطرات

/khâterât/ ▶ noun
memoirs

خارق العاده

/khâreghol'âde/ ▶ adjective
extraordinary

خاطرجمع

/khâterjam'/ ▶ adjective
sure

خاریدن

/khâridan/ ▶ verb
itch - tickle

خاطرخواه

/khâterkhâh/ ▶ adjective
lover

خاشاک

/khâshâk/ ▶ noun
brushwood

خاطره

/khâtere/ ▶ noun
memory - memoir - memento

خاشع

/khâshe'/ ▶ adjective
submissive

خاطی

/khâti/ ▶ adjective
trespasser

خاص

/khâs/ ▶ noun
particular - sacred - specific - special

خاک

/khâk/ ▶ noun
land - earth - dust - dirt - ground - grit -
clod - soil

(Idiom: با خاک یکسان شدن

Be razed to the ground)

خاصیت

/khâsiyat/ ▶ noun
property - nature - quale - virtue

خاک اره

/khâkare/ ▶ noun
sawdust

خاضع

/khâze'/ ▶ adjective
submissive

خاک رس

/khâke ros/ ▶ noun
pug - clay - bole

خاکروبه

/khâkrube/ ▶ noun
trash - rummage

خاکریز

/khâkriz/ ▶ noun
bulwark - moat - levee - fence - weir

خاکستر

/khâkestar/ ▶ noun
ash - cinder - slag

خاکی

/khâki/ ▶ adjective
mundane - worldly - earthy - earthly -
earthen - earthborn

خاکی کردن

/khâki kardan/ ▶ verb
soil

خاگینه

/khâgine/ ▶ noun
omelette

خال

/khâl/ ▶ noun
spot - speckle - dot - freckle

خال کوبیدن

/khâl kubidan/ ▶ verb
tattoo

خالص

/khâles/ ▶ adjective
absolute - downright - net - genuine -
pure

خالق

/khâlegh/ ▶ noun
maker - demiurge - creator - creative

خاله

/khâle/ ▶ noun
aunt

خاله زاده

/khâlezâd/ ▶ adjective
cousin

خالی

/khâli/ ▶ noun
vacant - unoccupied - empty - destitute

(Idiom: دق و دلی رو سر کسی خالی کردن
take it out on someone)

خالی کردن

/khâli kardan/ ▶ verb
empty - disgorge - discharge - deplete -
vent - vacate - hollow

خام

/khâm/ ▶ noun
raw - rude - crude - impolite - halfbaked

خامه

/khâme/ ▶ noun
cream

خاموش

/khâmush/ ▶ noun
silent - tacit - uncommunicative - quiet

خاموش شدن

/khâmush shodan/ ▶ verb
silence

خاموش کردن

/khâmush kardan/ ▶ verb
hush - quench - extinguish

خاموشی

/khâmushi/ ▶ noun
silence - mum

خامی

/khâmi/ ▶ noun
inexperience - crudity

خاندان

/khândân/ ▶ noun
house - clan - family

خانقاه

/khaneghâh/ ▶ noun
abbey

خانگی

/khânegi/ ▶ adjective
domestic - household - homelike

خانم

/khânom/ ▶ noun
lady - gentlewoman - wife – dame

(Idiom: یک پارچه خانم است

She is a real lady)

خانه

/khâne/ ▶ noun
house - home - domicile - room

خانه بدوش

/khâne bedush/ ▶ adjective
nomad - vagabond - tramp

خانه دار

/khânedâr/ ▶ adjective
thrifty - domestic - housekeeper - homey
- homemaker

خانه داری

/khânedâri/ ▶ noun
housekeeping - thrift

خانه مسکونی
/khâneye maskuni/ ► noun
manse

خانوادگی
/khânevâdegi/ ► noun
domestic

خانواده
/khânevâde/ ► noun
family - nation

خاور
/khâvar/ ► noun
east

خاوری
/khâvari/ ► adjective
oriental - eastern

خاویار
/khâviyâr/ ► noun
caviar

خایه
/khâye/ ► noun
testicle

خباز
/khabâz/ ► noun
baker

خبث
/khabs/ ► noun
vice

خبر
/khabar/ ► noun
news - advice - inkling - idea - hearsay - predicate

خبر داشتن
/khabar dâshtan/ ► verb
hear

خبرنامه
/khabarnâme/ ► noun
newsletter

خبرنگار
/khabarnegâr/ ► noun
reporter

خبره
/khebre/ ► adjective
expert - critic

خبری
/khabari/ ► adjective
news - predicate

خجالتی
/khejâlati/ ► adjective
unco - coy - shy - shamefaced

خجسته
/khojaste/ ► adjective
blest - auspicious

خجل
/khejel/ ► adjective
ashamed

خجول

/khajul/ ▶ adjective
shamefaced

خدمتگذار

/khedmatgozâr/ ▶ adjective
server

خدا

/khodâ/ ▶ noun
god - divinity - deity - holy

خدمتگزار

// ▶ adjective
housemaid

خداپرست

/khodâparast/ ▶ adjective
theist - deist

خر

/khar/ ▶ noun
donkey - ass - asinine

خداشناس

/khodâshenâs/ ▶ adjective
theologian - theist

خر کردن

/khar kardan/ ▶ verb
wheedle

خداوند

/khodâvand/ ▶ noun
god - lord

خراب

/kharâb/ ▶ adjective
ruinous - rotten

خدعه

/khod'e/ ▶ noun
trick - wile - ruse - deceit - lurch

خراب کردن

/kharâb kardan/ ▶ verb
destroy - demolish - corrupt - disfigure -
wreck - wrack - ruinate - ruin

خدمت

/khedmat/ ▶ noun
service - attendance - duty

خرابکاری کردن

/kharâbkâri/ ▶ verb
subvert - sabotage

خدمت کردن

/khedmat kardan/ ▶ verb
minister - serve

خرابه

/kharâbe/ ▶ adjective
ruin

خدمتکار

/khedmatkâr/ ▶ adjective
server - servant - chambermaid

خراج

/kharâj/ ▶ noun
tax - tribute - spendthrift - gavel - levy

خراش

/kharâsh/ ► noun
scotch - rift - graze - attrition - abrasion
- irritation

خراشاندن

/kharâshândan/ ► verb
porcupine

خراشیدن

/kharâshidan/ ► verb
graze - glance - chafe - rase - scrub -
scrape

خراط

/kharât/ ► noun
chipper

خرافات

/khorâfât/ ► noun
superstition

خرافاتی

/khorâfâti/ ► adjective
superstitious

خرج

/kharj/ ► noun
cost - expense - expenditure -
disbursement - disburse - outlay

خرج کردن

/kharj kardan/ ► verb
expend - disburse - outlay - spend

خرخر

/kher kher/ ► adjective
snort – rattle

خرد

/kherad/ ► noun
wisdom - reason - intellect

خرد

/khord/ ► adjective
tiny - retail - part - petty - minuscule

خرد کردن

/khord kardan/ ► verb
crushing

خردسال

/khorsâl/ ► adjective
minor - child

خردمند

/kheradmand/ ► adjective
wise - intellectual

خرده

/khorde/ ► adjective
small - shred - particle - bittock - bit -
vestige - grain

خرده ریز

/khorderiz/ ► adjective
trinkets - snippet - shard

خرف بودن

/kheref budan/ ▶ verb
senility

خرده سنگ

/khordesang/ ▶ noun
rubble

خرفت

/khereft/ ▶ adjective
imbecile - doter

خرده گیر

/khordigir/ ▶ adjective
censorious

خرقه

/kherghe/ ▶ noun
cloak - stole

خرده گیری

/khordegiri/ ▶ noun
cavil

خرقه پوش

/kherghepush/ ▶ adjective
cassock

خرده گیری کردن

/khordegiri kardan/ ▶ verb
cavil

خرک

/kharak/ ▶ noun
sawhorse

خرس

/khers/ ▶ noun
bear

خرگوش

/khargush/ ▶ noun
rabbit

خرسک

/khersak/ ▶ noun
badger

خرم

/khoram/ ▶ adjective
fresh

خرسند

/khorsand/ ▶ adjective
content - glad - happy

خرما

/khormâ/ ▶ noun
date

خرطوم

/khortum/ ▶ noun
proboscis

خرف

/kheref/ ▶ adjective
wacky - idiot - senile

خرمایی

/khormâyi/ ▶ adjective
brown - russet

خرمن
/kharman/ ► noun
shock - stack - harvest

خرمهره
/kharmohre/ ► noun
bead

خروج
/khoruj/ ► noun
exit - emersion - outgo - propulsion

خروش
/khorush/ ► noun
slogan - cry - roar

خروشیدن
/khorushidan/ ► verb
bubble - rage - roar

خرید
/kharid/ ► noun
buy - purchase

خرید کردن
/kharid kardan/ ► verb
shootinggallery

خریدار
/kharidâr/ ► adjective
shopkeeper - purchaser - buyer

خریداری
/kharidâri/ ► noun
purchase

خریدن
/kharidan/ ► verb
buy

خز
/khaz/ ► noun
zibelline - fur

خزان
/khazan/ ► adjective
autumn - fall

خزانه
/khazâne/ ► noun
thesaurus - treasury - treasure

خزنده
/khazande/ ► adjective
creeper - crawly - worm

خزه
/khaze/ ► noun
moss

خزیدن
/khazidan/ ► verb
slither - slime - creep - crawl - grovel - glide - ramp

خس خس
/khes khes/ ► adjective
wheeze

خس خس کردن
/khes khesh kardan/ ► verb
wheeze

خسارت
/khesârat/ ▶ noun
scathe - detriment - damage -
recompense - harm - lesion - loss

خستگی
/khastegi/ ▶ noun
exhaustion - boredom - tired - tedium

خستگی آور
/khastegi âvar/ ▶ adjective
irksome

خستگی ناپذیر
/khastegi nâpazir/ ▶ adjective
indefatigable - inexhaustible

خسته
/khaste/ ▶ adjective
spent - sear - tire - blown - weary

خسته شدن
/khaste shodan/ ▶ verb
runout - overweary - irk - bore

خسته و کوفته
/khaste va kufte/ ▶ adjective
stump

خسیس
/khasis/ ▶ adjective
sordid - skimpy - stringent - stingy -
niggardly - ungenerous - miserly

خسیسی
/khasisi/ ▶ noun
scotticism

خش خش کردن
/khesh khesh kardan/ ▶ verb
rustle

خشت
/khesht/ ▶ noun
adobe - brick - bat

خشک
/khoshk/ ▶ adjective
arid - abstract - mealy - husky

خشک کردن
/khoshk kardan/ ▶ verb
wipe - desiccation - dehumidify -
evaporate

خشکاندن
/khoshkândan/ ▶ verb
sear

خشکی
/khoski/ ▶ noun
welter - mainland - land - terrafirma

خشکیده
/khoshkide/ ▶ adjective
sear - hidebound - wizen

خشم

/khashm/ ▶ noun
rage - wrath - anger - irritation - ire -
indignation

خشم آلود

/khashmâlud/ ▶ adjective
fierce

خشم وغضب

/khashm va ghazab/ ▶ noun
dander

خشمگین

/khashmgin/ ▶ adjective
loathloth - irate - indignant

خشمگین ساختن

/khashmgin sâkhtan/ ▶ verb
snarl

خشمگین شدن

/khashmgin shodan/ ▶ verb
angry

خشمگینانه

/khashmginâne/ ▶ adverb
irate - angry

خشمناک

/khashmnâk/ ▶ adjective
angry - irate

خشمناک شدن

/khashmnâk shodan/ ▶ verb
rage

خشن

/khashen/ ▶ adjective
rude - harsh - unmennerly - unmannered
- unkempt - ungracious - brutish

خشنود

/khoshnud/ ▶ adjective
acquiescent

خشنود کردن

/khoshnud kardan/ ▶ verb
satisfy

خشوع کردن

/khosu' kardan/ ▶ verb
stoop

خشونت

/khoshunat/ ▶ noun
violence - discourtesy - rigor -
truculence - severity

خصم

/khasm/ ▶ noun
enemy - opponent

خصمانه

/khasmâne/ ▶ adverb
inimical

خصوصی

/khosusi/ ▶ adjective
private

خصوصیات

/khosusiyât/ ▶ noun
feature - quirk - pattern - particular

خطاب

/khatâb/ ▶ noun
address

خصوصیت

/khosusiyat/ ▶ noun
quality - intimacy

خطابه

/khatâbe/ ▶ noun
sermon - lecture - prelection - precept -
address - oration

خصومت

/khosumat/ ▶ noun
enmity - virulence

خطاط

/khat'tât/ ▶ noun
calligrapher

خصیصه

/khasise/ ▶ noun
trait

خطاطی

/khat'tâti/ ▶ noun
calligraphy

خط

/khat/ ▶ noun
line - ruck - streak - stoppage

خطاکار

/khatâkâr/ ▶ adjective
transgressor - wrongdoer

خط دار

/khatdâr/ ▶ adjective
streaky

خطاکاری

/khatâkâri/ ▶ noun
wrongdoing

خط کشیدن

/khat keshidan/ ▶ verb
line - tick

خطبه

/khotbe/ ▶ noun
sermon

خط ممتد

/khate momtad/ ▶ noun
stretch

خطر

/khatar/ ▶ noun
jeopardy - risk - danger - peril - hazard

خطا

/khatâ/ ▶ noun
error - wrong - slip - sinister -
transgression

خطرناک

/khatarnâk/ ▶ adjective
jeopardous - calamitous - venturesome -
malignant - perilous

خفت

/khefat/ ▶ noun
disgrace - contempt - noose -
opprobrium

خطه

/khete/ ▶ noun
territory

خفت آور

/khefat âvar/ ▶ adjective
derogatory

خطور

/khotur/ ▶ noun
haunt

خفتن

/khoftan/ ▶ verb
sleep

خطی

/khati/ ▶ adjective
linear - lineal

خفته

/khofte/ ▶ adjective
asleep

خطیب

/khatib/ ▶ noun
orator

خفگی

/khafegi/ ▶ noun
asphyxia

خطیر

/khatir/ ▶ adjective
serious - momentous

خفه

/khafe/ ▶ adjective
sultry - stuffy - pokey - muggy

خف کردن

/khef kardan/ ▶ verb
waylay

خفه شدن

/khafe shodan/ ▶ verb
smother

خفا

/khafâ/ ▶ noun
stealth - wrap

خفه شو

/khafe shô/ ▶ verb
shutup

خفاش

/khofâsh/ ▶ noun
bat

خلاف

/khalâf/ ▶ noun
misdeed - foul - contrary

خفه کردن

/khafe kardan/ ▶ verb
mute - scrag - throttle - suffocate -
strangulate

خلاف واقع

/khalâfe vâghe'/ ▶ noun
untrue

خفیف

/khafif/ ▶ noun
light - low - small

خلافکار

/khalâfkâr/ ▶ adjective
trespasser

خل

/khol/ ▶ adjective
fool - queer - screwy

خلال

/khelâl/ ▶ noun
peel - interval

خلا

/khala'/ ▶ noun
vacuum

خلال دندان

/khelâle dandân/ ▶ noun
toothpick - pick

خلاص کردن

/khalâs kardan/ ▶ verb
rid

خلبان

/khalabân/ ▶ noun
pilot

خلاصه

/kholâse/ ▶ noun
abstract - short - summary - extract -
digest - condensation - outline

خلخال

/khalkhâl/ ▶ noun
anklet

خلاصه ساختن

/kholâse sâkhtan/ ▶ verb
minute

خلط

/khelt/ ▶ noun
mucus - phlegm

خلاصه نمودن

/kholâse nemudan/ ▶ verb
sum

خلع

/khal'/ ▶ noun
deposition

خلع سلاح کردن
/khal' selâh kardan/ ► verb
unarm - disarm

خلوص
/kholus/ ► noun
sincerity - purity - candour - candor

خلع کردن
/khal' kardan/ ► verb
dethrone - depose

خلیج
/khalij/ ► noun
gulf

خلف
/kholf/ ► noun
successor

خلیفه
/khalife/ ► noun
caliph - vicar - prelate

خلق
/khalgh/ ► noun
people

خم شدن
/kham shodan/ ► verb
bow - lean - recline - wilt - decline

خلق
/kholgh/ ► noun
temper - mood

خم شده
/kham shode/ ► adjective
bent

خلق کردن
/khalgh kardan/ ► verb
make - create

خم کردن
/kham kardan/ ► verb
bend - incline - hunch - limber

خلقت
/khelghat/ ► noun
creation

خمار
/khomâr/ ► adjective
drunkard - languid

خلوت
/khalvat/ ► noun
solitude - sanctum - privacy

خمپاره
/khompâre/ ► noun
mortar

خلوتگاه
/khalvatgâh/ ► noun
den - boudoir – sanctum

خمره
/khomre/ ► noun
crock - vat

خمیر

/khamir/ ▶ noun
paste - unguent

خمیر زدن

/khamir zadan/ ▶ verb
paste

خمیر کردن

/khamir kardan/ ▶ verb
knead - masticate - mash - levigate -
leaven

خمیرمایه

/khamirmâye/ ▶ noun
leaven

خنثی

/khonsâ/ ▶ noun
inactive - hermaprodite - neutral - neuter
- eunuch

خنثی کردن

/khonsâ kardan/ ▶ verb
neutralize - neuter - negation - negate

خنثی نمودن

/khonsâ nemudan/ ▶ verb
annihilate

خنجر

/khanjar/ ▶ noun
dirk - daggar - bowieknife - bodkin

خمس

/khoms/ ▶ noun
quint

خموش

/khamush/ ▶ adjective
silent - hush - quiet

خمیازه

/khamiyâze/ ▶ noun
gape

خمیازه کشیدن

/khamiyâze keshidan/ ▶ verb
yawn - gape

خمیدگی

/khamidegi/ ▶ noun
loop - bent - bend - curvature - rake -
offset - stoop

خمیدن

/khamidan/ ▶ verb
retroflex - bend

خمیده

/khamide/ ▶ adjective
limber - embowed

خمیده بودن

/khamide budan/ ▶ verb
slouch

خمیده شدن

/khamide shodan/ ▶ verb
slump

خنجر زدن
/khanjar zadan/ ▶ verb
dirk

خنک کردن
/khonak kardan/ ▶ verb
cool - refrigerate - keel

خندان
/khandan/ ▶ adjective
smiling- laughing- riant

خنگ
/kheng/ ▶ adjective
stupid - dense

خندق
/khandagh/ ▶ noun
trig - trench - sike - ditch - graft - moat

خو
/khu/ ▶ noun
temper - habit

خنده
/khande/ ▶ noun
laughter - laugh

خو دادن
/khu dâdan/ ▶ verb
season - addict - inure

خنده آور
/khande âvar/ ▶ adjective
risible - droll - ludicrous - humorous -
howler

خو گرفتن
/khu gereftan/ ▶ verb
accustom

خنده دار
/khandedâr/ ▶ adjective
comic - ridiculous - waggish - queer -
laughable - hilarious

خواب
/khâb/ ▶ noun
nap - dream - asleep - sleep

خندیدن
/khandidan/ ▶ verb
laugh - chortle

خواب آلود
/khâbâlud/ ▶ adjective
soporific - somnolent - sleepy - heavy -
drowsy - dreamy

خنک
/khonak/ ▶ adjective
cool - fresh - flat - chilly - breezy -
vapid - icy

خواب دیدن
/khâb didan/ ▶ verb
dream

خواب رفتن
/khâb raftan/ ▶ verb
sleep

خواب کوتاه
/khâbe kutâh/ ▶ noun
snooze

خواباندن
/khâbândan/ ▶ verb
suppress - stop - embed - appease

خوابانیدن
/khâbânidan/ ▶ verb
soften - couch

خوابگاه
/khâbgâh/ ▶ noun
bedroom - dormitory - chamber

خوابیدن
/khâbidan/ ▶ verb
sleep - kip - lie

خوابیده
/khâbide/ ▶ adjective
torpid - sleeper - resting - recumbent -
asleep

خواجه
/khâje/ ▶ noun
eunuch - neuter

خوار
/khâr/ ▶ adjective
lowly - abject - wretch - despicable

خوار شمردن
/khâr shemordan/ ▶ verb
scorn - disdain - despise

خوار کردن
/khâr kardan/ ▶ verb
insult - reproach

خواربار
/khârobâr/ ▶ noun
grocery - viand

خواری
/khâri/ ▶ adjective
contempt - ignominy

خواست
/khâst/ ▶ noun
volition - wish - will - want

خواستار
/khâstâr/ ▶ adjective
demanding - wishful - volunteer

خواستار بودن
/khâstâr budan/ ▶ verb
solicit

خواستگار
/khâstegâr/ ▶ noun
suitor

خواستگاری
/khâstegâri/ ▶ noun
suit - court

خواهر

/khâhar/ ► noun
sister

خواستگاری کردن

/khâstegâri kardan/ ► verb
woo - suit

خواهر زن

/khâharzan/ ► noun
sisterinlaw

خواستن

/khâstan/ ► verb
intend - desire - wish - will - want

خواهر شوهر

/khâhar shohar/ ► noun
sisterinlaw

خواص

/khavâs/ ► noun
attribute

خواهرانه

/khâharâne/ ► adverb
sisterly

خوانا

/khânâ/ ► adjective
legible

خواهری

/khâhari/ ► adjective
sorority - sisterhood

خوانا بودن

/khânâ budan/ ► verb
legibility

خواهش

/khâhesh/ ► noun
wish - will - request

خوانایی

/khânâ'yi/ ► noun
legibility

خوب

/khub/ ► noun
fine - nice - good - okay - well - pretty

خواندن

/khândan/ ► verb
read - invite - intone

خوب کردن

/khub kardan/ ► verb
heal

خواننده

/khânde/ ► noun
reader - vocalist - singer

خوبترین

/khubtarin/ ► adjective
best

خواه

/khâh/ ► noun
or - whether

خوبرو
/khubru/ ▶ adjective
comely

خوبی
/khubi/ ▶ adjective
excellency - excellence - nicety - grace

خود
/khod/ ▶ pronoun
self - itself - own

خودبخود
/khod bekhod/ ▶ noun
spontaneous

خودبسندگی
/khodbasandegi/ ▶ noun
autarchy

خودبین
/khodbin/ ▶ adjective
smug - egocentric - presumptuous - vain
- arrogant

خودپرست
/khodparast/ ▶ adjective
selfish

خودپسند
/khodpasand/ ▶ adjective
selfish

خودپسندی
/khodpasandi/ ▶ noun
egocentric

خودخواه
/khodkhâh/ ▶ adjective
selfish

خوددار
/khod'dâr/ ▶ adjective
undemonstrative - continent

خودداری
/khod'dâri/ ▶ noun
restraint - refusal - composure -
equanimity - continence - abstinence

خودرو
/khodro/ ▶ noun
wild - weedy - automotive - automobile

خودستا
/khodsetâ/ ▶ adjective
vainglorious - bravado - bragger

خودستایی
/khodsetâyi/ ▶ noun
swagger - vainglory

خودستایی کردن
/khodsetâyi kardan/ ▶ verb
boast

خودسر
/khodsar/ ▶ adjective
stubborn - wilful - wayward -
headstrong - intractable - pertinacious

خودسرانه

/khodsarâne/ ► adverb
intractable

خور

/khor/ ► noun
inlet - cove

خودکار

/khodkâr/ ► noun
automatic

خوراک

/khorâk/ ► noun
nourishment - grub - feed - fare -
nutrition - repast - dish - cuisine

خودکامه

/khodkâme/ ► adjective
dictator

خوراکی

/khorâki/ ► noun
edible - chow - larder - meal

خودکشی

/khodkoshi/ ► noun
suicide

خورجین

/khorjin/ ► noun
kyack - cantina - bag - valise

خودکشی کردن

/khodkoshi kardan/ ► verb
suicide

خوردن

/khordan/ ► verb
eat - have - partake - abut - grub - feed

خودنما

/khodnamâ/ ► adjective
showy - jaunty - cocky - ostentatious -
blatant - airy - priggish - perky

خوردنی

/khordani/ ► adjective
edible - eatable

خودنمایی

/khodnamâyi/ ► noun
parade - ostentation

خوره

/khore/ ► noun
leprosy - leper - canker

خودنمایی کردن

/khodnamâyi kardan/ ► verb
parade

خوش

/khosh/ ► noun
jocund - sweet - good - gay - buxom -
blithe - blissful - merry - happy

خودی

/khodi/ ► adjective
relative - familiar – insider

خوش اقبال
/khosh eghbâl/ ► adjective
lucky

خوشامد
/khoshâmad/ ► noun
welcome

خوش بین
/khoshbin/ ► adjective
optimistic - optimist - roseate - upbeat

خوشامد گفتن
/khoshâmad goftan/ ► verb
welcome

خوش بینانه
/khoshbinâne/ ► adverb
optimistic

خوشایند
/khoshâyand/ ► adjective
gracious - welcome

خوش خیم
/khoshkhim/ ► adjective
benign

خوشبخت
/khoshbakht/ ► adjective
provident - blest

خوش زبان
/khosh zabân/ ► adjective
voluble

خوشبختی
/khoshbakhti/ ► noun
serendipity - luck

خوش فکر
/khoshfekr/ ► adjective
brainy

خوشبو
/khoshbu/ ► adjective
rosy - aromatic - scented

خوش لباس
/khoshlebâs/ ► adjective
dandy - gash - gallant

خوشحال
/khosh'hâl/ ► adjective
happy - merry - bouncy - wanton - glad - gay - sprightly - jolly

خوش نویس
/khosnevis/ ► noun
calligraphist - calligrapher

خوشحال کردن
/khosh'hâl kardan/ ► verb
gladden

خوش نویسی
/khoshnevisi/ ► noun
calligraphy

خوشحالی
/khosh'hâli/ ► noun
jocosity - mirth – glee

خوشحالی کردن

/khosh'hâli kardan/ ▶ verb
joy

خوشمزه

/khoshmaze/ ▶ adjective
delicious - taffeta

خوشدل

/khoshdel/ ▶ adjective
happy - buxom - buoyant

خوشنامی

/khoshnâmi/ ▶ noun
reputation

خوشرفتار

/khoshraftâr/ ▶ adjective
debonair

خوشنود

/khoshnud/ ▶ adjective
content - glad

خوشرو

/khoshru/ ▶ adjective
glad

خوشنود کردن

/khoshnud kardan/ ▶ verb
agree - gladden

خوشرویی

/khoshru'I/ ▶ noun
affability

خوشنودی

/khoshnudi/ ▶ noun
satisfaction

خوشگذران

/khoshgozarân/ ▶ adjective
luxuriate

خوشه

/khushe/ ▶ noun
cluster - clump - bunch - beard

خوشگذرانی

/khoshgozarâni/ ▶ noun
revelry

خوشه خوشه

/khushe khushe/ ▶ adjective
gregarious

خوشگل

/khoshgel/ ▶ adjective
beautiful

خوشوقت

/khoshvaght/ ▶ adjective
happy

خوشگلی

/khoshgeli/ ▶ noun
beauty

خوشی

/khoshi/ ▶ adjective
joyance - joy - delight - cheer - paradise
- bliss

خون ریزی
/khunrizi/ ▶ noun
hemorrhage

خوف
/khôf/ ▶ noun
scare - horror

خونابه
/khunâbe/ ▶ noun
serum - plasma

خوفناک
/khôfnâk/ ▶ adjective
macabre

خونبها
/khunbahâ/ ▶ noun
ransom

خوک
/khuk/ ▶ noun
pig

خونخوار
/khunkhâr/ ▶ adjective
bloody - gory

خوگیری
/khugiri/ ▶ noun
naturalization

خونخواه
/khunkhâh/ ▶ adjective
avenger

خون
/khun/ ▶ noun
sap - blood - gore

خونخواهی
/khunkhâhi/ ▶ noun
vengeance

خون آشام
/khunâshâm/ ▶ adjective
vampire

خونخواهی کردن
/khunkhâhi kardan/ ▶ verb
revenge - avenge

خون آلود
/khunâlud/ ▶ adjective
bloody

خونریز
/khunriz/ ▶ adjective
bloodthirsty

خون دماغ
/khundamâgh/ ▶ noun
nosebleed

خونریزی
/khunrizi/ ▶ noun
slaughter - carnage - bloodshed

خون ریختن
/khun rikhtan/ ▶ verb
bleed

خونسرد

/khunsard/ ► adjective
dispassionate - uninterested -
unconcerned - imperturbable

خونسردی

/khunsardi/ ► noun
phlegm - indifference - unconcern -
composure

خونگرم

/khungarm/ ► adjective
warm

خونی

/khuni/ ► adjective
sanguine - sanguinary - bloody - gory

خونین

/khunin/ ► adjective
red - mortal

خوی

/khuy/ ► noun
sweat - blood - navigate - nature - grain

خویش

/khish/ ► pronoun
self - kindred

خویشاوند

/khishâvand/ ► noun
relative - relation - kindred - kin

خویشاوندی

/khishâvandi/ ► noun
blood - cognation - kinship

خویشتن

/khishtan/ ► pronoun
self

خیابان

/khiyâbân/ ► noun
street - road

خیار

/khiyâr/ ► noun
cucumber - option

خیار ترشی

/khiyâr torshi/ ► noun
pickle - gherkin

خیاط

/khayât/ ► noun
tailor

خیال

/khiyâl/ ► noun
fiction - fancy - wraith - whim - notion -
imaginary

خیال اندیشی

/khiyalandishi/ ► noun
idealism

خیال باطل

/khiyâle bâtel/ ► noun

daydream

خیال داشتن

/khiyâl dâshtan/ ► verb
intend

خیال کردن

/khiyâl kardan/ ► verb
think - deem

خیالباف

/khiyâlbâf/ ► adjective
woolgatherer - whimsical

خیالی

/khiyâli/ ► adjective
dreamy - unrealistic - unreal - imaginary
- image

خیانت

/khiyânat/ ► noun
treason - treachery - betrayal - perfidy

خیانتکار

/khiyânatkâr/ ► adjective
treacherous - traitor - conspirator

خیر

/kheir/ ► noun
no - nay - good

خیرات

/kheirât/ ► noun
alms - charity

خیرخواه

/kheirkhâh/ ► adjective
propitious - gracious

خیرخواهی

/kheirkhâhi/ ► noun
benevolence - generosity - zeal

خیره

/khire/ ► noun
steadfast - agaze

خیره سر

/khiresar/ ► adjective
obstinate - pertinacious - intractable -
stubborn

خیره شدن

/khire shodan/ ► verb
stare

خیریه

/kheiriye/ ► noun
welfare

خیز

/khiz/ ► noun
leap - lunge - bound - edema - dropsy -
gradient - rise

خیس

/khis/ ► adjective
drunk - wet - rainy - soppy - sop - soggy
- sodden

خیس خوردن

/khis khordan/ ► verb
soak

خیس کردن

/khis kardan/ ▶ verb
drown - douse - swill - sluice

خیساندن

/khisândan/ ▶ verb
sop - soak - steep - poach - imbibe -
drench

خیلی

/kheili/ ▶ adverb
very - many

خیلی خوب

/kheili khub/ ▶ adjective
glorious - well - benedicite

خیمه

/kheime/ ▶ noun
tent - tabernacle - hovel - canopy

خیمه شب بازی

/kheime shab bâzi/ ▶ noun
puppetry

د

dâl /de/ ▶ tenth letter of the Persian alphabet

دائمی
/dâemi/ ▶ adjective
perennial - eternal - continual - constant - ceaseless

دائمی کردن
/dâemi kardan/ ▶ verb
perpetuate

داخل
/dâkhel/ ▶ noun
inside

داخل شدن
/dâkhel shodan/ ▶ verb
enter

داخلی
/dâkheli/ ▶ adjective
internal - interior - inner - innate - indoor

داد
/dâd/ ▶ noun
shout - squeal - justice - greet - outcry - ruction

داد زدن
/dâd zadan/ ▶ verb
shout - cry - root - roar - bawl

داد کشیدن
/dâd keshidan/ ▶ verb
roar

داد و بیداد
/dâdobidâd/ ▶ noun
scrimmage - jangle - squabble - uproar - broil - brawl - wrangle - riot - rampage

دادخواست
/dâdkhâst/ ▶ noun
plea - petition - suit

دادخواه
/dâdkhâh/ ▶ adjective
complainant - candidate - plaintiff

دادخواهی
/dâdkhâhi/ ▶ noun
lawsuit - complaint

دادرس
/dâdras/ ▶ adjective
judge - magistrate

دادگاه
/dâdgâh/ ▶ noun
courtroom - courthouse - court - forum

دارالتادیب
/dârolta'dib/ ► noun
penitentiary - reformatory

دادگر
/dâdgar/ ► adjective
just

دارای ابهام
/dârâye ebhâm/ ► adjective
equivocal

دادگستر
/dâdgostar/ ► noun
righter

دارایی
/dârâyi/ ► noun
thing - purse - property - asset -
possession - fortune - wealth - estate

دادگستری
/dâdgostari/ ► noun
justice

دادگیر
/dâdgir/ ► adjective
avenger - revenger

داربست
/dârbast/ ► noun
scaffold - trellis - stud

دادگیری کردن
/dâdgiri kardan/ ► verb
avenge

داربست بستن
/dârbast bastan/ ► verb
trellis

دادن
/dâdan/ ► verb
grant - give - concede - render - impute -
mind - mete - pay - afford - admit

دارو
/dâru/ ► noun
cure - drug - remedy - medicine -
medication

دار
/dâr/ ► noun
scaffold - gallows

داروخانه
/dârukhâne/ ► noun
pharmacy - drugstore

دارا
/dârâ/ ► adjective
possessor - wealthy

داروساز
/dârusâz/ ► noun
apothecary - pharmacist - chemist

دارا بودن
/dârâ budan/ ► verb
contain - encompass - own - have

داروسازی
/dârusâzi/ ▶ noun
pharmacy

داعی
/dâ'I/ ▶ noun
motive

داروغه
/dârughe/ ▶ noun
sheriff

داغ
/dâgh/ ▶ adjective
hot - mark

داروگر
/dârugar/ ▶ noun
druggist - pharmacist - apothecary

داغ کردن
/dâgh kardan/ ▶ verb
singe - brand - cauterize

دارویی
/dâruyi/ ▶ noun
medicinal - medic

داغدار
/dâghdâr/ ▶ adjective
scathing

داس
/dâs/ ▶ noun
sickle - scythe

دافع
/dâfe'/ ▶ noun
eductor - repulsive - repellent -
loathsome

داستان
/dâstân/ ▶ noun
narrative - fiction - fable - marchen -
tale - story

دالان
/dâlân/ ▶ noun
corridor - porch - hall

داستان سرا
/dâstânsarâ/ ▶ noun
storyteller

دام
/dâm/ ▶ noun
trap - toil - snare - noose - net - grin -
decoy - ambush - quicksand - pitfall

داستانی
/dâstâni/ ▶ adjective
story

داماد
/dâmâd/ ▶ noun
groom - birdegroom

داشتن
/dâshtan/ ▶ verb
bear - relieve - own

دامپزشک

/dâmpezeshk/ ▶ noun
veterinarian - vet

دامداری کردن

/dâmdâri kardan/ ▶ verb
ranch

دامگاه

/dâmgâh/ ▶ noun
stockyard - menagerie

دامن زدن

/dâman zadan/ ▶ verb
provoke

دامنه

/dâmane/ ▶ noun
skirt - amplitude - amplitude - hillside -
foot

دامنه کوه

/dâmaneye kuh/ ▶ noun
hillside - skirt

دانا

/dânâ/ ▶ adjective
savant - sage - sagacious - spry - astute -
wise

دانایی

/dânâyi/ ▶ noun
knowledge - wisdom - sagacity

دانستن

/dânestan/ ▶ verb

learn - have - ascribe - aim - adjudge -
account - con - cognize

دانش

/dânesh/ ▶ noun
science - scholarship - letter -
knowledge - witting - wisdom

دانشجو

/dâneshju/ ▶ noun
student - collegian

دانشسرا

/dâneshsarâ/ ▶ noun
trainingcollege

دانشگاه

/dâneshgâh/ ▶ noun
college - academy - university

دانشگاهی

/dâneshgâhi/ ▶ noun
varsity - collegiate

دانشمند

/dâneshmand/ ▶ noun
pundit - scientist - savant - erudite -
oracle

دانشنامه

/dâneshnâme/ ▶ noun
diploma

دانشور

/dâneshvar/ ▶ noun

scholar - master

دانگ

/dâng/ ► noun
toom - tone

دانمارکی

/dânmârki/ ► adjective
danish - dane

دانه

/dâneh/ ► noun
semen - seed - birdseed - bean - bait -
rash - kernel - granule - grain

داور

/dâvar/ ► noun
juror - arbiter - referee

داوری

/dâvari/ ► adjective
arbitration

داوطلب

/dâvtalab/ ► noun
volunteer - applicant - entrant -
candidate

داوطلب شدن

/dâvtalab shodan/ ► verb
volunteer

داوطلبانه

/dâvtalabâne/ ► adverb
Voluntary

داوطلبی

/dâvtalabi/ ► noun
candidacy

دایر

/dâyer/ ► noun
active - live - open

دایره

/dâyere/ ► noun
sphere - section - tambourine - rhomb -
compass - circle - roundel - disk -
bureau

دایره المعارف

/dâyerolma'âref/ ► noun
encyclopedia

دایره ای

/dâyere'I/ ► adjective
circular

دایی

/dâ'I/ ► noun
uncle

دبستان

/dabestân/ ► noun
school

دبه کردن

/dabe kardan/ ► verb
renege

دبیر
/dabir/ ▶ noun
teacher - secretary - actuary

دختر
/dokhtar/ ▶ noun
girl - daughter - quean - maid - lass -
sissy - sissified

دبیرخانه
/dabirkhâne/ ▶ noun
secretariat

دختر ساده
/dokhtare sâde/ ▶ noun
ingenue

دبیرستان
/dabirestân/ ▶ noun
gymnasium - school

دخترباز
/dokhtarbâz/ ▶ adjective
wencher

دچار
/dochâr/ ▶ noun
afoul - stricken

دختربچه
/dokhtarbache/ ▶ noun
girl

دچار کردن
/dochâr kardan/ ▶ verb
trouble - swamp - embroil

دخترک
/dokhtarak/ ▶ noun
doll - chit - pussy - puss

دچارشدن به
/dochâr shodan/ ▶ verb
catch

دختری
/dokhtari/ ▶ adjective
girlhood

دخالت
/dekhâlat/ ▶ noun
interference

دخل
/dakhl/ ▶ noun
pertinence - income

دخالت کردن
/dekhâlat kardan/ ▶ verb
interfere

دخمه
/dakhme/ ▶ noun
crypt

دخانیات
/dokhâniyât/ ▶ noun
tobacco

دخول
/dokhul/ ▶ noun
entry - entree - arrival - admission -
accession - inclusion

ددمنش

/dadmanesh/ ▶ noun
brutish

در

/dar/ ▶ preposition
to - door - at - about - plug - pearl - valve

در آمیختن

/darâmikhtan/ ▶ verb
commix

در آنجا

/darânja/ ▶ adverb
there

در ابتدا

/darebtedâ/ ▶ adverb
early

در اثنای

/darentehâye/ ▶ noun
meanwhile - meantime

در ازای

/dar ezâye/ ▶ noun
with

در اشتباه بودن

/dar eshtebâh budan/ ▶ verb
err

در اطراف

/dar atrâfe/ ▶ preposition
around

در افتادن

/daroftâdan/ ▶ verb
oppose

در امتداد خط

/dar emtedâde khat/ ▶ preposition
along

در اوایل

/dar avâyele/ ▶ adverb
early

در این باره

/darinbâre/ ▶ adverb
herein

در بر گرفتن

/darbar gereftan/ ▶ verb
snuggle - twine - encompass - embrace

در برابر

/darbarâbare/ ▶ preposition
to - versus - against - for

در تردید بودن

/dar tardid budan/ ▶ verb
hover

در تنگنا

/dar tangnâ/ ▶ adjective
strait

در تنگنا قرار دادن

/dar tangnâ gharâr dâdan/ ▶ verb
lockout - sandwich

در خاک نهادن

/dar khâk nahâdan/ ► verb
inter

در جاییکه

/darjâyike/ ► adverb
wherein

در خطا

/darkhatâ/ ► adjective
perverse

در جریان

/dar jariyân/ ► adverb
during - afoot

در خطر

/dar khatar/ ► adjective
subject

در جستجوی

/dar jostejuye/ ► noun
after

در خلال

/dar khelâle/ ► adverb
meanwhile - meantime

در جهت

/darjahate/ ► preposition
of - with

در دسترس

/dar dastres/ ► adjective
available - attainable - accessible

در جوار

/darjevâre/ ► adverb
besides

در رفتن

/dar raftan/ ► verb
escape - abscond - scuttle

در حالیکه

/darhâlike/ ► adverb
whereas

(Idiom: در رفتن
Take it on the lamb)

در حدود

/darhodude/ ► adverb
about - within

در صورتیکه

/darsuratike/ ► adverb
while - provided

در حرکت

/darharkat/ ► adverb
astir - agog - afloat

در ضمن

/dar zemn/ ► adverb
meanwhile - meantime - course

در حین

/darheine/ ► adverb
while

در معرض

/dar ma'raze/ ▶ adjective
disposable - subject

در مقابل

/dar moghâbele/ ▶ preposition
versus - against

در میان

/dar miyâne/ ▶ preposition
midst - between - among - amidst - amid
- across

در نظر داشتن

/dar nazar dâshtan/ ▶ verb
purpose - contemplate - envisage

در نظر گرفتن

/dar nazar gereftan/ ▶ verb
spot

در هر جا

/dar harjâ/ ▶ adverb
everywhere

در هر صورت

/dar har surat/ ▶ adverb
ever - anyway - anyhow

در واقع

/darvâghe/ ▶ adverb
indeed

در وسط

/darvasat/ ▶ adverb
midst

درآمد

/darâmad/ ▶ noun
revenue - emolument - income - mean -
admission

دراز

/derâz/ ▶ adjective
string - toom - prolix - longish - verbose
- linear - lengthy - oblong

دراز شدن

/derâz shodan/ ▶ verb
lengthen

دراز کردن

/derâz kardan/ ▶ verb
protract - prolong - extend - lengthen

درازا

/derâzâ/ ▶ noun
longitude - length

درام

/derâm/ ▶ noun
drama

درایت

/derâyat/ ▶ noun
tact

دراین جا

/darinjâ/ ▶ adverb
there

دربند
/darband/ ► noun
captive - canyon

دراین حدود
/darin hodud/ ► adverb
hereabout

درپوش
/darpush/ ► noun
bonnet - blind

درب
/darb/ ► noun
door - port

درج
/darj/ ► noun
interpolation

دربار
/darbâr/ ► noun
court

درجه
/daraje/ ► noun
degree - thermometer - proportion -
mark - point - peg - length - grade

درباره
/darbâreye/ ► noun
toward - on - of - re - about - inre

دربازکن
/darbâzkon/ ► noun
doorkeeper

درجه افتخاری
/darajeye eftekhâri/ ► noun
honorary

دربان
/darbân/ ► noun
janitor - doorkeeper - porter

درجه بندی
/daraje bandi/ ► noun
calibration - grade - gradation

دربدر
/darbedar/ ► adjective
gadabout - outcast - vagrant - vagabond

درجه دار
/darajedâr/ ► adjective
noncommissionedoffic - gaduate

دربدری
/darbedari/ ► noun
vagrancy

درجه دو
/daraje do/ ► adjective
second-rate

دربست
/darbast/ ► noun
lump - exclusive - enbloc

درجه یک

/daraje yek/ ▶ adjective
topnotch - classy

درخت

/derakht/ ▶ noun
tree

درخت بید

/derakhte bid/ ▶ noun
sallow - willow

درخت چنار

/derakhte chenâr/ ▶ noun
sycamore - plantain

درخت زیتون

/derakhte zeitun/ ▶ noun
olive

درختچه

/derakhtche/ ▶ noun
shrub

درخشان

/derakhshân/ ▶ adjective
shiny - shiner - illustrious - lucid -
ablaze - bright

درخشان ساختن

/derakhshân sâkhtan/ ▶ verb
illuminate

درخشان شدن

/derakhshân shodan/ ▶ verb
brighten

درخشش

/derakhshesh/ ▶ noun
scintillation - shine - sparkle - spangle -
luster - eclat - glitter

درخواست

/darkhâst/ ▶ noun
solicitation - suit - appeal - postulate -
request - demand

درد

/dard/ ▶ noun
shoot - pang - pain - ailment - agony -
distress

درد دندان

/darde dandân/ ▶ noun
toothache

درد شکم

/dardeshekam/ ▶ noun
cramp

درد کردن

/dard kardan/ ▶ adverb
shoot

درد کشیدن

/dard keshidan/ ▶ adverb
pain - twinge

دردآور

/dardâvar/ ▶ adjective
painful - achy

درددل

/dardedel/ ▶ noun
chat

درس دادن

/dars dâdan/ ▶ verb
teach

دردسر

/dardesar/ ▶ noun
inconvenience - headache

درست

/dorost/ ▶ adjective
true - correct - conscionable - exact -
entire - right - orthodox - whole -
genuine - veracious - valid

دردناک

/dardnâk/ ▶ adjective
angry - achy - painful - grievous - sore

درست کردن

/dorost kardan/ ▶ verb
make - build - mend - make - integrate -
organize

درز

/darz/ ▶ noun
suture - slit - seam - gap - crevice -
peephole - interstice

درستکار

/dorostkâr/ ▶ adjective
upright - right

درز دادن

/darz dâdan/ ▶ verb
seam

درستکاری

/dorostkâri/ ▶ noun
rectitude - honesty

درز لباس

/darze lebâs/ ▶ noun
seam

درستی

/dorosti/ ▶ noun
justice - truth - accuracy - precision -
legitimacy - integrity - honesty -
rectitude

درس

/dars/ ▶ noun
point - lesson - lecture - study

درس خوان

/dars khând/ ▶ adjective
studious

درشت

/dorosht/ ▶ adjective
sturdy - jumbo - harsh - large - lump -
abrupt - brutish - gruff - gross - rough

درس خواندن

/dars khândan/ ▶ verb
study

درصد

/darsad/ ► noun
percent

درگیر

/dargir/ ► adjective
outbreak

درصدد

/darsadad/ ► noun
after - about

درگیری

/dargiri/ ► noun
involvement

درصدد بودن

/darsadad budan/ ► verb
figure on

درمان

/darmân/ ► noun
treatment - remedy

درفش

/darafsh/ ► noun
banner - awl

درمان کردن

/darmân kardan/ ► verb
remedy - treat

درک

/dark/ ► noun
perception - uptake - realization - gusto

درمانکده

/darmânkade/ ► noun
polyclinic - policlinic

درک کردن

/dark kardan/ ► verb
apprehend - understand - perceive -
coneive - comprehend - realize

درمانگاه

/darmângâh/ ► noun
clinic - infirmary

درگاه

/dargâh/ ► noun
doorway

درنده

/darande/ ► adjective
fierce - predatory

درگذشت

/dargozasht/ ► noun
death

درنده خو

/darandekhu/ ► adjective
rapacious

درنگ

درگذشتن

/dargozashtan/ ► verb
passaway - die - decease

/derang/ ► noun
tarry - halt - pause

درو کردن
/dero kardan/ ► verb
reap - scythe

درنگ کردن
/derang kardan/ ► verb
tarry - linger - let

دروازه
/darvâze/ ► noun
goal - gateway - gate - portal

دره
/dare/ ► noun
valley - vale

درود
/dorud/ ► noun
salute - salutation - compliment - regard
- greet - hail

درهم
/darham/ ► adjective
shaggy - indistinct - mixed - mesh

درهم آمیختن
/darham âmikhtan/ ► verb
conjugate - interlace

درودگر
/dorudgar/ ► noun
carpenter

درهم پیچیدن
/darham pichidan/ ► verb
taut - tangle - intersubjective

درودگری
/dorudgari/ ► noun
carpentry

درهم ریختن
/darham rikhtan/ ► verb
pie - clutter

دروغ
/dorugh/ ► noun
fiction - false - fable - untrue - bung - lie

درهم شکستن
/darham shekastan/ ► verb
smash - scrunch - breakdown - vanquish
- overwhelm - force - crash

دروغ گفتن
/dorugh goftan/ ► verb
lie - belie - whiff - weasel

درهم کشیدن
/darham keshidan/ ► verb
puchery

دروغگو
/doroughgu/ ► adjective
liar

درهمه جا
/dar hamejâ/ ► adverb
everywhere

دروغگویی
/doroughguyi/ ► noun
lying - mendacity

دروگر
/derogar/ ▶ adjective
reaper

درون
/darun/ ▶ noun
inward - inside

درونی
/daruni/ ▶ adjective
inward - internal - interior - innermost -
inner - innate - inmost - indoor

دری وری گفتن
/dari vari goftan/ ▶ verb
tattle

دریا
/daryâ/ ▶ noun
sea

دریاچه
/daryâche/ ▶ noun
lake - laguna - pond - slew

دریاسالار
/daryâsâlâr/ ▶ noun
admiral

دریافت
/daryâft/ ▶ noun
comprehension - receipt - perception -
inception

دریافتن
/daryâftan/ ▶ verb
discover - comprehend - realize -
understand - apprehend - perceive

دریانورد
/daryânavard/ ▶ noun
shipper - shipman - seagoing - seafarer -
navigator

دریایی
/daryâyi/ ▶ adjective
nautical - maritime - marine

دریچه
/dariche/ ▶ noun
hatch - lid - porthole - vent - valve -
closure - choke - window

دریدگی
/daridegi/ ▶ noun
rift

دریدن
/daridan/ ▶ verb
slit - tear - lacerate - rip - rend

دریغ
/darigh/ ▶ noun
pity

دریغ داشتن
/darigh dâshtan/ ▶ verb
spare - withhold

دژ

/dezh/ ► noun
stronghold - citadel - castle - fort -
presidio

دریغا

/darighâ/ ► adverb
alas

دژخیم

/dezhkhim/ ► adjective
hangman - deathsman

دزد

/dozd/ ► noun
burglar - piker - picaroonp - peculator -
hobgoblin - robber - thief - stealer

(Idiom: تخم مرغ دزد شتر دزد میشود
Be the thin end of the wedge)

دسامبر

/desâmbr/ ► noun
december

دزد دریایی

/dozde daryâyi/ ► noun
pirate

دست

/dast/ ► noun
team - paw

دزدی

/dozdi/ ► noun
burglary - lift - larceny - robbery - nip -
thievery - theft

(Idiom: دست بالای دست بسیار است
The biter bit)

(Idiom: کسی را دست انداختن
Pull someone leg)

دزدی ادبی

/dozdiye adabi/ ► noun
plagiarism

دست آموز

/dast âmuz/ ► adjective
pet

دزدی کردن

/dozdi kardan/ ► verb
thieve

دست آورد

/dastâvard/ ► noun
consequence - result

دزدیدن

/dozdidan/ ► verb
steal - spoliate - thieve - purloin - rifle -
rob

دست انداز

/dastandâz/ ► noun
ramp – puddle

دست کم
/dastekam/ ► noun
leastwise

دست بند
/dastband/ ► noun
bracelet - wristband

دست نخورده
/dast nakhorde/ ► adjective
entire - whole - virgin - intact

دست پاچگی
/dastpâchegi/ ► noun
bafflement

دست نشانده
/dastneshande/ ► adjective
stooge - puppet

دست پاچه
/dastpâche/ ► adjective
hasty

دست و دلباز
/dasto delbâz/ ► adjective
spendthrift

دست پخت
/dastpokht/ ► noun
cuisine

دست یافتن
/dast yâftan/ ► verb
attain - achieve - accede

دست تنها
/dast tanhâ/ ► adjective
barehanded

دستار
/dastâr/ ► noun
turban

دست دادن
/dast dâdan/ ► verb
handclasp

دستاویز
/dastâviz/ ► noun
pretext - voucher - excuse - document

دست درازی کردن
/dast derâzi kardan/ ► verb
encroach

دستباف
/dastbâf/ ► adjective
handmade

دست زدن
/dast zadan/ ► verb
plaudit

دستبرد
/dastbord/ ► noun
robbery - defalcation - larceny

دست فروش
/dast forush/ ► noun
duffer - huckster

دسترسی

/dastresi/ ► noun
range - access

دسترنج

/dastranj/ ► noun
wage

دستشویی

/dastshuyi/ ► noun
lavatory - basin - washstand

دستفروش

/dastforush/ ► noun
badger - vendor

دستکاری کردن

/dastkâri kardan/ ► verb
retouch - manipulate

دستکش

/dastkesh/ ► noun
glove - gantlet - chevron

دستگاه

/dastgâh/ ► noun
system - mechanism - machinery -
machine

دستگیر کردن

/dastgiri/ ► verb
nab

دستگیره

/dastgire/ ► noun
catch - knob

دستبرد زدن

/dastbord zadan/ ► verb
steal - rob

دستبند

/dastband/ ► noun
shackle - lei - cuff

دستبند زدن

/dastband zadan/ ► verb
manacle

دستپاچگی

/dastpâchegi/ ► noun
hurry

دستپاچه

/dastpâche/ ► adjective
nervous - panicky

دستپاچه کردن

/dastpâche kardan/ ► verb
shend - baffle

دستخط

/dastkhat/ ► noun
manuscript - handwriting - hand -
longhand - script

دستخوش

/dastkhosh/ ► noun
prey

دسترس

/dastres/ ► noun
access - disposal

دستگیره در
/dastgireye dar/ ▶ noun
pin - pin

دستگیری
/dastgiri/ ▶ noun
charity - capture

دستمال
/dastmâl/ ▶ noun
napkin - kerchief - handkerchief

دستمال سفره
/dastmâle sofre/ ▶ noun
napkin

دستمال گردن
/dastmâle gardan/ ▶ noun
shawl - tie - handkerchief

دستمزد
/dastmozd/ ▶ noun
wage - stipend

دسته
/daste/ ▶ noun
set - section - sect - stud - stem - stack -
squad - team

دسته بندی
/daste bandi/ ▶ noun
junta - division

دسته بندی کردن
/dastebandi kardan/ ▶ verb
categorize - rank - grade

دسته جمعی
/dastejam'I/ ▶ noun
social - ensemble

دسته شدن
/daste shodan/ ▶ verb
shoal

دسته گل
/dastegol/ ▶ noun
bouquet - posy

دستور
/dastur/ ▶ noun
permission - injunction - direction -
regulation - rule - order

دستور دادن
/dastur dâdan/ ▶ verb
address

دستورالعمل
/dasturol'amal/ ▶ noun
recipe

دستوری
/dasturi/ ▶ adjective
imperative - ministry

دستی
/dasti/ ▶ adjective
handy - handmade - manual - portable

دستیار
/dastyâr/ ▶ noun
suffragan - assistant - ancillary

دستیاری

/dastyâri/ ▶ noun
assistance

دسر

/deser/ ▶ noun
dessert

دسیسه

/dasise/ ▶ noun
plot - machination - conspiracy

دسیسه کردن

/dasise kardan/ ▶ verb
angle - intrigue - cabal

دشت

/dasht/ ▶ noun
plain - moor - desert - flat - weald

دشمن

/doshman/ ▶ noun
antagonist - adversary - hostile - foe -
enemy

دشمنانه

/doshmanâne/ ▶ adverb
inimical

دشمنی

/doshmani/ ▶ adjective
odium - enmity - hatred - hate

دشنام

/doshnâm/ ▶ noun
abusive - curse

دشنام دادن

/doshnâm dâdan/ ▶ verb
mistreat - misname

دشنه

/deshne/ ▶ noun
stiletto - sticker - spit - dirk - bowieknife

دشوار

/doshvâr/ ▶ adjective
laborious - inexplicable - hard - uphill -
arduous - onerous - difficult - tough

دشواری

/doshvâri/ ▶ noun
difficulty

دعا

/do'â/ ▶ noun
prayer - vote - devotion

دعا کردن

/do'â kardan/ ▶ verb
bless - pray

دعوا

/da'vâ/ ▶ noun
strife - squeal - quarrel - discord -
contest

دعوت

/da'vat/ ▶ noun
invitation - call

دفاعیه

/defâ'iye/ ▶ noun
reply

دفتر

/daftar/ ▶ noun
tome - bureau - book - volume - cahier -
registry

دفتر یادداشت

/daftare yad'dâsht/ ▶ noun
notebook - folio

دفترچه

/daftarche/ ▶ noun
booklet

دفترخانه

/daftarkhâne/ ▶ noun
scriptorium - bureau

دفتردار

/daftardâr/ ▶ noun
clerk

دفع

/daf'/ ▶ noun
propulsion - expultion - excretion -
exclusion - repulse - repercussion

دفع حمله

/daf'e hamle/ ▶ noun
parry

دعوت کردن

/da'vat kardan/ ▶ verb
bid - ask - invite

دعوی

/da'vi/ ▶ noun
claim - case - pretension - lawsuit -
quarrel

دعوی کردن

/da'vi kardan/ ▶ verb
sue - quarrel - pretend

دغل

/daghal/ ▶ noun
dishonest

دغل باز

/daghalbâz/ ▶ adjective
idol - kite

دغلباز

// ▶ adjective
janusfaced

دفاع

/defâ'/ ▶ noun
pale - advocacy - munition - defence -
defense

دفاع کردن

/defâ' kardan/ ▶ verb
defence - defense - advocate - bield

دکان
/dokân/ ▶ noun
shootinggallery - store

دفع شدن
/daf' shodan/ ▶ verb
void

دکتر
/doktor/ ▶ noun
doctor - medico

دفن
/dafn/ ▶ noun
mortuary - interment - burial

دکمه
/dokme/ ▶ noun
tuber - button - knob

دفن کردن
/dafn kardan/ ▶ verb
sepulcher - grave - bury - lay

دکه
/dake/ ▶ noun
shootinggallery - kiosk

دق
/degh/ ▶ noun
percussion

دکور
/dekor/ ▶ noun
decor

دقت
/deghat/ ▶ noun
delicacy - certitude - nicety - attention -
accuracy - precision - severity

دگربار
/degarbâr/ ▶ noun
again

دقیق
/daghigh/ ▶ noun
precise - astute - astringent - accurate -
exquisite - wistful - watchful

دگردیسی
/degardisi/ ▶ noun
metastasis - metamorphosis

دقیق شدن
/daghigh shodan/ ▶ verb
attenuate

دگرگون
/degargun/ ▶ noun
dissimilar - vicissitudinous

دقیقه
/daghighe/ ▶ noun
hour

دگرگونی
/degarguni/ ▶ adjective
change - alteration - vicissitude -
variation - mutation - metamorphosis

دل

/del/ ► noun
spunk - midst - conscience

(Idiom: **اهل دل بودن**
Being a fun sucker)

دل درد

/deldard/ ► noun
bellyache

دل شکستگی

/delshekastegi/ ► noun
heartbreak

دل شکسته

/delshekaste/ ► adjective
heartsick

دل و جرات

/delojor'at/ ► noun
pluck - heart

دل واپسی

/delvâpasi/ ► noun
anxiety

دلار

/dolâr/ ► noun
dollar - buck

دلارام

/delârâm/ ► noun
sweetheart - belle

دلال

/dalâl/ ► noun
gobetween - dealer - middleman -
mediator - broker

دلالت

/delâlat/ ► noun
implication

دلاور

/delâvar/ ► adjective
warrior - knight - gallant - brave - hero

دلاوری

/delâvari/ ► noun
courage - gallantry - valor

دلباخته

/delbâkhte/ ► adjective
lovesick

دلبر

/delbar/ ► adjective
sweetheart - mistress

دلبستگی

/delbastegi/ ► noun
interest

دلپذیر

/delpazir/ ► adjective
gracious - graceful - melodious

دلپسند

/delpasand/ ► adjective
exquisite - nice

دلربایی

/delrobâyi/ ▶ noun
oomph - charm - mash

دلتنگ

/deltang/ ▶ adjective
sad - homesick - lone - nostalgic

دلسرد

/delsard/ ▶ adjective
despondent

دلتنگی

/deltangi/ ▶ noun
melancholia - anguish - ennui - tedium

دلسرد کردن

/delsard kardan/ ▶ verb
estrange - dissuade - disspirit -
dishearten - discourage

دلجویی

/delju'I/ ▶ noun
caress

دلسردی

/dalsardi/ ▶ noun
despondency

دلچسب

/delchasb/ ▶ adjective
hearty - meet

دلسوز

/delsuz/ ▶ adjective
sympathetic - piteous

دلخراش

/delkharâsh/ ▶ adjective
irritant

دلفریب

/delfarib/ ▶ adjective
lovely - cute

دلخواه

/delkhâh/ ▶ adjective
wish - ideal - arbitrary - accord

دلقک

/dalghak/ ▶ noun
jester - stooge - buffoon - pantaloon -
fool

دلخور

/delkhor/ ▶ adjective
sulky

دلخوری

/delkhori/ ▶ noun
annoyance - offense

دلکش

/delkesh/ ▶ adjective
attractive

دلربا

/delrobâ/ ▶ adjective
attractive

دلگیر

/delgir/ ▶ adjective
pokey

دلمه

/dolme/ ▶ noun
jelly - gelatin - clod

دلنواز

/delnavâz/ ▶ adjective
smooth

دله دزد

/daledozd/ ▶ noun
prig

دلهره

/delhore/ ▶ noun
presentiment

دلواپس

/delvâpas/ ▶ adjective
solicitous - anxious

دلواپسی

/delvâpasi/ ▶ noun
turpitude - worry

دلیر

/dalir/ ▶ adjective
brave - bold - intrepid - hardy - plucky -
gallant - courageous

دلیری

/daliri/ ▶ noun
spunk - spartanism - courage - glamor -
glamour - chivalry - bravery

دلیل

/dalil/ ▶ noun
proof - sake - symptom - reason -
agument

دم

/dom/ ▶ noun
train - tail - trice - instant - moment -
minute - at - breath - blast

دم زدن

/damzadan/ ▶ verb
respire - breathe

دم کردن

/dam kardan/ ▶ verb
stew - infuse - brew

دم کشیدن

/dam keshidan/ ▶ verb
pant

دماسنج

/damâsanj/ ▶ noun
thermometer

دماغ

/damâgh/ ▶ noun
genius

دماغه
/damâghe/ ▶ noun
headland - head - cape - nose

دنبل
/donbal/ ▶ noun
abscess

دمدمی مزاج
/damdami mezâj/ ▶ noun
cyclothyme - erratic - capricious - pliant

دنج
/denj/ ▶ noun
snug

دمر
/damar/ ▶ noun
prone

دندان
/dandân/ ▶ noun
tooth

دمساز
/damsâz/ ▶ adjective
helpmate - confidant - compatible

دندان آسیاب
/dandâne âsiyâb/ ▶ noun
molar - grinder - sectorial

دمل
/damal/ ▶ noun
boil - blotch - abscess - wen

دندان پیش
/dandâne pish/ ▶ noun
cutter

دموکراسی
/demokrâsi/ ▶ noun
democracy

دندان در آوردن
/dandân darâvardan/ ▶ verb
teethe

دمیدن
/damidan/ ▶ verb
bop - blow

دندان درد
/dandândard/ ▶ noun
toothache

دنبال
/donbâl/ ▶ noun
rear - pursuit

دندان شکن
/dandânshekan/ ▶ adjective
unanswerable - irrecusable

دنباله
/donbâle/ ▶ noun
sequel - suite - stem - train - trail - tail -
appendix

دندان عقل
/dandâne aghl/ ▶ noun
wisdomtooth

دندان گرد

/dandâ/ ▶ adjective
greedy

ده

/deh/ ▶ noun
village

دندانپزشک

/dandânpezeshki/ ▶ noun
dentist

ده

/dah/ ▶ noun
ten

دندانساز

/dandânsâz/ ▶ noun
prosthodontist - dentist

دهات

/dehât/ ▶ noun
country

دندانه

/dandâne/ ▶ noun
jag - tooth - tine - peg - leaf - cog - nick
- dent

دهاتی

/dehâti/ ▶ adjective
boorish - boor - peasant - villager -
hobnail - kern - clodhopper - rustic

دندانه دار

/dandânedâr/ ▶ adjective
toothy - jagged - dentate

دهان

/dahân/ ▶ noun
mouth - puss - jib

دندانه دندانه

/dandâne dandâne/ ▶ adjective
serrate - crinkle

دهانه

/dahâne/ ▶ noun
jet - throat - spout - inset - head - eye -
outfall

دنده

/dande/ ▶ noun
rib - gear

دهر

/dahr/ ▶ noun
universe

دنیا

/donyâ/ ▶ noun
universe - vale - macrocosm - world

دهشتناک

/dehshatnâk/ ▶ adjective
horrendous

دنیوی

/donyavi/ ▶ noun
secular - terrestrial - mundane - earthy

دهکده

/dehkade/ ► noun
stead - hamlet - village - borough

دوات

/davât/ ► noun
well - inkwell - inkstand

دهم

/dahom/ ► noun
tenth

دوازده

/davâzdah/ ► noun
twelve

دهنده

/dahande/ ► adjective
donor - giver

دوازدهم

/davâzdahom/ ► noun
twelfth

دهنه

/dahane/ ► noun
jet - line - muzzle - bit - gap

دوازدهمین

/davâzdahomin/ ► noun
twelfth

دهه

/dahe/ ► noun
decade

دوام

/davâm/ ► noun
substance - strength - persistence -
perpetuity - permanency - life -
continuity - continuance - durante

دو

/do/ ► noun
two

دوام داشتن

/davâm dâshtan/ ► verb
last

دو چندان

/dochandân/ ► adjective
reduplicate

دوبار

/dobâr/ ► adverb
twice

دو چندان کردن

/dochandân kardan/ ► verb
redouble

دوباره

/dobâre/ ► adverb
anew - again - afresh - bis

دوا

/davâ/ ► noun
medicine - medicament

دوبل

/dubl/ ► noun
duple

دوبیتی

/dobeiti/ ▶ adjective
couplet

دوپهلو

/dopahlu/ ▶ adjective
equivocal - ambiguous

دوتایی

/dotâyi/ ▶ adjective
binary - duplex - dual - couplement

دوجانبه

/dojânebe/ ▶ adjective
bilateral - reciprocal

دوجنسه

/dojense/ ▶ adjective
amphibious

دوختن

/dukhtan/ ▶ verb
sew - suture - steek - bind

دود

/dud/ ▶ noun
whiff - smoke

دود کردن

/dud kardan/ ▶ verb
smoke

دودخانه

/dudkhâne/ ▶ noun
smokehouse

دودکش

/dudkesh/ ▶ noun
chimney - funnel - uptake - tube - stack -
shaft

دودکننده

/dudkonande/ ▶ adjective
smoky

دودل

/dodel/ ▶ adjective
indecisive - hesitant

دودل بودن

/dodel budan/ ▶ verb
scruple - waver - vacillate

دودلی

/dodeli/ ▶ noun
indecision - hesitancy - doubt

دوده

/dude/ ▶ noun
grime - black - soot - smut

دوده زدن

/dude zadan/ ▶ verb
soot

دودی

/dudi/ ▶ adjective
smoky

دور

/dôr/ ▶ noun
circuit - orbit - wheel -

دور

/dur/ ▶ adjective
yonder - remote - race - distant - aloof - away

(Idiom: دوری و دوستی
Absence makes the heart grow fonder)

دور برداشتن

/dor bardâshtan/ ▶ verb
rev

دور زدن

/dôr zadan/ ▶ verb
skirt - twinge - compass - circle - round - revolve - recur

دور شدن

/durshodan/ ▶ verb
scat - recede

دور کردن

/durkardan/ ▶ verb
abduct - parry - estrange - distance - dispossess - oust - remove

دورادور

/durâdur/ ▶ noun
afar

دوران

/davarân/ ▶ noun
rotation

دوران

/dorân/ ▶ noun
season - vertigo

دورانی

/davarâni/ ▶ adjective
revolving

دوربین

/durbin/ ▶ noun
Camera

دورتر

/durtar/ ▶ adjective
yond - beyond - off

دورترین

/durtarin/ ▶ adjective
hindmost - utmost - ultimate

دوردست

/durdast/ ▶ adjective
far - remote

دورگه

/dorage/ ▶ adjective
mulatto - hybrid - crossover - crossbreed - cross

دورنگ

/dorang/ ▶ adjective
piebald

دورنما

/durnamâ/ ▶ noun
prospect - outlook - lookout - landscape

دوره تحصیلی
/doreye tahsili/ ▶ noun
session - schooltime

دوست داشتن
/dust dâshtan/ ▶ verb
savor - list - like - love - affect

دوره گرد
/doregard/ ▶ adjective
caird - huckster - itinerant - peripatetic -
badger

دوست داشتنی
/dust dâshtani/ ▶ noun
amiable - lovely - lovable - likeable -
likable - smacker

دورو
/doru/ ▶ adjective
januslike - janusfaced - hypocritical -
insincere

دوست صمیمی
/duste samimi/ ▶ noun
close friend

دورویی
/doruyi/ ▶ adjective
hyporisy - duplicity - guile

دوستان
/dustân/ ▶ noun
entourage

دوزخ
/duzakh/ ▶ noun
inferno - hell - pandemonium

دوستدار
/dustâr/ ▶ adjective
lover

دوزندگی
/duzandegi/ ▶ noun
sewing

دوستی
/dusti/ ▶ noun
haunt

دوست
/dust/ ▶ noun
schoolmate - friend - chum - leal -
amicable - ally

دوش
/dush/ ▶ noun
showerbath - shower - shoulder

دوش گرفتن
/dush gereftan/ ▶ verb
shower - douche

دوست پسر
/duste pesar/ ▶ noun
boyfriend

دوشاخه
/doshâkhe/ ▶ adjective
pitchfork - knee - fork - crutch - crotch

دوشنبه

/doshânbe/ ▶ noun
Monday

دوشیدن

/dushidan/ ▶ verb
milking

دوشیزه

/dushize/ ▶ noun
girl - damosel - damsel - maiden

دوقطبی

/do
bi/ ▶ adjective
bipolar

دوقلو

/dogholu/ ▶ adjective
twin - geminate

دوگانه

/dogâne/ ▶ adjective
twosome - twofold

دوگوشه

/dogushe/ ▶ adjective
bicuspid - diagonal

دولا

/dolâ/ ▶ adjective
geminate - dual - double

دولا کردن

/dolâ kardan/ ▶ verb
double - bend - ply

دولت

/dolat/ ▶ noun
state - respublica - government -
mammon

دولتمند

/dolatmand/ ▶ adjective
wealthy - rich - affluent

دولتی

/dolati/ ▶ adjective
state

دوم

/dovom/ ▶ adjective
second - sec

دومی

/dovomi/ ▶ adjective
latter - second

دون

/dun/ ▶ adjective
ribald - poor - lowly - low - sordid -
small - shabby - servile

دون پایه

/dunpâye/ ▶ adjective
understrapper - underling

دونده

/davande/ ▶ noun
runner

دونفره

/donafare/ ▶ adjective
twosome

دید زدن

/didzadan/ ▶ verb
sight - appraisal

دویدن

/davidan/ ▶ verb
run - race

دیدار

/didâr/ ▶ noun
visit

دیار

/diyâr/ ▶ noun
land - country

دیدبان

/didebân/ ▶ noun
watch

دیانت

/diyânat/ ▶ noun
honesty

دیدگاه

/didgâh/ ▶ noun
standpoint - sight - viewpoint - peephole
- lookout - beacon

دیباجه

/dibâche/ ▶ noun
preamble

دیدن

/didan/ ▶ verb
see - notice - observe - behold - look -
perceive - vision - view - eye

دیپلمات

/diplomât/ ▶ noun
diplomat

دیده بان

/didebân/ ▶ noun
sentinel - scout - lookout

دیپلماسی

/diplomâsi/ ▶ noun
diplomacy

دیر

/dir/ ▶ noun
late

دیپلمه

/diplome/ ▶ noun
diploma - gaduate

دیرباور

/dirbâvar/ ▶ adjective
unbelievin - unbeliever - incredulous

دید

/did/ ▶ noun
seeing - lookout - vision - visibility -
viewpoint - view - perspective

دیگ

/dig/ ► noun
cauldron - pot

(Idiom: دیگ به دیگ میگه روت سیاه
The pot calling the kettle black)

دیگران

/digarân/ ► noun
others - rest

دیگری

/digari/ ► adjective
another - other

دین

/din/ ► noun
liability - religion - faith - debt

دیندار

/dindâr/ ► adjective
religious - devout - pious

دیو

/div/ ► noun
spook - bogey - goblin - gnome

دیوار

/divâr/ ► noun
fence - wall - bulkhead

(Idiom: به در میگیم که دیوار بشنوه
Beating around the bush)

دیرک

/dirak/ ► noun
lug - mast

دیروز

/diruz/ ► noun
yesterday

دیرینه

/dirine/ ► noun
deepseated - old - chronic - ancient

دیزی

/dizi/ ► noun
cruse

دیسک

/disk/ ► noun
discus

دیشب

/dishab/ ► noun
yestreen

دیکتاتور

/diktâtor/ ► noun
dictator

دیکته

/dikte/ ► noun
dictation

دیکته کردن

/dikte kardan/ ► verb
dictate

دیواره

/divâre/ ▶ noun
rim - partition - parapet

دیوان

/divân/ ▶ noun
bureau

دیوان سالار

/divânsâlâr/ ▶ adjective
bureaucrat

دیوانگی

/divânegi/ ▶ noun
insanity - mania - amuck - delirium -
craze - rave - rage

دیوانه

/divâne/ ▶ adjective
mad - insane - crazy

ذ

zâl /ze/ ▶ eleventh letter of the Persian alphabet

ذات

/zât/ ▶ noun
substance - essence - navigate - nature

ذاتی

/zâti/ ▶ adjective
natural - inward - intuitive - intrinsic - innate - inherent - indigenous - substantial

ذبح

/zebh/ ▶ noun
slaughter - hew

ذبح کردن

/zebh kardan/ ▶ verb
slay

ذخیره

/zakhire/ ▶ noun
reservoir - reserve - reservation - hoard - store - stockpile - stock - spare

ذخیره سازی

/zakhire sâzi/ ▶ noun
storage

ذرات

/zarât/ ▶ noun
ingredient

ذره

/zare/ ▶ noun
shred - grain - dust - vestige - iota - particle - bit - ace

ذره بین

/zarebin/ ▶ noun
lens - microscope

ذغال سنگ

/zoghâlsang/ ▶ noun
collier

ذکاوت

/zekâvat/ ▶ noun
sagacity - brain - esprit - engine - witting

ذکر

/zekr/ ▶ noun
recitation - citation - mention - penis

ذکر کردن

/zekr kardan/ ▶ verb
cite - mingle - ming - mention - patter - assign

ذهن

/zehn/ ▶ noun
remembrance - mind - mentality

ذهنی

/zehni/ ▶ adjective
subjective - psychic - intrinsic -
intellectual

ذوب کردن

/zob kardan/ ▶ verb
found - melt

ذوذنقه

/zozanaghe/ ▶ noun
trapezoid - trapze

ذوق

/zôgh/ ▶ noun
zeal - taste - penchant - verve - gusto -
goo - relish

ذیل

/zeil/ ▶ noun
appendix - addendum

ذینفع

/zinaf'/ ▶ noun
nominee - beneficiary

ر

re /re/ ▶ twelfth letter of the Persian alphabet

رادمردی
/râdmardi/ ▶ noun
magnanimity

رادیاتور
/râdiyâtor/ ▶ noun
radiator

رابط
/râbet/ ▶ noun
liaison - gobetween - copulative

رادیو
/râdiyo/ ▶ noun
wireless - radio

رابطه
/râbete/ ▶ noun
tie - respect - bond - habit - linkage -
liaison

رادیواکتیو
/râdio aktiv/ ▶ noun
radioisotope - radioactive

رابطه داشتن
/râbete dâshtan/ ▶ verb
correspond

رادیوتراپی
/râdioterâpi/ ▶ noun
radiotherapy

رادیولوژی
/râdiolozhi/ ▶ noun
radiology

راحت
/râhat/ ▶ adjective
beforehand - cuddly - cozy - convenient
- well - comfortable - comfort

رادیویی
/râdio'i/ ▶ noun
radio

راحت طلبی
/râhat talabi/ ▶ noun
indolence

راز
/râz/ ▶ noun
secret - mystery - covert - cabal

رادار
/râdâr/ ▶ noun
radar

رازدار
/râzdâr/ ▶ adjective
secretary - repository - confident -
confidant

راضی شدن
/râzi shodan/ ▶ verb
supple - acquiesce - consent

راضی کردن
/râzi kardan/ ▶ verb
satisfy - sate - content - bate

رافع
/râfe'/ ▶ adjective
ablative

راکت
/râket/ ▶ noun
rocket - racket

راکتور
/reâktor/ ▶ noun
reactor

راکد
/râked/ ▶ adjective
stagnant - inert - dull - resting

راکد شدن
/râked shodan/ ▶ verb
statgnate

رام
/râm/ ▶ adjective
tame - meek - manageable - inward -
obedient - domestic - docile

رام کردن
/râm kardan/ ▶ verb
daunt - gentle - bridle - master - subdue

رازداری
/râzdâri/ ▶ noun
secrecy

راس
/ra's/ ▶ noun
top - tip - pinnacle - peak - vertex - head
- climax

راست
/râst/ ▶ noun
straightforward - straight - sheer - true -
erect - wooden - right

راستگو
/râstgu/ ▶ adjective
true - sooth - veracious

راستگویی
/râstguyi/ ▶ noun
veracity

راسخ
/râsekh/ ▶ adjective
firm

راضی
/râzi/ ▶ adjective
content - happy - acquiescent

راضی ساختن
/râzi sâkhtan/ ▶ verb
reconcile

راه آهن

/râh'âhan/ ► noun
railway - railroad - road

راه بندان

/râhbandân/ ► noun
blockade

راه پله

/râhpele/ ► noun
staircase

راه حل

/râhe hal/ ► noun
solution - out

راه رفتن

/râh raftan/ ► verb
traipse - tread - go - gait - walk

راه عبور

/râhe obur/ ► noun
transit - thoroughfare

راه یافتن

/râh yâftan/ ► verb
accede

راهب

/râheb/ ► noun
monk

راهبرد

/râhbord/ ► noun
guideline

ران

/rân/ ► noun
leg

راند

/rând/ ► noun
osmosis

راندگی

/rândegi/ ► noun
expultion

راندن

/rândan/ ► verb
drive - steer - unkennel - booh - poach -
pilot - force - whisk

رانده

/rânde/ ► adjective
outcast - castaway

رانش

/rânesh/ ► noun
buoyancy

رانندگی کردن

/rânandegi kardan/ ► verb
drive- chauffeur

راننده

/rânande/ ► adjective
helmsman - driver - repellent

راه

/râh/ ► noun
path - how - method - road - way

راهبه

/râhebe/ ▶ noun
religious - nun

راهی شدن

/râhi shodan/ ▶ verb
go - depart

راهپیمایی

/râhpeimâyi/ ▶ noun
demonstration - march

راوی

/râvi/ ▶ adjective
storyteller - narrator

راهپیمایی کردن

/râhpeimâyi kardan/ ▶ verb
demonstration

رای

/ra'y/ ▶ noun
sentence - judgment- poll - verdict -
vote- opinion

راهداری

/râhdâri/ ▶ noun
toll

رای دادن

/ra'y dâdan/ ▶ verb
sentence - election - resolve - vote

راهزن

/râhzan/ ▶ noun
brigand - bandit - robber

رای دهنده

/ra'y dahande/ ▶ adjective
voter

راهزنی

/râhzani/ ▶ noun
banditry

رایج

/râyej/ ▶ noun
current - brisk - prevalent

راهنما

/râhnamâ/ ▶ noun
signal - pacemaker - adviser - conductor
- key - guideline - guide - guidance

رایج شدن

/râyej shodan/ ▶ verb
pass

راهنمایی

/râhnamâyi/ ▶ noun
steerage - guidance - aim - instruction

رایحه

/râyehe/ ▶ noun
smell - scent - odor - aroma - breath

راهنمایی کردن

/râhnamâyi kardan/ ▶ verb
steer - guide - lead - instruct

رایزن

/râyzan/ ▶ adjective
adviser - counselor - consultant

رایزنی
/râyzani/ ▶ noun
counsel - advice

رباعی
/robâ'i/ ▶ noun
quatrain

رایگان
/râyegân/ ▶ adjective
free - gratuitous - gratis

ربایش
/robâyesh/ ▶ noun
snatch - seizure - rapture - grab

رایگانی
/râygâni/ ▶ noun
gratuity

رباینده
/robâyande/ ▶ adjective
snatcher

رب
/rab/ ▶ noun
god

ربط
/rabt/ ▶ noun
juncture - correlation - contiguity -
concern - relevance - rapport -
paraphrase

رب
/rob/ ▶ noun
sauce

ربطی
/rabti/ ▶ noun
copulative

ربا
/robâ/ ▶ noun
gavel

ربع
/rob'/ ▶ noun
quarter - redundancy

رباخوار
/robâkhâr/ ▶ adjective
usurious - usurer

ربودن
/robudan/ ▶ verb
rob - reave - ravish - hook - usurp -
abstract - abduct - betake - bag - purloin
- steal

رباخواری
/robâkhâri/ ▶ noun
usury

رباط
/robât/ ▶ noun
sinew - ligature - ligament

ربیعی
/rabi'i/ ▶ noun
vernal

رتبه

/rotbe/ ▶ noun
degree - rank - grade

رج

/raj/ ▶ noun
row

رجحان

/rejhân/ ▶ noun
privilege - preference - predominance -
predilection - excellence

رجحان دادن

/rejhân dâdan/ ▶ verb
prefer

رجز

/rajâz/ ▶ noun
warcry - epopee - paean

رجز خواندن

/rajâz khândan/ ▶ verb
brag - boast

رجعت

/rej'at/ ▶ noun
throwback - return

رجل سیاسی

/rajole siyâsi/ ▶ noun
diplomat - statesman

رجوع

/roju'/ ▶ noun
reversion - respect - referral - reference

رجوعی

/roju'i/ ▶ noun
reversional

رجیم

/rajim/ ▶ noun
cursed

رحم

/rahm/ ▶ noun
compunction - compassion - clemency -
ruth - uterus - mercy - matrix

رحمان

/rahmân/ ▶ adjective
clement

رحمت

/rahmat/ ▶ noun
mercy

رحیم

/rahim/ ▶ adjective
clement - humane - merciful

رخ

/rokh/ ▶ noun
visage - countenance - face - cleavage

رخ (شطرنج)

// ▶ noun
rook

رخ دادن

/rokh dâdan/ ▶ verb
befall - arise - pass - outcrop - occur

رخت

/rakht/ ► noun
clothes - garment - apparel

رخت کن

/rakhtkan/ ► noun
cloakroom - vestry

رختان

/rakhtân/ ► noun
commode

رختخواب

/rakhtekhâb/ ► noun
bed

رختشویی

/rakhtshuyi/ ► noun
wash

رخداد

/rokhdâd/ ► noun
occurrence

رخسار

/rokhsâr/ ► noun
visage - face

رخصت

/rokhsat/ ► noun
respite - reprieve - leave - permission

رخصت دادن

/rokhsat dâdan/ ► verb
allow

رخنه

/rekhne/ ► noun
crack - gap - chink - breach - leak -
influx

رخنه کردن

/rekhne kardan/ ► verb
transpire - penetrate

رخوت

/rekhvat/ ► noun
lethargy - lassitude - indolence -
paralysis

رد

/rad/ ► noun
repulse - rejection - refusal - rebuttal -
rebuff - exception - disproof - disavowal
- disavow - denial

رد کردن

/rad kardan/ ► verb
deny - decline - disprove - disapprove -
repudiate - repel - rejcet - refute - refuse

ردا

/radâ/ ► noun
toga - mantle - cloak - robe

رداع

/radâ'/ ► noun
obstacle

ردپا

/radepâ/ ► noun
vestige- track - trace

رژیم

/rezhim/ ▶ noun
regime

رده

/rade/ ▶ noun
class - category - regimen - echelon

رژیم گرفتن

/reshim gereftan/ ▶ verb
diet

رده بندی کردن

/radebandi/ ▶ verb
categorize - subsume

رسا

/resâ/ ▶ adjective
stentorian - audible - adequate - loud - expressive

ردیاب

/radyâb/ ▶ noun
tracer

رسالت

/resâlat/ ▶ noun
prophecy

ردیف

/radif/ ▶ noun
string - tier - run - row - rank - cue

رذالت

/rezâlat/ ▶ noun
blackguardism

رسالت کردن

/resâlat kardan/ ▶ verb
message

رسام

/resâm/ ▶ noun
tracer

رذل

/razl/ ▶ adjective
scoundrel

رزمجو

/razmju/ ▶ adjective
warrior - warlike

رسانا

/resânâ/ ▶ adjective
conductor - conductive

رزمگاه

/razmgâh/ ▶ noun
battlefield

رسانه

/resâne/ ▶ noun
vehicle - medium

رژه

/rezhe/ ▶ noun
parade - pageant - array - review

رستن

/rastan/ ▶ verb
escape - grow

رستنی

/rastani/ ▶ adjective
herb - plant - vegetable

رسم

/rasm/ ▶ noun
tradition - trace - order - wont - custom -
usage - mode

رسمی

/rasmi/ ▶ adjective
starchy - solemn - formal - ceremonious
- official

رسوا

/rosvâ/ ▶ adjective
blatant - ignominious - infamous -
opprobrious

خواهی نشوی رسوا همرنگ جماعت شو :Idiom)
When in Rome, do as the romans do)

رسوایی

/rosvâyi/ ▶ noun
notoriety

رسوب

/rosub/ ▶ noun
sediment - tartar

رسوخ

/rosukh/ ▶ noun
transfusion - sink - seepage - seep - ooze

رسول

/rasul/ ▶ noun
apostle - messenger

رسوم

/rosum/ ▶ noun
etiquette - mores - manner

رسید

/resid/ ▶ noun
receipt

رسیدن

/residan/ ▶ verb
attain - arrive - amount - aim - achieve -
accede - land - get - gain - receive

رسیده

/reside/ ▶ adjective
consummate - grown - ripe - full -
mellow - headed

رشادت

/reshâdat/ ▶ noun
heart - gallantry - courage

رشته

/reshte/ ▶ noun
branch - ligature - tract - tissue - thread -
sequence - system - suite - string

رشته عصبی

/reshteye asabi/ ▶ noun
nerve

رشد

/roshd/ ▶ noun
adolescence - increase - pickup - growth

رشد کردن

/roshd kardan/ ▶ verb
wax - grow - mature

رشک

/rashk/ ▶ noun
jealousy

رضایتبخش

/rezâyatbakhsh/ ▶ adjective
satisfactory

رشوه

/reshve/ ▶ noun
bribery - bribe - blackmail

رطوبت

/rotubat/ ▶ noun
moisture - humidity - wet - damp

رشوه خوار

/reshvekhâr/ ▶ adjective
venal - barrator

رعایا

/ro'âyâ/ ▶ noun
peasantry

رشوه خواری

/reshvekhâri/ ▶ noun
bribery

رعایت

/ra'âyat/ ▶ noun
regard - ovservation - observance - heed

رشید

/rashid/ ▶ adjective
high - adolescent

رعایت کردن

/ra'âyat kardan/ ▶ verb
observe

رضامندی

/rezâyatmandi/ ▶ noun
satisfaction

رعد

/ra'd/ ▶ noun
thunder

رضایت

/rezâyat/ ▶ noun
satisfaction - acquiescence - consent -
concurrence - satisfaction

رعشه

/ra'she/ ▶ noun
paralysis - tremor - tremble

رضایت دادن

/rezâyat dâdan/ ▶ verb
consent - assent - acquiesce - accede

رعیت

/ra'yat/ ▶ noun
cotter - citizen - vassal - peasant

رضایت نامه

/rezâyatnâme/ ▶ noun
testimonial

رفاقت

/refâghat/ ▶ noun
friendship - camaraderie

رفو

/rofu/ ▶ noun
darn

رفاه

/refâh/ ▶ noun
welfare - quiet

رفو کردن

/rofu kardan/ ▶ verb
mend - darn

رفت و آمد

/rafto âmad/ ▶ noun
traffic

رفیع

/rafi'/ ▶ adjective
skyscraper - sublime - lofty

رفتار

/raftâr/ ▶ noun
behavior - manner - conduct - gesture - comportment - comport - treatment

رفیق

/rafigh/ ▶ noun
friend - peer - mate - fere - comrade - comate

رفتار کردن

/raftâr kardan/ ▶ verb
demean - act - behave - handle - treat

رفیق بودن

/rafigh budan/ ▶ verb
chum

رفتگر

/roftegar/ ▶ noun
sweeper - dustman

رفیق شدن

/rafigh shodan/ ▶ verb
pal

رفتن

/raftan/ ▶ verb
go

رقابت

/reghâbat/ ▶ noun
contest - rivalry

رفتنی

/raftani/ ▶ adjective
doomed

رقاص

/raghâs/ ▶ noun
dancer

رفراندم

/refrândom/ ▶ noun
referendum

رقت

/reghat/ ▶ noun
sympathy

رفع

/raf'/ ▶ noun
obviation - removal

رقت آور

/reghat âvar/ ▶ adjective
lamentable

رقت انگیز

/reghat angiz/ ▶ adjective
pitiful - pitiable - piteous - pathetic -
deplorable

رقت بار

/reghatbâr/ ▶ adjective
pitiable - piteous

رقص

/raghs/ ▶ noun
dance - ball

رقصیدن

/raghsidan/ ▶ verb
dance

رقم

/ragham/ ▶ noun
type - brand - item - figure - number -
character - digit

رقمی

/raghami/ ▶ noun
digital

رقیب

/raghib/ ▶ noun
antagonist - adversary – rival

رقیب شدن

/raghib shodan/ ▶ verb
vie

رقیق

/raghigh/ ▶ adjective
watery - rare - attenuate

رقیق شدن

/raghigh shodan/ ▶ verb
dilution

رک

/rok/ ▶ adjective
frank - straightforward - straight - stark

رک گویی

/rokguyi/ ▶ noun
candour - candor

رکاب

/rekâb/ ▶ noun
stirrup - step

رکاب زدن

/rekâbzadan/ ▶ verb
pedal

رکن

/rokn/ ▶ noun
column - pillar

رکود

/rokud/ ▶ noun
slump - stagnancy - inactivity - inaction

رکورد

/rekord/ ▶ noun
record

رکیک

/rakik/ ▶ adjective
vulgar

رگ

/rag/ ▶ noun
streak - vessel

رگبار

/ragbâr/ ▶ noun
cloudburst - volley - spate - shower

رگه

/rage/ ▶ noun
grain - grain - rake - vein - thread -
streak - strain

رل

/rol/ ▶ noun
role

رم

/ram/ ▶ noun
scare - stampede - breakaway - rum

رم دادن

/ram dâdan/ ▶ verb
fright - rouse - hare

رمان

/ramâl/ ▶ noun
novel - romance

رمز

/ramz/ ▶ noun
mystery - enigma - crypt - cranny - code
- cipher - secret - symbol - token - trick

رمزی

/ramzi/ ▶ adjective
symbolic - undercover - allegorical -
figurative - occult - runic - esoteric

رمق

/ramagh/ ▶ noun
spirit - life

رمه

/rame/ ▶ noun
herd - drove - flock

رمیدن

/ramidan/ ▶ verb
wince - stampede

رنج

/ranj/ ▶ noun
toil - throe - tribulation - trial - bale -
agony - pain - labor - discomfort

نابرده رنج گنج میسر نمیشود :Idiom)
Nothing ventured, nothing gained)

رنج آور

/ranjâvar/ ▶ adjective
painful - troublesome

رنج بردن

/ranj bordan/ ▶ verb
suffer - travail - toil - rack

رنجاندن

/ranjândan/ ▶ verb
offend - annoy - irritate - irk - vex -
mortify

رنجبر

/ranjbar/ ▶ noun
toiler - durdge - painstaking

رنجش

/ranjesh/ ▶ noun
irritation - vexation - miff - pique -
bother - annoyance - acrimony

رنجور

/ranjur/ ▶ adjective
wretched - painful - ill - infirm

رنجیدن

/ranjidan/ ▶ verb
huff - miff

رنجیده

/ranjide/ ▶ adjective
sulky - angry - indignant - glum

رند

/rend/ ▶ adjective
rogue - knave

رندانه

/rendâne/ ▶ adverb
roguish

رنده

/rande/ ▶ noun
shaver

رنده کردن

/rande kardan/ ▶ verb
plane - bevel - grate - chip - shave

رنسانس

/ronesâns/ ▶ noun
renaissance

رنگ

/rang/ ▶ noun
paint - hue - indigo - dye - grain -
complexion - colony - speckle - shade

رنگ بنفش

/range banafsh/ ▶ noun
mauve

رنگ پریده

/rangparide/ ▶ adjective
pallid - pale - lurid - ghastly - wan -
colourless - sallowish

رنگ روغنی

/range roghani/ ▶ noun
oilcolor - oil

رنگ زدن

/rang zadan/ ▶ verb
tincture - dabber - complexion

رنگ زرد

/range zard/ ► noun
caramel

رنگ سبز

/range sabz/ ► noun
green

رنگ سیاه

/range siyah/ ► noun
sable - smut

رنگ صورتی

/range surati/ ► noun
pink

رنگ کمرنگ

/range kamrang/ ► noun
undertone

رنگارنگ

/rangârang/ ► adjective
colorful - varied - multicolored - motley

رنگی

/rangi/ ► adjective
colored - chromatic

رنگین

/rangin/ ► adjective
colored

ره آورد

/rahâvard/ ► noun
gift - present - souvenir

رها

/rahâ/ ► adjective
free

رها ساختن

/rahâ sâkhtan/ ► verb
indulge - redd

رها کردن

/rahâkardan/ ► verb
leave - surrender - drop - dispossess -
disentangle - release - extricate - liberate

رهانیدن

/rahânidan/ ► verb
rescue

رهایی

/rahâyi/ ► noun
escape - delivery - deliverance -
riddance - rescue - release

رهایی بخش

/rahâyibakhsh/ ► adjective
redeemer

رهایی بخشیدن

/rahâyi bakhshidan/ ► verb
save

رهایی جستن

/rahâyi jostan/ ► verb
escape

رهایی دادن

/rahâyi dâdan/ ▶ verb
rescue - redeem

رهنمون

/rahnemun/ ▶ noun
adviser - guideline

رهبر

/rahbar/ ▶ noun
leader - pilot

رهنورد

/rahnavard/ ▶ noun
roadster - wayfarer

رهبری

/rahbari/ ▶ noun
leadership

رو

/ru/ ▶ noun
top - face - uppermost - visage

رهبری کردن

/rahbari kardan/ ▶ verb
lead - conduce

رو دادن

/rudâdan/ ▶ verb
spoil

رهرو

/rahro/ ▶ adjective
wayfarer

روا

/ravâ/ ▶ noun
free - admissibll - admissible -
permissive - lawful

رهسپار شدن

/rahsepâr/ ▶ verb
leave - proceed - go

روا داشتن

/ravâdâshtan/ ▶ verb
approve

رهن دادن

/rahn dâdan/ ▶ verb
pawn

روا کردن

/ravâ kardan/ ▶ verb
permit

رهن کردن

/rahn kardan/ ▶ verb
bond

روابط

/ravâbet/ ▶ noun
term

رهنمود

/rahnemud/ ▶ noun
guidance

روانکاوی

/ravânkâvi/ ▶ noun
psychoanalysis

روانه ساختن

/ravâne sâkhtan/ ▶ verb
go

روانه کردن

/ravâne kardan/ ▶ verb
dispatch - dismiss

روانی

/ravâni/ ▶ adjective
bolubility - psychic

روایت

/ravâyat/ ▶ noun
story - narrative - cabal

روباه

/rubâh/ ▶ noun
reynard - fox

روتختی

/rutakhti/ ▶ noun
counterpane

روح

/ruh/ ▶ noun
spirit - umber - ghost - numen

روح پلید

/ruhe palid/ ▶ noun
devil

رواج

/ravâj/ ▶ noun
propagation - currency - vogue -
prevalence

رواج دادن

/ravâj dâdan/ ▶ verb
issue

روادید

/ravâdid/ ▶ noun
visa

روال

/revâl/ ▶ noun
zeitgeist - rubric

روان ساختن

/ravân sâkhtan/ ▶ noun
pour

روان شناسی

/ravânshenâsi/ ▶ noun
psychology

روانپزشک

/ravânpezeshk/ ▶ noun
psychiatrist

روانپزشکی

/ravânpezeshki/ ▶ noun
psychiatry

روانشناس

/ravânshenâs/ ▶ noun
psychologist

روز

/ruz/ ▶ noun
daytime - day

روز بعد

/ruze ba'd/ ▶ noun
tomorrow

روز پیش

/ruze pish/ ▶ noun
yesterday

روز تعطیل

/ruze ta'til/ ▶ noun
holiday

روز قیامت

/ruze ghiyâmat/ ▶ noun
resurrection - doomsday

روزگار

/ruzegâr/ ▶ noun
time - world - period

روزمره

/ruzmare/ ▶ adjective
routine

روزنامه

/ruznâme/ ▶ noun
journal - paper - newspaper - gazette

روزنه

/rôzane/ ▶ noun
hatch - pore - peephole - peep - aperture
- loophole - outlet - orifice - window

روحانی

/rôhâni/ ▶ adjective
priest - ethereal - religious - clergyman -
sacred

روحانیون

/rôhâniyun/ ▶ noun
clergy

روحی

/ruhi/ ▶ adjective
spiritual - intrinsic - inner - mental -
numinous

روحیه

/ruhiye/ ▶ noun
morale - moral - mentality - spirit - tuck

رود

/rud/ ▶ noun
stream - kil

رودخانه

/rudkhâne/ ▶ noun
river - strand

رودل

/rudel/ ▶ noun
indigestion

روده

/rude/ ▶ noun
bowel - gut - garbage

روزه

/ruze/ ▶ noun
fast

روزه گرفتن

/ruze gereftan/ ▶ verb
fast

روستا

/rustâ/ ▶ noun
village

روستایی

/rustâyi/ ▶ adjective
rustic - ruralist - rural - kern - bucolic -
boor - hobnail - peasant - villager

روسری

/rusari/ ▶ noun
scarf - hood - headgear - kerchief

روسی

/rusi/ ▶ adjective
russian

روش

/ravesh/ ▶ noun
method - manner - procedure - how -
demarche

روشن

/rôshan/ ▶ adjective
perspicuous - limpid - legible - vivid -
lucid - bright - alive - alight

روشن بین

/rôshanbin/ ▶ adjective
clairvoyant

روشن ساختن

/rôshan sâkhtan/ ▶ verb
picture

روشن شدن

/rôshan shodan/ ▶ verb
shine - kindle - open

روشن فکر

/rôshanfekr/ ▶ adjective
illuminate

روشن کردن

/rôshan kardan/ ▶ verb
alight - brighten - lighten - illuminate -
ignite - relume - refresh - clarify -
daylight - explain

روشنایی

/rôshanâyi/ ▶ noun
light - ray

روشنفکر

/rôshanfekr/ ▶ adjective
highbrow - liberal - intellectual

روشنگر

/rôshangar/ ▶ adjective
explanatory

روشنی

/rôshani/ ▶ adjective
shine - lucidity - glim - clarity

روکش متکا

/rukeshe mota'kâ/ ▶ noun
slipover

روشنی بخش

/rôshanibakhsh/ ▶ adjective
luminous

روکفشی

/rukafshi/ ▶ noun
galosh - overshoe

روشنی زا

/rôshanizâ/ ▶ adjective
photogenic

رولت

/rolet/ ▶ noun
jellyroll - roulette

روغن

/rôghan/ ▶ noun
ointment - oil - grease - butter - unguent
- unction - lubricant

روند

/ravand/ ▶ noun
process - procedure

روغن دان

/rôghandân/ ▶ noun
saucepan

رونق یافتن

/rônagh yâftan/ ▶ verb
thrive - prosper

روغنی

/rôghani/ ▶ adjective
unctuous - greasy - oily

رونوشت

/runevesht/ ▶ noun
counterpart - copy - transcript

روکش

/rukesh/ ▶ noun
slip - veneer - plate - blanket - coat

رونوشت برداشتن

/runevesht bardâshtan/ ▶ verb
transcribe

روکش زدن

/rukesh zadan/ ▶ verb
recap.

رونویس کردن

/runevis kardan/ ▶ verb
transcribe

روکش کردن

/rukesh kardan/ ▶ verb
face - coat - plate

روی

/ruye/ ▶ noun
upon - up - aboard - over

روی پا ایستادن

/ruye pâ istâdan/ ▶ verb
standup

روی دادن

/ruy dâdan/ ▶ verb
go - befall - happen

روی هم

/ruyeham/ ▶ adverb
sum

روی هم رفته

/ruheham rafte/ ▶ adverb
altogether- overall

رویا

/rôyâ/ ▶ noun
vision

رویارویی

/ruyâruyi/ ▶ noun
encounter

رویانیدن

/ruyôndan/ ▶ verb
grow

رویایی

/rôyâyi/ ▶ adjective
dreamy - visionary

رویت

/rô'yat/ ▶ noun
seeing

رویداد

/ruydâd/ ▶ noun
passage - event - circumstance -
occurrence

رویه

/raviye/ ▶ noun
scheme - tenor - tack - surface -
comportment - cover - upper - procedure

رویهم

/ruyeham/ ▶ noun
overhand - wholly

روییدن

/ruyidan/ ▶ verb
vegetate - grow

ریا

/riyâ/ ▶ noun
duplicity - hyporisy

ریاست

/riyâsat/ ▶ noun
presidency

ریاست کردن

/riyâsat kardan/ ▶ verb
superintend - chairman

ریاضت

/riyâzat/ ▶ noun
penance - austerity - abstinence

ریزریز کردن
/riz riz kardan/ ▶ verb
mince - comminute - chop

ریاضی دان
/riyâzidân/ ▶ noun
mathematician

ریزش
/rizesh/ ▶ noun
downfall - diffusion - gush - outflow -
catarrh -

ریاضیات
/riyâziyât/ ▶ noun
mathematics

ریزه کاری
/rizekâri/ ▶ noun
elegance - intricacy

ریاکار
/riyâkâr/ ▶ adjective
insincere - hypocritical

ریسک
/risk/ ▶ noun
venture - risk

ریاکاری
/riyâkâri/ ▶ noun
sham - hyporisy

ریسمان
/rismân/ ▶ noun
string - thread - line - cord - warp -
chord - rope

ریحان
/reihân/ ▶ noun
basil

ریختن
/rikhtan/ ▶ verb
shed - strew - dust - disgorge - found -
lave - infusion - infuse - pour

ریسنده
/risande/ ▶ adjective
spinner

ریدن
/ridan/ ▶ verb
Shit

ریش
/rish/ ▶ noun
whisker - beard - barb - ulcerous - ulcer
- sore

ریز
/riz/ ▶ adjective
tiny - small - atomic

ریش سفید
/rish sefid/ ▶ adjective
dean

ریزاندام
/rizandâm/ ▶ adjective
midget

ریشخند

/rishkhand/ ▶ noun
scoff - sarcasm - jeer - ridicule

ریوی

/riyavi/ ▶ noun
pulmonary

ریشه

/rishe/ ▶ noun
theme - tassel - stub - stem - germ -
pedigree

رییس

/re'is/ ▶ noun
boss - administer - principal - president -
master - chief - chairman - ruler

ریشه ای

/rishe'i/ ▶ adjective
thematic - comate - rooty

ریشه دار

/rishedâr/ ▶ adjective
stubby - rooty

ریشه دار کردن

/rishedâr kardan/ ▶ verb
root

ریشی

/rishi/ ▶ adjective
ulceration

ریگ

/rig/ ▶ noun
grit - gravel - pebble - sand

ریه

/riye/ ▶ noun
lung

ریواس

/rivâs/ ▶ noun
rhubarb

ز

ze /ze/ ▶ thirteenth letter of the Persian alphabet

زائر
/zâ'er/ ▶ noun
pilgrim

زاد
/zâd/ ▶ noun
son - birth

زادگاه
/zâdgâh/ ▶ noun
provenance - birthplace

زاده
/zâde/ ▶ adjective
fry - nee

زار
/zâr/ ▶ noun
deplorable - lamentable - vexation

زارع
/zâre'/ ▶ noun
sharecropper - tiller - planter

زاری
/zâri/ ▶ noun
whimper - moan - plaint

زاغ
/zâgh/ ▶ noun
alum

زال
/zâl/ ▶ noun
albino

زالو
/zâlu/ ▶ noun
leech - bloodsucker

زانو
/zânu/ ▶ noun
knee

زانو زدن
/zânu zadan/ ▶ verb
kneel

زاهد
/zâhed/ ▶ adjective
pious - votary - ascetic - devotee

زاهدانه
/zâhedâne/ ▶ adverb
ascetic

زاویه
/zâviye/ ▶ noun
canton - angle - in - hermitage

زاویه دار
/zâviyedâr/ ▶ adjective
embowed

زایا

/zâyâ/ ► adjective
zoogenic

زاید

/zâyed/ ► adjective
extra - waste - redundancy - further -
surplus - superfluous

زایدالوصف

/zâyedolvasl/ ► noun
unutterable

زایش

/zâyesh/ ► noun
get - birth

زایشگاه

/zâyeshgâh/ ► noun
maternity

زایمان

/zâyemân/ ► noun
throe - parturition - litter - childbirth

زاییدن

/zâyidan/ ► verb
birth - produce - teem

زباله

/zobâle/ ► noun
dump - rubbish - ordure - garbage

زبان

/zabân/ ► noun
tongue - language

(Idiom: زبانت را گاز بگیر
Bite your tongue)

زبان باز

/zabânbâz/ ► adjective
sophist

زبانه

/zabâne/ ► noun
tongue - prong - finger

زبده

/zobde/ ► adjective
elite - compendium

زبر

/zebr/ ► adjective
stubby - stark - shaggy - scaly - ragged -
coarse - russeting - russet - rough -
prickly

زبر و خشن

/zebrokhashen/ ▶ adjective
burly

زبردست

/zebardast/ ▶ adjective
dextrous - dexterous - deft - industrious
- proficient - adroit - adept

زبردستی

/zebardasti/ ▶ noun
sleight - skill - proficiency - dexterity

زبون

/zabun/ ▶ adjective
despicable - humble

زجر

/zajr/ ▶ noun
torture - torment

زجر دادن

/zajr dâdan/ ▶ verb
torture - torment

زحل

/zohal/ ▶ noun
satrun

زحمت

/zahmat/ ▶ noun
discomfort - difficulty - labor -
inconvenience - pain - torment - tug -
trouble

زحمت کشیدن

/zahmat keshidan/ ▶ verb
toil - plod - muck - labor

زحمتکش

/zahmatkesh/ ▶ adjective
sufferer - studious - toiler - workingman
- grub - plodder

زخم

/zakhm/ ▶ noun
gash - wound - scotch - trauma - sore

زخم زدن

/zakhm zadan/ ▶ verb
slash - stab - wound - gash - hack

زخم معده

/zakhme me'de/ ▶ noun
ulcer

زخمی

/zakhmi/ ▶ adjective
traumatic - ulcerous

زدن

/zadan/ ▶ verb
hit - whack - bruise - bop - beat

تو برجک کسی زدن :Idiom)

kicking someone's ass)

زدودن

/zedudan/ ▶ verb
efface - remove - clean - obliterate -
wipe - scrape - scour - purge - sweep -
swab – shuck

زردشت

/zardosht/ ► noun
zoroaster

زر

/zar/ ► noun
gold

زردی

/zardi/ ► adjective
autumn - yellow

زرادخانه

/zarâdkhâne/ ► noun
arsenal - armory

زرشکی

/zereshk/ ► adjective
purple

زراعت کردن

/zerâ'at kardan/ ► verb
till

زرق

/zargh/ ► noun
hyporisy

زرافه

/zarâfe/ ► noun
giraffe

زرگر

/zargar/ ► noun
goldsmith

زرپرست

/zarparast/ ► adjective
mammonite

زرنگ

/zerang/ ► adjective
adroit - bright - dapper - clever - nimble
- spry - snide - smart - slicker - shrewd -
shifty - jaunty

زرتشت

/zartosht/ ► noun
zoroaster

زرتشتی

/zartoshti/ ► adjective
parsi - zoroastrian

زرنگی

/zerangi/ ► noun
knack - sleight - promptitude

زرد

/zard/ ► adjective
wan - aquamarine - yellow

زره

/zereh/ ► noun
armor - armature - mail

زردآلو

/zardâlu/ ► noun
apricot

زگیل
/zegil/ ► noun
wart - tuber

زره پوش
/zerehpush/ ► adjective
ironclad

زلال
/zolâl/ ► adjective
lucid - limpid - crystal - clear

زرین
/zarin/ ► adjective
golden

زلزله
/zelzele/ ► noun
earthquake

زشت
/zesht/ ► adjective
hideous - heinous - bad - backhand -
awry - awkward - execrable - offensive

زلزله شناسی
/zelzeleshenâsi/ ► noun
seismology

زشتی
/zeshti/ ► noun
opprobrium - odium - obscenity -
inelegance - homeliness

زلف
/zolf/ ► noun
hair

زعفران
/za'ferân/ ► noun
saffron

زمام
/zemâm/ ► noun
helm - rein

زغال
/zoghâl/ ► noun
coal - char

زمامدار
/zemâmdâr/ ► noun
statesman

زغال فروش
/zoghâlforosh/ ► noun
charwoman

زمامداری
/zemâmdâri/ ► noun
statesmanship

زفاف
/zefâf/ ► noun
wedlock

زمان
/zamân/ ► noun
date - moment - time - zeitgeist

زمین شناسی
/zaminshenâsi/ ▶ noun
geology

زمانی
/zamâni/ ▶ noun
time

زمین گیر
/zamingir/ ▶ adjective
cripple

زمخت
/zomokht/ ▶ adjective
crude - crass - gross - coarse - clumsy -
rude - rough -blowsy - tough

زمین لرزه
/zaminlarze/ ▶ noun
earthquake

زمزمه
/zamzame/ ▶ noun
murmur - croon

زمینه
/zamine/ ▶ noun
basis - base - background - design -
context - conspectus - root - groundwork

زمزمه کردن
/zamzame kardan/ ▶ verb
croon - hum - murmur

زمینی
/zamini/ ▶ adjective
earthy - earthly - agrarian - territorial -
terrestrial

زمستان
/zemestân/ ▶ noun
winter

زمستانی
/zemestâni/ ▶ adjective
winter

زن
/zan/ ▶ noun
woman - wife

زمین
/zamin/ ▶ noun
territory - soil - earth - ground - globe -
acre - vale - land

زن باز
/zanbâz/ ▶ adjective
philander - gallant

زمین شناس
/zaminshenâs/ ▶ noun
geologist

زن برادر
/zane barâdar/ ▶ noun
sisterinlaw

زنانه
/zanâne/ ▶ adverb
womanly - womanish - wifely

زن پدر
/zane pedar/ ▶ noun
stepmother

زنبق
/zanbagh/ ▶ noun
flag - lily

زن پرست
/zanparast/ ▶ adjective
uxorious

زنبور
/zanbur/ ▶ noun
bee

زن فاسد
/zane fâsed/ ▶ noun
peat

زنبورعسل
/zanbure asal/ ▶ noun
bumblebee - bee

زنا
/zenâ/ ▶ noun
adultery

زنبیل
/zanbil/ ▶ noun
basket

زنازاده
/zenâzâde/ ▶ adjective
adulterate

زنجبیل
/zanjabil/ ▶ noun
ginger

زناشویی
/zanâshuyi/ ▶ noun
wedlock - matrimony - marriage

زنجیر
/zanjir/ ▶ noun
sling - manacle - link - hobble - bond - curb

زناکار
/zenâkâr/ ▶ adjective
adulterous - wencher

زنجیر کردن
/zanjir kardan/ ▶ verb
manacle

زنان
/zanân/ ▶ noun
feminine - womenfolk - womankind

زنانگی
/zanânegi/ ▶ noun
woman

زنجیره
/zanjire/ ▶ noun
continuum

زنده دل

/zendedel/ ► adjective
dashing - dapper

زندان

/zendân/ ► noun
jail - calaboose - prison

زنده شدن

/zende shodan/ ► verb
revive - quicken - liven

زندان کردن

/zendân kardan/ ► verb
lockup - prison - can

زنده ماندن

/zende mândan/ ► verb
survive

زندانی

/zendâni/ ► adjective
prisoner - inmate - jailbird

زنگ زدگی

/zangzadegi/ ► adjective
corrosion - stain

زندانی سیاسی

/zendâniye siyâsi/ ► noun
political prisoners

زنگ زدن

/zangzadan/ ► verb
smut - stain - oxidize - rust - ringer -
ring

زندانی کردن

/zendâni kardan/ ► verb
incarcerate

زندگی

/zendegi/ ► noun
existence - life - habitancy

زنگ زده

/zangzade/ ► adjective
rusty - rotten

زندگی بخشیدن

/zendegi bakhshidan/ ► verb
animate - enliven

زنگار

/zengâr/ ► noun
rust - blight - legging

زنده

/zende/ ► adjective
vivid - lively - alive - quick

زنگوله

/zangule/ ► noun
urceolate

یاد کسی را زنده نگه داشتن :Idiom)
Keep somebody's memory green)

زنگی

/zangi/ ► adjective
negro

زننده

/zanande/ ▶ adjective
nasty - garish - acrid - vile - poignant -
pitapat - striker - squalid - sharp

زنهار

/zenhâr/ ▶ noun
quarter

زه

/zeh/ ▶ noun
cord - chord - catgut - gut

زه کشی

/zeh keshi/ ▶ noun
canalization

زهر

/zahr/ ▶ noun
poison - venom

زهراب

/zahrâb/ ▶ noun
urine

زهردار

/zahrdâr/ ▶ adjective
venomous - poisonous

زهره

/zohre/ ▶ noun
gall - bile

زهکشی

/zehkeshi/ ▶ noun
sewerage - drainage

زهکشی کردن

/zehkeshi kardan/ ▶ verb
drain

زوال

/zavâl/ ▶ noun
chute - fall - decline - decay - decadence
- consumption - downfall - lapse

زواید

/zavâyed/ ▶ noun
excrement

زوج

/zôj/ ▶ noun
spouse - twin - even - couple - pair

زوجه

/jôje/ ▶ noun
spouse - wife - wedlock - lady

زود

/jud/ ▶ adjective
soon - early

زودباور

/zudbâvar/ ▶ adjective
credulous - untutored

زودتر

/zudtar/ ▶ adjective
junior

زودرس
/zudras/ ► adjective
unripe - hasty - precocious

زودگذر
/zudgozar/ ► adjective
perishable - memnetary - light - glint -
glancing - frail - shadowy

زور
/zur/ ► noun
vigor - might - power - energy - dint -
stunt - strength - push

زورآزمایی
/zurâzmâyi/ ► noun
match

زورگو
/zurgu/ ► adjective
unreasonable - incubus

زورمند
/zurmand/ ► adjective
vigorous - mighty

زوم
/zum/ ► noun
zoom

زیاد
/ziyâd/ ► adjective
very - vast - much - many - manifold

زیاد شدن
/ziyâdshodan/ ► verb
mount - increase - augment - grow -
gain - wax - proliferate

زیاد کردن
/ziyâd kardan/ ► verb
propagate - augment - add - increase -
heighten - enhance - raise

زیادتر
/ziyâdtar/ ► adjective
more

زیادترین
/ziyâdtarin/ ► adjective
most

زیاده
/ziyâde/ ► adjective
supernumerary

زیاده رو
/ziyâdero/ ► adjective
intemperate - indulgent

زیادی
/ziyâdi/ ► noun
surplus - superfluous - superfluity -
undue - excess

زیارت
/ziyârat/ ► noun
pilgrimage

زیارت کردن

/ziyârat kardan/ ▶ verb
visit

زیتون

/zeitun/ ▶ noun
olive

زیان

/ziyân/ ▶ noun
damage - evil - drawback - disservice -
disadvantage - washout - loss - harm

زیر

/zir/ ▶ preposition
bottom - beneath - under - nether

زیرآب زدن

/zirâb zadan/ ▶ verb
drain

زیان آور

/ziyânâvar/ ▶ adjective
pernicious - malignant - ill - bad -
nocuous - evil - deleterious

زیرا

/zirâ/ ▶ preposition
because

زیان بخش

/ziyânbakhsh/ ▶ adjective
obnoxious

زیراکه

/zirâke/ ▶ preposition
for - because

زیان زدن

/ziyân zadan/ ▶ verb
damage

زیربغل

/zirbaghal/ ▶ noun
armpit

زیبا

/zibâ/ ▶ adjective
picturesque - handsome - beautiful -
beauteous

زیربنا

/zirbanâ/ ▶ noun
infrastructure

زیبایی

/zibâyi/ ▶ noun
beauty - grace - glee - pulchritude -
sheen - seeming

زیرپوش

/zirpush/ ▶ noun
underwear - underpants - undergarment
- underclothing - underclothes

زیپ

/zip/ ▶ noun
zip

زیرپیراهنی

/zirpirâhani/ ▶ noun
underwaist - undershirt

زیرزمین

/zirzamin/ ▶ noun
cellar - basement - underground

زیرزمینی

/zirzamini/ ▶ adjective
suberranean

زیرک

/zirak/ ▶ adjective
subtle - smart - shrewd - sharp - astute -
alert - agile - adroit - acute – brilliant -
clever - keen

زیرکی

/ziraki/ ▶ noun
cogency - cunning - intelligence -
perspicacity - brilliance - agility -
subtlety - sagacity

زیرین

/zirin/ ▶ noun
beneath - underside - underneath - under

زیست

/zist/ ▶ noun
existence - work

زیست گاه

/zistgâh/ ▶ noun
settlement

زیستن

/zistan/ ▶ verb
exist - be - live - shack

زیلو

/zilu/ ▶ noun
carpet

زیور

/zivar/ ▶ noun
trangam - jollity - jewel

ژ

zhe /zhe/ ▶ forteenth letter of the Persian alphabet

ژاپن
/zhâpon/ ▶ noun
japan

ژاپنی
/zhâponi/ ▶ adjective
nipponese - japanese

ژاکت
/zhâkat/ ▶ noun
sweater - pullover - jacket

ژاله
/zhâle/ ▶ noun
dew - frost

ژانویه
/zhânviye/ ▶ noun
january

ژتون
/zheton/ ▶ noun
chip

ژرف
/zharf/ ▶ adjective
profound - unfathomable - deep

ژرفا
/zharfâ/ ▶ adjective
depth

ژرمنی
/zhermani/ ▶ adjective
germanic

ژست
/zhest/ ▶ noun
pose - gesture

ژن
/zhen/ ▶ noun
gene

ژنده
/zhende/ ▶ adjective
shabby - ragged

ژنراتور
/zhenerâtor/ ▶ noun
generator

ژنرال
/zhenerâl/ ▶ noun
general

ژوکر
/zhuker/ ▶ noun
joker

ژولیده
/zhulide/ ▶ adjective
draggy - disheveled - ragamuffin

ژیان

/zhiyân/ ► noun
fierce - rapacious

س - ـس

sin /se/ ▶ finteenth letter of the Persian alphabet

ساحل

/sâhel/ ▶ noun
shore - coast - beach - bank - littoral

ساحل دریا

/sâhele daryâ/ ▶ noun
seashore - seacoast

ساخت

/sâkht/ ▶ noun
manufacture - make - production - confection - workmanship - composition - structure

سابق

/sâbegh/ ▶ adjective
olden - former - predecessor - antecedent

ساختار

/sâkhtâr/ ▶ noun
structure

سابقا

/sâbeghan/ ▶ adverb
once - heretofore

ساختگی

/sâkhtegi/ ▶ adjective
apocryphal - quack - bogus - imitation - phony - made - false - whopper - sham

سابقه

/sâbeghe/ ▶ noun
background - antecedent - acquaintance - prehistory - precedence - intellect - history - record - scape - shaft

ساختمان

/sâkhtemân/ ▶ noun
structure - stance - skeleton - mechanism - make - anatomy - construction - frame

سابقی

/sâbeghi/ ▶ adjective
old - previous

ساختن

/sâkhtan/ ▶ verb
establish - build - invent - move - model - mint - manufacture - make

ساحر

/sâher/ ▶ noun
sorcerous - conjurer - necromancer - hex

سادگی

/sâdegi/ ▶ noun
unreserve - naivete - simplicity

ساحره

/sâhere/ ▶ adjective
hellcat - hag - witch

ساده

/sâde/ ▶ adjective
simple - plain - inexpensive - idiot -
homespun - untutored - unmeaning -
unceremonious - unassuming -

ساده دل

/sâde del/ ▶ adjective
simple - sheepish

ساده لوح

/sâdeloh/ ▶ adjective
dupe - oaf - nincompoop - sawney - sot -
simpleton

سار

/sâr/ ▶ noun
camel

ساربان

/sârebân/ ▶ noun
cameleer

سارق

/sâregh/ ▶ noun
thief - robber

ساز و برگ

/sâzobarg/ ▶ noun
outfit - ordnance - equipment

سازش

/sâzesh/ ▶ noun
collusion - agreement

سازگار

/sâzegar/ ▶ adjective
salubrious - compatible

سازگار کردن

/sâzegâr kardan/ ▶ verb
adjust

سازمان

/sâzemân/ ▶ noun
structure - infrastructure - organization

سازمان دادن

/sâzemân dâdan/ ▶ verb
organize

سازمان دهنده

/sâzemân dahande/ ▶ adjective
catalyst

سازنده

/sâzande/ ▶ adjective
composer - constituent - maker

ساس

/sâs/ ▶ noun
bug

ساطع

/sâte'/ ▶ noun
diffusive - radiant

ساطور

/sâtur/ ▶ noun
masher - whittle - cleaver - chopper

ساعت
/sâ'at/ ▶ noun
timer - timepiece - ticker - hour - watch

ساک
/sâk/ ▶ noun
bag

ساعت ساز
/sâ'at sâz/ ▶ adjective
watchmaker

ساکت
/sâket/ ▶ noun
silent - shush - serene - still - calm -
whist - imperturbable

ساعت شنی
/sâ'ate sheni/ ▶ noun
hourglass

ساکت بودن
/sâket budan/ ▶ verb
mum

ساغر
/sâghar/ ▶ noun
goblet - cup

ساکن
/sâken/ ▶ adjective
inmate - inhabitant - inert - habitant

ساق
/sâgh/ ▶ noun
stalk

ساکن بودن
/sâken budan/ ▶ verb
dwell

ساق پا
/sâghe pâ/ ▶ noun
shin - shank - leg

سال
/sâl/ ▶ noun
year

ساقه
/sâghe/ ▶ noun
stem - stalk - shank - leg

سالاد
/sâlâd/ ▶ noun
salad

ساقه گل
/sâgheye gol/ ▶ noun
peduncle

سالار
/sâlâr/ ▶ noun
head - chieftain - chief

ساقی
/sâghi/ ▶ noun
drawer - bung

سالخوردگی
/sâlkhordegi/ ▶ noun
senility

سانتی متر
/sântimetr/ ▶ noun
centimeter

سالخورده
/sâlkhorde/ ▶ adjective
elderly - old - hoary - senile

سانتیگراد
/sântigerâd/ ▶ noun
centigrade

سالک
/sâlek/ ▶ adjective
peripatetic - gradient

سانحه
/sânehe/ ▶ noun
accident

سالگرد
/sâlgard/ ▶ noun
anniversary - jubilee

ساندویچ
/sândevich/ ▶ noun
taco - sandwich

سالم
/sâlem/ ▶ adjective
well - lucid - intact - healthy - hale -
valid - sound - sane - salubrious - safe

سانسور
/sânsur/ ▶ noun
censorship

سالن
/sâlem/ ▶ noun
amphitheater - coliseum - gallery

سایبان
/sâyebân/ ▶ noun
sunshade - canopy - marquee - hovel -
parasol - umbrella - bower

سالنامه
/sâlnâme/ ▶ noun
annals - almanac - calendar - yearbook

سایرین
/sâyerin/ ▶ noun
others - rest

سالیانه
/sâliyâne/ ▶ adverb
yearly - annual

سایز
/sâyz/ ▶ noun
size

سامان
/sâmân/ ▶ noun
order - repose

سایش
/sâyesh/ ▶ noun
abrasion - erosion - grind - friction

ساینده

/sâyande/ ▶ adjective
grating - abrasive

سایه

/sâye/ ▶ noun
sunshade - shadow - shade - shade

سایه افکندن

/sâye afkandan/ ▶ verb
shade

سایه انداختن

/sâye andâkhtan/ ▶ verb
overcast - umber

سایه بان

/sâyebân/ ▶ adjective
shade

سایه مانند

/sâyemânand/ ▶ adjective
shadowy

ساییدگی

/sâyidegi/ ▶ noun
attrition - abrasion - gall - chafe -
erosion

ساییدن

/sâyidan/ ▶ verb
chafe - rub - grit - grind - grate - gnaw -
gall - levigate

ساییده شدن

/sâyide shodan/ ▶ verb
rub

سبب

/sabab/ ▶ noun
reason - causer - cause - account -
motive

سبد

/sabad/ ▶ noun
basket - kist

سبز

/sabz/ ▶ adjective
green

سبز کردن

/sabz kardan/ ▶ verb
green

سبزه

/sabze/ ▶ noun
greenery - green - grass - brunette -
vegetable

سبزی

/sabzi/ ▶ noun
vegetable - greenery

سبزیجات

/sabzijât/ ▶ noun
vegetables

سبقت

/sebghat/ ▶ noun
antedate

سبقت جستن

/sebghat jostan/ ▶ verb
transcend - outguess

سبقت گرفتن از

/sebghat gereftan az/ ▶ verb
pass

سبک

/sabok/ ▶ noun
soft - thin - levity - levigate - volatile -
portable

سبو

/sabu/ ▶ noun
crock - jar

سبوس

/sabus/ ▶ noun
slough - shuck - husk - bran - chaff

سبوسه

/sabuse/ ▶ noun
scruff

سبک

/sabk/ ▶ noun
style - structure - mode

سپاس

/sepâs/ ▶ noun
thank

سپاسگزار

/sepâsgozâr/ ▶ adjective
thankful

سپاسگزاری

/sepâsgozâri/ ▶ noun
gratuity - gratitude - thanksgiving -
thank

سپاسگزاری کردن

/sepâsgozâri kardan/ ▶ verb
thank

سپاه

/sepâh/ ▶ noun
army - host - corps

سپتامبر

/septâmbr/ ▶ noun
september

سپر

/separ/ ▶ noun
parapet - buffer - aegis - fence - shield

سپردن

/sepordan/ ▶ verb
surrender - award - reposit - commit -
depute - consign - confide - entrust

سپری کردن

/separi kardan/ ▶ verb
survive - while

ستاک
/setâk/ ▶ noun
stem

ستاندن
/setândan/ ▶ verb
take

ستایش
/setâyesh/ ▶ noun
worship - laud - praise - veneration -
panegyric - adoration - tribute

ستایش کردن
/setâyesh kardan/ ▶ verb
commend - kudos - glorify - eulogize -
laud

ستایشگر
/setâyeshgar/ ▶ adjective
ilolater - praiser

سترگ
/setorg/ ▶ adjective
large - huge

سترون
/setarvan/ ▶ noun
sterile - barren

ستم
/setam/ ▶ noun
oppression - cruelty - injustice - tyranny

سپس
/sepas/ ▶ adverb
therefore - thenceforth - then -
afterwards - next

سپهر
/sepehr/ ▶ noun
heaven

سپیدار
/sepidâr/ ▶ noun
poplar

سپیده دم
/sepide dam/ ▶ noun
cockcrow - daybreak - dawn - aurora -
streak

ستاره
/setâre/ ▶ noun
aster - shiner - star

ستاره شناس
/setâre shenâs/ ▶ noun
astronomer - astrologer

ستاره شناسی
/setâre shenâsi/ ▶ adjective
uranology - astronomy - astrology

ستاره قطبی
/setâreye ghotbi/ ▶ noun
northstar

ستم کردن

/setam kardan/ ▶ verb
tyrannize

ستمگر

/setamgar/ ▶ adjective
tyrant - tyrannous - oppressor -
dispiteous - despot - cruel - atrocious -
unjust

ستمگرانه

/setamgarâne/ ▶ adverb
tyrannous - tyrannical

ستمگری

/setamgari/ ▶ noun
ravage - tyranny

ستودنی

/setudani/ ▶ noun
laudable - praiseworthy - admirable -
commendable

ستوده

/setude/ ▶ adjective
exemplary - honorable - laudable

ستون

/sotun/ ▶ noun
column - pillar - pile - pier - jamb -
staple - shaft

ستون فقرات

/sotune fagharât/ ▶ noun
spine - backbone

ستیز

/setiz/ ▶ noun
toil - struggle - battle - warfare - combat

ستیزجو

/setizeju/ ▶ adjective
querulous

ستیزگر

/setizegar/ ▶ adjective
contentious - warlike - militant -
quarrelsome

ستیزه

/setize/ ▶ noun
strife - squabble - quarrel - melee -
dispute - disputation - controversy -
contention - conflict

ستیزه جو

/setizeju/ ▶ adjective
currish - contestant - contentious -
intractable - quarrelsome - scrappy -
pugilist - striver

ستیزه جویی

/setizejuyi/ ▶ noun
pugnacity

سحر

/sahar/ ▶ noun
spell - incantation - magic - charm -
wizardry

سحرآمیز

/sehrâmiz/ ▶ adjective
magical - magic - sorcerous

سحرخیز

/saharkhiz/ ▶ adjective
riser

سخاوت

/sekhâvat/ ▶ noun
generosity - bounty

سخاوتمندانه

/sekhâvatmandâne/ ▶ adverb
handsomely

سخاوتمندی

/sekhâvatmandi/ ▶ noun
benevolence

سخت

/sakht/ ▶ adjective
troublesome - strong - steely - sore -
severe - serious - difficult

سخت کردن

/sakht kardan/ ▶ verb
intensify - harden - ossify

سخت گیر

/sakhtgir/ ▶ adjective
strict - severe - difficult - unrelenting -
astringent - priggish - intransigent - hard

سخت گیری

/sakhtgiri/ ▶ noun
tax - severity - stricture

سختگیر

/sakhtgir/ ▶ adjective
taskmaster - stringent

سختگیری

/sakhtgiri/ ▶ noun
rigor - stringency

سختی

/sakhti/ ▶ adjective
solidity - severity - hardship - duration -
difficulty - granite - rigidity - resistance

سخن

/sokhan/ ▶ noun
speech - pronunciation - yap - utterance
- locution - lip - word - redundancy

سخن تند

/sokhane tond/ ▶ noun
vitriolic

سخن چین

/sokhanchin/ ▶ noun
telltale - informer

سخن سرایی

/sokhansârâyi/ ▶ noun
elocution

سخنران

/sokhanrân/ ▶ adjective
lecturer - orator - spokesman

سخنگو

/sokhangu/ ► noun
talker - spokesman - speaker

سد

/sad/ ► noun
sluice - stoppage - stank - dike - dam -
pile - barrier

سد کردن

/sad kardan/ ► verb
stop

سدراه

/saderâh/ ► noun
blockade

سده

/sade/ ► noun
century - centennial - centenary

سدیم

/sodyom/ ► noun
sodium

سر

/sar/ ► noun
head - end - corona - top

(Idiom: سر به سر کسی گذاشتن
Do not pick on me)

(Idiom: سرو مورو گنده
alive and kicking)

سر

/ser/ ► noun
secret- mystery

سر آشپز

/sarâshpaz/ ► noun
chef

سر بریدن

/sar boridan/ ► verb
behead - decollate

سر خوردن

/sor khordan/ ► verb
skid - skate - glide

سر راست

/sar'râst/ ► adjective
straightforward - stark - upstanding

سر زدن

/sar zadan/ ► verb
rise - amount

سر سپردن

/sarsepordan/ ► verb
commit

سر کشیدن

/sarkeshidan/ ► verb
swill - quaff - lap - guzzle

سر و صدا

/saro sedâ/ ► noun
noise

سراب

/sarâb/ ▶ noun
mirage

سرازیر

/sarâzir/ ▶ noun
steep - ramp

سرازیر شدن

/sarâriz shodan/ ▶ verb
top - slope - plummet - ramp

سرازیری

/sarâziri/ ▶ adjective
slope - slide - tilt - bent - pitch -
downhill - dip - declivity

سراسر

/sarâsar/ ▶ noun
throughout - quite - whole

سراسیمگی

/sarâsimegi/ ▶ noun
scurry

سراسیمه

/sarâsime/ ▶ adjective
unaware - unawares - headlong

سراشیبی

/sarâshibi/ ▶ noun
abrupt - slide

سراغ

/sorâgh/ ▶ noun
scent

سرافکندگی

/sarafkandegi/ ▶ noun
dejection

سرافکنده

/sarafkande/ ▶ adjective
ashamed - abject

سرانجام

/saranjam/ ▶ noun
upshot

سرایت

/seryâyat/ ▶ noun
transmittal - transmission - contagion

سرایدار

/serâyedâr/ ▶ noun
janitor - caretaker - custodian

سراینده

/sorâyande/ ▶ adjective
singer - vocalist - warbler - composer

سرب

/sorb/ ▶ noun
plumb

سرباز

/sarbâz/ ▶ noun
soldier - private

سرباز زدن

/sarbâz zadan/ ▶ verb
refuse

سربازی
/sarbâzi/ ► noun
military

سربراه
/sarberâh/ ► noun
tractable - docile

سربسر
/sarbesar/ ► noun
endwise - endways

سربلند
/sarboland/ ► adjective
proud - elate

سربی
/sorbi/ ► adjective
leaden

سرپرست
/sarparast/ ► noun
supervisor - protector - caretaker -
overseer - warden - attendant - headman

سرپوش
/sarpush/ ► noun
lid - valve - cover - casquet - capsule -
cap

سرپوشیده
/sarpushide/ ► adjective
porch

سرپیچی
/sarpichi/ ► noun
refusal - disobedience - transgression

سرپیچی کردن
/sarpichi kardan/ ► verb
disobey - challenge

سرتاپا
/sartâpâ/ ► noun
capapie

سرتاسر
/sartâsar/ ► noun
through - crossways - crosswise -
overall - across

سرجمع
/sarjam'/ ► noun
total - tot - overhead

سرچشمه
/sarcheshme/ ► noun
fountain - root - original - derivation -
springhead - spring - source

سرحال
/sarehâl/ ► noun
cheery - game - wholesome - jink - trig

سرحد
/sarhad/ ► noun
demarcation - bound - border - mete

سرخ
/sorkh/ ▶ adjective
sanguine - rosy - red

سرد کردن
/sard kardan/ ▶ verb
refrigerate - chill

سرخ جامه
/sorkhjâme/ ▶ adjective
scarlet

سرداب
/sardâb/ ▶ noun
basement - cellar

سرخ شدگی
/sorkhshodegi/ ▶ noun
scarlet

سردار
/sardâr/ ▶ noun
headed

سرخ کردن
/sorgh kardan/ ▶ verb
saute - fry - ruddy - rose - pan - brown

سردبیر
/sardabir/ ▶ noun
redactor

سرخاب
/sorkhâb/ ▶ noun
rouge

سردخانه
/sardkhâne/ ▶ noun
springhouse - fridge

سرخر
/sarekhar/ ▶ adjective
killjoy

سردر
/sardar/ ▶ noun
portal

سرخرگ
/sorang/ ▶ noun
artery

سردرد
/sardard/ ▶ noun
headache

سرخک
/sorkhak/ ▶ noun
measles

سردرگم
/sardargom/ ▶ noun
amaze

سرد
/sard/ ▶ adjective
cold - cool - arctic

سردسته
/sardaste/ ▶ noun
protagonist - leader - marshal - chieftain
- ringleader - drillmaster

سردستی

/sardasti/ ▶ noun
sketchy

سردکن

/sardkon/ ▶ noun
cooler

سردی

/sardi/ ▶ noun
ice

سررسید

/sar resid/ ▶ noun
maturity - usance

سررشته

/sar reshte/ ▶ noun
scent - competence

سرزده

/sarzade/ ▶ adjective
uninvited

سرزمین

/sarzamin/ ▶ noun
territory - clime - region - land

سرزندگی

/sarzendegi/ ▶ noun
vivacity - esprit

سرزنده

/sarzende/ ▶ adjective
alive - vivacious - lively - live

سرزنش

/sarzanesh/ ▶ noun
remonstrance - rail - censure - obloquy -
demerit - blame - vituperation

سرسام

/sarsâm/ ▶ noun
delirium - maze

سرسخت

/sarsakht/ ▶ adjective
tenacious - stubborn - stark - dour -
headstrong

سرسرا

/sarsarâ/ ▶ noun
gallery - hall - portico

سرسره

/sorsore/ ▶ noun
slide

سرشار

/sarshâr/ ▶ adjective
profuse - alive - opulence - galore

سرشب

/sareshab/ ▶ noun
evening

سرشت

/seresht/ ▶ noun
temperament - make - nature

سرشک

/sereshk/ ▶ noun
tear

سرشماری

/sarshomâri/ ▶ noun
census - capitation - statistic

سرصفحه

/sarsafhe/ ▶ noun
headline - head

سرطان

/saretân/ ▶ noun
cancer

سرطانزا

/saretânzâ/ ▶ adjective
carcinogen

سرعت

/sor'at/ ▶ noun
speed

سرفه

/sorfe/ ▶ noun
cough

سرقت

/serghat/ ▶ noun
thievery - theft - prowl - lift - larceny -
robbery

سرقت کردن

/serghat kardan/ ▶ verb
lift

سرک

/sarak/ ▶ noun
slippage

سرکار

/sarekâr/ ▶ noun
overseer - taskmaster

سرکارگر

/sarkârgar/ ▶ noun
joss

سرکردگی

/sarkardegi/ ▶ noun
command

سرکرده

/sarkarde/ ▶ adjective
commander - captain

سرکش

/sarkesh/ ▶ adjective
turbulent - malignant - malcontent -
irrepressible - insubordinate - inelastic -
rebellious - rebel

سرکشی کردن

/sarkeshi kardan/ ▶ verb
inspect - visit

سرکه

/serke/ ▶ noun
pickle - vinegar

سرکوبی

/sarkubi/ ▶ noun

squelch - repression

سرلوحه
/sarlôhe/ ▶ noun
caption - epigraph - signboard

سرکوفت
/sarkuft/ ▶ noun
rail

سرم
/serom/ ▶ noun
serum

سرگذشت
/sargozasht/ ▶ noun
event - adventure - act - memoir

سرما
/sarmâ/ ▶ noun
cold - chill

سرگرد
/sargord/ ▶ noun
major

سرما زدن
/sarmâ zadan/ ▶ verb
frost

سرگردان
/sargardân/ ▶ adjective
erratic - discursive - wanderer -
gadabout - rambler - adrift

سرماخوردگی
/sarmâkhordegi/ ▶ noun
cold

سرگردان شدن
/sargardân shodan/ ▶ verb
roil - stray

سرمایه
/sarmâye/ ▶ noun
turnover - stock - asset - capital

سرگردانی
/sargardâni/ ▶ noun
quandary - divagation - ramble - roam

سرمست
/sarmast/ ▶ adjective
maudlin

سرگرمی
/sargarmi/ ▶ noun
recreation - fun - game - diversion -
pastime - avocation - hobbyhorse -
hobby

سرمشق
/sarmashgh/ ▶ noun
example - lead - model - pacemaker

سرگیجه
/sargije/ ▶ noun
vertigo

سرمقاله
/sarmaghâle/ ▶ noun
editorial

سرنج

/soranj/ ▶ noun
putty

سرنگ

/sorang/ ▶ noun
syringe

سرنگونی

/sarneguni/ ▶ noun
debacle

سرنوشت

/sarnevesht/ ▶ noun
lot - portion - fate - dole - destiny -
destination

سرهنگ

/sarhang/ ▶ noun
colonel

سرو

/sarv/ ▶ noun
cedar

سرود

/sorud/ ▶ noun
song - sing - hymn - anthem - warble -
chant - canto

سرودن

/sorudan/ ▶ verb
sing - compose

سرور

/sarvar/ ▶ noun
overlord - joy

سروری کردن

/sarvari kardan/ ▶ verb
prince

سروش

/sorush/ ▶ noun
oracle - gabriel

سرویس

/servis/ ▶ noun
service

سری

/seri/ ▶ adjective
undercover - esoteric - crypt - occult

سریال

/seryâl/ ▶ noun
serial

سریر

/sarir/ ▶ noun
throne

سریع

/sari'/ ▶ adjective
swift - sudden - speedy - prompt - quick
- precipitate - rapid

سریع تر

/sari'tar/ ▶ adjective
rather

سطحی

/sathi/ ▶ adjective
surface - superficial - sketchy - shallow - planar

سزا

/sezâ/ ▶ noun
punishment - retribution

سطر

/satr/ ▶ noun
line

سزاوار

/sezâvar/ ▶ noun
worthy - worth

سطل

/satl/ ▶ noun
kit - pail - bucket - bail

سزاوار بودن

/sezâvâr budan/ ▶ verb
deserve

سعادت

/sa'âdat/ ▶ noun
felicity - welfare - paradise - bliss

سست

/sost/ ▶ adjective
loose - atonic – inactive - mild - weak - rickety - remiss

سعادتمند

/sa'âdatmand/ ▶ adjective
happy - blissful

سست شدن

/sost shodan/ ▶ adjective
unclinch - unclench - weaken - flag

سعی

/sa'y/ ▶ noun
endeavor - effort - assay

سستی

/sosti/ ▶ noun
lassitude - insecurity - indolence - inaction - droop - sloth

سعی کردن

/sa'y kardan/ ▶ verb
try

سطح

/sath/ ▶ noun
surface - sheet - external

سفارت

/sefârat/ ▶ noun
embassy

سطح زمین

/sathe zamin/ ▶ noun
earth

سفارشی

/sefâreshi/ ▶ adjective
bespoke

سفال

/sofâl/ ▶ noun
shard - tile - clay - earthenware

سفالگری

/sofâlgari/ ▶ noun
pottery

سفالی

/sofâli/ ▶ adjective
earthen - bat

سفالین

/sofâlin/ ▶ adjective
earthenware

سفاهت

/sefâhat/ ▶ noun
idiotism

سفت

/seft/ ▶ adjective
stiff - tough - tight - hard

سفت شدن

/seft shodan/ ▶ verb
toughen - tighten

سفت کردن

/seft kardan/ ▶ verb
stiff - jell - toughen - tone - tighten - fix
- firm - congeal

سفته باز

/saftebâzi/ ▶ adjective
speculator

سفته بازی کردن

/zaftebâzi kardan/ ▶ verb
kite - speculate

سفر

/safar/ ▶ noun
voyage - junket - journey - trip - tour

سفرنامه

/safarnâme/ ▶ noun
itinerary

سفره

/sofre/ ▶ noun
tablecloth - table

سفید

/sefid/ ▶ adjective
snowy - hoary

سفید شدن

/sefid shodan/ ▶ verb
whiten

سفیدپوست

/sefidpust/ ▶ adjective
caucasian

سفیر

/safir/ ▶ noun
ambassador

سفینه

/safine/ ▶ noun
ship

سقز
/saghez/ ▶ noun
turpentine - galipot

سقف
/saghf/ ▶ noun
soffit - ceiling - roof - loft

سقوط
/soghut/ ▶ noun
crash - elapse - downfall - fall

سکان
/sokân/ ▶ noun
steerage - helm

سکته
/sekte/ ▶ noun
apoplexy - halt - caesura

سکس
/seks/ ▶ noun
sex

سکسکه کردن
/sekseke kardan/ ▶ verb
hiccough - hiccup

سکنی
/soknâ/ ▶ noun
habitancy - occupancy

سکه
/seke/ ▶ noun
shiner - coin - poke - piece - money

سکوت
/sokut/ ▶ noun
mum - calm - reticence - doldrums -
silence - still

سکون
/sokun/ ▶ noun
equilibrium - lull - quiet - inaction -
inertia - slack - stay - station

سکونت
/sokunat/ ▶ noun
habitancy - occupancy

سگ
/sag/ ▶ noun
dog

سگ آبی
/sage âbi/ ▶ noun
beaver

سگال
/segâl/ ▶ noun
intention

سگک
/sagak/ ▶ noun
tach - buckle

سلاح
/selâh/ ▶ noun
weapon - armor - armament - arm

سلام
/salâm/ ► noun
greet - regard - salute - salutation

سلام کردن
/salâm kardan/ ► verb
hello - hail

سلامت
/salâmat/ ► noun
safety - health

سلامتی
/salâmati/ ► noun
peace

سلب کردن
/salb kardan/ ► verb
devest

سلب مالکیت
/salbe mâlekiyat/ ► noun
dispossession

سلحشور
/selahshur/ ► adjective
squire - warrior - knight - rink

سلسله
/selsele/ ► noun
string - phylum - dynasty - gradation -
genealogy - rank - flight - chain

سلطان
/soltân/ ► noun
king - monarch - potentate - sultan

سلطنت
/saltanat/ ► noun
sultanate - reign - dominion - majesty

سلطنتی
/saltanati/ ► adjective
royal - rial - regnal

سلطه
/solte/ ► noun
yoke - ascendency - mastery

سلطه جو
/solteju/ ► adjective
aggressive

سلمانی
/salmâni/ ► noun
barber - haircut - shaver

سلمانی کردن
/salmâni kardan/ ► verb
barber

سلوک
/soluk/ ► noun
demeanour - conduct - behavior

سلول
/selul/ ► noun
cell

سلیس

/salis/ ▶ adjective
fluent - versatile - liquid - voluble -
smooth

سمج

/semej/ ▶ adjective
stubborn - stickler - pertinacious

سمسار

/semsâr/ ▶ noun
broker

سلیس بودن

/salis budan/ ▶ verb
flow

سلیقه

/salighe/ ▶ noun
elegance - style - taste - tact

سمعک

/sam'ak/ ▶ noun
earphone

سم

/sam/ ▶ noun
hoof - poison - venom - nail

سمفونی

/samfoni/ ▶ noun
symphony

سمند

/samand/ ▶ noun
dun

سم پاش

/sampâsh/ ▶ noun
sprayer

سم پاشی

/sampâshi/ ▶ noun
spray

سمی

/sami/ ▶ adjective
toxic - poisonous - poison - venomous

سماجت

/semâjat/ ▶ noun
pertinacity - persistence

سمینار

/seminâr/ ▶ noun
seminar

سمت

/samt/ ▶ noun
side - set

سن

/sen/ ▶ noun
age

سمت

/semat/ ▶ noun
job - title

سنبه

/sonbe/ ▶ noun
piston - ramrod

سنت

/sonat/ ▶ noun
tradition - custom

سنجاق

/sanjâgh/ ▶ noun
pin

سنجش

/sanjesh/ ▶ noun
assay - ponder - comparison - evaluation

سنجیدن

/sanjidan/ ▶ verb
deliberate - counterweight - evaluate -
essay - weigh - assay - ponder - meter -
measure

سنجیده

/sanjide/ ▶ adjective
weighty

سند

/sanad/ ▶ noun
title - script - instrument - voucher - bill
- act - writ - document - deed

سندیت

/sanadiyat/ ▶ noun
authenticity

سندیکا

/sendikâ/ ▶ noun
syndicate

سنگ

/sang/ ▶ noun
rock - stone

سنگ بزرگ نشانه نزدن است :Idiom)

All bark and no bite)

سنگ پا

/sangepâ/ ▶ noun
pumice

سنگدل

/sangdel/ ▶ adjective
obdurate - unholy - ungodly - unfeeling
- inexorable - implacable - implacability

سنگر

/sangar/ ▶ noun
trench - stronghold - blind - parapet -
fort - citadel

سنگریزه

/sangrize/ ▶ noun
slither - grit - gravel - pebble

سنگسار کردن

/sangsâr kardan/ ▶ verb
stone

سنگفرش
/sangfarsh/ ▶ noun
pavement - cobblestone

سنگلاخ
/sanglâkh/ ▶ adjective
stony - rocky

سنگواره
/sangvâre/ ▶ noun
fossil

سنگی
/sangi/ ▶ adjective
stone

سنگین
/sangin/ ▶ adjective
weighty - heavy - unwieldy - lumpy -
burdensome

سنگین کردن
/sangin kardan/ ▶ verb
heavy - gravitate - weight - load - ballast

سنگینی
/sangini/ ▶ noun
ballast - avoirdupois - lethargy - weight
- gravity

سه
/se/ ▶ noun
three

(Idiom: تا سه نشه بازی نشه
third time lucky)

سه برابر
/sebarâbar/ ▶ adjective
threefold - triplicate - triple - treble

سه پایه
/sepâye/ ▶ noun
andiron - trivet - tripod

سه پهلو
/sepahlu/ ▶ adjective
triangle

سه جانبه
/se jânebe/ ▶ adjective
tripartite - trilateral

سه رنگ
/serang/ ▶ adjective
tricolor

سه قلو
/segholu/ ▶ adjective
triplet

سه گانه
/segâne/ ▶ adjective
threefold - triplet - triple

سهام
/sahâm/ ▶ noun
portfolio - liquidate - stock

سهل
/sahl/ ▶ adjective
eath - easy

سهل انگار
/sahlengar/ ▶ adjective
nonchalant - inconsiderate - lax

سهل انگاری
/sahlengâri/ ▶ noun
indifference - nonchalance

سهم
/sahm/ ▶ noun
proportion - contribution - ration - ratio - portion

سهم بندی کردن
/sahiyebandi kardan/ ▶ verb
lot - portion

سهمگین
/sahmgin/ ▶ adjective
horrible - hideous

سهمیه
/sahmiye/ ▶ noun
scantling - quota - ration

سهو
/sahv/ ▶ adjective
error - oversight - wrong - goof - slip

سهولت
/sohulat/ ▶ noun
ease

سهیم
/sahim/ ▶ noun
sharer - participant

سو
/su/ ▶ noun
half - side

سوء تفاهم
/su'e tafâhom/ ▶ noun
gaingiving - imbroglio - misapprehension

سوء تفاهم
/su'e tafâhom/ ▶ noun
embroglio

سوء ظن
/su'ezan/ ▶ noun
umbrage

سوا کردن
/savâ kardan/ ▶ verb
detach - disassemble - isolate - unlink - sort - separate

سوابق
/savâbegh/ ▶ noun
data - dossier - information

سواد
/savâd/ ▶ noun
transcript - literacy

سوار
/savâr/ ▶ noun
trooper - horseback

سوارکار
/savârkâr/ ► noun
rider - horseman

سواری
/savâri/ ► adjective
ride - cavalcade

سواری کردن
/savâr kardan/ ► verb
saddle - jumble - drive

سوال
/soâl/ ► noun
question - query

سوت
/sut/ ► noun
whistler - whistle

سوت زدن
/sut zadan/ ► verb
whistle

سوخت
/sukht/ ► noun
stoker - fuel - combustion

سوخت گیری
/sukhgir/ ► noun
refuelling

سوختگی
/sukhtegi/ ► noun
scorch - scald

سوختن
/sukhtan/ ► verb
consumption - combustion - burn - broil
- singe

سود
/sud/ ► noun
interest - profit - grist - good - gain -
fruit - dividend

سود بردن
/sud bordan/ ► verb
gain - profit

سودآور
/sudâvar/ ► adjective
profitable

سودا
/sôdâ/ ► noun
trade - bargain - melancholy -
melancholia

سوداگر
/sôdâgari/ ► adjective
tradesman - trader - merchant

سودجو
/sudju/ ► adjective
jobber

سودجویی
/sudjuyi/ ► noun
jobbery

سودسهام

/sudesahâm/ ▶ noun
dividend - revenue

سودمند

/sudmand/ ▶ adjective
commodious - useful - beneficial

سودمند بودن

/sudmand budan/ ▶ verb
avail - advantage

سور

/sur/ ▶ noun
banquet

سور دادن

/sur dâdan/ ▶ verb
regale

سوراخ

/surâkh/ ▶ noun
puncture - overture - outage - orifice -
leak - hole - mesh - pigenhole

سوراخ بینی

/surâkhe bini/ ▶ noun
snuffer - nostril

سوراخ کردن

/surâkh kardan/ ▶ verb
delve - stick - steek - stab - spit

سوریه ای

/suriye'i/ ▶ adjective
syrian

سوریه

/suriye/ ▶ noun
syria

سوز

/suz/ ▶ noun
blast

سوزان

/suzân/ ▶ adjective
scathing - torrid - perfervid - ardent -
alight - acrimonious - ablaze - fervid

سوزاندن

/suzândan/ ▶ verb
fry - cauterize - burn - blast - incinerate -
incense - sear - scorch

سوزاننده

/suzânande/ ▶ adjective
torrid - acrid

سوزش

/suzesh/ ▶ noun
sting - twinge - irritation - ignition - nip

سوزش آور

/suzeshâvar/ ▶ adjective
caustic - abrasive - irritant

سوزن

/suzan/ ▶ noun
stylus - needle

سوزناک

/suznâk/ ► adjective
pungent - pathetic - plaintive

سوگ

/sug/ ► noun
sorrow

سوس

/sos/ ► noun
sauce

سوگلی

/sôgoli/ ► noun
pet - favorite

سوسک

/susk/ ► noun
beetle - dorbeetle

سوگنامه

/sugnâme/ ► noun
jeremiad

سوسمار

/susmâr/ ► noun
lizard - crocodile - worm

سوگند

/sôgand/ ► noun
oath - sanction - sacrament

سوسو

/susu/ ► noun
gleam - flicker

سوگند خوردن

/sôgand khordan/ ► verb
swear

سوسیالیزم

/susyâlizm/ ► noun
socialism

سوگندنامه

/sôgandnôme/ ► noun
affidavit

سوسیالیست

/susyâlist/ ► noun
socialist

سوگوار

/sugvâr/ ► adjective
rueful - mournful

سوسیس

/sosis/ ► noun
weeny - sausage

سوگواری

/sugvâri/ ► noun
jeremiad - lament

سوغات

/sôghât/ ► noun
souvenir

سوم

/sevom/ ► noun
third

سومی
/sevomi/ ▶ adjective
third

سیاحت
/siyâhat/ ▶ noun
journey - tourism - tour

سومین
/sevomin/ ▶ adjective
tertiary

سیاحت کردن
/siyâhat kardan/ ▶ verb
rubberneck - explore - tour - safari

سوهان
/sôhân/ ▶ noun
rasp

سیار
/sayâr/ ▶ adjective
ambulatory - migrant - itinerant -
wanderer - rover

سوهان زدن
/sôhân zadan/ ▶ verb
rasp - float

سیارک
/sayârak/ ▶ noun
asteroid

سوی
/suye/ ▶ noun
to- unto

سیاست
/siyâsat/ ▶ noun
diplomacy - policy

سویا
/sôyâ/ ▶ noun
soya

سیاستمدار
/siyâsatmadâr/ ▶ noun
politician - diplomat

سی
/si/ ▶ noun
thirty

سیاسی
/siyâsi/ ▶ adjective
politic

سی ام
/siyom/ ▶ adjective
thirtieth

سیال
/sayâl/ ▶ adjective
fluor - mobile

سی امین
/siyomin/ ▶ adjective
thirtieth

سیاه
/siyâh/ ▶ adjective
jetty - sooty - black - negro - grimy

سیخونک
/sikhunak/ ► noun
prick - poke - jag

سیاه پوست
/siyâhpust/ ► adjective
negro - ethiopian

سیر
/sir/ ► noun
garlic

سیاه رنگ
/siyâhrang/ ► adjective
black

سیر کردن
/sir kardan/ ► verb
saturate - satiate - sate - englut - glut -
revolve - cloy - roam

سیاه کردن
/siyâh kardan/ ► verb
blacken - black - denigrate

سیرک
/sirk/ ► noun
circus

سیاهرگ
/siyâhrag/ ► noun
vein

سیری
/siri/ ► adjective
amplitude - full

سیاهی
/siyâhi/ ► adjective
black

سیب
/sib/ ► noun
apple

سیزده
/sizdah/ ► noun
thirteen

سیبک
/sibak/ ► noun
tuber

سیزدهم
/sizdahom/ ► adjective
thirteenth

سیخ
/sikh/ ► noun
stiff - spur - broach - erect - wooden -
grid - goad - gad - ramrod

سیزدهمین
/sizdahomin/ ► adjective
thirteenth

سیخ زدن
/sikh zadan/ ► verb
yerk - prod - poke - gig

سیگار

/sigâr/ ▶ noun
cigarette - cigar

سیگار کشیدن

/sigâr keshidan/ ▶ verb
smoke

سیل

/seil/ ▶ noun
overflow - flood - spate - torrent

سیلندر

/silandr/ ▶ noun
cylinder

سیلی

/sili/ ▶ noun
slog - slap - spat - buffet - box

سیلی زدن

/sili zadan/ ▶ verb
slap

سیلیس

/silis/ ▶ adjective
silica

سیلیکا

/silikâ/ ▶ noun
silica

سیم

/sim/ ▶ noun
wire - cord - line - string - silver

سیما

/simâ/ ▶ noun
aspect - appearance - air - brow - visage
- mien - expression - countenance -
feature

سیمان

/simân/ ▶ noun
cement

سیمرغ

/simorgh/ ▶ noun
roc

سیمکش

/simkesh/ ▶ noun
wirepuller

سینما

/sinamâ/ ▶ noun
picture - movie - cinema

سینه

/sine/ ▶ noun
bust - breast - bosom - heart

سینه بند

/sineband/ ▶ noun
napkin

سینه پهلو

/sinepahlu/ ▶ noun
pneumonia

سینی

/sini/ ► noun
tray - paten - dish

ش – شـ

shin /shin/ ▶ sixteenth letter of the Persian alphabet

شأن
/sha'n/ ▶ noun
dignity - rank - grandeur - importance - their - status

شاخ
/shâkh/ ▶ noun
horn - branch

شاخ زدن
/shâkh zadan/ ▶ verb
push - butt - gore

شاخدار
/shâkhdâr/ ▶ adjective
cuspidate - cornuted

شاخص
/shâkhes/ ▶ noun
tyupical - indicator - index - dial

شاخک
/shâkhak/ ▶ noun
antenna

شاخه
/shâkhe/ ▶ noun
sprout - tributary - wing - grain - limb - bough - arm

شاد
/shâd/ ▶ adjective
joyful - merry - exultant - happy - cheery - glad - debonair

شاداب
/shâdâb/ ▶ adjective
lush - succulent - juicy

شادابی
/shâdâbi/ ▶ noun
succulence

شادکام
/shâdkâm/ ▶ adjective
upbeat - merry

شادکامی
/shâdkâmi/ ▶ noun
welfare

شادمان
/shâdemân/ ▶ adjective
upbeat

شادی
/shâdi/ ▶ noun
jubilation - joyance - mirth - curvet - glee - gala - caper

شاق
/shâgh/ ► adjective
onerous - astringent - burdensome - tall - severe - stark

شادی بخش
/shâdibakhsh/ ► adjective
breezy

شاکر
/shâker/ ► adjective
thankful

شادی کردن
/shâdi kardan/ ► verb
joy - revel - rejoice - exult

شاکی
/shâki/ ► adjective
complainant - actor - plaintiff - squawker

شارع
/shâre'/ ► noun
lawyer

شاگرد
/shâgerd/ ► noun
pupil - protege - student - disciple - apprentice - mate - votary

شارلاتان
/shârlâtân/ ► adjective
charlatan

شاگردی
/shâgerdi/ ► adjective
journeywork

شاش
/shâsh/ ► noun
piss - urine

شال
/shâl/ ► noun
wraparound - shawl

شاشیدن
/shâshidan/ ► verb
piss - urinate

شاعر
/shâ'er/ ► noun
poet

شالوده
/shâlude/ ► adjective
base - infrastructure - pedestal - texture - sole - skeleton

شام
/shâm/ ► noun
supper - meat - dinner

شاعری
/shâ'eri/ ► adjective
poesy

شاغل
/shâghel/ ► noun
practitioner

شامپانزه

/shâmpânze/ ▶ noun
chimpanzee

شانسی

/shânsi/ ▶ adjective
lottery

شامگاه

/shâmgâh/ ▶ noun
eventide - eve

شانه

/shâne/ ▶ noun
shoulder - comb - pitchfork - heckle

شامل

/shâmel/ ▶ noun
inclusive - in

شاه

/shâh/ ▶ noun
sceptered - king

شامل بودن

/shâmel budan/ ▶ verb
comprise - contain - consist - entail - encompass

شاه توت

/shâhtut/ ▶ noun
blackberry

شانزده

/shânzdah/ ▶ noun
sixteen

شاهانه

/shâhâne/ ▶ adverb
sceptered - royal - majestic

شانزدهم

/shânzdahom/ ▶ adjective
sixteenth

شاهد

/shâhed/ ▶ noun
theme - testimonial - instance - voucher

شانزدهمین

/shânzdahomin/ ▶ adjective
sixteenth - sixteen

شاهراه

/shâhrâh/ ▶ noun
superhighway - turnpike - thoroughfare - freeway - highway

شانس

/shâns/ ▶ noun
odds - chance - fortune - fortuity - luck

شاهرگ

/shâhrag/ ▶ noun
artery - aorta

شانس یک بار در خونه آدم رو می زنه :Idiom)
take a chance while it is available)

شاهزاده

/shâhzâde/ ▶ noun
lord - prince

شاهکار

/shâhkâr/ ► adjective
stunt - exploit - masterwork -
mesterpiece - performance

شاهنامه

/shâhnâme/ ► noun
epopee

شاهنشاهی

/shâhanshâhi/ ► adjective
imperial

شاهین

/shâhin/ ► noun
hawk

شایان

/shâyân/ ► noun
worthy - considerable

شایبه

/shâ'ebe/ ► noun
alloy

شاید

/shâyad/ ► adverb
maybe - may - perhaps - perchance -
peradventure - like - lest

شایستگی

/shâyestegi/ ► noun
sufficiency - competence - desert -
decency - eligibility - pertinence - merit
- aptness - aptitude - adequacy - ability

شایستگی داشتن

/shâyestegi dâshtan/ ► verb
able - deserve

شایسته

/shâyeste/ ► noun
proper - worthy - fit - competent -
intrinsic - meritorious - meet - becoming
- apt

شایسته بودن

/shâyeste budan/ ► verb
adequate - merit

شایسته ترین

/shâyestetarin/ ► adjective
best

شایع

/shâye'/ ► adjective
incident - prevalent - current - rife -
rampant - widespread

شایع شدن

/shâye' shodan/ ► verb
prevail

شایعات

/shâye'ât/ ► noun
canard - murmur

شایعه

/shâye'e/ ► noun
buzz - hearsay - grapevine

شب

/shab/ ▶ noun
eve - night

شب نشینی

/shabneshini/ ▶ noun
wake

شبان

/shabân/ ▶ noun
pastor - looker

شبانگاه

/shabângâh/ ▶ noun
nightfall

شبانه

/shabâne/ ▶ adjective
overnight - nocturnal - nightly

شباهت

/shabâhat/ ▶ noun
semblance - proportion - propinquity -
resemblance - equality - likeness -
analogy - analog - analogue

شبح

/shabah/ ▶ noun
sprite - spook - spectrum - ghost - wraith
- phantom - umbra - umber

شبکه

/shabake/ ▶ noun
trellis - lattice - mesh - plexus - network
- net - grille - grating - grate

شبکه ارتباطی

/shabakeye ertebâti/ ▶ noun
network

شبگرد

/shabgard/ ▶ noun
hobgoblin

شبنم

/shabnam/ ▶ noun
dew - frost

شبه

/shabah/ ▶ noun
quasi

شبه قاره

/shebhe ghâre/ ▶ noun
subcontinent

شبهه

/shobhe/ ▶ noun
doubt - misgiving

شبیه

/shabih/ ▶ noun
simile - similar - quasi - alike - likeness
- like - medal - make - rival - equal

شبیه سازی

/shabihsâzi/ ▶ noun
imagery

شپش

/shepesh/ ▶ noun
louse

شپشه

/shishe/ ▶ noun
weevil - louse

شتا

/shetâ/ ▶ noun
winter

شتاب

/shetâb/ ▶ noun
tilt - speed - velocity - pelt - hustle -
hurry - haste - dispatch

شتاب دادن

/shetâb dâdan/ ▶ verb
accelerate

شتاب زده

/shetâbzade/ ▶ adjective
hasty

شتابان

/shetâbân/ ▶ noun
expedite

شتافتن

/shetâftan/ ▶ verb
hasten

شتر

/shotor/ ▶ noun
camel

شتر در خواب بیند پنبه دانه :Idiom)
The cat dreams of mice)

شجاع

/shojâ'/ ▶ adjective
stark - gallant - valiant - intrepid - brave

شجاعت

/shojâ'at/ ▶ noun
courage - gallantry - heroism - pluck -
valor - manhood - bravery

شجره نامه

/shajarenâme/ ▶ noun
pedigree - genealogy

شخص

/shakhs/ ▶ noun
subject - specimen - dude - cove - figure
- one - guy - individual - person - man

شخصی

/shakhsi/ ▶ adjective
someone - somebody - own - one -
personal - personable

شخصیت

/shakhsiyat/ ▶ noun
self - character - personality - personage
- identity - individuality

شخم

/shokhm/ ▶ noun
plough - plow

شخم زدن

/shokhm zadan/ ▶ verb
husband - plough - plow

شخم کردن

/shokhm kardan/ ▶ verb
plough - plow

شدت

/shedat/ ▶ noun
severity - stringency - duress - gravity -
acrimony - intensity - violence -
vehemence - extremity

شدت داشتن

/shedat dâshtan/ ▶ verb
rage

شدت عمل

/shedate amal/ ▶ noun
arrogance - force

شدن

/shodan/ ▶ verb
wind - grow - lapse - branch - become -
be

شدنی

/shodani/ ▶ adjective
precipitant - possible

شدید

/shadid/ ▶ adjective
rigorous - hard - intensive - vigorous -
vehement - strenuous - stalwart -
sopping - severe - tough

شدید شدن

/shadid shodan/ ▶ verb
intensify

شدید کردن

/shadid kardan/ ▶ verb
keen - heighten

شدیدالحن

/shadidolahn/ ▶ adjective
overtone

شراب

/sharâb/ ▶ noun
wine

شرارت

/sherârat/ ▶ noun
iniquity - villainy - mischief -
malfeasance - depravity

شرافت

/sherâfat/ ▶ noun
honor

شرافتمند

/sherâfatmand/ ▶ adjective
upstanding

شرافتمندانه

/sherâfatmandâne/ ▶ adverb
honorable

شرایط

/sharâyet/ ▶ noun
term - qualification

شربت

/sharbat/ ▶ noun
juice - beverage - nectar

شرح

/sharh/ ▶ noun
description - explanation - gloss -
geography - tale - treatise - sketch

شرح حال

/sharhe hâl/ ▶ noun
memoir

شرح دادن

/sharh dâdan/ ▶ verb
explain - detail - describe - depict -
demonstrate - relate - narrate - give -
illustrate

شرشر

/shorshor/ ▶ adjective
gurgle

شرط

/shart/ ▶ noun
condition - reservation - clause

شرطی

/sharti/ ▶ adjective
provisional - eventual - conditional

شرعی

/shar'i/ ▶ adjective
legal - canonical - juridical - judicial
(ary)

شرف

/sharif/ ▶ noun
honor

شرق

/shargh/ ▶ noun
east - orient

شرقی

/sharghi/ ▶ adjective
oriental - eastward - eastern

شرکت

/sherkat/ ▶ noun
corporation - firm - cahoot - hand -
bodycorporate - unity

شرکت کردن

/sharkat kardan/ ▶ verb
participate - partake

شرکتی

/sharkati/ ▶ adjective
joint

شرم

/sharm/ ▶ noun
shame - pudency

شرم آور

/sharmâvar/ ▶ adjective
petulant - inglorious - indecent - gross -
shameful

شرمسار

/sharmsâr/ ▶ adjective
ashamed

شرمنده شدن

/sharmande/ ► verb
blush - bash

شرمنده کردن

/sharmande kardan/ ► verb
shame - abash

شروع

/shoru'/ ► noun
start - inception - resumption - onset

شروع کردن

/shoru' kardan/ ► verb
start - launch - begin - embark -
commence

شریان

/shariyân/ ► noun
artery

شریانی

/shariyâni/ ► adjective
arterial

شریف

/sharif/ ► adjective
patrician - honorable - noble

شریک

/sherik/ ► adjective
partner - participant - pal - complier -
copartner - consort

شریک کردن

/sherik kardan/ ► verb
associate

شست

/shast/ ► noun
thumb

شستشو

/shostoshu/ ► noun
wash - rinse - lavation - launder - bathe -
bath - ablution - lotion - souse

شستشو دادن

/shostoshu dâdan/ ► verb
wash

شستن

/shostan/ ► verb
scour - wash - leach - launder

شستنی

/shostani/ ► adjective
washable

شش

/shesh/ ► noun
six - lung

شش گانه

/sheshgâne/ ► adjective
sextet

شش گوشه

/sheshgushe/ ► adjective
hesagonal

شش ماهه

/sheshmâhe/ ► adjective
semiannual

ششم

/sheshom/ ► adjective
sixth

ششمین

/sheshomin/ ► adjective
sixth - six

شصت

/shast/ ► noun
sixty

شصتم

/shastom/ ► adjective
sixtieth

شصتمین

/shastomin/ ► adjective
sixtieth

شطرنج

/shatranj/ ► noun
chess

شطرنجی کردن

/shatranji kardan/ ► verb
checker

شعار

/sho'âr/ ► noun
slogan - motto - emblem - device - catch

شعاعی

/sho'â'i/ ► adjective
radiant - radial

شعبده

/sho'bade/ ► noun
juggle - legerdemain

شعبده باز

/sho'badebâz/ ► adjective
juggler

شعر

/she'r/ ► noun
song - rime - rhyme - poetry - poesy -
poem - verse - measure

شعله

/sho'le/ ► noun
flame

شعله ور

/sho'levar/ ► adjective
inflammable - alight - aflame - afire -
garish

شعور

/sho'ur/ ► noun
sense - reason

شغل

/shoghl/ ► noun
profession - position - vocation - employ
- occupation - job

شفته
/shefte/ ► adjective
vexatious - mortar

شفا
/shafâ/ ► noun
cure

شفق
/shafagh/ ► noun
twilight

شفا دادن
/shafâ dâdan/ ► verb
cure - heal - mend - medicate

شفیق
/shafigh/ ► adjective
sympathetic

شفابخش
/shafâbakhsh/ ► adjective
medicinal - medic - remedial - curative

شق شدن
/shagh shodan/ ► verb
erect

شفادهنده
/shafâd dahande/ ► adjective
healer

شک
/shak/ ► noun
skepticism - doubt - uncertainty

شفاعت
/shafâ'at/ ► noun
intervention - intercession

شک داشتن
/shak dâshtan/ ► verb
doubt - suspect

شفاف
/shafâf/ ► adjective
transparent - sleek - elucidate -
crystalline - crystal - lucid - perspicuous

شکار
/shekâr/ ► noun
prey - predatin - hunt - hank - quarry

شفاهی
/shafâhi/ ► noun
oral - verbal - unwritten

شکاربان
/shekârbân/ ► adjective
gamekeeper

شفتالو
/shaftâlu/ ► noun
peach

شکارچی
/shekârchi/ ► adjective
jaeger - hunter - woodman – gunner

شکارگاه
/shekârgâh/ ▶ noun
preserve

شکر
/shekar/ ▶ noun
sugar

شکاف
/shekâf/ ▶ noun
crack - notch - rake - fracture - fraction -
clef - chink - chasm - chap -

شکر
/shokr/ ▶ noun
thank

شکست
/shekast/ ▶ noun
breakage - break - washout - reverse -
refraction - fracture - setback

شکاف دادن
/shekâf dâdan/ ▶ verb
slash - shear - chap

شکافتن
/shekâftan/ ▶ verb
split - slit - slat - pierce - excision -
fracture - cleave - chink - rive

شکست دادن
/shekast dâdan/ ▶ verb
defeat - drub - floor - outdo - worst -
vanquish

شکافنده
/shekâfande/ ▶ adjective
ripping - cleaver

شکست فاحش
/shekaste fâhesh/ ▶ noun
lurch

شکاکی
/shakâki/ ▶ noun
incredulity

شکستن
/shekastan/ ▶ verb
break - crackle - nick - cleave - chop -
refract - fracture - fraction

شکایت
/shekâyat/ ▶ noun
grievance - complaint - rumble -
murmur - moan

شکستنی
/shekastani/ ▶ noun
breakage - breakable

شکایت کردن
/shekâyat kardan/ ▶ verb
bitch - complain

شکسته
/shekaste/ ▶ adjective
zigzag

شکسته نفسی
/shekaste nafsi/ ▶ noun
modesty

شکم درد
/shekamdard/ ▶ noun
bellyache

شکفتگی
/shekoftegi/ ▶ noun
efflorescence

شکمی
/shekami/ ▶ adjective
gastric - uterine - abdominal - ventral

شکفتن
/shekoftan/ ▶ verb
burst - nip - open - dehisce

شکن
/shekan/ ▶ noun
plica - crease

شکل
/shekl/ ▶ noun
shape - schema - configuration - form -
figure - image

شکنجه
/shekanje/ ▶ noun
torture - torment - rack

شکل دادن
/skhel dâdan/ ▶ verb
crystallize - model

شکنجه کردن
/shekanje kardan/ ▶ verb
excruciate

شکل گرفتن
/shekl gereftan/ ▶ verb
form

شکنندگی
/shekanandegi/ ▶ noun
frangibility

شکلک
/sheklak/ ▶ noun
grimace

شکننده
/shekanande/ ▶ adjective
brittle - plucky - frail

شکوفایی
/shokufâyi/ ▶ noun
efflorescence

شکم
/shekam/ ▶ noun
gorge - paunch - bulge - breadbasket -
bowel - belly - ventricle

شکوفه
/shekufe/ ▶ noun
blossom - bloom - chrysalis - flower

شکوفه دادن

/shekufe dâdan/ ► verb
flower

شگفت

/shegeft/ ► noun
surprise - stupendous - muse -
prodigious - wonder

شکوفه کردن

/shekufe kardan/ ► verb
bud - bloom

شگفت آور

/shegeftâvar/ ► adjective
extraordinary - exclamatory

شکوه

/shokuh/ ► noun
glory - refulgence - magnitude -
magneficence - pomp

شگفت انگیز

/shegeftangiz/ ► adjective
phenomenal - stupendous

شکوه کردن

/shekve kardan/ ► verb
gripe - plain

شگون

/shogun/ ► noun
presage - auspices - augur

شکیب

/shakib/ ► adjective
patience

شل

/shol/ ► adjective
slack - ramshackle - knockkneed - limp -
lax - loose - baggy

شکیبا

/shakibâ/ ► adjective
tolerant - patient

شل کردن

/shol kardan/ ► verb
relax - unstring - unloose - unhook -
unbrace - unbind - unbend - loosen

شکیبایی

/shakibâyi/ ► noun
fortitude - patience - sufferance

شلاق

/shalâgh/ ► noun
scourge - whiplash - whip - horsewhip -
lash - lambaste

شکیل

/shakil/ ► adjective
shapely - pretty

شگرف

/shegarf/ ► adjective
excellent - wondrous - fine - prodigious

شلاق زدن

/shalâgh zadan/ ► verb
whiplash - whip - belt - belabor - beat -
baste - leather

شمارشگر
/shomâreshgar/ ► noun
numerator

شلنگ
/shelang/ ► noun
hose

شماره
/shomâre/ ► noun
issue - numeral - number

شلوار
/shalvâr/ ► noun
pants - pantaloon

شمال
/shomâl/ ► noun
north

شلوغ
/sholugh/ ► adjective
messy - unquiet - busy - tumult

شمال باختری
/shomâle bâkhtari/ ► adjective
northwest

شلوغی
/sholughi/ ► noun
jumble - crowd - chaos - bustle

شمال خاوری
/shomâle khâvari/ ► adjective
northeast

شلی
/sholi/ ► adjective
slack

شمال شرق
/shomâle shargh/ ► noun
northeast

شلیل
/shalil/ ► noun
nectarine

شمال شرقی
/shomâle sharghi/ ► adjective
northeast

شما
/shomâ/ ► noun
you

شمال غرب
/shomâle gharb/ ► noun
northwest

شمار
/shomâr/ ► noun
count - unit

شمال غربی
/shomâle gharbi/ ► adjective
northwest

شمارش
/shomâresh/ ► noun
computation

شمالی
/shomâli/ ▶ adjective
northern

شمول
/shomul/ ▶ noun
incurrence - inclusion - liability

شمردن
/shemordan/ ▶ verb
enumerate - count - figure - number -
repute

شن
/shen/ ▶ noun
sand - grit - gravel

شمش
/shemsh/ ▶ noun
bullion - bar

شن پاشیدن
/shen pâshidan/ ▶ verb
gravel - sand

شمشیر
/shamshir/ ▶ noun
sword - steel - spurtle - blade

شن زار
/shenzâr/ ▶ noun
beach

شمشیرباز
/shamshirbâz/ ▶ noun
swordsman

شنا
/shenâ/ ▶ noun
swim

شمشیربازی
/shamshirbâzi/ ▶ noun
fencing

شنا کردن
/shenâ kardan/ ▶ verb
swim

شمشیرزن
/shamshirzan/ ▶ noun
swordsman

شناخت
/shenâkht/ ▶ noun
cognition - recognition

شمع
/sham'/ ▶ noun
stanchion

شناختن
/shenâkhtan/ ▶ verb
identify - notice - know - recognize

شمعدان
/sham'dân/ ▶ noun
candlestick

شناسایی
/shenâsâyi/ ▶ noun
identity - cognizance - recognition

شناکننده
/shenâ konande/ ▶ adjective
swimmer

شنونده
/shenavande/ ▶ noun
listener - auditor

شناگر
/shenâgar/ ▶ adjective
swimmer

شنیدن
/shenidan/ ▶ verb
hear - listen

شناور
/shenâvar/ ▶ adjective
afloat - adrift - buoyant

شنیدنی
/shenidani/ ▶ adjective
audible

شناور شدن
/shenâvar shodan/ ▶ verb
swim - float

شنیع
/shani'/ ▶ adjective
foul - nefarious - bawdy - hideous -
heinous

شنبه
/shanbe/ ▶ noun
sabbath

شهاب
/shahâb/ ▶ noun
meteor

شنگول
/shangul/ ▶ adjective
sprightly - sappy

شهادت
/shahâdat/ ▶ noun
testimony - testimonial - evidence -
martyrdom

شنل
/shenel/ ▶ noun
cape

شنوا
/shenavâ/ ▶ adjective
receptive

شهامت
/shahâmat/ ▶ noun
dare

شنوایی
/shenavâ'i/ ▶ noun
audition - hearing - ear

شهبانو
/shahbânu/ ▶ noun
empress - queen

شهد
/shahd/ ▶ noun
honey - molasses - ambrosia - ooze -
nectar

شهر
/shahr/ ▶ noun
town - city - parish

شهرت
/shohrat/ ▶ noun
notability - fame - reputation - renown -
attribute

شهرت داشتن
/shohrat dâshtan/ ▶ verb
repute

شهردار
/shahrdâr/ ▶ noun
municipality - mayor - provost

شهرستان
/shahrestân/ ▶ noun
township - county - parish

شهرک
/shahrak/ ▶ noun
town

شهرنشین
/shahrneshin/ ▶ noun
urbanite - urban

شهروند
/shahrvand/ ▶ noun
national - citizen

شهری
/shahri/ ▶ adjective
towny - twonsman - urban - civic

شهریار
/shahriyâr/ ▶ noun
sovereign - king - monarch

شهریه
/shahriye/ ▶ noun
salary

شهوانی
/shahvâni/ ▶ noun
lustful - lecherous - lascivious -
voluptuous - carnal - ruttish

شهوت
/shahvat/ ▶ noun
rut - lust

شهوت انگیز
/shahvatangiz/ ▶ adjective
sexy - voluptuous - lascivious - lusty -
luscious

شهوتران
/shahvatrân/ ▶ adjective
salacious - oversexed - voluptuous -
licentious - lecher

شهوترانی
/shahvatrâni/ ▶ noun
pleasure - lechery

شورانگیز
/shurangiz/ ► adjective
sensational

شهود
/shohud/ ► noun
intuition

شوربخت
/shurbakht/ ► adjective
unhappy

شهید
/shahid/ ► noun
martyr

شورش
/shuresh/ ► noun
riot - revolution - revolt - rebellion - uproar

شوالیه
/shovâliye/ ► noun
knight - cavalier

شوخ
/shukh/ ► adjective
joker - jocularity - jocular - jester

شورشی
/shureshi/ ► adjective
insurgent - rioter - rebel

شوروی
/shôravi/ ► noun
soviet

شوخ بودن
/shukh budan/ ► verb
joviality

شوخی
/shukhi/ ► noun
joke - jocosity - pleasantry - curvet - fun

شوری
/shuri/ ► noun
salinity

شوخی کردن
/shukhi kardan/ ► verb
joke - jest - trick - lark - indulge - fun

شوریدگی
/shuridegi/ ► noun
snarl

شور کردن
/shur kardan/ ► verb
salt

شوریدن
/shuridan/ ► verb
revolt - rebel

شورا
/shôrâ/ ► noun
council

شوریده
/shuride/ ► adjective
phrenetic - berserk - distraught - crazy

شیار
/shiyâr/ ▶ adjective
thread - ruck - rake

شوفر
/shufer/ ▶ noun
driver - chauffeur

شیب
/shib/ ▶ noun
declivity - gradient - rake - tilt - slope

شوق
/shôgh/ ▶ noun
zeal - ardor - delight

شیب دار
/shibdâr/ ▶ adjective
gradient - slope - shelvy

شوک
/shok/ ▶ noun
thistle

شوم
/shum/ ▶ adjective
unlucky - infelicitous - inauspicious -
ghastly - ominous

شیب داشتن
/shib dâshtan/ ▶ verb
tilt

شوهر
/shôhar/ ▶ noun
husband

شیب ملایم
/shibe molâyem/ ▶ noun
espianade

شوهردار
/shôhardâr/ ▶ adjective
married

شیپور
/sheipur/ ▶ noun
trumpet - bugle - horn - clarion

شوی
/shuy/ ▶ noun
husband

شیخ
/sheikh/ ▶ noun
patriarch

شیاد
/shayâd/ ▶ adjective
trickster

شیدا
/sheidâ/ ▶ adjective
manic - lovelorn

شیادی
/shayâdi/ ▶ noun
abusive - juggle

شیر

/shir/ ▶ noun
lion - milk

شیراب

/shirâb/ ▶ noun
tap - spout - spigot

شیرجه

/shirje/ ▶ noun
dive - plunge

شیرزن

/shirzan/ ▶ adjective
heroine

شیره

/shire/ ▶ noun
juice - syrup - extract - ooze - molasses

شیره ای

/shire'i/ ▶ adjective
junkie

شیری رنگ

/shiri rang/ ▶ adjective
milky

شیرینی

/shirini/ ▶ noun
cookie - confection - pastry - amiability
- bonbon

شیشه

/shishe/ ▶ noun
glass - bottle

شیشه آلات

/shishe'âlât/ ▶ noun
glass

شیشه بر

/shishebor/ ▶ noun
glazier

شیطان

/sheitân/ ▶ noun
devil - deuce - naughty

شیطنت

/sheitanat/ ▶ noun
mischief - shenanigan

شیطنت آمیز

/sheitanatâmiz/ ▶ adjective
sly

شیطنت کردن

/sheitanat kardan/ ▶ verb
monkey

شیفتگی

/shiftegi/ ▶ noun
preoccupation

شیفتن

/shiftan/ ▶ verb
charm - captivate - allure - mash

شیفته

/shifte/ ▶ adjective
amorous - fond - captive

شیک

/shik/ ► adjective
scrumptious - trig - swell - suave -
stylish - snappy

شیک پوش

/shikpush/ ► adjective
ritzy - dandy

شیمی دان

/shimidân/ ► noun
chemist

شیمیایی

/shimiyâyi/ ► noun
chemical

شیوا

/shivâ/ ► adjective
eloquent

شیوع

/shoyu'/ ► noun
prevalence - outbreak

شیون

/shivan/ ► noun
whimper

شیوه

/shive/ ► noun
method - pace - device - style -
technique

ص ‑صـ

sâd /se/ ▶ seventeenth letter of the Persian alphabet

صابون
/sâbun/ ▶ noun
soap

صاحب
/sâheb/ ▶ noun
master - owner - lord

صاحبخانه
/sâhebkhâne/ ▶ noun
host - landlord

صادر کردن
/sâder kardan/ ▶ verb
export

صادرات
/sâderât/ ▶ noun
export

صادرکننده
/sâder konande/ ▶ adjective
exporter

صادق
/sâdegh/ ▶ adjective
sincere - honest - leal - loyal

صادقانه
/sâdeghâne/ ▶ adverb
loyal - truly

صاعقه
/sâ'eghe/ ▶ noun
thunderbolt

صاف
/sâf/ ▶ adjective
plain - explicit - even - glossy - flat -
clear

صاف شدن
/sâf shodan/ ▶ verb
fine - smooth

صاف کردن
/sâf kardan/ ▶ verb
strain - smooth - sleek - serene - clear

صافی
/sâfi/ ▶ noun
gloss - leach - purity - strainer - serenity
- serene - scumble

صالح
/sâhel/ ▶ adjective
righteous

صامت
/sâmet/ ▶ noun
silent - speechless - mute - consonantal

صحرا
/sahrâ/ ▶ noun
desert - wilderness

صبح
/sobh/ ▶ noun
morning - daybreak

صحرایی
/sahrâyi/ ▶ adjective
outdoor

صبحانه
/sobhâne/ ▶ noun
breakfast

صحن
/sahn/ ▶ noun
apron

صبر
/sabr/ ▶ noun
patience

صحنه
/sahne/ ▶ noun
scene - arena

صبر کردن
/sabr kardan/ ▶ verb
wait

صحنه سازی
/sahnesâzi/ ▶ noun
histrionics - scenery

صبور
/sabur/ ▶ adjective
patient

صحه
/sehe/ ▶ noun
signature

صحبت
/sohbat/ ▶ noun
talk - speech - dialogue - converse -
colloquy

صحیح
/sahih/ ▶ adjective
right - correct - exact - safe - true

صحت
/sehat/ ▶ noun
rectitude - authenticity - accuracy -
precision - verity - veracity

صخره
/sakhre/ ▶ noun
cliff - rock - roach

صد
/sad/ ▶ noun
hundred

صدا

/sedâ/ ▶ noun
sound - tone - tingle - noise - voice -
vocation - vocal

صدا زدن

/sedâ zadan/ ▶ verb
hail - call

صدا کردن

/sedâ kardan/ ▶ verb
cry - click - clang - rustle

صداخفه کن

/sedâ khafekon/ ▶ noun
muffler - silencer

صدادار

/sedâdâr/ ▶ adjective
vowel - phonetic - sonorous - sonant

صداقت

/sedâghat/ ▶ noun
truth - loyalty - honesty - veracity

صدراعظم

/sadre'azam/ ▶ noun
chancellor

صدساله

/sadsâle/ ▶ adjective
centennial - centenary

صدف

/sadaf/ ▶ noun
shard - shale - pearl

صدق

/sedgh/ ▶ noun
truth - verity

صدقه

/sadaghe/ ▶ noun
charity - alms

صدمه

/sadame/ ▶ noun
injury - indemnity - hurt - harm

صدمه دیدن

/sadame didan/ ▶ verb
miscarry

صدمه زدن

/sadame zadan/ ▶ verb
scathe - nip - offend - damnify - harm -
maul - mar

صدور

/sodur/ ▶ noun
emission - issuance

صراحت

/serâhat/ ▶ noun
speciosity - precision

صراف

/sarâf/ ▶ adjective
banker - usurer - moneychanger

صرافی

/sarâfi/ ▶ noun
exchange

صرف

/sarf/ ▶ noun
expenditure

صرفا

/serfan/ ▶ adverb
alone - downright - only

صرفنظر

/sarfenazar/ ▶ noun
surrender - waiver

صرفه

/sarfe/ ▶ noun
gain - advantage

صرفه جو

/sarfeju/ ▶ adjective
thrifty - inexpensive - parsimonious

صریح

/sarih/ ▶ adjective
frank - definite - express - explicit -
abstract - unequivocal

صریحا

/sarihan/ ▶ adverb
expressly

صعب العبور

/sa'bol obur/ ▶ noun
impassable

صعود کردن

/so'ud kardan/ ▶ verb
soar - mount - up - ascend - climb - rise
- ramp

صغر

/seghr/ ▶ noun
imfancy

صغیر

/saghir/ ▶ verb
underage - lowly - lesser

صف

/saf/ ▶ noun
tier - muster - queue - array - army - cue
- rank - row

صف آرایی

/safârâyi/ ▶ noun
embattle

صف بستن

/saf bastan/ ▶ verb
cue

صفا

/safâ/ ▶ noun
ingenuity - candour - candor - serenity -
purity

صفت

/sefat/ ▶ noun
quality - qualification - adjective

صفحه

/safhe/ ▶ noun
folio - leaf - brede - page - sheet - tablet

صفر

/sefr/ ▶ noun
zero - null - nothing

صفرا

/safrâ/ ▶ noun
bile - gall - yellowbile

صفیر

/safir/ ▶ noun
whistle - whish

صلاحدید

/salâhdid/ ▶ noun
discretion - government

صلاحیت

/salâhiyat/ ▶ noun
qualification - competence - capacity -
capability

صلاحیتدار

/salâhdid/ ▶ adjective
capable

صلح

/solh/ ▶ noun
peace

صلح آمیز

/solhâmiz/ ▶ adjective
peaceful

صلح جو

/solhju/ ▶ adjective
pacifier - pacific

صلیب

/salib/ ▶ noun
cross

صمیمانه

/samimâne/ ▶ adverb
hearty - earnest

صمیمی

/samimi/ ▶ adjective
sincere - unaffected - privy - heartfelt -
hailfellow - intimate - cordial - warm

صمیمیت

/samimiyat/ ▶ noun
sincerity - devotion - confidence -
intimacy

صندل

/sandal/ ▶ noun
sandal

صندلی

/sandali/ ▶ noun
chair - seat

صندوق خانه

/sandoghkhâne/ ▶ noun
closet

صندوقچه
/sandoghche/ ► noun
ark - kist

صندوقدار
/sandoghdâr/ ► noun
cashier

صنعت
/san'at/ ► noun
industry

صنعتی
/san'ati/ ► adjective
industrial

صنف
/senf/ ► noun
order - guild - caste

صنوبر
/senobar/ ► noun
spruce - pinon - pine

صوت
/sôt/ ► noun
phoneme - voice

صوتی
/sôti/ ► adjective
sonic - sonant - vowel - vocal -
phomenic

صورت
/surat/ ► noun
roll - figure - face - aspect - visage -
medal - phase - list

با سیلی صورت خود را سرخ نگه داشتن :Idiom)
Live in genteel poverty)

صورت غذا
/surate ghazâ/ ► noun
menu

صورت گرفتن
/surat gereftan/ ► verb
accomplish

صوری
/suri/ ► noun
superficial - simulate - nominal -
ostensible

صومعه
/sôme'e/ ► noun
monastery - abbey - convent - cloister

صیاد
/sayâd/ ► noun
hunter

صید
/seid/ ► noun
quarry - prey - predatin - raven

صیغه
/sighe/ ► noun
concubine

صیقل
/seighal/ ► noun
burnish - varnish

صیقلی

/sheighali/ ► adjective
smooth - slight - sleek - shiny - levigate
- glossy - reflective

ض – ضـ

zâd /ze/ ► eighteenth letter of the Persian alphabet

ضابط

/zâbet/ ► noun
archivist - constable

ضابطه

/zâbete/ ► noun
criterion - topic

ضامن

/zâmen/ ► adjective
sponsor - guarantor - guarantee

ضایع

/zâye'/ ► adjective
lost

ضایع شدن

/zâye' shodan/ ► verb
rot

ضایعات

/zâye'ât/ ► noun
culch - garble - wastage - loss

ضبط

/zabt/ ► noun
retention - record - seizure

ضخامت

/zekhâmat/ ► noun
diameter

ضخیم

/zakhim/ ► adjective
squatty - russeting - russet - gross

ضد

/zed/ ► noun
opposite - opponent - foe - hostile -
antagonist - adversary

ضدآب

/zede'âb/ ► adjective
waterproof

ضدصدا

/zede'sedâ/ ► adjective
soundproof

ضدیت

/zediyat/ ► noun
opposition

ضدیخ

/zedeyakh/ ► noun
antifreeze

ضرب العجل

/zarbolajal/ ► noun
deadline

ضرب المثل

/zarbolmasal/ ▶ noun
proverb - sooth - byword

ضرب کردن

/zarb kardan/ ▶ verb
muliply

ضرب و جرح

/zarbo jarh/ ▶ noun
maim - battery

ضربان قلب

/zarabâne ghalb/ ▶ noun
heartbeat

ضربت

/zarbat/ ▶ noun
crack - coup - contusion - whack -
knock - pound - pounce - plunk

ضربه

/zarbe/ ▶ noun
impact - hook - hew - hack - lash

ضربه زدن

/zarbe zadan/ ▶ verb
dabber - layon - butt

ضرر

/zarar/ ▶ noun
harm - loss - detriment - washout

ضرورت

/zarurat/ ▶ noun
cogency - necessity - exigency - urgency

ضروری

/zaruri/ ▶ adjective
urgent - obligate - needful - necessary

ضریب

/zarib/ ▶ noun
coefficient

ضعف

/za'f/ ▶ noun
swoon - languor - infirmity -
depauperation

ضعیف

/za'if/ ▶ adjective
weak - pusillanimous - puny - slender -
slack - shaky

ضعیف شدن

/za'if shodan/ ▶ verb
weaken

ضمانت

/zemânat/ ▶ noun
guaranty - guarantee - warranty -
responsibility - sponsorship

ضمانت کردن

/zemânat kardan/ ▶ verb
insure - guarantee - sponsor

ضمایم

/zamâ'em/ ▶ noun
paraphernalia - complement

ضمنا

/zemnan/ ▶ adverb
tacit - meanwhile - meantime

ضمنی

/zemni/ ▶ noun
tacit - accident - incident

ضمیر

/zamir/ ▶ noun
conscience - ego

ضمیمه

/zamime/ ▶ noun
supplement - enclosure - appurtenance -
appendix - appendage - annex

ضیافت

/ziyâfat/ ▶ noun
repast - banquet - symposium

ط

tâ /te/ ▶ ninteenth letter of the Persian alphabet

طاس
/tâs/ ▶ adjective
dibs - bald

طاعون
/tâ'un/ ▶ noun
plague - pest

طاق
/tâgh/ ▶ noun
roof - arch - arc - azygos - vault

طاق زدن
/tâgh zadan/ ▶ verb
roof

طاقت
/tâghat/ ▶ noun
lip - patience - nerve - gut - sufferance - stamina

طاقت داشتن
/tâghat dâshtan/ ▶ verb
tolerate

طاقت فرسا
/tâghatfarsâ/ ▶ adjective
onerous - cumbersome - severe - troublous - tiresome

طاقچه
/tâghche/ ▶ noun
niche - ledge

طالب
/tâleb/ ▶ adjective
wishful - applicant

طالبی
/tâlebi/ ▶ noun
cantaloupe

طالع
/tâle'/ ▶ adjective
horoscope - fortune

طاهر
/tâher/ ▶ noun
clean

طاووس
/tâvus/ ▶ noun
peacock

طایفه
/tâyefe/ ▶ noun
tribe - phyle - nation - race - clan

طب
/teb/ ▶ noun
medicine - physic

طبال

/tabâl/ ▶ noun
beater

طبع

/tab'/ ▶ noun
impression - impress

طبق

/tebghe/ ▶ noun
tray

طبقه

/tabaghe/ ▶ noun
sort - estate - order - grain - genus - race
- class

طبقه بندی

/tabaghe bandi/ ▶ noun
taxonomy - division - bracket

طبل

/tabl/ ▶ noun
drum

طبله

/table/ ▶ noun
belly

طبی

/tebi/ ▶ adjective
medical

طبیب

/tabib/ ▶ noun
leech - medico - medic

طبیعت

/tabi'at/ ▶ noun
temperament - quality - inclination -
navigate - nature

طبیعی

/tabi'i/ ▶ adjective
physical - intrinsic - innate - indigenous
- real - normal - natural

طحال

/tahâl/ ▶ noun
lien

طراح

/tarâh/ ▶ noun
drawer - draftsman - designer - tracer -
sketcher

طراوت

/tarâvat/ ▶ noun
effervescence

طرب

/tarab/ ▶ noun
joviality - jollification - jocularity

طرح

/tarh/ ▶ noun
pattern - plot - model - layout - outline -
skeleton - proposal - scheme - schema

طرح ریزی

/tarhrizi/ ▶ noun
skeleton - schematization - projection

طرح کردن

/tarh kardan/ ► verb
advance - manoeuvre - draft - frame -
chart - cast

طرفدار بودن

/tarafdâr budan/ ► verb
adhere

طرد

/tard/ ► noun
ostracism

طرفداری

/tarafdâri/ ► noun
adhesion - devotion

طرد کردن

/tard krdan/ ► verb
excommunicate

طره

/tare/ ► noun
crimp - ringlet - whisker - tuft

طرز

/tarz/ ► noun
method - manner - rate - garb - order -
way

طریق

/tarigh/ ► noun
way - road

طرزتفکر

/tarze fekr/ ► noun
ideology

طریقت

/tarighat/ ► noun
path

طرزکار

/tarzekâr/ ► noun
workmanship

طریقه

/tarighe/ ► noun
system - form - way - mode - method -
manner

طرف

/taraf/ ► noun
opponent - party - avuncular - hand -
half - side

طشت

/tasht/ ► noun
tub

طعم

/ta'm/ ► noun
taste - savor - palate - relish - flavor -
gusto - odor

طرفدار

/tarafdâr/ ► adjective
proponent - cohort - votary - advocate -
party - partisan - partial

طعمه

/to'me/ ▶ noun
prey - victim

طعنه

/ta'ne/ ▶ noun
sikt - scoff - satire - sarcasm - jest - jeer

طغیان

/toghyân/ ▶ noun
tornado - revolt - rebellion - overflow -
outflow - outburst - outbreak - uprising

طغیان کردن

/toghyân kardan/ ▶ verb
muitiny - arise - uprise - overflow - rise
- flood

طفره

/tafre/ ▶ noun
jink - subterfuge - stall - procrastination
- evasion - fetch

طفره رفتن

/tafre raftan/ ▶ verb
parry - pussyfoot - prolong - jink

طفل

/tefl/ ▶ noun
baby - babe - peewee - infant - child -
tyke

طفولیت

/tofuliat/ ▶ noun
childhood

طلا

/talâ/ ▶ noun
gold

طلاق

/talâgh/ ▶ noun
divorce

طلایی

/talâyi/ ▶ adjective
auburn - golden - gilt

طلب

/talab/ ▶ noun
demand - quest

طلب کردن

/talab kardan/ ▶ verb
invoke - fish

طلبکار

/talabkâr/ ▶ adjective
creditor

طلبیدن

/talabidan/ ▶ verb
seek - ask - invite - crave

طلسم

/telesm/ ▶ noun
glamor - glamour - charm - incantation -
talisman

طلق

/talgh/ ▶ noun
talc - isinglass

طلوع

/tolu'/ ▶ noun
dawn - rise - break - peep

طهارت

/tahârat/ ▶ noun
purity

طماع

/tam'mâ'/ ▶ noun
greedy - avaricious

طوافی کردن

/tavâfi kardan/ ▶ verb
hawk - vend - peddle

طمع

/tama'/ ▶ noun
greed - avidity - avarice

طور

/tôr/ ▶ noun
sort

طناب

/tanâb/ ▶ noun
tow - line - rope - reeve

طوفان

/tufân/ ▶ noun
deluge - gale - flood - cataclysm -
hurricane

طناز

/tanâz/ ▶ adjective
coquette

طوفانی

/tufâni/ ▶ adjective
foul - windy

طنازی کردن

/tanâzi kardan/ ▶ verb
coquette

طوقه

/tôghe/ ▶ noun
torque - ring

طنز

/tanz/ ▶ noun
scoff - satire - jeer - irony - quip

طوقی

/tôghi/ ▶ noun
torpid

طنین

/tanin/ ▶ noun
sonance - ring - resonance - noise

طول

/tul/ ▶ noun
abscissa - length

طنین افکندن

/tanin afkandan/ ▶ verb
din

طولانی

/tulâni/ ▶ adjective
prolix - long - great

طولی

/tuli/ ► noun
linear

طومار

/tumâr/ ► noun
roll - role - scroll

طویل

/tavil/ ► adjective
major - long - lengthy

طویله

/tavile/ ► noun
stable - barn

طی

/tei/ ► noun
duration

طی شدن

/tei shodan/ ► verb
blowover

طی کردن

/tei kardan/ ► verb
traverse - negotiate - cover

طیاره

/tayâre/ ► noun
aircraft - aeroplane

طیف

/teif/ ► noun
spectrum

ظ

zâ /ze/ ► twentieth letter of the Persian alphabet

ظالم
/zâlem/ ► adjective
cruel - wroth - grim - remorseless - ruthless - incubus - heinous

ظالمانه
/zâlemâne/ ► adverb
tyrannous - tyrannical - burdensome - outrageous

ظاهر
/zâher/ ► noun
face - outside - ostensible - mien - hue - habit - look - aspect - appearance

ظاهر شدن
/zâher shodan/ ► verb
seem - spring - out - look

ظاهرسازی
/zâhersâzi/ ► adjective
histrionics

ظاهرنما
/zâhernamâ/ ► adjective
seeming

ظاهری
/zâheri/ ► adjective
outwards - seeming - surface - superficial

ظرافت
/zerâfat/ ► noun
precision - nicety - grace - delicacy - elegance

ظرف
/zarf/ ► noun
dish - container - can - repository - receptacle - adverb - vessel - vase

ظرفشویی
/zarfshuyi/ ► noun
dishwasher

ظروف
/zoruf/ ► noun
utensil

ظریف
/zarif/ ► adjective
capillary - delicate - slender - sheer

ظفر
/zafar/ ► noun
victory

ظلم
/zolm/ ► noun
cruelty - injustice - tyranny

ظلمانی

/zolmâni/ ▶ noun
tenebrific

ظن

/zan/ ▶ noun
conjecture - guess - hunch - surmise

ظن داشتن

/zan dâshtan/ ▶ verb
mistrust

ظنین

/zanin/ ▶ adjective
suspicious

ظهر

/zohr/ ▶ noun
midday - meridian - noontide - noon

ظهور

/zohur/ ▶ noun
outburst - outbreak - emersion - income
- peep - appearance

ظواهر

/zavâher/ ▶ noun
external

ع – عـ

ein /e/ ▶ twenty-first letter of the Persian alphabet

عابد
/âbed/ ▶ adjective
votary - devout

عابر
/âber/ ▶ noun
passer - passenger

عاج
/â'j/ ▶ noun
tusk - ivory

عاجز
/âjez/ ▶ adjective
septum - unable - incapable - determinant - cripple

عاجل
/âjel/ ▶ adjective
prompt

عاجلانه
/âjelâne/ ▶ adverb
pronto

عادت
/âdat/ ▶ noun
addict - accustom - hank - vogue - rut - rote - wont - custom

عادت دادن
/âdat dâshtan/ ▶ verb
accustom

عادت کردن
/âdat kardan/ ▶ verb
get

عادل
/âdel/ ▶ adjective
righteous

عادلانه
/âdelâne/ ▶ adverb
square

عادی
/â'di/ ▶ adjective
usual - uncritical - habitual - customary - ornery - ordinary - normal - naked - common - rife - regular

عارضه
/âreze/ ▶ noun
phenomenon

عاری
/âri/ ▶ noun
bare - devoid

عاطفه

/â'tefe/ ▶ noun
heart - sentiment

عاری از

/âri az/ ▶ noun
void

عاطل

/â'tel/ ▶ adjective
unemployed

عاریه

/âriye/ ▶ noun
loan

عاقبت

/âghebat/ ▶ noun
finale

عازم

/âzem/ ▶ adjective
off

عاقل

/âghel/ ▶ adjective
sane - sage - sagacious - sober - wise -
canny

عازم شدن

/âzem shodan/ ▶ verb
pullout - start - leave - embark

عاشق

/âshegh shodan/ ▶ adjective
paramour - lover – amorous

عاقلانه

/âghelane/ ▶ adverb
wise

(Idiom: یک دل نه صد دل عاشق کسی بودن
Love somebody head over heels)

عالم

/âlem/ ▶ adjective
scientist - universe - erudite - orb -
world

عاشق بودن

/âshegh budan/ ▶ verb
love

عالمگیر

/âlamgir/ ▶ adjective
epidemic - universal

عاشقانه

/âsheghâne/ ▶ adverb
amorous

عالی

/âli/ ▶ adjective
supreme - superb - super - remarkable -
exquisite - excellent

عاصی

/â'si/ ▶ adjective
sinner - sinful

عالی مقام

/âlimaghâm/ ▶ adjective
dignitary

عالیرتبه

/âlirotbe/ ▶ adjective
official

عام

/âm/ ▶ adjective
ecumenical - generic

عامل

/âmel/ ▶ noun
operative - element - doer - potential -
agent

عامی

/âmi/ ▶ adjective
layman - laic - illiterate - secular

عامیانه

/âmiyâne/ ▶ adverb
slangy - vulgar

عایدی

/âyedi/ ▶ noun
revenue - income - mean

عایق

/âyegh/ ▶ adjective
damper - brake - insulator - impediment
- pawl

عبا

/abâ/ ▶ noun
cloak

عبادت

/ebâdat/ ▶ noun
worship

عبارت

/ebârat/ ▶ noun
term - diction - quotation - word -
phrase

عبارت بودن از

/ebârat budan az/ ▶ verb
consist

عبث

/abas/ ▶ noun
vain - absurd

عبرت

/ebrat/ ▶ noun
example - byword

عبور

/obur/ ▶ noun
transmittal - transmission - transit -
passage - pass

عبور و مرور

/oburo morur/ ▶ noun
traffic

عبوس
/abus/ ▶ adjective
rusty - grim - lower - morose - moody - peevish - sullen - sulky - stern

عبوس بودن
/abus budan/ ▶ verb
gloom

عبوسانه
/abusâne/ ▶ adverb
sullen - black

عتاب
/atâb/ ▶ noun
pounce

عتیق
/atigh/ ▶ noun
early

عتیقه
/atighe/ ▶ adjective
antique - relic - curio

عتیقه شناس
/atigheshenâs/ ▶ noun
antiquarian

عجب
/ajab/ ▶ noun
benedicite

عجبا
/ajabâ/ ▶ adverb
zounds - zooks

عجز
/ajz/ ▶ noun
intolerance - insufficiency - insufficience - inability - paralysis

عجله
/ajale/ ▶ noun
snap - speed - expediency - post - hustle - hurry - haste

عجله کردن
/ajale kardan/ ▶ verb
hurry - haste

عجوزه
/ajuze/ ▶ adjective
mare - hellcat - hag - trot

عجول
/ajul/ ▶ adjective
rash - headlong - hasty - madbrained

عدالت
/edâlat/ ▶ noun
equanimity - justice

عداوت
/edâvat/ ▶ noun
hatred - odium - rancor - enmity

عدد
/adad/ ▶ noun
tot - digit - figure - number - piece - head

عدد زوج
/adade zôj/ ▶ noun
even

عراق
/adasi/ ▶ noun
Iraq

عددی
/adadi/ ▶ adjective
numeral

عراقی
/arâghi/ ▶ adjective
Iraqi

عدسی
/adasi/ ▶ noun
glass - lens

عرب
/arab/ ▶ noun
Arab

عدل
/adl/ ▶ noun
bale

عربی
/arabi/ ▶ adjective
arabian - arabic

عدم
/adam/ ▶ noun
want - nought - nonentity - naught

عرش
/arsh/ ▶ noun
height - heaven

عدم رضایت
/adame rezâyat/ ▶ noun
dissatisfaction

عرشه
/arshe/ ▶ noun
shipboard

عده
/ed'e/ ▶ noun
force

عرصه
/orze/ ▶ noun
arena - ring - compound

عدو
/adu/ ▶ noun
foe - enemy

عرض
/arz/ ▶ noun
width - breadth

عذاب
/azâb/ ▶ noun
torture - torment - tribulation

عرضه
/arze/ ▶ noun
offer - proffer - presentation

عرضی	عروس
/arzi/ ▶ adjective phenomenal	/arus/ ▶ noun bride
عرعر	عروسک
/ar'ar/ ▶ adjective bray	/arusak/ ▶ noun toy - puppet - doll
عرف	عروسک بازی
/orf/ ▶ noun tradition - custom - institution - usance - usage - ure - unwrittenlaw	/arusakbâzi/ ▶ noun puppetry
عرفان	عروسی
/erfân/ ▶ noun theosophy	/arusi/ ▶ noun wedding- matrimony - marriage
عرق	عریان
/aragh/ ▶ noun sweat - distillate - arrack	/oryân/ ▶ adjective naked - nude
عرق کردن	عریب
/aragh kardan/ ▶ verb sweat	/orib/ ▶ noun unaccountable
عرق گیر	عریض
/araghgir/ ▶ noun pullover - sweater	/ariz/ ▶ adjective wide - broad
عرقچین	عریضه
/araghchin/ ▶ noun skullcap	/arize/ ▶ noun petition
عروج	عزادار
/oruj/ ▶ noun ascent	/azâdâr/ ▶ adjective weepy - mournful - plaintful

عشوه
/eshve/ ▶ noun
ogle

عزت
/ezat/ ▶ noun
honor

عشوه گر
/eshvegar/ ▶ adjective
coquettish - coquette

عزل
/azal/ ▶ noun
deposition

عشیره
/ashire/ ▶ noun
tribe - phyle

عزل کردن
/azl kardan/ ▶ verb
dethrone

عصا
/asâ/ ▶ noun
cane - rod - wand - bat - stick

عزم
/azm/ ▶ noun
purpose - avow - impetus - resolution -
decision

عصاره
/osâre/ ▶ adjective
extract - distillate - sap - juice

عزیز
/aziz/ ▶ adjective
dear - darling - chary

عصب
/asab/ ▶ noun
nerve - chord

عزیمت
/azimat/ ▶ noun
departure - outgo - flight

عصبانیت
/asabâni/ ▶ noun
chafe - huff - heat - ire

عزیمت کردن
/azimat kardan/ ▶ verb
start - vamoose - pike - go

عصبی
/asabi/ ▶ adjective
neurotic - overwrought

عسل
/asal/ ▶ noun
honey

عصر
/asr/ ▶ noun
age - afternoon - period - era - epoch

عطسه
/atse/ ▶ noun
sniffle - sneeze

عصیان
/osyân/ ▶ noun
sin

عطسه کردن
/atse kardan/ ▶ verb
sneeze

عضلانی
/azolâni/ ▶ adjective
muscular

عطش
/atash/ ▶ noun
thirst

عضله
/azole/ ▶ noun
muscle

عطف
/atf/ ▶ noun
reference

عضو
/ozv/ ▶ noun
organ - limb - member - part

عظیم الجثه
/azimoljose/ ▶ adjective
monster - gargantuan - whale

عضویت
/ozviyat/ ▶ noun
membership

عفت
/efat/ ▶ noun
purity - honor - virtue - modesty

عطا
/atâ/ ▶ noun
grant

عفو
/afv/ ▶ noun
remission

عطا کردن
/atâ kardan/ ▶ verb
betake

عفو کردن
/afv kardan/ ▶ verb
forgive - absolve

عطار
/atâr/ ▶ noun
grocer

عفونت
/ofunat/ ▶ noun
putrefaction

عطر
/atr/ ▶ noun
smell - scent - odor - ambrosia - perfume

عقب نشاندن
/aghab neshândan/ ► verb
retreat - drive

عفونی کردن
/ofuni kardan/ ► verb
infect

عقب نشینی
/aghabneshini/ ► noun
scuttle - retreat - recess

عفیف
/afif/ ► adjective
clean - chaste - virtuous - virgin - honest

عقبه
/aghabe/ ► noun
sequel

عقاب
/oghâb/ ► noun
eagle

عقد کردن
/aghd kardan/ ► verb
espouse

عقب
/aghab/ ► noun
rear - behind - back - abaft - tail

عقده
/oghde/ ► noun
knot

عقب افتادگی
/aghab oftâdegi/ ► noun
leeway

عقده روحی
/oghdeye ruhi/ ► noun
obsession

عقب تر
/aghabtar/ ► adjective
yond - latter - posterior

عقرب
/aghrab/ ► noun
scorpion

عقب کشیدن
/aghabkeshidan/ ► verb
recede - shrink - setback

عقربه
/aghrabe/ ► noun
hand - poniter

عقب ماندگی
/aghabmândegi/ ► noun
lag

عقل
/aghl/ ► noun
tact - sagacity - reason - wisdom - intellect

عقب مانده
/aghabmânde/ ► adjective
behind - backward - laggard

عقلانی
/aghlâni/ ▶ adjective
intellectual - rational

عقلانیت
/aghlâniyat/ ▶ noun
rationality

عقیده
/aghide/ ▶ noun
thought - doctrine - faith - opinion -
belief - viewpoint

عقیده داشتن
/aghide dâshtan/ ▶ verb
have

عقیم
/aghim/ ▶ adjective
sterile - barren - abortive

عکاس
/akâs/ ▶ noun
photographer

عکاسی
/akâsi/ ▶ noun
photography

عکس
/aks/ ▶ noun
shot - vignette - picture - photograph

عکس العمل
/aksol'amal/ ▶ noun
repercussion - reaction

عکس بردار
/aksbardâr/ ▶ noun
photographer

علاج
/alâj/ ▶ noun
cure - remedy

علاج بخش
/alâjbakhsh/ ▶ adjective
curative

علاقمند
/alâghemand/ ▶ adjective
fond

علاقمند بودن
/alâghemand budan/ ▶ verb
care - like

علاقه
/alâghe/ ▶ noun
interest - bind

علاقه مند
/alâghemand/ ▶ adjective
enthusiastic - enthusiast

علامت
/alâmat/ ▶ noun
signal - sign - showing - symptom –
symbol - marker - mark

علامت گذاری
/alâlamtgozari/ ▶ noun
demarcation

علامت گذاشتن

/alâmat gozâshtan/ ▶ verb
trig - mark

علت

/elat/ ▶ noun
reason - cause - disease - motive

علف

/alaf/ ▶ noun
herb - vegetable - grass

علف چیدن

/alaf chidan/ ▶ verb
mow

علف چین

/alafchin/ ▶ noun
haymaker - mower

علف خشک

/alafe khoshk/ ▶ noun
hay

علف خوردن

/alaf khordan/ ▶ verb
grass

علفزار

/alafzâr/ ▶ noun
meadow - lawn - arbor

علم

/elm/ ▶ noun
science - knowledge

علم غیب

/elme gheib/ ▶ noun
prescience

علم نجوم

/elme nojum/ ▶ noun
astronomy

علنی

/alani/ ▶ adjective
aboveboard

علو

/alô/ ▶ noun
excellency - predominance - ascendency

علوفه

/olufe/ ▶ noun
provender - feed

علوم انسانی

/olume ensâni/ ▶ noun
humanism

علوی

/alavi/ ▶ noun
astral - ethereal - empyreal - celestial

علی رغم

/alâraghm/ ▶ preposition
notwithstanding

علیحده

/alâ'ede/ ▶ preposition
another - separate

علیرغم
/alâraghm/ ▶ preposition
never&eless

عمارت
/emârat/ ▶ noun
edifice - construction - hall

عمامه
/amâme/ ▶ noun
sash - turban

عمده
/omde/ ▶ adjective
significant - major - main - principal -
prime - primary - predominant -
essential - dominant

عمده فروش
/omdeforush/ ▶ noun
wholesaler

عمده فروشی
/omdeforushi/ ▶ noun
wholesale

عمدی
/amdi/ ▶ adjective
studied - intentional - deliberate

عمر
/omr/ ▶ noun
age - lifetime - life

عمق
/omgh/ ▶ noun
depth

عمقی
/omghi/ ▶ adjective
deepseated

عمل
/amal/ ▶ noun
act - function - operation - work -
exploit - experiment

عمل آوردن
/amal âvardan/ ▶ verb
treat

عمل جراحی
/amale jarâhi/ ▶ noun
surgery - operation

عمل کردن
/amal kardan/ ▶ verb
act - exercise - do - work - function

عملکرد
/amalkard/ ▶ noun
turnover - work

عمله
/amale/ ▶ noun
laborer - labor - worker

عملی
/amali/ ▶ adjective
practical - practicable - operative

عناصر

/anâsor/ ▶ noun
ingredient

عملی بودن

/amali budan/ ▶ verb
practicability

عنان

/anân/ ▶ noun
rein - bridle

عمه

/ame/ ▶ noun
aunt

عنتر

/antar/ ▶ noun
wanderoo

عمو

/amu/ ▶ noun
uncle

عنصر

/onsor/ ▶ noun
element

عمود

/amud/ ▶ noun
staple

عنف

/onf/ ▶ noun
force

عموزاده

/amuzâde/ ▶ noun
german

عنقریب

/angharib/ ▶ noun
soon

عموم

/omum/ ▶ noun
public

عنکبوت

/ankabut/ ▶ noun
insect

عمومی

/omumi/ ▶ noun
public - common - general - universal

عهد

/ahd/ ▶ noun
time - testament - promise - vow - pact -
avow - word - clause - era - covenant

عمیق

/amigh/ ▶ adjective
profound - recondite - deep

عهد شکستن

/ahdshekan/ ▶ verb
perjure

عناد

/enâd/ ▶ noun
malice - animus

عهدشکن
/ahd shekastan/ ► adjective
trespasser

عهده
/ohde/ ► noun
responsibility

عوارض
/avârez/ ► noun
toll - imposition - duty - due

عواقب
/avâgheb/ ► noun
backwash

عوام
/avâm/ ► noun
community - popular - laity

عوامانه
/avâmâne/ ► adverb
common - vulgar

عوامل
/avâmel/ ► noun
factors

عود
/ôd/ ► noun
reversion - relapse - regression -
recurrence - lute

عودت
/ôdat/ ► noun
relapse

عوض
/avaz/ ► noun
surrogate - substitute - stead - lieu -
reparation - recompense

عوض شدن
/avaz shodan/ ► verb
change

عوض کردن
/avaz kardan/ ► verb
exchange - remodel - change - alter -
vary

عوض و بدل
/avazo badal/ ► noun
alternate

عوعو
/ô'ô/ ► noun
bark

عوعو کردن
/ô'ô kardan/ ► verb
yowl - yip - yap - snap - bay

عیادت
/ayâdat/ ► noun
visit

عیادت کردن
/ayâdat kardan/ ► verb
visit

عید
/eid/ ► noun
tide

عیار
/ayâr/ ► noun
carat - rover - alloy

عید پاک
/eide pâk/ ► noun
easter

عیاشی
/ayâshi/ ► noun
jollity - binge - mask - debauchery -
debauch - revelry

عید فطر
/eide fetr/ ► noun
passover

عیاشی کردن
/ayâshi kardan/ ► verb
revel

عیسی
/isâ/ ► noun
jesus - christ

عیب
/eib/ ► noun
taint - defect - gall - vice - blot

عیش
/eish/ ► noun
luxury - mirth - pleasure

عیب جویانه
/eibjuyâne/ ► adverb
censorious

عین
/ein/ ► noun
exact - self

عیبجو
/eibju/ ► adjective
cynical - nag

عینا
/einan/ ► adverb
plumb - exact

عیبجویی
/eibjuyi/ ► noun
knock - denunciation - criticism

عینک
/einak/ ► noun
glass

عیبجویی کردن
/eibjuyi kardan/ ► verb
pick - henpeck - nag

عینک سازی
/einaksâzi/ ► noun
optometry

عینی بودن

/eini budan/ ► verb
objectivity

عینیت

/einiyat/ ► noun
identity

غ – غـ

ghein /ghe/ ▶ twenty-second letter of the Persian alphabet

غار
/ghâr/ ▶ noun
cave - grotto - vault

غارت
/ghârat/ ▶ noun
predatin - plunderage - plunder - pillage - ravage - despoliation

غارتگر
/ghâratgar/ ▶ adjective
robber - predatory - marauder

غارتگری
/ghâratgari/ ▶ noun
sack - rapacity

غارغار کردن
/ghâr ghâr kardan/ ▶ verb
croak

غارنشین
/ghârneshin/ ▶ noun
caveman

غاز
/ghâz/ ▶ noun
venue - goose

غاصب
/ghâseb/ ▶ adjective
usurper - impostor - violator

غافلگیر
/ghâfelgir/ ▶ adjective
aback

غافلگیر کردن
/ghâfelgir kardan/ ▶ verb
surprise

غالب
/ghâleb/ ▶ adjective
dominant - conqueror - overbearing - predominant

غالب اوقات
/ghâlebe ôghât/ ▶ noun
often

غالبا
/ghâleban/ ▶ adverb
freuqently

غامض
/ghâmez/ ▶ noun
unintelligible - abstruse - problematic - knotty

غایب
/ghâyeb/ ► adjective
absent - away - away

غایب شدن
/ghâyeb shodan/ ► verb
disappear

غبار
/ghobâr/ ► noun
mist - film - dust

غبطه
/ghebte/ ► noun
grudge

غبطه خوردن
/ghebte khordan/ ► verb
begrudge

غبغب
/ghabghab/ ► noun
lob

غدر
/ghadar/ ► noun
treason - treachery

غده
/ghode/ ► noun
tumor - wen - knot - gland

غذا
/ghaza/ ► noun
food - dish - viand - meat - meal

غرامت
/gherâmat/ ► noun
damage - repayment - fine - indemnity

غرامت پرداختن
/gherâmat pardâkhtan/ ► verb
recompense

غرب
/gharb/ ► noun
occident - west

غرب گرایی
/gharbgarâyi/ ► noun
westernization

غربال
/gharbâl/ ► noun
screen - scalp - jigger - sieve - harp

غربال کردن
/gharbâl kardan/ ► verb
sieve - screen - winnow

غربی
/gharbi/ ► adjective
western - westerner

غرض
/gharaz/ ► noun
spite - prejudice - peeve - intention - grudge

غرض ورزی
/gharazvarzi/ ► adjective
prejudice

غرغره کردن
/gherghere kardan/ ▶ verb
gurgle - gargle

غرولند
/ghoroland/ ▶ noun
rumble

غرفه
/ghorfe/ ▶ noun
stall - booth - loge

غریب
/gharib/ ▶ adjective
stranger - eccentric - unusual - unmoral

غرفه نمایشگاه
/ghorfeye namâyeshgâh/ ▶ noun
pavilion

غریبه
/gharibe/ ▶ noun
stranger - strange

غرق
/ghargh/ ▶ noun
shipwreck

غریزی
/gharizi/ ▶ noun
innate

غرق شدن
/ghargh shodan/ ▶ verb
merge - drown - sink

غریو
/ghariv/ ▶ noun
outcry - uproar - boom

غرق کردن
/ghargh kardan/ ▶ verb
flood - deluge - drown

غزال
/ghazâl/ ▶ noun
gazelle

غره
/ghore/ ▶ noun
cocksure

غزل
/ghazal/ ▶ noun
ode - sonnet

غروب
/ghorub/ ▶ noun
night - evening - sundown

غزل خوان
/ghazalkhâni/ ▶ adjective
songster

غرور
/ghorur/ ▶ noun
assumption - insolence - pride - vanity -
vainglory - conceit - ruffe

غسل
/ghosl/ ▶ noun
soak - ablution - wash – dip

غسل دادن

/ghosl dâdan/ ▶ verb
souse

غش

/ghash/ ▶ noun
fit - syncope - swoon

غش کردن

/ghash kardan/ ▶ verb
swoon - collapse

غصب

/ghazab/ ▶ noun
confiscation - usurpation - violence

غصه

/ghose/ ▶ noun
sorrow - grief - woe - heartache

غصه خوردن

/ghose khordan/ ▶ verb
pine

غضب

/ghazab/ ▶ noun
anger - huff - rage - outrage - outburst -
wrath

غضب کردن

/ghazab kardan/ ▶ verb
rage

غضبناک

/ghazabnâk/ ▶ adjective
vehement - wroth

غفلت

/gheflat/ ▶ noun
default - omission - negligence - neglect
- forget

غل خوردن

/ghel khordan/ ▶ verb
trundle

غلاف

/ghalâf/ ▶ noun
sheathe - sheath - casing - pod - vagina

غلام

/gholâm/ ▶ noun
slave

غلبه

/ghalabe/ ▶ noun
conquest - dominance - victory - beat

غلتاندن

/ghaltândan/ ▶ verb
turnover - trundle - roll

غلتیدن

/ghaltidan/ ▶ verb
wallow - roll - slither

غلط

/ghalat/ ▶ noun
inaccurate - inaccuracy - phony - error -
erroneous - foul - false

غلطگیر

/ghalatgir/ ▶ noun
corrector

غلیظ کردن

/ghaliz kardan/ ▶ verb
thicken

غلظت

/ghelzat/ ▶ noun
density

غم

/gham/ ▶ noun
sorrow - despondency - remorse - rue -
grief

غلغلک

/ghelghelak/ ▶ noun
tickle

غم انگیز

/ghamangiz/ ▶ adjective
tragic - somber - lugubrious -
burdensome

غله

/ghale/ ▶ noun
corn - cereal

غم خوردن

/gham khordan/ ▶ verb
care

غلو

/gholov/ ▶ noun
hyperbole

غم و اندوه

/ghamo anduh/ ▶ noun
sorrow - anguish - pine

غلو کردن

/gholov kardan/ ▶ verb
overstate - overestimate - overcharge

غمخوار

/ghamkhâr/ ▶ adjective
sympathetic

غلیان

/ghelyân/ ▶ noun
spout - seethe

غمگین

/ghamgin/ ▶ adjective
sad - sorry - dyspeptic - woeful -
heartsick - melancholy

غلیظ

/ghaliz/ ▶ adjective
heavy - caliginous - dense - thick - slab

غمناک

/ghamnâk/ ▶ adjective
sad

غلیظ شدن

/ghaliz shodan/ ▶ verb
thicken

غنایم
/ghanâ'em/ ► noun
trophy

غوغا کردن
/ghôghâ kardan/ ► verb
jangle

غنچه
/ghonche/ ► noun
button - bud

غیاب
/ghâyeb/ ► noun
absence

غنی کردن
/ghani kardan/ ► verb
enrich

غیب شدن
/gheib shodan/ ► verb
vanish

غنیمت
/ghanimat/ ► noun
spoil - prize - plunder

غیبت
/gheibat/ ► noun
absence

غواص
/ghavâs/ ► noun
diver

غیبت کردن
/gheibat kardan/ ► verb
backbite

غواصی کردن
/ghavâsi kardan/ ► verb
dive

غیبگو
/gheibgu/ ► adjective
seer - necromancer

غوطه
/ghute/ ► noun
soak - plunge - duck

غیبگویی
/gheibguyi/ ► noun
prophecy - divination

غوطه ورشدن
/ghutevar shodan/ ► verb
dip

غیر
/gheir/ ► adjective
other

غوغا
/ghôghâ/ ► noun
uproar - affray - hubbub - mob - melee -
peal - clamor - rumpus - turmoil

غیراخلاقی
/gheireakhlâghi/ ► adjective
unmoral - amoral

غیرارادی

/gheire erâdi/ ▶ adjective
involuntary - automatic

غیراز

/gheiraz/ ▶ adjective
than - except

غیرانسانی

/gheir ensâni/ ▶ adjective
inhuman

غیرت

/gheirat/ ▶ noun
zealotry - zeal - enthusiasm - mettle -
ardor

غیررسمی

/gheire rasmi/ ▶ adjective
unofficial - informal

غیرضروری

/gheire zaruri/ ▶ adjective
superfluous - unnecessary - unessential -
undue - uncalledfor - dispensable

غیرطبیعی

/gheire tabi'i/ ▶ adjective
preposterous - unnatural - uncanny -
sophisticated - subnormal

غیرقابل جبران

/gheire ghâbele jobrân/ ▶ adjective
irrecoverable

غیرقابل حل

/gheire ghâbele hal/ ▶ adjective
indissoluble

غیرقابل فسخ

/gheire ghâbele faskh/ ▶ adjective
irrevocable

غیرمادی

/gheire mâdi/ ▶ adjective
spiritual - immaterial

غیره

/gheire/ ▶ adverb
etc. - whatnot

غیره مترقبه

/gheire moteraghebe/ ▶ noun
unexpected

غیض

/gheiz/ ▶ noun
resentment

غیور

/ghayur/ ▶ adjective
spunky - zealous - zealot - zeal - jealous
- warm

ف – ف

fe /fe/ ▶ twenty-third letter of the Persian alphabet

فارسی
/fârsi/ ▶ noun
Persian - Persian

فارغ التحصیل
/fâreghotahsil/ ▶ noun
gaduate - alumnus

فاتح
/fâteh/ ▶ adjective
conqueror - winner - victorious - victor

فارغ التحصیل شدن
/fâreghotahsil shodan/ ▶ verb
gaduate

فاتح شدن
/fâteh shodan/ ▶ verb
win

فارق
/fâregh/ ▶ noun
separator

فاتحه
/fâtehe/ ▶ noun
requiem

فاسد
/fâsed/ ▶ adjective
immoral - villainous - vile - vicious

فاجعه
/fâje'e/ ▶ noun
tragedy - catastrophe - calamity

فاسد شدن
/fâsed shodan/ ▶ verb
spoil - putrefy - gangrene - canker - degenerate - decay - vitiate

فاحش
/fâhesh/ ▶ adjective
heavy - egregious - tremendous

فاسد کردن
/fâsed kardan/ ▶ verb
taint - spoil - bastardize - vitiate - canker - ruin - rot - deprave - debauch - corrupt

فاحشه خانه
/fâheshe/ ▶ noun
brothel - whorehouse - callhouse

فاسق
/fâsegh/ ▶ adjective
goat - paramour - lover - lecher

فاخر
/fâkher/ ▶ adjective
fine - costly

فاعلی
/fâeli/ ► adjective
subjective - nominative

فاش
/fâsh/ ► adjective
overt

فاقد
/fâghed/ ► adjective
without - toom

فاش شدن
/fâsh shodan/ ► verb
transpire - out

فاکتور
/fâktor/ ► noun
invoice

فاش کردن
/fâsh kardan/ ► verb
betray - utter - disclose - reveal -
giveaway - squeal - tell - tattle

فال
/fâl/ ► noun
omen - auspices

فاصله
/fâsele/ ► noun
space - distance - hiatus - lacuna

فال بین
/fâlbin/ ► noun
augur

فاصله دار
/fâseledâr/ ► adjective
distant - away

فالگیر
/fâlgir/ ► noun
augur

فاصله داشتن
/fâsele dâshtan/ ► verb
space

فامیلی
/fâmili/ ► adjective
family

فاضل
/fâzel/ ► adjective
residue

فانوس
/fânus/ ► noun
louver - lantern - lamp

فاضلاب
/fâzelâb/ ► noun
sewerage - sewage

فانی
/fâni/ ► adjective
transitory - transient - earthborn - mortal
- memnetary

فاعل
/fâel/ ► noun
doer - subject

فایده

/fâyede/ ► noun
avail - advantage - utter - use - profit -
fruit

فتنه انگیز

/fetne'angiz/ ► adjective
incentive

فتنه جویی

/fetnejuyi/ ► noun
sedition

فایده بردن

/fâyede bordan/ ► verb
gain - benefit

فتور

/fotur/ ► noun
languor

فایده رساندن

/fâyede resândan/ ► verb
profit - benefit

فتوکپی

/fotokopi kardan/ ► noun
photocopy

فایق

/fâ'egh/ ► noun
paramount - prevalent

فتوی

/fatvâ/ ► noun
sentence - judgment (gement) - verdict

فایق آمدن

/fâ'egh âmadan/ ► verb
surmount - get

فتوی دادن

/fatvâ dâdan/ ► verb
arbitrate - adjudicate - judge

فتح

/fath/ ► noun
triumph - win - victory

فتیله

/fetile/ ► noun
wick

فتح کردن

/fath kardan/ ► verb
conquer - reduce

فجر

/fajr/ ► noun
dawn - aurora

فترت

/fetrat/ ► noun
interval - interregnum - recess

فجیع

/faji'/ ► adjective
tragic - calamitous - disastrous

فتنه

/fetne/ ► noun
sedition - riot - muitiny - insurrection

فحاش

/fahâsh/ ▶ adjective
blackguardly - vilifier - reviler

فر

/fer/ ▶ noun
splendor - curl

فحاشی

/fahâshi/ ▶ noun
scurrility

فر دادن

/fer dâdan/ ▶ verb
curl

فخر

/fakhr/ ▶ noun
glory - pride

فرآور

/farâvar/ ▶ noun
productive - producer

فدا کردن

/fadâ kardan/ ▶ verb
immolate - give - devote

فرآورده

/farâvarde/ ▶ noun
supply - production - product

فداکاری

/fadâkâri/ ▶ noun
sacrifice

فرآوری

/farâvari/ ▶ noun
production

فداکاری کردن

/fadâkâri kardan/ ▶ verb
sacrifice

فرآیند

/farâyand/ ▶ noun
process

فدایی

/fadâyi/ ▶ adjective
zealous - devotee - immolate - martyr

فرا خواندن

/farâ khândan/ ▶ verb
evoke - recall - muster - summon

فدرال

/federâl/ ▶ noun
federal

فرابنفش

/farâbanafsh/ ▶ adjective
ultraviolet

فدرالیسم

/fedelâlizm/ ▶ noun
federalism

فراخ

/farâkh/ ▶ adjective
spacious - ample - wide

فراخور

/farâkhor/ ▶ noun
worthy - proportionate - suitable

فراگیر

/farâgir/ ▶ adjective
pervasive

فرار

/farâr/ ▶ noun
scape - guy - desertion - evasive -
escape - lam - breakaway

فراموشکار

/farâmushkâr/ ▶ adjective
slack - oblivious

فرار کردن

/farâr kardan/ ▶ verb
skedaddle - stampede - scape - abscond -
escape - elope - flight

فراموشکاری

/farâmushkâri/ ▶ noun
negligence

فرارو

/farâru/ ▶ noun
transgressor

فراموشی

/farâmushi/ ▶ noun
amnesia - forget - oblivion

فراروی

/farâravi/ ▶ noun
transgression - ultraism

فراهم

/farâham/ ▶ noun
whorl - available

فراز

/farâz/ ▶ noun
phrase - loft - ascent - ascendency -
altitude - accolade

فراهم آمدن

/farâham âmadan/ ▶ verb
troop

فراست

/farâsat/ ▶ noun
sagacity - intuition - intelligence -
insight - perspicacity

فراهم آوردن

/farâham âvardan/ ▶ verb
assemble

فراوان

/farâvân/ ▶ adjective
copious - plenty - very - exuberant -
bounteous - ample - affluent - abundant

فراغت

/ferâghat/ ▶ noun
opportunity - relief - leisure

فراوان بودن
/farâvân budan/ ▶ verb
teem

فرد
/fard/ ▶ noun
odd - unit - unique - azygos - individual
- singular - single - subject - specimen

فراوانی
/farâvâni/ ▶ adjective
superabundance - redundancy -
amplitude - affluence - abundance -
plenty

فردا
/fardâ/ ▶ noun
tomorrow

فربه
/farbe/ ▶ adjective
fat - obese - hammy - plump

فردگرا
/fardgarâ/ ▶ adjective
individualist

فردوس
/ferdôs/ ▶ noun
paradise

فرجام
/farjâm/ ▶ noun
end

فردی
/fardi/ ▶ adjective
subjective

فرح بخش
/farahbakhsh/ ▶ adjective
pleasurable

فردیت
/fardiyat/ ▶ noun
individuality

فرحناک
/farahnâk/ ▶ adjective
jocund

فرز
/ferz/ ▶ adjective
swift - spry - agile - quick - nimble

فرخ
/farokh/ ▶ adjective
auspicious

فرزانگی
/farzânegi/ ▶ noun
wisdom

فرخنده
/farkhonde/ ▶ adjective
jubilant - happy - beatific - auspicious

فرزانه
/farzâne/ ▶ adjective
wise

فرسایش
/farsâyesh/ ▶ noun
scuff - erosion

فرستادن
/ferestâdan/ ▶ verb
forward - dispatch - ship - send

فرستاده
/ferestâde/ ▶ adjective
sent - messenger - apostle - emissary

فرستنده
/ferestande/ ▶ adjective
transmitter - sender

فرسودگی
/farsudegi/ ▶ noun
exhaustion

فرسوده
/farsude/ ▶ adjective
effete - rusty - old - timeworn

فرش
/farsh/ ▶ noun
carpet

فرش کردن
/farsh kardan/ ▶ verb
spread - pave - rug

فرشته
/fereshte/ ▶ noun
angel – intelligence

فرصت
/forsat/ ▶ noun
opportunity - chance - vantage - leisure - breather

(Idiom: فرصتها را غنیمت شمردن
Take advantage of an opportunity to do something!)

فرض
/farz/ ▶ noun
supposition - thesis - assumption - hypothesis - presumption - posit - guess

فرض کردن
/farz kardan/ ▶ verb
suppose - assume - aim - adjudge - imagine - hypothesize - presume

فرضی
/farzi/ ▶ adjective
supposition - obligatory - hypothetical

فرضیه
/farziye/ ▶ noun
hypothesis

فرع
/far'/ ▶ noun
sub - branch - outgrwth - offshoot

فرعون
/fer'ôn/ ▶ noun
pharaoh

فرقان
/forghân/ ▶ noun
wheelbarrow

فرعی
/far'i/ ▶ adjective
sideway - secondary - ancillary - adjunct
- accessory

فرقه
/ferghe/ ▶ noun
sect - heresy

فرفره
/ferfere/ ▶ noun
gig - whirligig - spin

فرکانس
/ferekâns/ ▶ noun
frequency

فرفری
/ferferi/ ▶ adjective
curly - kinky

فرگشت
/fargasht/ ▶ noun
evolution

فرق
/fargh/ ▶ noun
top - vertex - head - inequality - odds –
difference

فرم
/form/ ▶ noun
form

فرق داشتن
/fargh dâshtan/ ▶ verb
vary - differ

فرمان
/farmân/ ▶ noun
errand - ordinance - word - commission
- commandment - command

فرمان دادن
/farmân dâdan/ ▶ verb
ordain - officer - command

فرمانبردار
/farmânbordâr/ ▶ adjective
subordinate - obedient

(Idiom: یک دنیا باهم فرق داشتن
Be as different as chalk and cheese)

فرمانبرداری کردن
/farmânbordâri kardan/ ▶ verb
obey

فرق سر
/farghe sar/ ▶ noun
crown - peak

فرماندار

/farmândâr/ ▶ noun
governor

فرهنگ

/farhang/ ▶ noun
lexicon - dictionary - culture

فرمانداری

/darmândâri/ ▶ noun
government

فرهیختن

/farhikhtan/ ▶ verb
educate

فرمانده

/farmânde/ ▶ noun
leader - admiral - commander -
commandant - chief - governor

فرو بردن

/foru bordan/ ▶ verb
swallow - devour - ram - gulp - immerse
- imbibe - plunge - aspire - absorb

فرمانروا

/farmânravâ/ ▶ noun
lord - ruler

فرو رفتن

/foru raftan/ ▶ verb
sink - stick - merge

فرمانروایی

/farmânravâyi/ ▶ noun
rule

فرو نشاندن

/foruneshândan/ ▶ verb
tranquilize - soften - slack - relieve -
calm

فرمایش

/farmâyesh/ ▶ noun
order - command

فرو نشستن

/foruneshastan/ ▶ verb
abate - sag - slake - subside

فرمودن

/farmudan/ ▶ verb
bid

فروتن

/forutan/ ▶ adjective
modest - humble - daft - courteous -
slight - submissive

فرمول

/formul/ ▶ noun
frame

فروتنی کردن

/forutani kardan/ ▶ verb
humble - condescend

فرنگی

/farangi/ ▶ noun
european

فروشندگی

/forushandegi/ ► noun
solicitorship - salesmanship

فروختن

/forukhtan/ ► verb
sell - vend - market - hawk

فروشنده

/forushande/ ► noun
vendor - dealer - salesman - seller

فروختنی

/forukhtani/ ► noun
saleable - salable

فروغ

/forugh/ ► noun
shine - light - blaze

فرود آمدن

/forud âmadan/ ► verb
shore - alight - perch - ground - descend

فروکش

/forukesh/ ► noun
refluence - ebb - deflation - letup

فرودگاه

/forudgâh/ ► noun
landingfield - airport - airfield

فروکش کردن

/forukesh kardan/ ► verb
subside - lower - abate - ebb

فرورفتگی

/foruraftegi/ ► adjective
dip - notch

فروگذار کردن

/forugozâr/ ► verb
neglect

فرورفته

/forurafte/ ► adjective
sunken

فروگذاری

/forugozâri/ ► noun
silence - omission - neglect

فروزان

/foruzân/ ► adjective
luminous - ablaze

فروماندگی

/forumândegi/ ► noun
inability - intolerance

فروش

/forush/ ► noun
sale

فرومایه

/forumâye/ ► adjective
currish - brassy - abject - vile - ignoble

فروشگاه

/forushgâh/ ► noun
salesroom - store - shootinggallery

فروهر

/foruhar/ ▶ adjective
essence

فریاد

/faryâd/ ▶ noun
shout - gaff - cry

فریاد زدن

/faryâd zadan/ ▶ verb
yell - shout - bawl - howl - hoot - cry

فریب

/farib/ ▶ noun
temptation - abusive - defraud - deceit -
cheat

فریب خوردگی

/faribkhordegi/ ▶ noun
deception

فریب خوردن

/farib khordan/ ▶ verb
beguile

فریبا

/faribâ/ ▶ adjective
deceptive

فریبکار

/faribkâr/ ▶ adjective
japer - tortuous

فریبکاری

/faribkâri/ ▶ noun
japery

فریبندگی

/faribandegi/ ▶ noun
charm - grace - glamor - glamour

فریبنده

/faribande/ ▶ adjective
sophisticate - tempter - attractive -
deceptive - witch - glamorous - captious

فریفتن

/fariftan/ ▶ verb
entice - enchant - seduce

فزونی

/fozuni/ ▶ adjective
excess - amplitude - intensity -
prepayment - extreme

فساد

/fesâd/ ▶ noun
spoil - vice - depravity - degeneration -
decay - decadence - corruption

فسخ

/faskh/ ▶ noun
revoke - revocation - repeal - recision -
waiver

فسخ کردن

/faskh kardan/ ▶ verb
terminate - cancel - countermand -
dissolve - disannul

فسفردار

/fosfordâr/ ▶ adjective
phosphorous

فسفری

/fosfori/ ▶ adjective
phosphorous - phosphoric

فسق

/fesgh/ ▶ noun
debauchery

فسیل

/fosil/ ▶ noun
fossil

فشار

/feshâr/ ▶ noun
press - zip - thrust - tension - stress -
strain - squeeze

فشار آوردن

/feshâr âvardan/ ▶ verb
wrest

فشار دادن

/feshâr dâdan/ ▶ verb
squeeze - yerk - hustle

فشارسنج

/feshârsanj/ ▶ noun
indicator

فشاندن

/feshândan/ ▶ verb
erupt

فشردگی

/feshordegi/ ▶ noun
jam

فشردن

/feshordan/ ▶ verb
pressure - wring - wad - crush - squeeze
- tighten - twitch

فشرده

/feshorde/ ▶ adjective
succinct - squeeze - massive

فشفشه

/feshfeshe/ ▶ noun
squib - rocket

فشنگ

/feshang/ ▶ noun
cartridge

فصل

/fasl/ ▶ noun
term - season - article

فصل بهار

/fasle bahâr/ ▶ noun
springtime - springtide

فصلی

/fasli/ ▶ adjective
seasonal

فصیح
/fasih/ ► adjective
eloquent - fluent - communicative

فضا
/fazâ/ ► noun
space - place - area - room - region

فضاپیما
/fazâpeimâ/ ► noun
spacecraft

فضاحت
/fezâhat/ ► noun
disgrace - scandalization

فضانورد
/fazânavard/ ► noun
astronaut - spaceman

فضایی
/fazâyi/ ► noun
spatial

فضل و دانش
/fazlo dânesh/ ► noun
erudition

فضله
/fazle/ ► noun
excrement

فضول
/fozul/ ► adjective
inquisitive - meddlesome - officious

فضول را بردند جهنم گفت هیزمش تره (Idiom:
Curiosity killed the cat)

فضولات
/fozulât/ ► noun
refuse - garble - garbage

فضولی
/fozuli/ ► noun
gallimaufry - impertinence - pry

فضیلت
/fazilat/ ► noun
prepayment - accomplishment -
excellence

فطرت
/fetrat/ ► noun
temperament - mould - mettle

فطری
/fetri/ ► adjective
innate - ingrown - indigenous - inborn

فعال
/fa'âl/ ► adjective
active - pragmatic - energetic

فعال سازی
/fa'âl sâzi/ ► noun
activation

فعال شدن
/fa'âl shodan/ ► verb
activation

فعالیت
/fa'âliyat/ ▶ noun
stir - activity

فقه
/fegh'h/ ▶ noun
jurisprudence

فعل
/fe'l/ ▶ noun
act

فقهی
/feghhi/ ▶ adjective
juridical - juratory

فعلا
/fe'lan/ ▶ adverb
now - nonce

فقیر
/faghir/ ▶ adjective
poor - penurious

فعلی
/fe'li/ ▶ adjective
now - verbal

فقیه
/faghih/ ▶ noun
jurisconsult - lawyer

فغان
/faghân/ ▶ noun
shout - whine

فک
/fak/ ▶ noun
chaw - jowl - jaw

فقدان
/foghdân/ ▶ noun
loss - absence - lack - want

فکاهی
/fokâhi/ ▶ noun
jocular - jocose - humorous

فقر
/faghr/ ▶ noun
depauperation - poverty

فکاهی نویس
/fokâhinevis/ ▶ noun
humorist

فقره
/faghare/ ▶ noun
episode - entry - item - vertebrate -
vertebra - piece - paragraph

فکر
/fekr/ ▶ noun
thought - concept - notion - opinion -
mind - idea

فقط
/faghat/ ▶ noun
but - alone - mere - only

فکربکر
/fekre bekr/ ▶ noun
mastermind

فكور
/fakur/ ► adjective
thoughtful - thinker

فلات
/falât/ ► noun
plateau

فلاحت
/falâhat/ ► noun
husbandry

فلاسک
/felâsk/ ► noun
thermos

فلاکت
/felâkat/ ► noun
adversity - poverty

فلان
/felân/ ► noun
whatnot

فلج
/falaj/ ► noun
paralysis - palsy

فلج شدن
/falaj shodan/ ► verb
freeze

فلزکاری
/felezkâri/ ► noun
metallurgy

فلسفی
/falsafi/ ► noun
philosophic

فلفل
/felfel/ ► noun
pepper

فلفل پاشیدن
/felfel pâshidan/ ► verb
pepper

فلفلی
/felfeli/ ► adjective
pepper

فلک
/falak/ ► noun
sphere - sky - orbit - bastinado - heaven

فلوت
/folut/ ► noun
pipe

فلوت زدن
/folut zadan/ ► verb
pipe

فن
/fan/ ► noun
art

(Idiom: فوت و فن چیزی را بلد بودن
Know the ins and outs of something)

فنری

/fanari/ ► adjective
elastic - bouncy - springy

فنا

/fanâ/ ► noun
doom

فنون

/fonun/ ► noun
technology - tactics

فنا کردن

/fanâ kardan/ ► verb
ruin

فنی

/fani/ ► adjective
technical

فناپذیر

/fanâpazir/ ► adjective
mortal

فهرست

/fehrest/ ► noun
list

فناناپذیر

/fanâ nâpazir/ ► adjective
undying - indestructible - immortal -
eternal

فهرست کردن

/fehrest kardan/ ► verb
list - catalogue - catalog

فنجان

/fenjân/ ► noun
calix - cupule

فهم

/fahm/ ► noun
understanding - intelligence - intellect -
mind - grasp - savvy

فندق

/fandogh/ ► noun
hazelnut

فهماندن

/fahmândan/ ► verb
show - purporst - clear - represent

فندک

/fandak/ ► noun
lighter

فهمیدن

/fahmidan/ ► verb
understand - gripe - grasp - get - realize
- comprehend - compass

فنر

/fanar/ ► noun
spring - coil

فهمیدنی

/fahmidani/ ▶ adjective
intelligible

فهمیده

/fahmide/ ▶ adjective
understanding

فواره

/favâre/ ▶ noun
waterwheel - fountain - springhead -
spout - jet

فوت

/fôt/ ▶ noun
death - gust - puff - snuff

فوت کردن

/fôt kardan/ ▶ verb
die

فوتبال

/futbâl/ ▶ noun
soccer

فورا

/fôran/ ▶ adverb
straightaway - fast - expressly - anon -
instant

فوران

/favarân/ ▶ noun
eruption - gush - outburst - spurt - spout
- jet

فوران کننده

/favarân konande/ ▶ adjective
effusive

فوری

/fôri/ ▶ adjective
immediate - urgent - sudden - spot -
spontaneous

فوریت

/fôriyat/ ▶ noun
urgency - immediacy

فوق

/fôgh/ ▶ noun
upon

فوق الذکر

/fôgholzekr/ ▶ noun
aforesaid

فوق العاده

/fôghol'âde/ ▶ noun
supernatural - strenuous - terrific -
extraordinary - precious

فوقانی

/fôghâni/ ▶ adjective
upside - uppish - upper - capital

فولاد

/fulâd/ ▶ noun
steel

فیصله دادن
/feisale dâdan/ ▶ verb
evict

فی الواقع
/felvâghe/ ▶ noun
indeed

فیض
/feiz/ ▶ noun
grace

فیبر
/fibr/ ▶ noun
fiber

فیلسوف
/filsuf/ ▶ noun
philosopher

فیروز
/firuz/ ▶ adjective
jubilant

فیمابین
/fimâbein/ ▶ noun
interim

فیزیک
/fizik/ ▶ noun
physics - physic

فین
/fin/ ▶ noun
snivel

فیزیک دان
/fizikdân/ ▶ noun
physicist

فیزیکی
/fiziki/ ▶ noun
physical

فیزیولوژی
/fiziyolozhi/ ▶ noun
physiology

فیس
/fis/ ▶ noun
vainglory

فیش
/fish/ ▶ noun
strap

ق – ﻕ

ghâf /ghe/ ▶ twenty forth letter of the Persian alphabet

قاب

/ghâleb/ ▶ noun
pan - case

قابل

/ghâbel/ ▶ noun
good - capable - apt - able

قابل اتکا

/ghâbele etekâ/ ▶ adjective
reliable

قابل اثبات

/ghâbele esbât/ ▶ adjective
provable

قابل احترام

/ghâbele ehterâm/ ▶ adjective
respectable

قابل استفاده

/ghâbele estefâde/ ▶ adjective
utilizable - available - handy -
instrumental

قابل قبول

/ghâbele ghabul/ ▶ adjective
tolerable - admissible - acceptable -
passable - receivable

قابله

/ghâbele/ ▶ noun
obstetrician - midwife

قابلیت

/ghâbeliyat/ ▶ noun
sufficiency - ability - capability

قاپ

/ghâp/ ▶ noun
knucklebone

قاپ بازی

/ghâp bâzi/ ▶ noun
dib

قاپ زدن

/ghâp zadan/ ▶ verb
snap

قاپ زنی

/ghâp zani/ ▶ noun
snatch

قاپیدن

/ghâpidan/ ▶ verb
yerk

قاتل

/ghâtel/ ▶ noun
murderer - assassin - killer

قادرمتعال
/ghâdere mota'âl/ ► noun
omnipotent

قاتی
/ghâti/ ► adjective
mixed

قارچ
/ghârch/ ► noun
mushroom

قاتی کردن
/ghâti kardan/ ► verb
mix

قارقار کردن
/ghâr ghâr kardan/ ► verb
plunk

قاچ
/ghâch/ ► noun
plug

قاره
/ghâre/ ► noun
mainland - continent

قاچ کردن
/ghâch kardan/ ► verb
plug

قاری
/ghâri/ ► noun
reader

قاچاق
/ghâchâgh/ ► noun
swindler - contraband - illicit

قاز
/ghâz/ ► noun
goose

قاچاق کردن
/ghâchâgh kardan/ ► verb
smuggle

قاش
/ghâsh/ ► noun
sliver - slice - plug

قاچاقچی
/ghâchâghchi/ ► noun
racketeer - smuggler

قاش کردن
/ghâsh kardan/ ► verb
sliver - slice

قاچاقی
/ghâchâghi/ ► adjective
underthecounter - wildcat

قاشق
/ghâshogh/ ► noun
spoon

قادر بودن
/ghâder budan/ ► verb
may

قاصد
/ghâsed/ ▶ noun
courier - herald - harbinger

قاصدک
/ghâsedak/ ▶ noun
dandelion

قاصر
/ghâser/ ▶ adjective
short

قاضی
/ghâzi/ ▶ noun
arbiter - pretor - judge

قاطر
/ghâter/ ▶ noun
mule

قاطع
/ghâte'/ ▶ adjective
decisive - conclusive - overbearing -
clincher - categorical

قاطع بودن
/ghâte' budan/ ▶ verb
predominate

قاعدگی زنان
/ghâedegiye zanân/ ▶ noun
fluor

قاعده
/ghâede/ ▶ noun
theorem - law - norm - rule - regulation -
frame

قافله
/ghâfele/ ▶ noun
convoy

قافیه
/ghâfiye/ ▶ noun
rime

قافیه دار
/ghâfiyedâr/ ▶ adjective
rimy

قال گذاشتن
/ghâl gozâshtan/ ▶ verb
walkouton

قالب
/ghâleb/ ▶ noun
mould - mold - model - pat - cast - case

قالب زنی
/ghâleb zani/ ▶ noun
snap

قالب کردن
/ghâleb zadan/ ▶ verb
cake - found - form - block - bloc- shove
over

قالب گرفتن

/ghâleb gereftan/ ▶ verb
die

قالی

/ghâli/ ▶ noun
carpet

قالیچه

/ghâliche/ ▶ noun
rug

قامت

/ghâmat/ ▶ noun
stature

قاموس

/ghâmus/ ▶ noun
lexicon - thesaurus

قانع کردن

/ghâne' kardan/ ▶ verb
satisfy - convince - content

قانون

/ghânun/ ▶ noun
statute - law - edict - regulation - code -
rule

قانون شکن

/ghânun shekan/ ▶ adjective
scofflaw - lawbreaker - outlaw

قانون شکنی

/ghânunshekani/ ▶ noun
offense

قانونی

/ghânuni/ ▶ adjective
juridical - statutory - standard -
canonical - legitimate - legal - lawful -
valid

قانونی بودن

/ghânuni budan/ ▶ verb
legitimacy - legality

قاه قاه

/ghâh ghâh/ ▶ noun
guffaw

قاه قاه خندیدن

/ghâh ghâh khandidan/ ▶ verb
guffaw

قاهر

/ghâher/ ▶ adjective
violent

قایق

/ghâyegh/ ▶ noun
outboard - ark - boat

قایقران

/ghâyeghrân/ ▶ noun
sculler - boatman

قایل

/ghâyel/ ▶ noun
teller

قایم
/ghâ'em/ ► noun
upstanding - orthogonal - erect

قبل
/ghabl/ ► adverb
former - ago - before

قایم مقام
/ghâ'em'maghâm/ ► noun
deputy - vicar - surrogate - successor

قبل از
/ghabl az/ ► adverb
before

قبا
/ghabâ/ ► noun
cassock

قبلا
/ghablan/ ► adverb
beforehand - already - heretofore

قباحت
/ghebâhat/ ► noun
obscenity

قبلی
/ghabli/ ► adjective
fore - prior - previous - predecessor

قباله
/ghabâle/ ► noun
deed

قبول
/ghabul/ ► noun
agreement - adoption - admission - compliance - reception

قبر
/ghabr/ ► noun
grave - sepulcher - tomb

قبول کردن
/ghabul kardan/ ► verb
entertain - matriculate - adopt - accord - accept

قبرستان
/ghabrestân/ ► noun
cemetery - graveyard

قبولی
/ghabuli/ ► adjective
approbation - ratification

قبض
/ghabz/ ► noun
bill

قبیح
/ghabih/ ► adjective
objcetionable

قبضه
/ghabze/ ► noun
hilt

قبيح دانستن

/ghabih dânestan/ ► verb
deprecate

قبيله

/ghabile/ ► noun
phylum - clan - caste - tribe

قبيله ای

/ghabile'i/ ► adjective
tribal

قتل

/ghatl/ ► noun
homicide - murder

قتل عام

/ghatloâm/ ► noun
slaughter - genocide - carnage -
holocaust

قتل عام کردن

/ghatloâm kardan/ ► verb
massacre

قحطی

/ghahti/ ► noun
starvation - hunger

قحطی زدگی

/ghahtizadegi/ ► noun
starvation

قد

/ghad/ ► noun
length - size

قدام

/ghadâm/ ► noun
foreside

قدبلند

/ghadboland/ ► adjective
tall

قدح

/ghadah/ ► noun
bowl

قدر

/ghadar/ ► adjective
value - importance - quantity - esteem -
deal - significance

قدرت

/ghodrat/ ► noun
authority - power - potency - posse - vis
- vim - might

قدرت داشتن

/ghodrat dâshtan/ ► verb
can

قدرت مطلق

/ghodrate motlagh/ ► noun
omnipotence

قدردانی

/ghadrdâni/ ► noun
gratitude

قدردانی کردن

/ghadrdâni kardan/ ► verb
value - acknowledge

قدس

/ghods/ ► noun
sanctum

قدغن

/ghadeghan/ ► noun
interdict - injunction - prohibition

قدغن کردن

/ghadeghan kardan/ ► verb
ban - veto

قدقد

/ghodghod/ ► noun
cluck

قدقدکردن

/ghodghod kardan/ ► verb
squawk - cluck

قدم

/ghadam/ ► noun
stride - step - foot - pace

قدم آهسته

/ghadam âheste/ ► noun
trudge

قدم رو

/ghadamrô/ ► noun
march

قدم زدن

/ghadam zadan/ ► verb
walk

قدمت

/ghedmat/ ► noun
archaism - antiquity

قدوس

/ghodus/ ► noun
sacrosanct

قدیم

/ghadim/ ► noun
primitive - aborigine

قدیمی

/ghadimi/ ► adjective
outdated - olden - old - bygone - archaic
- ancient

قر زدن

/ghor zadan/ ► verb
bitch

قرآن

/ghor'ân/ ► noun
koran - quran

قرابت

/gherâbat/ ► noun
propinquity - imminence

قرار

/gharâr/ ► noun
agreement - appointment

قرار دادن

/gharâr dâdan/ ► verb
set - put - fix

قرص

/ghors/ ► noun
tablet - cake - disk - pellet - brede

قرارداد

/gharârdâd/ ► noun
treaty - bond

قرص نان

/ghorse nân/ ► noun
loaf

قراردادی

/gharârdâdi/ ► adjective
formal - arbitrary - bespoke

قرض

/gharz/ ► noun
debt - loan - prest

قراضه

/ghorâze/ ► noun
rattletrap - scrap

قرض دادن

/gharz dâdan/ ► verb
lend

قراول

/gharâvol/ ► noun
sentry - sentinel - warden

قرض کردن

/gharz kardan/ ► verb
loan

قربانی

/ghorbâni/ ► adjective
sacrifice - victim - prey

قرض گرفتن

/gharz gereftan/ ► verb
borrow

قربانی دادن

/ghorbâni dâdan/ ► verb
sacrifice

قرضه

/gharze/ ► noun
prest - loan

قربانی شدن

/ghorbâni shodan/ ► verb
immolate

قرعه

/ghor'e/ ► noun
grace - lottery - lot

قربانی کردن

/ghorâani kardan/ ► verb
victimize

قرعه کشی

/ghor'e keshi/ ► noun
lottery - draw

قرعه کشیدن
/ghor'e keshidan/ ▶ verb
ballot

قرقچی
/ghoroghchi/ ▶ adjective
gamekeeper

قرقره
/gherghere/ ▶ noun
spool - pulley - bobbin - hasp - hank

قرمز
/ghermez/ ▶ adjective
sanguine - vermilion - ponceau - bloody
- bloodshot - red

قرمز شدن
/ghermez shodan/ ▶ verb
glow - redden

قرمز کردن
/ghermez kardan/ ▶ verb
crimson - redden

قرمزرنگ
/ghermezrang/ ▶ adjective
ruddy

قرن
/gharn/ ▶ noun
century

قرنطینه
/gharantine/ ▶ noun
quarantine

قرنطینه کردن
/gharantine kardan/ ▶ verb
quarantine

قریب
/gharib/ ▶ adjective
nigh - near - about

قریب الوقوع
/gharibolvoghu/ ▶ adjective
imminent

قریحه
/gharihe/ ▶ noun
initiative

قرین
/gharin/ ▶ noun
tally - doublet - counterpart - correlate -
pendant - peer - like

قرینه
/gharine/ ▶ noun
symmetry - proportion

قریه
/ghar'ye/ ▶ noun
village

قزل
/ghazal/ ▶ noun
roan

قزل آلا
/ghezel'âlâ/ ▶ noun
salmon

قشر

/gheshr/ ▶ noun
stratum - shell - crust - cortex - rind -
peeling - hull

قساوت

/ghesâvat/ ▶ noun
atrocity

قشنگ

/ghashang/ ▶ adjective
sprucy - spruce - beautiful - beauteous -
pretty - pert - cheesy

قسط

/ghest/ ▶ noun
payment

قسم

/ghasam/ ▶ noun
oath

قشنگتر

/ghâshangtar/ ▶ adjective
natty

قسم

/ghesm/ ▶ noun
type - species - sort - kind - genus

قشو

/ghashô/ ▶ noun
currycomb

قسم خوردن

/ghasam khordan/ ▶ verb
oath

قشو کردن

/ghashô kardan/ ▶ verb
currycomb

قسم دادن

/ghasam dâdan/ ▶ verb
swear - adjure

قصاب

/ghasâb/ ▶ noun
butcher

قسم دروغ

/ghasame dorugh/ ▶ noun
swearword

قصاب خانه

/ghasâbkhâne/ ▶ noun
slaughterhouse

قسمت

/ghesmat/ ▶ noun
division - ratio - portion - slice

قسمت کردن

/ghesmat kardan/ ▶ verb
Divide

قصابی

/ghasâbi/ ▶ adjective
carnage

قصابی کردن
/ghasâbi kardan/ ► verb
butcher

قصیده
/ghaside/ ► noun
ode

قصاص
/ghesâs/ ► noun
nemesis

قضا
/ghazâ/ ► noun
mishap

قصد
/ghasd/ ► noun
will - intention - intent - pretension -
assumption - thought - purpose

قضاوت
/ghezâvat/ ► noun
witting - view - verdict - sentence -
judgeship

قصد داشتن
/ghasd dâshtan/ ► verb
purpose - aim - mean - intend

قضاوت کردن
/ghezâvat kardan/ ► verb
judge - advise

قصر
/ghasr/ ► noun
castle

قضایی
/ghazâyi/ ► adjective
juridical - juratory

قصه
/ghese/ ► noun
fiction - narrative - marchen - tale

(Idiom: قصه حسین کرد شبستری گفتن
Tell a cock and bull story)

قضیه
/ghaziye/ ► noun
thesis - theorem - proposition - clause -
case

قطار
/ghatâr/ ► noun
train - tandem - string

قصه گو
/ghesegu/ ► adjective
storyteller

قطب
/ghotb/ ► noun
pole - hub - axis

قصور
/ghosur/ ► noun
shortcoming - delinquency - default -
debt - negligence

قطب نما

/ghotbnamâ/ ▶ noun
compass

قطبی

/ghotbi/ ▶ adjective
polar

قطر

/ghatar/ ▶ noun
Qatar

قطر

/ghotr/ ▶ noun
diagonal

قطری

/ghatari/ ▶ noun
Qatari

قطری

/ghotri/ ▶ adjective
diametrical

قطع

/ghat'/ ▶ noun
cut - recision - rupture - excision -
dissection

قطع جریان

/ghat'e jariyân/ ▶ noun
cutout - cutoff

قطع کردن

/ghat' kardan/ ▶ verb
cut - cross

قطعه

/ghet'e/ ▶ noun
segment - section - piece - fragment

قطعه قطعه

/ghet'e ghet'e/ ▶ noun
sectional

قطعه یخ

/ghet'e yakh/ ▶ noun
icicle

قطعیت

/ghat'iyat/ ▶ noun
pragmatism

قطور

/ghatur/ ▶ adjective
punch

قعر

/gha'r/ ▶ noun
depth

قفس

/ghafas/ ▶ noun
birdhouse - coop - cage

قفسه

/ghafase/ ▶ noun
cupboard - cabinet - wardrobe

قفسه سینه
/ghafaseye sine/ ▶ noun
kist - ribcage - chest

قفسه کتاب
/ghafaseye ketâb/ ▶ noun
bookcase

قفل
/ghofl/ ▶ noun
lock - padlock

قفل ساز
/ghoflsâz/ ▶ noun
locksmith

قفل شدن
/ghofl shodan/ ▶ verb
lock

قلاب
/gholâb/ ▶ noun
clasp - buckle - uncus - pennant - link -
hook - hank

قلابدوزی
/gholâbduzi/ ▶ noun
patchwork - crocket - embroidery

قلابی
/gholâbi/ ▶ adjective
sham - quack - bogus - adulterate -
pasteboard - false

قلب
/ghalb/ ▶ noun
spurious - midst - heart - anagram -
brassy - counterfeit

(Idiom: قلب کسی تو دهنش آمدن
قالب تهی کردن
One's heart in their mouth)

قلدر
/gholdor/ ▶ adjective
bully

قلع
/ghal'/ ▶ noun
tin

قلعه
/ghal'e/ ▶ noun
castle - fort - munition

قلق
/ghelegh/ ▶ noun
temper

قلم
/ghalam/ ▶ noun
entry - pen - shaft - style

قلم زدن
/ghalam zadan/ ▶ verb
engrave - enchase

قلم مو
/ghalam'mu/ ▶ noun
brush

قلمبه

/gholombe/ ► adjective
snob

قلمرو

/ghalamrô/ ► noun
scope - zone - territory - dominion -
orbit - circle - milieu

قلمه درخت

/ghalameye derakht/ ► noun
sapling

قلمه زدن

/ghalame zadan/ ► verb
propagate

قلنبگی

/gholonbegi/ ► noun
protuberance

قلنبه

/gholonbe/ ► adjective
lumpy - lump - bombastic - hunch - nub
- stodgy - stilted - sonorous

قله

/ghole/ ► noun
zenith - top - summit - peak - acme - pap
- culmination - crest - knoll - climax

قله یخ

/gholeye yakh/ ► noun
icicle

قلوه

/gholve/ ► noun
kidney

قلوه سنگ

/gholve sang/ ► noun
cobblestone - rubble

قلیل

/ghalil/ ► adjective
scrimp - scarce - scant - slight - slender -
skimpy

قمار

/ghomâr/ ► noun
gamble - die - hazard

قمار کردن

/ghomâr kardan/ ► verb
gamble

قمارباز

/ghomârbâz/ ► adjective
gambler

قماش

/ghomâsh/ ► adjective
cloth - fabric

قمپز

/ghompoz/ ► noun
bluff

قمری

/ghamari/ ► adjective
dove - lunar

قمقمه

/ghomghome/ ► noun
thermos - canteen

قنات

/ghanât/ ► noun
aqueduct

قناری

/ghanâri/ ► noun
canary

قنداق تفنگ

/ghondâghe tofang/ ► noun
stock

قنداق کردن

/ghondâgh kardan/ ► verb
wrap - swathe - swath - swaddle

قندی

/ghandi/ ► noun
sugary

قهر

/ghahr/ ► noun
tantrum - sulky - sulk - miff - wrath

قهر کردن

/ghahr kardan/ ► verb
huff - miff

قهرمان

/ghahremân/ ► adjective
champion - champ - knight - victor -
hero

قهرمانانه

/ghahremânâne/ ► adverb
heroic

قهرمانی

/ghahremâni/ ► noun
heroism

قهقهه

/ghahghahe/ ► noun
horselaugh - gaff

قهوه

/ghahve/ ► noun
coffee

قهوه ای

/ghahve'i/ ► adjective
brown

قهوه جوش

/ghahve jush/ ► noun
percolator

قهوه خانه

/ghahvekhâne/ ► noun
teashop - coffeehouse

قواره

/ghavâre/ ► noun
shape - lot - configuration

قوانین

/ghavânin/ ► noun
regulations

قوس
/ghôs/ ▶ noun
archer - arch - arc - bow - chord

قوت
/ghovat/ ▶ noun
strength - punch - nourishment - nutrition - bread

قوش
/ghush/ ▶ noun
hawk

قوچ
/ghuch/ ▶ noun
buck - ram

قوطی
/ghuti/ ▶ noun
package - box - canister - can

قورباغه
/ghurbâghe/ ▶ noun
greenback - frog

قول
/ghôl/ ▶ noun
promise - avow - vow - word

قورت
/ghurt/ ▶ noun
gulp

قول دادن
/ghôl dâdan/ ▶ verb
engage - undertake - promise

قورت دادن
/ghurt dâdan/ ▶ verb
poop - englut - gulp - gobble

قول مردانه
/ghôle mardâne/ ▶ noun
parole

قوری
/ghuri/ ▶ noun
pot

قولنج
/ghôlanj/ ▶ noun
colic - gripe - bellyache

قوز
/ghuz/ ▶ noun
hunch - hump

قوم
/ghôm/ ▶ noun
nation - race - people

قوز کردن
/ghuz kardan/ ▶ verb
squat - hump

قوه
/ghove/ ▶ noun
strength

قوزک
/ghuzak/ ▶ noun
ankle

قوه ابتکار
/ghoveye ebtekâr/ ► noun
ingenuity - creativity

قوی
/ghavi/ ► adjective
overtone - lusty - boisterous - vigorous -
strong

قوی بودن
/ghavi budan/ ► verb
dow

قوی هیکل
/ghavi heikal/ ► adjective
giant - robust - sturdy

قی
/ghei/ ► noun
puke

قیاس
/ghiyâs/ ► noun
deduction - parable - analogy -
proportion - syllogism

قیاسی
/ghiyâsi/ ► adjective
schematic - categorical - analogical -
analog - inductive

قیافه
/ghiyâfe/ ► noun
mien - leer - look - countenance -
expression - gesture - sight - semblance

قیام
/ghiyâm/ ► noun
uprising - insurrection - insurgency -
insurgence

قیام کردن
/ghiyghiyâm kardan/ ► verb
arise

قیچی
/gheichi/ ► noun
scissors - tweezer

قیچی کردن
/gheichi kardan/ ► verb
snip - shear - share

قیچی کننده
/gheichi konande/ ► adjective
clincher

قید
/gheid/ ► noun
tie - bind - assurance - adverb -
encumbrance -

قیر زدن
/ghir zadan/ ► verb
tar

قیری
/ghiri/ ► adjective
tarry

قیصر
/gheisar/ ► noun
czar - kaiser

قیف

/ghif/ ▶ noun
hopper - funnel

قیمومت

/ghayumiyat/ ▶ noun
tutelage - protectorate - patronage -
mandate

قیم

/ghayem/ ▶ adjective
executor - guardian - protector

قیمت

/gheimat/ ▶ noun
price - value - worth - estimate

قیمت داشتن

/gheimat dâshtan/ ▶ verb
cost

قیمت کردن

/gheimat kardan/ ▶ verb
value - apprise - evaluate

قیمت گذاشتن

/gheimat gozâshtan/ ▶ verb
price

قیمتی

/gheimati/ ▶ adjective
valuable

قیمه

/gheime/ ▶ noun
executrix - mince

قیمه کردن

/gheime kardan/ ▶ verb
mince

ک - ک

kâf /ke/ ► twenty fifth letter of the Persian alphabet

کادر
/kâdr/ ► noun
cadre

کاذب
/kâzeb/ ► adjective
liar

کاباره
/kâbâre/ ► noun
cabaret

کار
/kâr/ ► noun
task - job - avocation - appointment - affair - vocation - work

کاربردی
/kârbari/ ► adjective
practical

کار کردن
/kâr kardan/ ► verb
act - go - work

کاپیتان
/kâpitân/ ► noun
capitan

کارایی
/kârâyi/ ► adjective
efficiency - proficiency

کاتالوگ
/kâtâlog/ ► noun
repertory - catalogue - catalog

کاربار
/kârbâr/ ► noun
workload

کاتب
/kâteb/ ► noun
ascribe

کاربرد
/kârbord/ ► noun
usage

کاتولیک
/kâtolik/ ► noun
catholic

کاربری
/kârbari/ ► noun
control

کاخ
/kâkh/ ► noun
palace

کارپرداز
/kârpardâz/ ▶ noun
supplier

کاردان
/kârdân/ ▶ noun
resourceful - deft - technician

کارپردازی
/kârpardâzi/ ▶ noun
jobprocessing

کاردانی
/kârdâni/ ▶ noun
policy - resource - tact - skill

کارت پستال
/kârt postâl/ ▶ noun
postcard

کاردینال
/kârdinâl/ ▶ noun
cardinal

کارت عضویت
/kârte ozviyat/ ▶ noun
membership card

کارشناس
/kârshenâs/ ▶ noun
expert - judge

کارت ویزیت
/kârte vizit/ ▶ noun
pasteboard

کارفرما
/kârfarmâ/ ▶ noun
taskmaster - employer - master

کارتن
/kârton/ ▶ noun
carton

کارکرد
/kârkerd/ ▶ noun
function

کارچاق کن
/kârchâghkon/ ▶ verb
jobber

کارکن
/kârkon/ ▶ adjective
purge - purgative - workable

کارخانه
/kârkhâne/ ▶ noun
studio - mill - plant - housework - firm -
factory

کارکنان
/kârkonân/ ▶ noun
personnel

کارد
/kârd/ ▶ noun
knife - gully

کارگاه
/kârgâh/ ▶ noun
workshop - workroom

کارگاه بافندگی

/kârgâhe bâfandegi/ ▶ noun
loom

کاروانسرا

/kârevânsarâ/ ▶ noun
inn

کارگر

/kârgar/ ▶ noun
labor - worker - employee

کاریکاتور

/kârikâtor/ ▶ noun
cartoon - caricature

کارگشا

/kârgoshâ/ ▶ noun
entrepreneur

کاسب

/kâseb/ ▶ noun
tradesman

کارمزد

/kârmozd/ ▶ noun
journeywork - wage

کاسبی

/kâsebi/ ▶ noun
trade

کارمند

/kârmand/ ▶ noun
employee - member

کاست

/kâset/ ▶ noun
cassette

کارنامه

/kârnâme/ ▶ noun
workbook - log

کاستن

/kâstan/ ▶ verb
subtract - shorten - pare - abate - lighten
- lessen - detract - decrease - decline

کارناوال

/kârnâvâl/ ▶ noun
carnival

کاستی

/kâsti/ ▶ adjective
shortcoming - defect

کاروان

/kârevân/ ▶ noun
convoy - caravan

کاسکت

/kâsket/ ▶ noun
casquet

کاسه

/kâse/ ▶ noun
socket - bowl - chalice - cupule

كافه
/kâfe/ ► noun
restaurant - cafe - buffet

كاسه كوزه ها رو سر كسی شكستن (Idiom:
Put the blame on somebody)

كاش
/kâsh/ ► preposition
if - wish

كافی
/kâfi/ ► noun
adequate - enough

كاشانه
/kâshâne/ ► noun
shack - hut

كافی بودن
/kâfi budan/ ► verb
suffice

كاشت
/kâsht/ ► noun
implant

كاكائو
/kâkâ'u/ ► noun
cocoa - coca - chocolate - cacao

كاشتن
/kâshtan/ ► verb
seed - grow - plant - inseminate -
implant - husband

كاكتوس
/kâktus/ ► noun
cactus

كاكل
/kâkol/ ► noun
topknot - scalplock - peak

كاشف
/kâshef/ ► noun
pathfinder

كالا
/kâlâ/ ► noun
product - object - commodity

كاغذ
/kâghaz/ ► noun
letter - paper

كالبد
/kâlbad/ ► noun
framework - chassis - mould - mold -
skeleton - shell

كافر
/kâfer/ ► noun
impious - heathen - infidel - paynim -
pagan - ethnic

کاملا

/kâmelan/ ▶ adverb
through - quite - outright - wholly

کامیاب

/kâmyâb/ ▶ adjective
prosperous - palmy

کامیاب شدن

/kâmyâb shodan/ ▶ verb
succeed - thrive - prosper

کامیابی

/kâmyâbi/ ▶ noun
good - glee - palm - prosperity - success
- speed

کامیون

/kâmiyun/ ▶ noun
truck

کانادایی

/kânâdâyi/ ▶ adjective
canadian

کانال

/kânâl/ ▶ noun
conduit - gullet - groove

کاندید

/kândid/ ▶ noun
candidate - nomination

کانون

/kânun/ ▶ noun
club

کالری

/kâlori/ ▶ noun
heatunit - calory - calorie

کالیبر

/kâlibr/ ▶ noun
caliber

کام

/kâm/ ▶ noun
desire - wish - palate

کامروایی

/kâmravâyi/ ▶ noun
success

کامکار

/kâmkâr/ ▶ adjective
prosperous

کامکار شدن

/kâmkâr shodan/ ▶ verb
prosper

کامکاری

/kâmkâri/ ▶ noun
prosperity

کامل

/kâmel/ ▶ noun
perfect - complete - whole - exact -
culminant - thorough

کامل شدن

/kâmel shodan/ ▶ verb
ripen

کانی

/kâni/ ► noun
inorganic - mineral

کاه

/kâh/ ► noun
straw - pug - chaff

کاهش

/kâhesh/ ► noun
decrease - decline - diminution -
wastage - reduction - rebate

کاهش بها

/kâheshe bahâ/ ► noun
depreciation

کاهش دادن

/kâhesh dâdan/ ► verb
lessen

کاهش یافتن

/kâhesh yâftan/ ► verb
slake

کاهگل

/kâhgel/ ► noun
thatch

کاهل

/kâhel/ ► noun
laze - slothful

کاهلی

/kâheli/ ► adjective
sloth

کاهنده

/kâhande/ ► adjective
reducer - ablative

کاهیدن

/kâhidan/ ► verb
detract

کاوشگر

/kâvoshgar/ ► noun
excavator

کاویدن

/kâvidan/ ► verb
rummage - excavate - drag

کباب

/kabâb/ ► noun
barbecue

کباب کردن

/kabâb kardan/ ► verb
roast - grid - broil - barbecue

کبد

/kabed/ ► noun
liver

کبره

/kebre/ ► noun
crust

کبره بستن

/kebre bastan/ ► verb
crust

کبیر

/kabir/ ▶ adjective
great - major - adult

کپر

/kapar/ ▶ noun
shed

کپسول

/kapsul/ ▶ noun
capsule - cachet

کپک

/kapak/ ▶ noun
mould - mildew

کپک زدن

/kapak zadan/ ▶ verb
mould - mildew

کپل

/kopol/ ▶ noun
buttock - butt - behind

کپه

/kope/ ▶ noun
congeries - ruck - heap - pile - mass

کپور

/kapur/ ▶ noun
minnow - carp

کپی

/kopi/ ▶ noun
kepi

کبریت

/kebrit/ ▶ noun
match - lighter - light

کبوتر

/kabutar/ ▶ noun
pigeon

(Idiom: کبوتر با کبوتر باز با باز – کند همجنس با همجنس پرواز
Birds of a feather flock together)

کبوترخانه

/kabutarkhâne/ ▶ noun
loft - penthouse

کبود

/kabud/ ▶ adjective
gray - livid

کبود شدن

/kabud shodan/ ▶ verb
bruise

کبودشدگی

/kabudshodegi/ ▶ noun
bruise

کت

/kot/ ▶ noun
coat

کتاب

/ketân/ ▶ noun
book

کتاب خوان

/ketâbkhân/ ▶ adjective
studious

کتاب داستان

/ketâbe dâstân/ ▶ noun
novel

کتاب درسی

/ketâbe darsi/ ▶ noun
textbook - text

کتاب راهنما

/ketâbe râhnamâ/ ▶ noun
guidebook - guide - handbook - manual

کتابچه

/ketâbche/ ▶ noun
cahier - booklet

کتابخانه

/ketâbkhâne/ ▶ noun
library

کتابدار

/ketâbdâr/ ▶ noun
curator - librarian

کتابفروش

/ketâbforush/ ▶ noun
bookseller - bookman

کتابفروشی

/ketâbforushi/ ▶ noun
bookstore

کتان

/katân/ ▶ noun
linen - bombast

کتری

/ketri/ ▶ noun
skillet - pot - kettle

کتف

/ketf/ ▶ noun
shoulder - scapular - scapula

کتک

/kotak/ ▶ noun
smacker

کتک زدن

/kotak zadan/ ▶ verb
beat - mug - drub - clobber - thrash - smack

کتلت

/kotlet/ ▶ noun
cutlet

کتمان

/ketmân/ ▶ noun
reservation

كتيبه
/katibe/ ▶ noun
epigraph - cornice - coping - inscription

كثافت
/kesâfat/ ▶ noun
dirt - guck - impurity - pollution - muck
- mire

كثرت
/kesrat/ ▶ noun
multiplicity - intensity

كثيف
/kasif/ ▶ adjective
dirty - amiss - lousy - impure - mussy -
messy - sordid

كثيف كردن
/kasif kardan/ ▶ verb
dirty - soil

كج
/kaj/ ▶ adjective
indirect - lopsided - gauche - devious

كج شدن
/kaj shodan/ ▶ verb
lurch - heel - lean - careen - tilt - swerve

كج نهادن
/kaj nahâdan/ ▶ noun
cock

كج و معوج
/kajo ma'vaj/ ▶ noun
zigzag

كجا
/kojâ/ ▶ adverb
whither - where - where

كجى
/kaji/ ▶ adjective
slope - slant - skew - hade - list -
curvature - obliquity

كچل
/kachal/ ▶ noun
bald

كحالى
/kahâli/ ▶ noun
ophthalmology

كدام
/kodâm/ ▶ adverb
any - which - what

كدبانو
/kadbânu/ ▶ noun
dame - housewife - mistress - matron

كدخدا
/kadkhodâ/ ▶ noun
sheriff - reeve

کرانه

/karâne/ ▶ noun
littoral - mete - strand - shore

کدر

/keder/ ▶ adjective
glum - opaque - turbid

کراوات

/kerâvât/ ▶ noun
necktie - tie

کدر کردن

/keder kardan/ ▶ verb
tarnish

کرایه

/kerâye/ ▶ noun
portage - hire - lease - rent - freight -
fare

کدو

/kadu/ ▶ noun
gourd

کرایه کردن

/kerâye kardan/ ▶ verb
rent - lease - hire

کدورت

/kodurat/ ▶ noun
miff - tiff

کرباس

/karbâs/ ▶ noun
burlap - sackcloth

کذایی

/kazâyi/ ▶ noun
socalled - eventful

کرپ

/kerep/ ▶ noun
crepe - crape

کذب

/kezb/ ▶ noun
false - untruth (ful) - mendacity - lie

کرخ

/kerekh/ ▶ adjective
numbing - numb

کر کردن

/ker kardan/ ▶ verb
deafen

کردار

/kerdâr/ ▶ noun
jest - act - issue - exploit - deed

کرارا

/kerâran/ ▶ adverb
often - freuqently

کردن

/kardan/ ▶ verb
do - perform - peer

کرامت

/kerâmat/ ▶ noun
munificence

کرنا

/kernâ/ ► noun
horn - trumpet

کرسی

/korsi/ ► noun
stool

کره

/kore/ ► noun
sphere - globe

کرفس

/karafs/ ► noun
celery

کره زمین

/koreye zamin/ ► noun
earth

کرک

/kerk/ ► noun
pubes - pile - wool - fuzz

کروکی

/koruki/ ► noun
top

کرگدن

/kargadan/ ► noun
rhino - behemoth - hippopotamus

کروی

/koravi/ ► adjective
spherical - globular - global

کرم

/kerm/ ► noun
worm

کریدور

/koridor/ ► noun
hallway

کرم ابریشم

/kerme abrisham/ ► noun
silkworm

کریه

/karih/ ► adjective
detestable - offensive - nasty - unsightly
- ugly

کرم رنگ

/kerem rang/ ► adjective
cream

کزاز

/kozâz/ ► noun
tetanus

کرم روده

/kerme rude/ ► noun
helminth

کس

/kas/ ► noun
person

کرم کدو

/kerme kadu/ ► noun
jointworm - measles

كساد

/kesâd/ ► adjective
sluggish - slack - stagnant - tight -
insensitive - inactive - off

كساد شدن

/kesâd shodan/ ► verb
statgnate

كسادی

/kesâdi/ ► adjective
depression - recession - stringency -
slack

كسالت

/kesâlat/ ► noun
disorder

كسب

/kasb/ ► noun
traffic - trade - avocation - metier -
vocation

كسب تكليف

/kasbe taklif/ ► noun
referendum

كسب كردن

/kasb kardan/ ► verb
gain

كسر

/kasr/ ► noun
deficit - deficiency - deduction -
diminution - leakage - under

كسر درآمد

/kasre darâmad/ ► noun
deficit

كسر كردن

/kasr kardan/ ► verb
mute - detract - deduct

كسری

/kasri/ ► adjective
shortage - leakage - lack

كسل

/kesel/ ► adjective
weary - exanimate

كسل كننده

/kesle konande/ ► adjective
tedious - prosaic - irksome - drowsy -
drab

كسوت

/kesvat/ ► noun
garb

كسی

/kasi/ ► pronoun
someone - somebody - some - anybody -
one

كسی كه

/kasike/ ► pronoun
whom

كش آمدن
/kesh âmadan/ ► verb
stretch

كش دادن
/kesh dâdam/ ► verb
protract - stretch - strain

كش دار
/keshdâr/ ► adjective
supple - tensile

كشاكش
/keshâkesh/ ► noun
struggle - strife - conflict

كشاورز
/keshâvarz/ ► noun
yeomanly - yeoman - tiller - husband -
planter - peasant - agronomist - farmer

كشاورزی
/keshâvarzi/ ► noun
agronomy - husbandry

كشت كردن
/kesht kardan/ ► verb
cultivate

كشتار
/koshtâr/ ► noun
carnage - murder - massacre - planter

كشتارگاه
/koshtârgâh/ ► noun
abattoir - slaughterhouse - shambles

كشتكار
/keshtkâr/ ► noun
tiller - cultivator

كشتكاری
/keshtkâri/ ► noun
husbandry

كشتن
/koshtan/ ► verb
extinguish - out - doin - dispatch -
butcher - amortize - administer - murder

كشتی
/keshti/ ► noun
ship

كشتیران
/keshtirân/ ► noun
navigator

كشتیرانی
/keshtirâni/ ► noun
sailing

كشتیرانی كردن
/keshtirâni kardan/ ► verb
navigate

كشدار
/keshdâr/ ► adjective
elastic

كشسان
/keshsân/ ► adjective
elastic

كشش

/keshesh/ ▶ noun
pull - twitch - tug - magnetism -
inducement - haulage - haul - extension

كششی

/kesheshi/ ▶ noun
tensional

كشف

/kashf/ ▶ noun
detection - discovery - overture -
intuition

كشف رمز كردن

/kashfe ramz kardan/ ▶ verb
decode

كشف كردن

/kashf kardan/ ▶ verb
spot - uncover - discover - detect -
decode - decipher

كشک

/kashk/ ▶ noun
whey - curd

كشمش

/keshmesh/ ▶ noun
raisin

كشو

/keshô/ ▶ noun
drawer - slide - till

كشور

/keshvar/ ▶ noun
territory - state - soil - commonwealth -
nation - kingdom - country

كشورداری

/keshvardâri/ ▶ noun
statecraft

كشورگشا

/keshvargoshâ/ ▶ adjective
conqueror

كشیدگی

/keshidegi/ ▶ noun
elongation

كشیدن

/keshidan/ ▶ verb
pull - strain - lengthen - lave - heave -
haul - figure - weigh - entrain - draw -
drag

كشیده

/keshide/ ▶ adjective
oblong - extensive - long - linear - taut

كشیش

/keshish/ ▶ noun
priest - ecclesiastic - divine - cleric -
clergyman - cassock

كشیک

/keshik/ ▶ noun
sentry - sentinel - vigilance - picket -
watch

كف

/kaf/ ▶ noun
foam - bottom - silt - scum

كفگير

/kafgir/ ▶ noun
splatter - spatula

كف آلود

/kafâlud/ ▶ adjective
sudsy - scummy

كفن

/kafan/ ▶ noun
shroud

كف بين

/kafbin/ ▶ noun
palmist

كفن كردن

/kafan kardan/ ▶ verb
shroud

كفالت

/kefâlat/ ▶ noun
bail

كفه

/kafe/ ▶ noun
pan

كفايت كردن

/kefâyat kardan/ ▶ verb
do - suffice

كفيل

/kafil/ ▶ adjective
surety - sponsor - guarantor - bondsman
- bond

كفر

/kofr/ ▶ noun
atheism - infidelity - heresy

كل

/kol/ ▶ noun
total

كفر آميز

/kofrâmiz/ ▶ adjective
profane - unholy - unhallowed -
unhallow

كلاس

/kelâs/ ▶ noun
class

كفرگويی

/kofrguyi/ ▶ noun
swearword - profanity

كلاس درس

/kelâse dars/ ▶ noun
classroom

كفش

/kafsh/ ▶ noun
shoe

كلاغ

/kalâgh/ ▶ noun
crow

كلاف
/kalâf/ ▶ noun
skein - hasp - hank

كلافه
/kalâfe/ ▶ noun
hank

كلام
/kalâm/ ▶ noun
language

كلان
/kalân/ ▶ noun
massive - immense - huge

كلان شهر
/kalânshahr/ ▶ noun
metropolis

كلانتر
/kalântar/ ▶ noun
sheriff - reeve - marshal

كلانتری
/kalântari/ ▶ noun
policestation - commissariat

كلاه
/kolâh/ ▶ noun
cap - hat

كلاه بردار
/kolâhbardâr/ ▶ adjective
swindler - crook

كلاه برداری
/kolâhbardâri/ ▶ noun
swindle

كلاه خود
/kolâhkhud/ ▶ noun
helmet

كلاه گذاشتن
/kolâh gozâshtan/ ▶ verb
welsh

كلاهبردار
/kolâhbardâri/ ▶ adjective
rook - hustler

كلاهک
/kolâhak/ ▶ noun
warhead - cap - cupule - bonnet - lid

كلبه
/kolbe/ ▶ noun
cottage - cabin - cabana - hut - hull -
hovel - lodge

كلروفيل
/kolorofil/ ▶ noun
chlorophyl

كلسيم
/kalsiyom/ ▶ noun
calcium

كلفت
/koloft/ ▶ noun
housemaid - charwoman - stocky

کلک

/kalak/ ► noun
pen

کلکسیون

/koleksiyon/ ► noun
collection

کلم

/kalam/ ► noun
cabbage

کلمه

/kalame/ ► noun
word

کلنگ

/kolang/ ► noun
hack - pick

کله

/kale/ ► noun
head - brain - pate - pash

کلوخ

/kolukh/ ► noun
clod

کلی

/koli/ ► noun
universal - material - generic - general -
totality - total

کلیت

/koliyat/ ► noun
totality - universalization - universality -
universalism

کلید

/kelid/ ► noun
passport - key

کلیسا

/kelisa/ ► noun
church - abbey

کلیشه

/kelishe/ ► noun
stereotype - type

کلیمی

/kalimi/ ► noun
jew

کلیه

/koliye/ ► noun
kidney - all

کم

/kam/ ► noun
small - slight - little - low

کم آب

/kamâb/ ► adjective
shallow

کم ارزش

/kam arzesh/ ► adjective
cheap

كماج
/komaj/ ▶ adjective
shortbread

كم پشت
/kamposht/ ▶ adjective
sparse - thin

كمال
/kamâl/ ▶ noun
sophistication - amplitude -
accomplishment - prime - period -
perfection - maturity - integrity

كم خونى
/kamkhuni/ ▶ noun
anemia - anaemia

كم داشتن
/kam dâshtan/ ▶ verb
lack

كماندار
/kamândâr/ ▶ noun
archer

كم دوام
/kam davâm/ ▶ adjective
memnetary - weak

كمانه
/kamâne/ ▶ noun
ricochet

كم رو
/kamru/ ▶ adjective
weak

كمانه كردن
/kamâne kardan/ ▶ verb
ricochet

كم رويى
/kamruyi/ ▶ noun
diffidence

كمباين
/kombâin/ ▶ noun
combine

كم عقل
/kam aghl/ ▶ adjective
vacuous

كمبود
/kambud/ ▶ adjective
shortcoming - shortage - leakage -
deficit - deficiency - dearth

كم كردن
/kam kardan/ ▶ verb
subtract - detract - deduct - deduce - cut
- extenuate - drawoff - retrench - reduce

كمپرسور
/komperesor/ ▶ noun
compressor

كم و كاستى
/kamo kasti/ ▶ noun
wane

کمربند
/kamarband/ ► noun
belt

کمردرد
/kamardard/ ► noun
backache

کمرنگ
/kamrang/ ► adjective
inconspicuous - pale - lunar

کمرو
/kamru/ ► adjective
shy - sheepish - timid - coy - chicken -
chary - cagey - meticulous - unassertive

کمک
/komak/ ► noun
assistance - assist - help

کمک کردن
/komak kardan/ ► verb
help - hand - boost - aid - relieve -
redound

کمک هزینه
/komakhazine/ ► noun
subvention

کمکی
/komaki/ ► adjective
secondary - subsidiary - auxiliary

کمند
/kamand/ ► noun
noose - lasso - lariat - snarl - snare -
tether

کمپوت
/komput/ ► noun
compote

کمتر
/kamtar/ ► adjective
lesser - less

کمتر از
/kamtar az/ ► adjective
under

کمتر کردن
/kamtar kardan/ ► verb
lessen

کمترین
/kamtarin/ ► adjective
least

کمد
/komod/ ► noun
dresser - commode

کمدی
/komodi/ ► adjective
comedy

کمر
/kamar/ ► noun
meddle - loin - crag - girdle - waistline

کمند انداختن
/kamand andâkhtan/ ► verb
lasso

کمونیسم
/komonism/ ► noun
communism - communalism

کمی
/kami/ ► adjective
paucity - peep - insufficiency -
infrequency - deficiency

کمیاب
/kamyâb/ ► adjective
rare - curiosity - infrequent - uncommon
- scarce

کمیابی
/kamyâbi/ ► noun
scarcity - paucity - poverty -
infrequency - rarity

کمیت
/kamiyat/ ► noun
quantity

کمیسیون
/komisiyon/ ► noun
committee - commission

کمین
/kamin/ ► noun
ambush

کمین کردن
/kamin kardan/ ► verb
stalk - waylay - lurk - ambush

کنار
/kenâr/ ► noun
shunt - by - brink - brim - besides - bank
- away - apart - list - lip - limit - verge -
margin - recess - rand - next

کنار رفتن
/kenâr raftan/ ► verb
sheer

کناره
/kenâre/ ► noun
edge - border

کناره گرفتن
/kenâre gereftan/ ► verb
resign

کناره گیری کردن
/kenâregiri kardan/ ► verb
secede - abdicate - retire

کنایه
/kenâye/ ► noun
jest - squib - quibble - allusion - allegory
- metaphor - lampoon - innuendo - quip

کنایه آمیز
/kenâye âmiz/ ► adjective
wry - snide - sardonic

کنذهن
/kondzehn/ ▶ adjective
imbecile - obtuse - dimwit - stupid

کنایه زدن
/kenâye zadan/ ▶ verb
squib

کندن
/kandan/ ▶ verb
dig - cutout - mine - pick - peel - trench - pull

کنترل
/kontorol/ ▶ noun
rein - control

کندو
/kandu/ ▶ noun
apiary - beehive - hive

کنتور
/kontor/ ▶ noun
meter

کنسرت
/konsert/ ▶ noun
concert

کنج
/konj/ ▶ noun
corner - angle

کنسرو
/konserv/ ▶ noun
conserve

کنجکاو
/konjkâv/ ▶ adjective
curious - prowler

کنسول
/konsul/ ▶ noun
consul

کنجکاوی
/konjkâvi/ ▶ noun
pry

کنسولگری
/konsulgari/ ▶ noun
consulate

کنجکاوی کردن
/konjkâvi kardan/ ▶ verb
poke

کنسولی
/konsuli/ ▶ noun
consular

کند
/kond/ ▶ adjective
slow - heavy - haunt - leaden - lazy - late

کنش
/konesh/ ▶ noun
action - act

کند کردن
/kond kardan/ ▶ verb
rebate

کنش گر
/koneshgar/ ▶ adjective
active

کنفرانس
/konferâns/ ▶ noun
conference - lecture

کنکاش کردن
/kankâsh kardan/ ▶ verb
deliberate - consult

کنگره
/kongere/ ▶ noun
congress

کنونی
/konuni/ ▶ adjective
modern - current

کهربا
/kahrobâ/ ▶ adjective
amber

کهکشان
/kahkeshân/ ▶ noun
galaxy

کهن
/kohan/ ▶ adjective
hoary - ancient - olden

کهن سال
/kohansâl/ ▶ adjective
old

کهنگی
/kohnegi/ ▶ noun
archaism - obsolescence

کهنه
/kohne/ ▶ adjective
old - obsolete - obsolescent - antique -
ancient

کهنه کار
/kohnekâr/ ▶ adjective
old - veteran

کهولت
/kohulat/ ▶ noun
senility

کو
/ku/ ▶ preposition
where?

کوارتز
/kovârtz/ ▶ noun
quartz

کوبنده
/kubande/ ▶ adjective
knocker - pounder - masher

کوبیدن
/kubidan/ ▶ verb
bruise - beat - hammer - mallet - knock

کوپال
/kupâl/ ▶ noun
mace

کوپن

/kopon/ ▶ noun
coupon

کوتاه

/kutâh/ ▶ adjective
short - succinct - stunt - stocky - low -
little - concise

کوتاه قد

/kutâhghad/ ▶ adjective
stump

کوتاه کردن

/kutâh kardan/ ▶ verb
abridge - abbreviate - shorten - short -
stag

کوتاه و مختصر

/kutâh va mokhtasar/ ▶ adjective
curt

کوته بین

/khutahbin/ ▶ adjective
sectarian

کوته فکر

/khutahfekr/ ▶ adjective
lowminded - dogmatic - prude -
provincial

کوته فکری

/kutahfekri/ ▶ noun
prudery

کوته نظر

/kutahnazar/ ▶ adjective
hidebound - parochial - lowminded -
smug

کوتوله

/kutule/ ▶ noun
stub - dwarf - grub - gnome - runt

کوچ

/kuch/ ▶ noun
departure - migration

کوچ دادن

/kuch dâdan/ ▶ verb
transplant - transmigrate

کوچ نشین

/kuchneshin/ ▶ noun
immigrant

کوچک

/kuchak/ ▶ adjective
small - short - thumbnail -little

کوچک شدن

/kuchak shodan/ ▶ verb
shrink

کوچکتر

/kuchektar/ ▶ adjective
lesser - less - minor - beneath

کوچکترین

/kuchektarin/ ▶ adjective
least

کوچه

/kuche/ ▶ noun
alley - lane - street

کور

/dur/ ▶ adjective
sightless - blind

کوچولو

/kuchulu/ ▶ adjective
tiny - kid - wee

کوره

/kure/ ▶ noun
stove - chimney - oven - kiln - manhole

کوچیدن

/kuchidan/ ▶ verb
migrate

کوزه

/kuze/ ▶ noun
urn - pitcher - cruse - jug

کود

/kud/ ▶ noun
dung - muck

کوژ

/kuzh/ ▶ adjective
convex

کود دادن

/kud dâdan/ ▶ verb
manure - dung - compost

کوسن

/kôsan/ ▶ noun
cushion - squab

کودتا

/kudetâ/ ▶ noun
coup

کوشا

/kushâ/ ▶ adjective
industrious - diligent - studious

کودک

/kudak/ ▶ noun
kid - chit - child - baby - babe - infant

کوشش

/kushesh/ ▶ noun
effort - attempt - assay - bustle - muss - labor

کودکی

/kudaki/ ▶ noun
childhood - imfancy

کوشیدن

/kushidan/ ▶ verb
tug - try - strive - endeavor

کودن

/kôdan/ ▶ adjective
dull - unintelligent - unapt - lug - birdbrain - backward

کوفتن

/kuftan/ ▶ verb
oppress

کوک

/kudak/ ▶ noun
stitch

کولی

/kuli/ ▶ noun
gypsy - gipsy - hungarian

کوک کردن

/kuk kardan/ ▶ verb
crank - key

کون

/kun/ ▶ noun
ass

کوکب

/kôkab/ ▶ noun
star

کون و مکان

/kônomakân/ ▶ noun
universe

کول

/kul/ ▶ noun
piggyback - pickaback

کوه

/kuh/ ▶ noun
mountain

کول کردن

/kul kardan/ ▶ verb
piggyback - pickaback

کوه پیما

/kuhpeimâ/ ▶ noun
mountaineer

کولاک

/kulâk/ ▶ noun
storm - blizzard

کوهان

/kuhân/ ▶ noun
hunch - hump

کولر

/kuler/ ▶ noun
cooler

کوهستانی

/kuhestân/ ▶ adjective
mountainous - mountain

کوله بار

/kulebâr/ ▶ noun
knapsack

کوهنورد

/kuhnavard/ ▶ noun
mountaineer

کوله پشتی

/kuleposhti/ ▶ noun
pack - knapsack

کی

/ki/ ▶ preposition
who

کیفری

/keifari/ ▶ noun
pnitive - retribution - penal

کیاست

/kiyasat/ ▶ noun
perspicacity

کیفیت

/keifiyat/ ▶ noun
quality

کیر

/kir/ ▶ noun
penis

کیک

/keik/ ▶ noun
cake

کیسه

/kise/ ▶ noun
bag - capsule - bung

کیلوگرم

/kilugaram/ ▶ noun
kilogram

کیسه پول

/kiseye pul/ ▶ noun
purse

کیلومتر

/kilumetr/ ▶ noun
kilometer

کیش

/kish/ ▶ noun
religion - faith

کیلووات

/kiluvât/ ▶ noun
kilowatt

کیف

/kif/ ▶ noun
bag

کیمیاگری

/kimiyâgari/ ▶ noun
alchemy

کیف کردن

/keif kardan/ ▶ verb
please

کیمیایی

/kimiyâyi/ ▶ noun
chemical

کیفر

/keifar/ ▶ noun
retribution - penalty

کینه

/kine/ ▶ noun
enmity - onomastic - hatred - peeve

کیفر دادن

/keifar dâdan/ ▶ verb
punish

کینه توز

/kinetuz/ ► adjective
spiteful - dispiteous - venomous -
vengeful - implacable

کینه توزی

/kinetuzi/ ► noun
implacability - malice

کینه جو

/kineju/ ► adjective
virulent - malignant

کینه جویی

/kinejuyi/ ► noun
nemesis

کینه جویی کردن

/kinejuyi kardan/ ► verb
revenge

کینه ورزیدن

/kinevarzi/ ► verb
hate

کیهان

/keihân/ ► noun
universe - cosmos

کیهان شناس

/keihânshenâs/ ► noun
cosmographer

کیهان شناسی

/keihânshenâsi/ ► noun
cosmology - cosmogony

کیهانی

/keihâni/ ► adjective
cosmic

گ - گ

gâf /ge/ ► twenty-sixth letter of the Persian alphabet

گاراژ

/gârâzh/ ► noun
garage

گارانتی

/gârânti/ ► noun
warranty

گارد

/gârd/ ► noun
lifeguard - guard

گاری

/gâri/ ► noun
cart

گاز

/gâz/ ► noun
bite - gas

گاز زدن

/gâz zadan/ ► verb
nibble

گاز گرفتن

/gâz gereftan/ ► verb
bite

گاز معده

/gâzeme'de/ ► noun
gas

گازانبر

/gâzanbor/ ► noun
pincer - calliper - caliper

گازدار

/gâzdâr/ ► adjective
gaseous

گازسوز

/gâzsuz/ ► adjective
gaslight

گازی

/gâzi/ ► adjective
gaseous

گال

/gâl/ ► adjective
scabies

گالری

/gâleri/ ► noun
gallery

گالن

/gâlon/ ► noun
gallon

گاوصندوق

/gâvsandugh/ ▶ noun
strongbox - safedeposit

گام

/gâm/ ▶ noun
step - pace - gamut - gait

گپ

/gap/ ▶ noun
chat

گام برداشتن

/gâm bardâshtan/ ▶ verb
gait

گپ زدن

/gap zadan/ ▶ verb
chat

گاه

/gâh/ ▶ noun
time - period

گچ

/gach/ ▶ noun
chalk

گاه شمار

/gâhshomâr/ ▶ noun
timepiece

گچ بری

/gachbori/ ▶ noun
tore

گاه و بیگاه

/gâhobigâh/ ▶ noun
occasionally - sporadic

گچی

/gachi/ ▶ adjective
chalky

گاهگاهی

/gâhgâhi/ ▶ adverb
sometime

گدا

/gedâ/ ▶ noun
beggar - pauper

گاهی

/gâhi/ ▶ adverb
somewhen

گداخانه

/gedâkhâne/ ▶ noun
poorhouse - almshouse

گاو

/gâv/ ▶ noun
cow

گداختن

/godâkhtan/ ▶ verb
thaw - smelt - dissolve - liquefy - melt

گاوآهن

/gâvâhan/ ▶ noun
plough - plow

گذر

/gozar/ ▶ noun
transit - passage - pass

گذران

/gozarân/ ▶ adjective
maintenance

گذران کردن

/gozarân kardan/ ▶ verb
subsist - fare

گذراندن

/gozarândan/ ▶ verb
survive - fare - outwear - while

گذرگاه

/gozargâh/ ▶ noun
defile - causeway - gangway - pathway -
passageway - passage - pass

گذرنامه

/gozarnâme/ ▶ noun
passport - pass

گذشت

/gozasht/ ▶ noun
remission - amnesty - pardon

گذشت زمان

/gozashte zamân/ ▶ noun
lapse

گذشت کردن

/gozasht kardan/ ▶ verb
remise

گداخته

/godâkhte/ ▶ adjective
molten

گداخته شدن

/godâkhte shodan/ ▶ verb
smelt

گداز

/godâz/ ▶ noun
melt

گداز آتشفشانی

/godâzeye âtashfeshâni/ ▶ noun
slag

گدازه

/godâze/ ▶ noun
lava

گدایی کردن

/gedâyi kardan/ ▶ verb
beg

گذاردن

/gozârdan/ ▶ verb
set - repose - pose - imprint - lay - invest

گذاشتن

/gozâshtan/ ▶ verb
attach - lodge - let - leave - infiltrate -
have - place - deposit - cut - stead -
shunt

گذشتن
/gozashtan/ ▶ verb
pass - blowover - elapse - cross - go

گرانبها
/gerânbahâ/ ▶ adjective
valuable - lief - inestimable - rich

گذشته
/gozashte/ ▶ adjective
late - bygone - back - past - old

گرانیت
/gerânit/ ▶ noun
granite

گر
/gor/ ▶ adjective
scab - mangey - mangy - mange

گرایش
/gerâyesh/ ▶ noun
tendency - propensity - attitude - ism

گراز
/gorâz/ ▶ noun
hog - pork - pig

گراییدن
/gerâyidan/ ▶ verb
join

گرافیک
/gerâfik/ ▶ noun
graph

گربه
/gorbe/ ▶ noun
cat

گرامافون
/gerâmâfon/ ▶ noun
gramophone - phonograph

گربه وحشی
/gorbeye vahshi/ ▶ noun
wildcat

گرامی
/gerâmi/ ▶ adjective
dear

گرچه
/garche/ ▶ preposition
though

گران
/gerân/ ▶ adjective
expensive - exclusive - costly - onerous
- high - heavy - sumptuous - prohibitive

گرد
/gard/ ▶ noun
powder- flour

گرانبار
/gerânbâr/ ▶ adjective
burdensome

گرد آمدن
/gerdâmadan/ ▶ verb
flock - gather - convene - constringe -
herd - assemble - agglomerate

گردانیدن

/gardânidan/ ▶ verb
wield

گردباد

/gerdbâd/ ▶ noun
tornado - typhoon - twister - hurricane -
cyclone - whirlwind

گردش

/gardesh/ ▶ noun
circulation - meander - period -
operation - wrest - gyration - rev - race -
canter - roll

گردشگاه

/gardeshgâh/ ▶ noun
promenade - park - walkway - walk -
espianade

گردشی

/gardeshi/ ▶ adjective
rotatory - ambulatory

گردن

/gardan/ ▶ noun
neck

گردن بند

/gardanband/ ▶ noun
collar - necklace

گردن زدن

/gardan zadan/ ▶ verb
decollate - decapitate - behead

گرد آوردن

/gerdâvardan/ ▶ verb
troop - assemble - amass - compile -
collect

گرد و خاک

/gardokhâk/ ▶ noun
dust

گرد و خاکی

/gardokhâki/ ▶ noun
dusty

گردآوری

/gerdâvari/ ▶ noun
compilation - collection

گرداب

/gerdâb/ ▶ noun
vortex - whirlpool - gulf - gourd

گرداگرد

/gerdâgerd/ ▶ noun
around - about

گردان

/gordân/ ▶ noun
battalion - versatile - winch

گرداندن

/gardândan/ ▶ verb
operate - wheel - manage - turquoise

گرداننده

/gardânande/ ▶ adjective
operator

گردن کلفت

/gardankoloft/ ▶ adjective
stodgy - thug - bully - dumpy - ruffian -
roughneck

گردن نهادن

/gardan nahâdan/ ▶ verb
submit

گردنکش

/gardankesh/ ▶ adjective
turbulent - disobedient - refractory

گردنکشی

/gardankeshi/ ▶ noun
turbulence

گردنه

/gardane/ ▶ noun
neck - cervix - defile - stem

گرده

/gorde/ ▶ noun
kidney

گردو

/gerdu/ ▶ noun
walnut

گردون

/gardun/ ▶ noun
sphere - heaven

گردونه

/gardune/ ▶ noun
pass

گرز

/gorz/ ▶ noun
maul - mallet - wand - club

گرسنگی

/gorosnegi/ ▶ noun
hunger - starvation

گرسنگی دادن

/gorosnegi dâdan/ ▶ verb
starve - hunger

گرسنه

/gorosne/ ▶ noun
hungry

گرفتار

/gereftâr/ ▶ adjective
afoul - captive

گرفتار کردن

/gereftâr kardan/ ▶ verb
entangle - enmesh - incriminate -
implicate - hook - involve

گرفتارساختن

/gereftâr sâkhtan/ ▶ verb
gin

گرفتاری

/gereftâri/ ▶ noun
constraint - encumbrance - mire - plight
- involvement

گرفتگی

/gereftegi/ ▶ noun
melancholia - eclipse - congestion -
obstruction - jamming

گرفتن

/gereftan/ ▶ verb
hold - catch - capture - grab - obturate -
obtain - engage - educe - devest

گرگ

/gorg/ ▶ noun
wolf

گرم

/garm/ ▶ noun
hot - warm

گرم

/geram/ ▶ noun
gram

گرم شدن

/garm shodan/ ▶ verb
thaw - warm

گرم کردن

/garm kardan/ ▶ verb
heat - braise - anneal - warm

گرم کننده

/garm konande/ ▶ adjective
warmer

گرم و نرم

/garmo narm/ ▶ adjective
snug - cozy

گرما

/garmâ/ ▶ noun
heat - therm

گرمابه

/garmâbe/ ▶ noun
bathroom - bath

گرمایی

/garmâyi/ ▶ noun
thermal

گرمخانه

/garmkhâne/ ▶ noun
stove - greenhouse

گرمسیر

/garmsir/ ▶ adjective
tropic

گرمسیری

/garmsiri/ ▶ noun
tropic

گرمی

/garmi/ ▶ noun
heat - warmth - glow - rut

گره

/gere/ ▶ noun
tie - lump - burr - knot - knob - ganglion

گره خوردن

/gere khordan/ ▶ verb
knot - snarl

گروه بندی

/goruhbandi/ ▶ noun
regimentation

گره دار

/geredâr/ ▶ adjective
burly - knotty

گروه بندی کردن

/goruhbandi kardan/ ▶ verb
group

گره زدن

/gere zadan/ ▶ verb
twitch - truss - tie - loop - ruffle - knot

گروهی

/goruhi/ ▶ noun
gregarious - republican

گره گشایی

/geregoshâyi/ ▶ noun
relief

گرویدن

/geravidan/ ▶ verb
gravitate

گره گشودن

/gere goshudan/ ▶ verb
unweave

گریان

/geryân/ ▶ adjective
weepy - moist

گرو

/gerô/ ▶ noun
deposit - encumbrance

گریبان

/garibân/ ▶ noun
collar

گرو گذاشتن

/gerô gozâshtan/ ▶ verb
engage - pledge - pawn

گریختن

/gorikhtan/ ▶ verb
slip - skedaddle - shun - escape - desert - runaway - abscond

گروگان

/gerôgân/ ▶ noun
hostage

گریزان

/gorizân/ ▶ adjective
runaway - evasive - elusive

گروه

/goruh/ ▶ noun
group - team - flock - company - cohort - cluster - clinch - class

گریس

/gris/ ▶ noun
grease

گریه

/gerye/ ▶ noun
sob - tear - cry - greet

گزارش

/gozâresh/ ▶ noun
story - report - inkling - hearing -
account

گزارش دادن

/gozâresh dâdan/ ▶ verb
report - relate

گزارشگر

/gozâreshgar/ ▶ noun
reporter

گزاره

/gozâre/ ▶ noun
predicate

گزاف

/gazâf/ ▶ noun
extravagant - - exorbitant - costly -
rodomontade - unconscionable

گزاف گویی

/gazâfguyi/ ▶ noun
extravaganza - hyperbole - bounce

گزاف گویی کردن

/gazâfguyi kardan/ ▶ verb
bounce

گزافه گو

/gazâfegu/ ▶ adjective
braggart - braggadocio

گزافه گویی کردن

/gazâfeguyi kardan/ ▶ verb
rodomontade - overstate - exaggerate

گزند

/gazand/ ▶ noun
harm - detriment

گزندگی

/gazandegi/ ▶ noun
bite

گزنده

/gazande/ ▶ adjective
damage - piquant

گزنه

/gazne/ ▶ noun
nettle

گزیدن

/gazidan/ ▶ verb
select - sting - bite - choose

گزیر

/gozir/ ▶ noun
remedy

گزینش

/gozinesh/ ▶ noun
election

گزینشی

/gozineshi/ ▶ adjective
selective - elective

گس

/gas/ ▶ adjective
astringent - acrid

گستاخ

/gostâkh/ ▶ adjective
rude - insolent - unabashed - brash -
boldface - bold - barefaced - arrogant

گستاخ شدن

/khostâkh shodan/ ▶ verb
wanton

گستاخی

/gostâkhi/ ▶ noun
impudence - impertinence - insolence -
presumption

گستاخی کردن

/gostâkhi kardan/ ▶ verb
brazen - blab

گستردن

/gostardan/ ▶ verb
spread - propagate - layon

گسترده

/gostarde/ ▶ adjective
widespread - splay

گسترده کردن

/gostarde kardan/ ▶ verb
explode

گسترش

/gostaresh/ ▶ noun
propagation - spread - deploy -
extension - expanse

گسستگی

/gosastegi/ ▶ noun
rupture

گسستن

/gosastan/ ▶ verb
tear - disconnect - cut - rupture

گسیختگی

/gosikhtegi/ ▶ noun
rupture

گشاد

/goshâd/ ▶ adjective
loose - broad - wide - spacious - slack

گشادگی

/goshâdegi/ ▶ noun
aperture

گشادن

/goshâdan/ ▶ verb
solve - evolve - open

گشاده
/goshâde/ ▶ adjective
patent

گفت
/goft/ ▶ verb
said

گشاینده
/goshâyande/ ▶ adjective
opener

گفت و شنود
/gofto shenud/ ▶ noun
dialogue

گشت
/gasht/ ▶ noun
tour - veer

گفتار
/goftâr/ ▶ adjective
speech - sermon - article - word

گشت زدن
/gasht zadan/ ▶ verb
cruise - patrol

گفتگو
/goftogu/ ▶ noun
talk - parlance - dialogue - converse -
conversation - conference - discussion

گشتاوری
/gashtâvari/ ▶ noun
torque

گفتگویی
/goftoguyi/ ▶ noun
colloquial

گشتن
/gashtan/ ▶ verb
search - swirl - turquoise - trundle - troll

گفتن
/goftan/ ▶ verb
say - tell - relate - rehearse - cite -
observe - intimate - inform

گشتی
/gashti/ ▶ noun
patrolman - patrol

گل
/gel/ ▶ noun
mud

گشودن
/goshudan/ ▶ verb
untie - unlace - open

گل
/gol/ ▶ noun
flower - blossom

گشوده
/goshude/ ▶ adjective
open - unbutton

گلابتون
/golâbatun/ ► noun
purl - braid

گل رس
/gole ros/ ► noun
bole

گلادیاتور
/gelâdiyâtor/ ► noun
gladiator

گل زدن
/gol zadan/ ► verb
goal

گلاویز شدن
/galâviz shodan/ ► verb
wrestle - grapple

گل کردن
/gol kardan/ ► verb
flower

گلبرگ
/golbarg/ ► noun
calycle

گل لاله
/gole lâle/ ► noun
tulip

گلبن
/golbon/ ► noun
shrub

گل میخک
/gole mikhak/ ► noun
clove

گلبول
/golbul/ ► noun
globule

گل مینا
/gole minâ/ ► noun
aster

گلبول سفید خون
/golbule sefide khun/ ► noun
leukocyte

گل نسترن
/gole nastaran/ ► noun
jonquil

گلچهره
/golchehre/ ► noun
ruddy

گلاب
/golâb/ ► noun
rosewater

گلچین
/golchin/ ► noun
elite

گلاب پاش
/golâbpâsh/ ► noun
sprinkler

گلنگدن

/galangadan/ ▶ noun
spanner

گله

/gale/ ▶ noun
grumble - flock - quarrel - herd

گلو

/galu/ ▶ noun
gullet - gorge - lane - throttle - throat

گلوبند

/galuband/ ▶ noun
bangle

گلوکز

/golokoz/ ▶ noun
glucose

گلوگاه

/galugâh/ ▶ noun
gorge

گلوله

/golule/ ▶ noun
shot - bullet - cartridge - gunshot

گلوله کردن

/golule kardan/ ▶ verb
ball

گلی

/geli/ ▶ adjective
muddy - earthen - draggy - roseate

گلچین کردن

/golchin kardan/ ▶ verb
tab - cull - excerpt - pluck

گلچینی

/golchini/ ▶ adjective
eclecticism

گلخانه

/golkhâne/ ▶ noun
nursery - greenhouse - greenery -
glasshouse

گلدان

/goldân/ ▶ noun
jardiniere - urn - vase - pot

گلدوزی

/golduzi/ ▶ noun
needlework

گلر

/goler/ ▶ noun
goalkeeper

گلستان

/golestân/ ▶ noun
rosery - rosary

گلکاری کردن

/golkâri kardan/ ▶ verb
flower

گلگون

/golgun/ ▶ adjective
ruddy - rosy - roseate

گلی شدن

/geli shodan/ ▶ verb
drabble

گماشت

/gomâsht/ ▶ noun
duty - appointment

گماشتن

/gomâshtan/ ▶ verb
charge - designate - assign - appoint

گماشته

/gomâshte/ ▶ adjective
agent

گمان

/gomân/ ▶ noun
supposition - idea - belief - assumption -
aim - doubt - guess - opinion

گمان کردن

/gomân kardan/ ▶ verb
think - suspect - suppose - reckon

گمانه

/gamâne/ ▶ noun
bore

گمانه زدن

/gamâne zadan/ ▶ verb
sound

گمراه

/gomrâh/ ▶ adjective
devious - perverse - heterodox - astray

گمراه شدن

/gomrâh shodan/ ▶ verb
stray - err - pervert

گمراه کردن

/gomrâh kardan/ ▶ verb
seduce - mislead - misinform - misguide
- misdirect

گمراه کننده

/gomrâh konande/ ▶ adjective
sinuous - sinister - seducer - screwy

گمراهی

/gomrâhi/ ▶ noun
slip - obliquity - loss

گمرک

/gomrok/ ▶ noun
custom

گمنام

/gomnâm/ ▶ adjective
obscure - inglorious - unknown -
scrubby

گمنام کردن

/gomnâm kardan/ ▶ verb
obscure

گمنامی

/gomnâmi/ ▶ noun
anonymity - obscurity - oblivion

گناه
/gonâh/ ▶ noun
sin - transgression - crime - guilt - vice -
misdemeanor - misdeed - blame

گناهکار
/gonâhkâr/ ▶ adjective
guilty - wicked - unrighteous -
unregenerate - sinner - sinful

گنبد
/gonbad/ ▶ noun
dome - cupola - vault

گنج
/ganj/ ▶ noun
treasury - treasure - hoard

گنجانیدن
/gonjânidan/ ▶ verb
lug

گنجایش
/gonjâyesh/ ▶ noun
content - capacity - module - inclusion -
aptitude - burden

گنجینه
/ganjine/ ▶ noun
thesaurus - trove - treasury - treasure

گند
/gand/ ▶ adjective
stink - stench

گنداب
/gandâb/ ▶ noun
bog - sewer - sewage

گندم
/gandom/ ▶ noun
wheat

گنده
/gonde/ ▶ adjective
whopper - unwieldy - massive - huge

گندیدگی
/gandidegi/ ▶ noun
putrefaction

گندیدن
/gandidan/ ▶ verb
putrefy

گنگ
/gong/ ▶ adjective
incommensurable - mute - unvocal -
whist

گهواره
/gahvâre/ ▶ noun
cradle

گوارا
/govârâ/ ▶ adjective
salubrious - tasty - soft - digestive -
digestible

گوارش

/govâresh/ ▶ noun
digestion

گوارشی

/govâreshi/ ▶ noun
digestive

گواه

/govâh/ ▶ noun
proof - voucher - evidence

گواهی

/govâhi/ ▶ noun
testimony - warrant - deposition -
evidence

گواهی دادن

/govâhi dâdan/ ▶ verb
testify

گواهینامه

/govâhinâme/ ▶ noun
certificate - diploma - affidavit

گوجه

/gôje/ ▶ noun
sloe - plum

گود

/gôd/ ▶ adjective
dished - deep - ring - arena

گود کردن

/gôd kardan/ ▶ verb
scoop - gull - deepen

گودال

/gôdâl/ ▶ noun
trench - puddle - swag - sinus - grave -
cavity - cavern - vesicle - pit - hole

گودی

/gôdi/ ▶ adjective
valley - lacuna - dint - depth - dent -
delve - groove

گور

/gur/ ▶ noun
tomb

گورستان

/gurestân/ ▶ noun
cemetery

گورکن

/gurkan/ ▶ noun
sexton - badger - pitman

گوریل

/guril/ ▶ noun
gorilla

گوزیدن

/guzidan/ ▶ verb
poop

گوژپشت

/guzhposht/ ▶ noun
crookback - humpback

گوساله

/gusâle/ ▶ noun
veal - calf

گوسفند

/gusfand/ ▶ noun
mutton

گوش

/gush/ ▶ noun
ear

(Idiom: یاسین به گوش خر خواندن
Waste one's breathe on somebody)

(Idiom: گوش به زنگ بودن
Keep one's ear to the ground)

گوش بر

/gushbor/ ▶ adjective
swindler

گوش بری

/gushbori/ ▶ noun
shark

گوش بزنگ

/gushbezang/ ▶ noun
alert - vigilant - wakeful

گوش خراش

/gushkharâsh/ ▶ adjective
strident - loud

گوش دادن

/gush dâdan/ ▶ verb
listen

گوش کردن

/gush kardan/ ▶ verb
hear

گوشت

/gusht/ ▶ noun
bully - brawn - viand

گوشتخوار

/gushtkhâr/ ▶ adjective
zoophagous

گوشتی

/gushti/ ▶ verb
meaty

گوشخراش

/gushkhârâsh/ ▶ adjective
earsplitting

گوشمال دادن

/gushmâl dâdan/ ▶ verb
punish

گوشمالی

/gushmâli/ ▶ adjective
rebuke - scourge - punishment

گوشه

/gushe/ ▶ noun
jest - angle - lobe - nook - quip - recess - corner

گوناگون

/gunâgun/ ▶ adjective
diverse - varied

گوشه نشین

/gusheneshin/ ▶ adjective
solitudinarian - solitary - unsociable - recluse

گونه

/gune/ ▶ noun
type - sort - species - navigate - nature - kind

گوشواره

/gushvâre/ ▶ noun
earring - eardrop

گونی

/guni/ ▶ noun
sacking - sack - gunny

گوشی

/gushi/ ▶ noun
receiver - aural

گوه

/goh/ ▶ noun
gad - cleat - slice - sprag

گوشی تلفن

/gushiye telefon/ ▶ noun
phone

گوهر

/gôhar/ ▶ noun
essence - navigate - nature - gem - jewel

گوگرد

/gugerd/ ▶ noun
brimstone

گوی

/guy/ ▶ noun
sphere - orb - globe - ball

گول

/gul/ ▶ noun
deception - crimp - cheat - cajolery - cajole - gull - humbug - bilk - jape

گویا

/guyâ/ ▶ adjective
perhaps - communicative

گویش

/guyesh/ ▶ noun
dialect

گول زدن

/gul zadan/ ▶ verb
deceive - cheat - cajole - rogue - fool

گوینده

/guyande/ ▶ noun
teller - speaker - announcer - narrator

گیاه
/giyâh/ ▶ noun
vegetable - plant - herb

گیاه شناس
/giyâhshenâs/ ▶ noun
botanist

گیاه شناسی
/giyâhshenâsi/ ▶ noun
botany

گیاهخواری
/giyâhkhâri/ ▶ noun
vegetarian

گیتار
/gitâr/ ▶ noun
guitar

گیتار زدن
/gitâr zadan/ ▶ verb
guitar

گیتی
/giti/ ▶ noun
universe - world

گیج
/gij/ ▶ noun
stupid - hazy - harebrained - astray - astound

گیج خوردن
/gij khordan/ ▶ verb
reel - stagger

گیج شدن
/gij shodan/ ▶ verb
dizzy

گیج کننده
/gij konande/ ▶ adjective
hectic - problematic - stunner - stickler

گیجی
/giji/ ▶ adjective
stupefaction - stun - razzledazzle - muddle - quandary - bafflement

گیج کردن
/gij kardan/ ▶ verb
mystify - puzzle

گیر
/gir/ ▶ noun
gripe - fix - impediment - impasse - hitch

گیر آوردن
/gir âvardan/ ▶ verb
grasp - hook

گیر دادن
/gir dâdan/ ▶ verb
engage

گیر کردن
/gir kardan/ ▶ verb
stymie - stick

گیرا

/girâ/ ▶ adjective
impressive

گیرایی

/girâyi/ ▶ noun
charisma

گیرنده

/girande/ ▶ adjective
recipient - receptor - receiver - holder

گیره

/gire/ ▶ noun
pincer - pin - pin - pawl - bend - retainer
- cleat - clamp - nip - dog - jaw - trigger

گیره سر

/gireye sar/ ▶ noun
pin

گیسو

/gisu/ ▶ noun
hair

گیلاس

/gilâs/ ▶ noun
glass

گیوتین

/giyutin/ ▶ noun
guillotine

ل - L

lâm /le/ ▶ twenty seventh letter of the Persian alphabet

لابد

/lâbod/ ▶ noun
maybe

لات

/lât/ ▶ noun
scoundrel

لاتین

/lâtin/ ▶ noun
latin

لاجورد

/lâjavard/ ▶ adjective
azure

لاجوردی

/lâjavardi/ ▶ adjective
azure

لازم

/lâzem/ ▶ adjective
necessary - requirement

لازم الاجرا

/lâzemol'ejrâ/ ▶ adjective
indispensable

لازم بودن

/lâzem budan/ ▶ verb
require

لازم داشتن

/lâzem dâshtan/ ▶ verb
need - want

لازمه

/lâzeme/ ▶ noun
prerequisite

لاس زدن

/lâs zadan/ ▶ verb
flirt

لاستیک

/lâstik/ ▶ noun
tire - caoutchouc - rubber

لاستیک چرخ

/lâstike charkh/ ▶ noun
tire

لاشخور

/lâshkhor/ ▶ noun
buzzard - lammergeyer

لاشه

/lâshe/ ▶ noun
corpse - body

لامپ
/lâmp/ ► noun
tube - lamp

لاغراندام
/lâgharandâm/ ► adjective
lithe

لامذهب
/lâmazhab/ ► adjective
ungodly

لاف
/lâf/ ► noun
boast - vainglory

لانه
/lâne/ ► noun
nest - den - lair

لاف زدن
/lâf zadan/ ► verb
puff - yelp - rodomontade - brag

(Idiom: لاف زدن، غلو کردن
Shoot off one's mouth)

لانه ساختن
/lâne sâkhtan/ ► verb
nest

لاف زن
/lâfzan/ ► adjective
idol - bouncer

لایتناهی
/lâyatanâhi/ ► noun
infinite

لاک پشت
/lâkposht/ ► noun
turtle - tortoise

لایحه قانونی
/lâyeheye ghânuni/ ► noun
legal bill

لاکی
/lâki/ ► adjective
crimson

لایق
/lâyegh/ ► adjective
competent - capable - worthy

لال
/lâl/ ► noun
speechless - mute

لایق بودن
/lâyegh budan/ ► verb
deserve - able

لالایی
/lâlâyi/ ► noun
lullaby

لاینحل
/lâyanhal/ ► adjective
insoluble

لاینفک
/lâyanfak/ ► adjective
essential - innate

لاینقطع
/lâyanghat'/ ► adjective
incessant

لایه
/lâye/ ► noun
pad - leaf - layer

لایه دار
/lâyedâr/ ► adjective
zonate

لایه روبی
/lâyerubi/ ► noun
layer removal

لب
/lab/ ► noun
lip - brink - bank - puss

لب زدن
/lab zadan/ ► verb
taste

لب کلام
/lobe kalâm/ ► noun
gist - heart

لباس
/lebâs/ ► noun
clothing - dress - costume - attire -
vestment

لباس ابریشمی
/lebâse abrishami/ ► noun
silk

لباس پوشاندن
/lebâs pushândan/ ► verb
dress - attire

لباس پوشانیدن
/lebâs pushânidan/ ► verb
dress

لباس پوشیدن
/lebâs pushidan/ ► verb
dress

لباس رسمی
/lebâse rasmi/ ► noun
tuxedo

لباس زیر
/lebâse zir/ ► noun
underwear - underclothing -
underclothes

لباس فروش
/lebâsforush/ ► noun
clothier

لباس مبدل
/lebâse mobadal/ ► noun
disguise - guise - masquerade

لباسشویی
/lebâsshuyi/ ► noun
laundry

لبخند

/labkhand/ ▶ noun
smile

لبخند زدن

/labkhand zadan/ ▶ verb
smile

لبریز

/labriz/ ▶ adjective
replete - full - awash - large - profuse

لبلاب

/labâlab/ ▶ adjective
ivy

لبنیاتی

/labaniyât/ ▶ noun
dairy - creamery

لبه

/labe/ ▶ noun
ledge - wayside - border - ridge - edge

لثه

/lase/ ▶ noun
gingiva

لج

/laj/ ▶ noun
spite - grudge - grouch

لجاجت

/lejâjat/ ▶ noun
pertinacity - obstinacy - obduracy -
grouch

لجاجت کردن

/lejâjat kardan/ ▶ verb
grudge

لجام

/lejâm/ ▶ noun
rein - bit - line

لجام گسیخته

/lejâm gosikhte/ ▶ adjective
ungovernable - unbridle

لجباز

/lajbâz/ ▶ adjective
headstrong

لجبازی

/lajbâzi/ ▶ noun
pertinacity

لجن

/lajân/ ▶ noun
slobber - slob - silt - lair - mud - mire

لجن زار

/lajanzâr/ ▶ adjective
bog - marsh - swampy

لجن مال

/lajanmâl/ ▶ adjective
slimy

لجوج

/lajuj/ ▶ adjective
stubborn - headstrong - obstreperous -
obstinate

لجوجانه

/lajujâne/ ► adverb
intractable

لحاظ

/lahâz/ ► noun
viewpoint - phase - perspective - light

لحاف

/lahâf/ ► noun
quilt - coverlet

لحظه

/lahze/ ► noun
instant - moment - minute - flash

لحظه ای

/lahze'i/ ► adjective
wee

لحظه بحرانی

/lahzeye bohrâni/ ► noun
zerohour

لحن

/lahn/ ► noun
tone - tune

لحیم

/lehim/ ► noun
solder

لحیم کردن

/lehim kardan/ ► verb
solder

لخت

/lokht/ ► adjective
naked - nude - stodgy

لخت شدن

/lokht shodan/ ► verb
unclothe

لخت کردن

/lokht kardan/ ► verb
skin - strip - doin - rob - rifle - ransack -
harry - pluck

لخته

/lakhte/ ► noun
lobe - clod

لخته خون

/lakhteye khun/ ► noun
clot

لخته شده

/lakhte shodan/ ► adjective
gory

لذت

/lezat/ ► noun
joy - pleasure - delight

لذت بخش

/lezatbakhsh/ ► adjective
pleasurable

لذت بردن

/lezat bordan/ ► verb
pleasure - enjoy - revel

لذیذ

/laziz/ ► adjective
delicious - pleasurable - palatable -
luscious

لرز

/larz/ ► noun
tremble - thrill - shiver - shake

لرزان

/larzân/ ► adjective
vibrant - unsteady - unstable - wobbly

لرزاندن

/larzândan/ ► verb
jar - tremble - wangle

لرزاننده

/larzânande/ ► adjective
shaker

لرزش

/larzesh/ ► noun
quake - shake

لرزش داشتن

/larzesh dâshtan/ ► verb
quake - shimmy

لرزش صدا

/larzeshe sedâ/ ► noun
trill

لرزه

/larze/ ► noun
vibration - quake - thrill - jar - tremor

لرزیدن

/larzidan/ ► verb
vibrate - trill - tremble - throb - shudder
- shake

لزج

/lezej/ ► noun
slimy - slab

لزره نگار

/larzenegâr/ ► noun
seismograph

لزوم

/lozum/ ► noun
supply - need - necessity - exigency -
incumbency

لژ

/lozh/ ► noun
box - loge - stall

لژ سلطنتی

/lozhe saltanati/ ► noun
podium

لسان

/lesân/ ► noun
language

لشکر

/lashkar/ ► noun
corps

لشگر

/lashgar/ ▶ noun
army

لطافت

/letâfat/ ▶ noun
subtlety - elegance - rosewater

لطف

/lotf/ ▶ noun
boon - ethereal - kindness

لطف کردن

/lotf kardan/ ▶ verb
oblige - indulgence

لطفا

/lotfan/ ▶ adverb
please

لطمه

/latme/ ▶ noun
brunt - shock - stroke

لطیف

/latif/ ▶ adjective
tender - subtle - soft - rare - fine -
rosewater - gossamer - gentle

لطیفه

/latife/ ▶ noun
joke - jest - jape - epigram - witticism -
quip

لطیفه گو

/latifegu/ ▶ noun
humorist - witty - japer

لعاب

/la'âb/ ▶ noun
mucilage - glaze - slime

لعاب دادن

/la'âb dâdan/ ▶ verb
glaze

لعابی

/la'âbi/ ▶ adjective
overglaze

لعابی کردن

/la'âbi kardan/ ▶ verb
glaze

لعل

/la'l/ ▶ noun
ruby - garnet

لعن

/la'n/ ▶ noun
imprecation - ban

لعنت

/la'nat/ ▶ noun
damn - cuss - curse

لعنت کردن

/la'nat kardan/ ▶ verb
damn

لعنتی

/la'nati/ ► adjective
darn - damnable

لغت

/loghat/ ► noun
verb - vocabulary - word

لغزان

/laghzân/ ► adjective
slippery

لغزش

/laghzesh/ ► noun
slither - slippage - slip - slide

لغزش خوردن

/laghzesh khordan/ ► verb
trip

لغزنده

/laghzande/ ► adjective
slippery - slipper - slipover - slide -
rattletrap

لغزیدن

/laghzidan/ ► verb
tumble - stumble - slip - slide - skid

لغو

/laghv/ ► noun
waiver - revocation - repeal

لغو کردن

/laghv kardan/ ► verb
annul - abrogate - disannul - cancel -
revoke - repeal - nullify

لغوی

/loghavi/ ► noun
lexical

لفاظی

/lafâzi/ ► adjective
rhetoric - verbiage

لفاف

/lafâf/ ► noun
padding - envelope

لفافه

/lafâfe/ ► noun
shroud - mask - paraphernalia

لفظ

/lafz/ ► noun
particle - word

لفظی

/lafzi/ ► adjective
textual - literal - verbal

لق

/lagh/ ► noun
wobbly - rickety - unsteady - loose -
jiggly

لکه

/lake/ ▶ noun
stain - spot - dot - dirt - glob - gall

لق بودن

/lagh budan/ ▶ verb
wobble

لکه ننگ

/lakeye nang/ ▶ noun
slur - stigma

لقاح

/leghâh/ ▶ noun
zygosis

لگد

/lagad/ ▶ noun
yerk - trample - kick - hurl

لقب

/laghab/ ▶ noun
label - title - surname - sobriquet

لگد کردن

/lagad kardan/ ▶ verb
tread

لقب دادن

/laghab dâdan/ ▶ verb
entitle - title - surname

لگدپرانی

/lagadparâni/ ▶ noun
wince

لقمه

/loghme/ ▶ noun
morsel - bit - snap

لگدکوب

/lagadkub/ ▶ noun
stampede

لک

/lak/ ▶ noun
stain - speck - smudge - blot

لگدمالی

/lagadmâli/ ▶ noun
padding

لک کردن

/lak kardan/ ▶ verb
smudge - blur

لگن

/lagân/ ▶ noun
basin

لکنت

/loknat/ ▶ noun
stutter - stammer

لم

/lam/ ▶ noun
trick - loll

لکنت داشتن

/loknat dâshtan/ ▶ verb
stutter - stumble

لم دادن

/lam dâdan/ ▶ verb
lounge - loll

لنگیدن

/langidan/ ▶ verb
stagger - hobble - halt - limp - lag - clop

لم یزرع

/lamyazra'/ ▶ adjective
wasteland - arid - barren

له

/leh/ ▶ adjective
pro

لمس

/lams/ ▶ noun
handle

له کردن

/leh kardan/ ▶ verb
quash - rase - pummel - squelch -
squeeze - squash

لمس کردن

/lams kardan/ ▶ verb
feel - palpate - stroke - touch - take

لهجه

/lahje/ ▶ noun
dialect - intonation - accent

لمیدن

/lamidan/ ▶ verb
recline - lounge - loll

لوازم

/lavâzem/ ▶ noun
accessories - apparatus - service

لنگ

/lang/ ▶ adjective
cripple - limp

لواط

/lavât/ ▶ noun
sodomyh - pederasty

لنگ بودن

/lang budan/ ▶ verb
woke - wobble

لوبیا

/lubiyâ/ ▶ noun
bean

لنگرگاه

/langargâh/ ▶ noun
harbor - port

لوث

/lôs/ ▶ noun
pollution

لنگه

/lenge/ ▶ noun
bale - mate - match - pendant - leaf -
doublet

لوچ

/luch/ ▶ noun
squint - crosseyed - cockeyed

لوستر

/luster/ ▶ noun
luster

لوچی

/luchi/ ▶ adjective
squint

لوطی

/luti/ ▶ adjective
ruffian

لوح

/lôh/ ▶ noun
brede - plate - tablet - table

لوکوموتیو

/lokomotiv/ ▶ noun
locomotive

لوح یادبود

/lôhe yâdbud/ ▶ noun
memorial

لولا

/lôlâ/ ▶ noun
band - hinge - joint - joint

لودگی

/lôdegi/ ▶ noun
badinage - tomfoolery

لوله

/lule/ ▶ noun
cylinder - cannon - roll - pipe - spout - tube

لوده

/lôde/ ▶ adjective
fool - clown

لوزالمعده

/lôzolmede/ ▶ noun
sweetbread

لوله تفنگ

/luleye tofang/ ▶ noun
barrel

لوزی

/lôzi/ ▶ noun
diamond - rhombic - lozenge

لوله کش

/lulekesh/ ▶ noun
plumber - piper

لوس

/lus/ ▶ adjective
gaudy - chilish

لوله کشی

/lulekeshi/ ▶ noun
canalization - pipeline

لوس کردن

/lus kardan/ ▶ verb
spoil

لولو
/lôlô/ ► noun
scarecrow - bugbear - bugaboo -
bogeyman - pearl - hobgoblin

لوند
/lavand/ ► noun
coquette

لی لی کردن
/lei lei kardan/ ► verb
sikt - skip - hop - hip

لیاقت
/liyâghat/ ► noun
merit - potency - autarchy - aptitude -
ability

لیتر
/litr/ ► noun
liter

لیز
/liz/ ► adjective
slippery - slimy - slick - slab

لیز خوردن
/liz khordan/ ► verb
slip

لیس
/lis/ ► noun
lick

لیس زدن
/lis zadan/ ► verb
lap

لیسانس
/lisâns/ ► noun
bachelor

لیست
/list/ ► noun
list

لیست حقوق
/liste hoghugh/ ► noun
payroll

لیسه
/lise/ ► noun
lick

لیسیدن
/lisidan/ ► verb
lick

لیف
/lif/ ► noun
filament - brush

لیمو
/limu/ ► noun
lemon

لیموترش
/limutorsh/ ► noun
lime - lemon

لیموناد

/limunâd/ ▶ noun
lemonade - soda - sherbet

لیوان

/livân/ ▶ noun
tumbler - glass - mug

م - ﻤ

mim /me/ ▶ twenty eighth letter of the Persian alphabet

ما

/mâ/ ▶ pronoun
we - kiss

مابه التفاوت

/mâbetafâvot/ ▶ noun
margin

مابین

/mâbein/ ▶ adverb
betwixt - between - medial

مات

/mât/ ▶ adjective
dumbstruck - quizzical - opaque - aghast

ماتم

/mâtam/ ▶ noun
dole

ماجرا

/mâjarâ/ ▶ noun
adventure

ماجراجو

/mâjarâju/ ▶ adjective
venturer - adventurer

ماجراجویی

/mâjarâjuyi/ ▶ noun
adventure

ماچ

/mâch/ ▶ noun
smack

ماچ کردن

/mâch kardan/ ▶ verb
kiss

ماخذ

/ma'khaz/ ▶ noun
source - datum - basis - alloy

مادام

/mâdâm/ ▶ adjective
while - mademe

مادام العمر

/mâdâmol'omr/ ▶ adjective
lifetime

مادامیکه

/mâdâmike/ ▶ adverb
while

مادر

/mâdar/ ▶ noun
mother - matriarch

مادرانه

/mâdarâne/ ▶ adverb
maternal

مادرزاد

/mâdarzâd/ ▶ adjective
innate

مادری

/mâdari/ ▶ adjective
motherhood - maternity - maternal

ماده

/mâde/ ▶ noun
metal - material - point - paragraph -
article - abscess - provision - substance -
stuff

مادون

/mâdun/ ▶ noun
subordinate - subject - sub - below

مادی

/mâdi/ ▶ noun
corporeal - earthen - worldly - material -
physical

مادیان

/mâdiyân/ ▶ noun
mare

مار

/mâr/ ▶ noun
serpent - worm

مارپیچ

/mârpich/ ▶ adjective
spire - spiral - coil

مارپیچی

/mârpichi/ ▶ noun
spiral - sinuous - whorl

مارک

/mârk/ ▶ noun
stripe - score - brand

مارکبری

/mâre kobrâ/ ▶ noun
cobra

مارگزیدگی

/mârgazidegi/ ▶ noun
snakebite

مارماهی

/mârmâhi/ ▶ noun
lamprey

مارمولک

/mârmulak/ ▶ noun
gecko- lizard

ماری جوانا

/mâri jo'vânâ/ ▶ noun
grass - marijuana

مازاد

/mâzâd/ ▶ noun
surplus - rejcet

ماساژ

/mâsâzh/ ▶ noun
massage

ماساژ دادن
/mâsâzh dâdan/ ▶ verb
massage

ماسک
/mâsk/ ▶ noun
mask - guise

ماسک زدن
/mâsk zadan/ ▶ verb
mask

ماسه
/mâse/ ▶ noun
gravel - sand

ماسوره
/mâsure/ ▶ noun
spool - reel - bobbin - hasp - hank

ماسیدن
/mâsidan/ ▶ verb
jell - congeal - harden

ماشه
/mâshe/ ▶ noun
pincer

ماشین
/mâshin/ ▶ noun
engine - apparatus - motor - mill -
mechanism - machine - plant

ماشین بخار
/mâshine bokhâr/ ▶ noun
steamer - engine

ماشین تحریر
/mâshine tahrir/ ▶ noun
typewriter

ماشین ظرفشویی
/mâshine zarfshuyi/ ▶ noun
dishwasher

ماشینی
/mâshini/ ▶ adjective
mechanic

ماضی
/mâzi/ ▶ noun
past

ماضی بعید
/mâziye ba'id/ ▶ noun
pastperfect

مافوق
/mâfogh/ ▶ adjective
superior - dominant - overlord - above -
upmost - ultra

ماقبل
/mâghabl/ ▶ adjective
past - precedency

ماکارونی
/kâkâroni/ ▶ noun
noodle - macaroni

ماکسیم
/mâksimom/ ▶ noun
maximum

ماکول

/ma'kul/ ▶ noun
edible - eatable

ماکیان

/mâkiyân/ ▶ noun
hen - poultry

مال

/mâl/ ▶ noun
property - fortune - for - wealth - lucre

مال آنها

/mâle ânhâ/ ▶ pronoun
their

مال او

/mâle to/ ▶ pronoun
whose - its - her- his

مال چه کسی

/mâle che kasi/ ▶ pronoun
whose

مال من

/mâle man/ ▶ pronoun
my - mine

مالاریا

/mâlâriyâ/ ▶ noun
malaria

مالش

/mâlesh/ ▶ noun
scrub - friction - attrition

مالش دادن

/mâlesh dâdan/ ▶ verb
chafe

مالک

/mâlek/ ▶ adjective
landlord - possessor - lord - angel -
owner - proprietor

مالک بودن

/mâlek budan/ ▶ verb
own

مالکیت

/mâlekiyat/ ▶ noun
ownership - possession

ماله

/mâle/ ▶ noun
trowel - malay

مالی

/mâli/ ▶ noun
financial - pecuniary

مالیات

/mâliyât/ ▶ noun
tax - scot - scat - imposition - levy

مالیخولیا

/mâlikhuliyâ/ ▶ adjective
melancholy - melancholia - mare -
hypochondria

مالیخولیایی

/mâlikhuliyâyi/ ▶ noun
hypochondriac

ماندن

/mândan/ ▶ verb
subsist - stay - stand - stall - settle -
remain - be - abide - lie

مالیدن

/mâlidan/ ▶ verb
rub - knead - daub - curry - blob

ماندنی

/mândani/ ▶ noun
permanent - viable

مامان

/mâmân/ ▶ noun
mammy

مانده

/mânde/ ▶ adjective
remainder - remain

مامن

/ma'man/ ▶ noun
port - mine

مانع

/mâne'/ ▶ noun
setback - stay - brake - barricade - bar -
balk - impediment - hurdle - hindrance -
hinder - obstacle

مامور

/ma'mur/ ▶ noun
envoy - officer - agent

مانع شدن

/mâne' shodan/ ▶ verb
prevent - inhibit - impede - holdup -
hinder - resist - obturate - obstruct

ماموریت

/ma'muriyat/ ▶ noun
tour - errand - duty - function - mission -
assignment - agency

مانکن

/mânkan/ ▶ noun
dummy - mannequin - manikin

ماندگار

/mândegâr/ ▶ adjective
settler - indelible - immanent -
indissoluble

مانند

/mânand/ ▶ noun
similar - analogue - analogous - like

ماندگاری

/mândegâri/ ▶ noun
insolubility

مانند بودن

/mânand budan/ ▶ verb
simulate - similarity – resemble

ماه عسل
/mâhe asal/ ▶ noun
honeymoon

ماندهم
/mânande ham/ ▶ adjective
alike

ماهتاب
/mâhtâb/ ▶ noun
moonshine - moonbeam

مانور
/mânovr/ ▶ noun
manoeuvre

ماهر
/mâher/ ▶ adjective
skillful - jimmy - dextrous - dexterous -
proficient - adroit

مانور دادن
/mânovr dâdan/ ▶ verb
manoeuvre

مانوس
/ma'nus/ ▶ noun
familiar - habitue

ماهرانه
/mâherâne/ ▶ adverb
workmanlike - subtle

مانوس شدن
/ma'nus shodan/ ▶ verb
acclimate

ماهواره
/mâhvâre/ ▶ noun
satellite

مانویت
/ma'naviyat/ ▶ noun
manichaeanism

ماهوت
/mâhut/ ▶ noun
broadcloth

مانیکور
/mânikor/ ▶ noun
manicure

ماهور
/mâhur/ ▶ noun
knoll - dale - mound - barrow

مانیکور زدن
/mânikor zadan/ ▶ verb
manicure

ماهی
/mâhi/ ▶ noun
lunar - fish

ماه
/mâh/ ▶ noun
satellite - moon - month - acolyte

ماهیانه
/mâhiyâne/ ► adverb
monthly

مایل بودن
/mâyle budan/ ► verb
like

ماهیت
/mâhiyat/ ► noun
navigate - nature - essence

مایل شدن
/mâyle shodan/ ► verb
decline

ماهیچه
/mâhiche/ ► noun
muscle

مایه
/mâye/ ► noun
nestegg - resource

ماهیخوار
/mâhikhâr/ ► noun
ichthyophagous- heron

مایه تاسف
/mâye'e ta'asof/ ► adjective
unfortunate

ماورای
/mâvarâye/ ► noun
past - ultra

مایه عبرت
/mâye'e ebrat/ ► adjective
gazingstock

مایحتاج
/mâyahtâj/ ► noun
needful

مایوس
/ma'yus/ ► adjective
chill

مایع
/mâye'/ ► noun
liquid - water

مایوس شدن
/ma'yus shodan/ ► verb
despair

مایع زدن
/mâye' zadan/ ► verb
liquor

مایوس کردن
/ma'yus kardan/ ► verb
disappoint

مایل
/mâyel/ ► adjective
solicitous - desirous - gauche - oblique -
wilful - fond

مایونز
/mâyonez/ ► noun
mayonnaise

مباحثه

/mobâhese/ ▶ noun
disputation - discussion - discourse - controversy - agument

مباحثه کردن

/mobâhese kardan/ ▶ verb
dissert - dispute - debate

مبادا

/mabâdâ/ ▶ preposition
lest

مبادرت

/mobâderat/ ▶ noun
venture

مبادله

/mobâdele/ ▶ noun
exchange

مبادی

/mobâdi/ ▶ noun
Ports

مبادی آداب

/mobâdiye âdâd/ ▶ adjective
tactful - polite

مبارز

/mobârez/ ▶ adjective
warrior - comatant - defiant - adversary

مبارزه

/mobâreze/ ▶ noun
battle - champion

مبارزه طلبی

/mobârezetalabi/ ▶ noun
defiance

مبارزه کردن

/mobâreze kardan/ ▶ verb
joust - combat - conflict

مبارک

/mobârak/ ▶ adjective
auspicious - blest

مباشر

/mobâsher/ ▶ noun
supervisor - steward - overseer - manager

مباشرت

/mobâsherat/ ▶ noun
stewardship

مباشرت کردن

/mobâsherat kardan/ ▶ verb
steward

مبالغه

/mobâleghe/ ▶ noun
bombast

مبالغه آمیز

/mobâlegheâmiz/ ▶ adjective
superlative

مباهات

/mobâhât/ ▶ noun
brag - boast - pride

مبتدی
/mobtadi/ ▶ noun
novice - neophyte - greenhorn -
beginner - youngling - tyro

مبرا
/mobarâ/ ▶ adjective
innocent

مبرا کردن
/mobarâ kardan/ ▶ verb
exonerate - absolve

مبتذل
/mobtazal/ ▶ adjective
humdrum - vulgar - pedestrian - banal -
commonplace

مبرم
/mobram/ ▶ adjective
sore - imperious - urgent - demanding

مبتکر
/mobtaker/ ▶ adjective
inventor - originator - ingenious

مبصر
/mobser/ ▶ noun
monitor

مبتلا
/mobtalâ/ ▶ noun
stricken - given

مبلغ
/mablagh/ ▶ noun
quantity - amount

مبحث
/mabhas/ ▶ noun
topic - subject

مبلغ مذهبی
/mobaleghe mazhabi/ ▶ noun
missioner - missionary

مبدا
/mabâdâ/ ▶ noun
source - era - offspring - offset

مبله کردن
/moble kardan/ ▶ verb
furnish

مبدا تاریخ
/mabda'e târikh/ ▶ noun
epoch

مبهم
/mobham/ ▶ adjective
obscure - ambiguous - vague -
mysterious - misty - imprecise

مبدل
/mobadel/ ▶ noun
converter

مبهم کردن
/mobham kardan/ ▶ verb
obscure - adumbrate

مبهوت

/mabhut/ ▶ noun
agape - quizzical

متابعت

/motâbe'at/ ▶ noun
follow

متاثر

/mote'aser/ ▶ adjective
sorry - dull - regretful

متاثر شدن

/mote'aser shodan/ ▶ verb
pity - touch

متاخر

/mote'akher/ ▶ noun
recent

متارکه

/motâreke/ ▶ noun
separate - quit

متارکه کردن

/motâreke kardan/ ▶ verb
leave

متاسف

/mote'asef/ ▶ adjective
sorry - afraid

متاسفانه

/mote'asefâne/ ▶ adverb
unfortunately

متانت

/metânat/ ▶ noun
sobriety - serene - equanimity -
calmness

متاهل

/mote'ahel/ ▶ noun
married

متبادل

/motebâdel/ ▶ noun
alternate

متبحر

/motebaher/ ▶ adjective
conversant - erudite

متبسم

/motebasem/ ▶ adjective
riant

متبلور

/motebalver/ ▶ adjective
crystalline

متجانس

/motejanes/ ▶ adjective
congruent

متجاوز

/motejavez/ ▶ adjective
aggressor - aggressive- offender

متجدد

/motejaded/ ▶ adjective
ultramodern - mewfangled

متحد

/motahed/ ► noun
conjunct - confederate - one - allied

متحد شدن

/motahed shodan/ ► verb
band - combine

متحد کردن

/motahed kardan/ ► verb
incorporate - herd - unite - unify - ally -
band

متحدالشکل

/motahedolshekl/ ► adjective
uniform

متحدالقول

/motahedolghôl/ ► adjective
unisonous (onal-onant

متحرک

/moteharek/ ► adjective
gradient - remote - versatile - mobile -
locomotive

متحمل

/motehamel/ ► noun
sufferer

متحمل شدن

/motehamel shodan/ ► verb
sustain - defray - incur

متحیر

/motehayer/ ► adjective
astound - amaze - dumbstruck

متخاصم

/motekhâsem/ ► adjective
hostile - party - belligerent - adversary

متخصص

/motekhases/ ► noun
specialist - expert - adhoc - proficient

متخلف

/motekhalef/ ► adjective
offender - wrongdoer - transgressor -
trespasser

متد

/metod/ ► noun
method

متداول

/motedâvel/ ► adjective
standard - current - general - ordinary -
usual - uptodate - vogue - prevalent

متر

/metr/ ► noun
meter

مترادف

/moterâdef/ ► noun
synonymous - equivalent

متراکم

/moterâkem/ ► adjective
aggregate - voluminous - compact -
dense - cumulous

متزلزل

/motezalzel/ ► adjective
shaky - seismic - ramshackle - giddy -
unstable - insecure

متراکم شدن

/moterâkem shodan/ ► verb
agglomerate

متزلزل شدن

/motezalzel shodan/ ► verb
waver - totter

متراکم کردن

/moterâkem kardan/ ► verb
jam - condense - inflame - amass

متشابه

/moteshâbeh/ ► adjective
analogous - homonym - like

مترجم

/motarjem/ ► noun
translator - interpreter - dragoman

متشخص

/moteshakhesh/ ► adjective
magnate

مترسک

/matarsak/ ► noun
scarecrow

متشکر

/khoteshaker/ ► adjective
thankful

مترقی

/moteraghi/ ► adjective
progressive

متشنج

/moteshanej/ ► adjective
nervous

مترو

/metro/ ► noun
subway

متصاعد شدن

/motesâed shodan/ ► verb
reek

متروک

/matruk/ ► adjective
desolate - derelict - bleak - lonely

متصدی

/motesadi/ ► noun
officer - titular

متروکه

/matruke/ ► adjective
obsolete - disuse

متصرف

/motesaref/ ► adjective
possessor - proprietor

متصل شدن

/motasel shodan/ ► verb
adjoin

متصل کردن

/motasel kardan/ ► verb
join - joggle - connect - link - apply -
adjoin

متصنع

/motesane'/ ► adjective
hypocrite

متضاد

/motezâd/ ► noun
antonym - polar

متضمن

/motezamen/ ► noun
pergnant - underlying

متضمن بودن

/motezamen budan/ ► verb
entail - embody - include - presuppose

متظاهر

/motezâher/ ► adjective
simulator - prude - braggadocio -
hypocritical - ostentatious - ostensive

متعادل

/mote'âdel/ ► adjective
dominant

متعارف

/mote'âref/ ► adjective
standard - common

متعاقب

/mote'âgheb/ ► adjective
pursuant - subsequent

متعال

/mota'âl/ ► adjective
excelsior - eminent - sublimate

متعجب ساختن

/mote'ajeb sâkhtan/ ► verb
surprise - admire

متعجب شدن

/mote'ajeb shodan/ ► verb
swan

متعدد

/mote'aded/ ► adjective
multiple - several

متعدی

/mote'adi/ ► noun
active

متعصب

/mote'aseb/ ► adjective
dogmatic - rabid - intolerant - bigot -
zeal

متفرق ساختن
/motefaresh sâkhtan/ ▶ verb
disperse

متفرق شدن
/motefaregh shodan/ ▶ verb
straggle

متفرق کردن
/motefaregh kardan/ ▶ verb
intersperse - scatter

متفرقه
/motefareghe/ ▶ noun
sundries - miscellaneous

متفق
/motafegh/ ▶ adjective
confederate

متفق القول
/motafegholghôl/ ▶ adjective
unanimous

متفکر
/motefaker/ ▶ adjective
pensive - thoughtful - thinker

متقابل
/moteghâbel/ ▶ noun
reciprocal - polar

متقارن
/moteghâren/ ▶ adjective
concurrent - polar

متعفن
/mote'afen/ ▶ adjective
smelly - putrid - rancid

متعلق
/mote'alegh/ ▶ adjective
dependent

متعلقات
/mote'aleghât/ ▶ noun
paraphernalia - appurtenance

متعهد
/mote'ahed/ ▶ adjective
underwriter - undertaking - undertaker - guarantor

متعهد شدن
/mote'ahed shodan/ ▶ verb
plight - pledge - undertake - oblige

متغیر
/moteghayer/ ▶ adjective
shifty - variant - variable - unsteady - uncertain

متغیر کردن
/moteghayer kardan/ ▶ verb
offend

متفاوت
/motefâvet/ ▶ noun
away - different - other

متقارن ساختن
/moteghâren sâkhtan/ ► verb
symmetrize

متکبرانه
/motekaberâne/ ► adverb
arrogance

متقارن کردن
/moteghâren kardan/ ► verb
polarize - proportion

متکلم
/motekalem/ ► noun
speaker

متقاضی
/moteghâzi/ ► noun
suppliant - applicant

متکی
/motaki/ ► adjective
pending - reliant

متقاطع
/moteghâte'/ ► noun
crossover - crisscross - intercepter -
transverse - secant

متکی شدن
/motaki shodan/ ► verb
lean

متقبل
/moteghâbel/ ► noun
sponsor

متل
/motel/ ► noun
motel

متقلب
/moteghaleb/ ► adjective
shark - swindler - dishonest - gyp

متلاشی
/motelâshi/ ► adjective
disjointed - disjoin

متکا
/motakâ/ ► noun
slip - cushion - bolster - backrest -
pillow

متلاشی شدن
/motelâshi shodan/ ► verb
collapse - decompose - crackup

متلاطم
/motelâtem/ ► adjective
turbulent - unruly - lumpy - heavy

متکبر
/motekaber/ ► adjective
imperious - high - haughty - perky -
arrogant - proud

متلک
/matalak/ ► noun
josh

متمايز

/motemâyez/ ▶ adjective
diverse - different

متمايل

/motemâyel/ ▶ noun
tendentious - prone - like - apt

متمدن

/motemaden/ ▶ adjective
civilized

متمدن شدن

/motemaden shodan/ ▶ verb
civilize

متمدن كردن

/motemaden kardan/ ▶ verb
civilize

متمرد

/motemared/ ▶ adjective
disobedient - outlaw - wayward -
recusant - recalcitrant - rebellious - rebel

متمركز

/motemarkez/ ▶ adjective
intensive

متمركز كردن

/motemarkez kardan/ ▶ verb
concentrate - epitomize - localize

متمسك شدن

/motemasek shodan/ ▶ verb
truss

متملق

/motemalegh/ ▶ adjective
sycophant

متمم

/motamam/ ▶ noun
complementary - supplementary -
supplement - subsidiary

متموج

/motemavej/ ▶ adjective
wavy

متن

/matn/ ▶ noun
text - version

متناسب

/motenâseb/ ▶ adjective
proportionate - commensurate

متناسب بودن

/motenâseb budan/ ▶ verb
harmonize

متناقض

/motenâghez/ ▶ adjective
repugnant - anomalous - inconsistent -
incommensurable - incoherent

متناوب

/motenâveb/ ▶ adjective
periodic - intermittent - alternative -
alternating - alternate - alternate

متناوبا

/motenâveban/ ► adverb
alternatively

متنفر

/motenafer/ ► adjective
irksome - averse

متنفر ساختن

/motenafer sâkhtan/ ► verb
nauseate

متنوع

/motenave'/ ► adjective
variety - varied

متنوع ساختن

/motenave' sâkhtan/ ► verb
vary

متنی

/matni/ ► adjective
textual

مته

/mate/ ► noun
auger - bore - gimlet - drill

مته زدن

/mate zadan/ ► verb
drill

مته کردن

/mate kardan/ ► verb
gimlet

متهم

/motaham/ ► adjective
culprit

متهم ساختن

/motaham sâkhtan/ ► verb
charge

متهور

/motehaver/ ► adjective
brash - bold - audacious - venturer -
intrepid - hardy

متوازی

/motevâzi/ ► adjective
collateral - parallel

متواضع

/motevâze'/ ► adjective
humble - unselfish

متوالی

/motevâli/ ► noun
continuous - consecutive - reel

متوجه

/motevajeh/ ► noun
tendentious - heedful - attentive - wistful

متوجه ساختن

/motevajeh sâkhtan/ ► verb
address - point - direct

متوجه شدن

/motevajeh shodan/ ► verb
pay attention

متوجه کردن

/motevajeh kardan/ ▶ verb
divert - lend

متورق

/motevaregh/ ▶ noun
sheet - laminate

متورم

/motevarem/ ▶ adjective
turgid - protuberant - gouty

متوسط

/motevaset/ ▶ noun
normal - medium - mediocre - medial -
mean - mean - intermediate - average

متوسل شدن

/motevasel shodan/ ▶ verb
resort

متوسل شدن به

/motevasel shodan be/ ▶ verb
recourse

متوفیات

/motevafiyât/ ▶ noun
mortality

متوقف ساختن

/motevaghef sâkhtan/ ▶ verb
layoff

متوقف کردن

/motevaghef kardan/ ▶ verb
gravel

متولد

/motevaled/ ▶ noun
born

متولی

/motevali/ ▶ adjective
trustee - custodian - proctor

متین

/matin/ ▶ adjective
sober - serene - sedate - placid - douce -
demure

مثال

/mesâl/ ▶ noun
example - parable - instant - instance

مثال ادبی

/mesâle adabi/ ▶ noun
locus

مثانه

/masâne/ ▶ noun
cyst

مثبت

/mosbat/ ▶ adjective
positive - plus

مثل

/masal/ ▶ noun
proverb

مثل

/mesl/ ▶ noun
example - adage - parable - like

مثل آب خوردن :Idiom)
Something that is very easy to do)

مجازاتی
/mojâzâti/ ► noun
pnitive - penal - retribution

مثلا
/masalan/ ► adverb
like - say - thus

مجازی
/majâzi/ ► noun
virtual

مثلث
/mosalas/ ► noun
triangle

مجال
/majâl/ ► noun
time - leisure - chance - room -
opportunity

مجاب کردن
/mojâb kardan/ ► verb
confute - assure

مجانی
/majâni/ ► adjective
free

مجادله
/mojâdele/ ► adjective
toil - tussle - contention

مجاهد
/mojâhed/ ► noun
zealous - zealot - devotee

مجاز
/mojâz/ ► adjective
free - allowable - admissibll - admissible
- permissive - licensable - lawful

مجاهدت
/mojâhedat/ ► noun
industry

مجاز کردن
/mojâz kardan/ ► verb
permit

مجاهدین
/mojâhedin/ ► noun
militia

مجازات
/mojâzât/ ► noun
punishment - penalty - retribution -
reprimand

مجاور
/mojâver/ ► adjective
contiguous - nigh - next - neighbor -
against - adjacent

مجازات کردن
/mojâzât kardan/ ► verb
lynch - punish

مجذوب کردن
/majzub kardan/ ▶ verb
witch - engage

مجذور
/majzur/ ▶ noun
square

مجرا
/majrâ/ ▶ noun
vessel - cullis - conduit - duct - channel -
runway - gully - gullet - tube - strand

مجرد
/mojarad/ ▶ noun
solitary - single - bachelor - abstract -
absolute - lone - immaterial - discrete

مجرم
/mojrem/ ▶ adjective
guilty - wrongdoer - culpable - convict

مجروح
/majruh/ ▶ adjective
ulcerous

مجری
/mojri/ ▶ noun
executor - executive

مجزا
/mojazâ/ ▶ adjective
separable - apart - knockdown - ditinct -
discrete

مجاور بودن
/mojâver budan/ ▶ verb
bound - border - abut

مجاورت
/mojâverat/ ▶ noun
juxtaposition - proximity - propinquity -
neighborhood - contiguity - vicinity -
adjacency

مجبور ساختن
/majbur sâkhtan/ ▶ verb
impel

مجبور کردن
/majbur kardan/ ▶ verb
compel - oblige - necessitate - enforce -
bludgeon

مجتهد
/mojtahed/ ▶ noun
priest

مجدد
/mojadad/ ▶ noun
second - further

مجذوب
/majzub/ ▶ adjective
spellbound - engross - rapt

مجذوب ساختن
/majzub sâkhtan/ ▶ verb
attract

مجزا کردن
/mojazâ kardan/ ► verb
discrete - disassemble - knockdown -
insulate

مجسم ساختن
/mojasam sâkhtan/ ► verb
image

مجسم کردن
/mojasam kardan/ ► verb
depict - epitomize - embody - incarnate -
image - portray

مجسمه
/mojasame/ ► noun
statue

مجسمه سازی
/mojasame sâzi/ ► noun
imagery - plastic - sculpture

مجلد
/mojalad/ ► noun
tome - book

مجلس
/majles/ ► noun
council - convocation - congress -
parliament

مجلس سنا
/majlese senâ/ ► noun
senate

مجلس شورا
/majlese shorâ/ ► noun
parliament

مجلسی
/majlesi/ ► adjective
parliamentary

مجلل
/mojalal/ ► adjective
sumptuous - illustrious - plush -
luxurious - luxuriant - grand - gorgeous
- glorious - gala - royalty

مجله
/majale/ ► noun
review - gazette - magazine - journal

مجمع
/majma'/ ► noun
society - convention - convent

مجمل
/mojmal/ ► noun
abstract - inconclusive - compendious -
synopsis - succinct

مجموع
/majmu'/ ► noun
tote - totality - total - ensemble - lump -
altogether - aggregate

مجموعه
/majmu'e/ ► noun
complex - collection - caboodle -
repertory - bundle - scrapbook - yardage
- set

مجنون

/majnun/ ▶ adjective
lunatic - amok - loco - insane - maniac - demented

مجهز ساختن

/majahaz sâkhtan/ ▶ verb
prime

مجهز کردن

/mojahaz kardan/ ▶ verb
equip - dight - furnish - imp - prepare

مجهول

/majhul/ ▶ noun
secret - unknown - unbeknownst - unbeknown

مجوز

/mojavez/ ▶ noun
justification

مچ

/moch/ ▶ noun
wrist

مچاله

/mochâle/ ▶ adjective
crumple

مچاله شدن

/mochâle shodan/ ▶ verb
snuggle

مچاله کردن

/mochâle kardan/ ▶ verb
rumple - crumple - tousle - scrunch

محارب

/mohâreb/ ▶ noun
warrior - comatant

محاربه

/mohârebe/ ▶ noun
warfare - war

محاسبه

/mohâsebe/ ▶ noun
computation - calculation

محاسبه کردن

/mohâsebe kardan/ ▶ verb
calk

محاصره

/mohâsere/ ▶ noun
siege - blockage - blockade

محاصره کردن

/mohâsere kardan/ ▶ verb
surround - siege - encompass - gird - blockade

محافظ

/mohâfez/ ▶ adjective
preservative

محافظت

/mohâfezat/ ▶ noun
shelter - preservation

محافظت کردن
/mohâfezat kardan/ ► verb
keep - guard - shelter

محبوس شدن
/mahbus shodan/ ► verb
lock

محاکمه
/mohâkeme/ ► noun
trial

محبوس کردن
/mahbus kardan/ ► verb
stash - confine

محبت
/mohabat/ ► noun
amour - love - glow

محتاج
/mohtâj/ ► adjective
dependent

محبت آمیز
/mohabatâmiz/ ► adjective
tender

محتاج بودن
/mohtâj budan/ ► verb
want

محبس
/mahbas/ ► noun
dungeon - calaboose - gaol - prison - jail

محتاط
/mohtât/ ► adjective
scrupulous - demure - considerate -
chary - cautious - gingerly

محبوب
/mahbub/ ► adjective
lovable - beloved - lief - popular -
favorite - chary - dear - darling

محترق
/mohtaregh/ ► adjective
torrid

محبوبه
/mahbube/ ► noun
lief - ladylove - pigeon

محترق شدن
/mohtargh shodan/ ► verb
explode

محبوبیت
/mahbubiyat/ ► noun
amicability - popularity

محترقه
/mohtareghe/ ► adjective
igneous

محبوس
/mahbus/ ► adjective
jailbird - convict

محترم
/mohtaram/ ► adjective
reverent - respectable - honorable

محترمانه

/mohtaramâne/ ▶ adverb
deferential

محتکر

/mohtaker/ ▶ adjective
speculator - hoarder

محتمل

/motehamel/ ▶ adjective
apt - probable - plausible - likely - soso

محتوی

/mohtavi/ ▶ noun
container

محتوی بودن

/mohtavi budan/ ▶ verb
contain

محجر

/mahjar/ ▶ noun
fence - peel - parapet

محجوب

/mahjub/ ▶ adjective
timid - unobtrusive - unassertive -
diffident - decent

محجوبیت

/mahbubiyat/ ▶ noun
decency

محدب

/mohadab/ ▶ noun
convex

محدود

/mahdud/ ▶ adjective
bound - parochial - moderate - narrow -
determinate

محدود ساختن

/mahdud sâkhtan/ ▶ verb
trammel

محدودسازی

/mahdudsâzi/ ▶ noun
limitation

محدوده

/mahdude/ ▶ noun
confine

محدودیت

/mahdudiyat/ ▶ noun
limitation - restriction

محراب

/mehrâb/ ▶ noun
altar

محرک

/moharek/ ▶ adjective
motive - irritant - stimulus - stimulant

محرم اسرار

/mahrame asrâr/ ▶ adjective
secretary - confidant - privy

محرم ساختن

/mahram sâkhtan/ ▶ verb
intimate

محرمانه

/mahramâne/ ▶ adverb
surreptitious - secret - esoteric -
backstage - backside - private

محصول

/mahsul/ ▶ noun
vintage - product - produce - harvest -
crop - yield - turnover

محروم کردن

/mahrum kardan/ ▶ verb
bereave - devest - deprive - exclude -
evacuate - divest - dispossess -
disappoint - geld

محض

/mahz/ ▶ adjective
strict - sheer - downright - only - mere

محضر

/mahzar/ ▶ noun
registry

محرومیت

/mahrumiyat/ ▶ noun
proscription - reprobate - privation

محفل

/mahfel/ ▶ noun
ring - clique - circle

محزون

/mahzun/ ▶ adjective
somber - sad - tragic - minor - plaintive -
pensive - despondent

محفوظ

/mahfuz/ ▶ adjective
safe

محسوس

/mahsus/ ▶ adjective
tangible - sensible - phenomenal - patent

محفوظ کردن

/mahfuz kardan/ ▶ verb
elate - immune

محشر

/mahshar/ ▶ noun
doomsday - doom

محصور

/mahsur/ ▶ adjective
pent

محق

/mohegh/ ▶ adjective
rightful

محقر

/mohaghar/ ▶ adjective
small - little - humble - unpretentious

محصور کردن

/mahsur kardan/ ▶ verb
yard - compass - close - wall - pale -
inclose

محقق

/mohaghegh/ ▶ noun
prober - positive - incontestable -
scholar - sure

محک

/mahak/ ▶ noun
shibboleth - test - proof - criterion -
examination - acid

محک زدن

/mahak zadan/ ▶ verb
assay - test

محکم

/mohkam/ ▶ adjective
firm - tough - tight - tenacious - secure -
substantial - sturdy - strong - steady -
stable

محکم شدن

/mohkam shodan/ ▶ verb
anchor

محکم کردن

/mohkam kardan/ ▶ verb
tighten - consolidate - reinforce - fix -
clinch - rivet - gird

محکم گرفتن

/mohkam gereftan/ ▶ verb
hug - gripe - grip - clutch - clip - clam

محکمه

/mahkame/ ▶ noun
forum

محکوم

/mahkum/ ▶ adjective
guilty - fey

محکوم کردن

/mahkum kardan/ ▶ verb
sentence - adjudge - convict - condemn

محکومیت

/mahkumiyat/ ▶ noun
condemnation - proscription

محل

/mahal/ ▶ noun
stead - spot - situation - site - place -
location - locality - locale - room

محل عبور

/mahale obur/ ▶ noun
passageway

محله

/mahale/ ▶ noun
sector - parish - quarter

محلول

/mahlul/ ▶ noun
solvable - solution - soluble

محلی

/mahali/ ▶ adjective
vernacular - autochthonous - residential
- native - territorial

محموله
/mahmule/ ▶ noun
shipment - consignment - good

محنت
/mehnat/ ▶ noun
bale - pain - hardship - distress -
tribulation - toil

محو
/mahv/ ▶ adjective
pallid - nebulous - obscure - deletion

محو کردن
/mahv kardan/ ▶ verb
blur - expunge - erase - eliminate -
efface - deface - raze - obliterate -
washout

محور
/mehvar/ ▶ noun
pivot - pedestal - hinge - axle - axis

محوری
/mehvari/ ▶ noun
radial - rotate - pivotal

محوطه
/mohavate/ ▶ noun
lot - precinct - enclosure - close - run

محول کردن
/mohaval/ ▶ verb
relegate - devolve - vest

محیط
/mohit/ ▶ noun
circumference - environment -
entourage - periphery - perimeter -
milieu - lap - sphere

محیط دایره
/mohite dâyere/ ▶ noun
circumference - circle

مخ
/mokh/ ▶ noun
marrow - brain

مخابره
/mokhâbere/ ▶ noun
transmittal - traffic

مخابره کردن
/mokhâbere kardan/ ▶ verb
dispatch - wire

مخارج
/makhârej/ ▶ noun
expenditure

مخارج کلی
/makhâreje koli/ ▶ noun
overhead

مخاط
/mokhât/ ▶ noun
phlegm

مختار

/mokhtâr/ ▶ noun
free

مخترع

/mokhtare'/ ▶ adjective
inventor - ingenious

مختصات

/mokhtâsât/ ▶ noun
coordinate

مختصر

/mokhtasar/ ▶ adjective
short - synopsis - summary - sum -
succinct - terse - little - compendium -
epitome - concise

مختصر کردن

/mokhtasar kardan/ ▶ verb
simplify - shorten - abridge - abbreviate

مختصرا

/mokhtaseran/ ▶ adverb
nutshell

مختل کردن

/mokhtal kardan/ ▶ verb
queer - unhinge - hamper - violate -
disorganize - disorder - disarrange

مختلس

/mokhtales/ ▶ adjective
grafter - peculator

مخاطره

/mokhâtere/ ▶ noun
jeopardy - risk - hazard - venture -
menace - peril - adventure

مخاطره آمیز

/mokhâtere âmiz/ ▶ adjective
perilous

مخاطی

/mokhâti/ ▶ noun
pituitary - mucous

مخالف

/mokhâlef/ ▶ adjective
contrary - opponent

مخالف بودن

/mokhâlef budan/ ▶ verb
disagree

مخالفت

/mokhâlefat/ ▶ noun
resistance - repugnance - remonstrance -
opposition - objection - gainsay -
aversion

مخالفت کردن

/mokhâlefat kardan/ ▶ verb
blackball - controvert - oppose - object -
withstand

مخبر

/mokhber/ ▶ adjective
informer - informant

مختلط
/mokhtalet/ ► adjective
motley - medley

مخصوص
/makhsus/ ► noun
specific - special - particular - favorite

مختلف
/mokhtalef/ ► noun
several - diverse - dissimilar - disparate -
off - various - variant

مخصوصا
/makhsusan/ ► adverb
special - chiefly

مخچه
/mokhche/ ► noun
cerebellum

مخفی
/makhfi/ ► adjective
closet - clandestine - invisible - hid -
undercover - slinky - secret

مخدر
/mokhader/ ► adjective
narcotic - opiate

مخفی کردن
/makhfi kardan/ ► verb
submerge - stow - occult - camouflage -
huddle

مخرب
/mokhareb/ ► adjective
wrecker - destroyer - mortal

مخفیگاه
/makhfigâh/ ► noun
sanctuary

مخرج
/makhraj/ ► noun
denominator - outlet - outgo - port - vent

مخل
/mokhel/ ► adjective
intruder

مخروط
/makhrut/ ► noun
cone

مخلص
/mokhles/ ► adjective
sincere - devotee

مخزن
/makhzan/ ► noun
reservoir - depository

مخزن آب
/makhzane âb/ ► noun
cistern - reservoir

مخلوط
/makhlut/ ► noun
mixture - mixed - hash - admixture -
blend - compost - composite

مخلوط کردن

/makhlut kardan/ ▶ verb
commix - roil

مخلوق

/makhlugh/ ▶ noun
creature

مخمر

/mokhamer/ ▶ adjective
zymogenic - yeast

مخمصه

/makhmase/ ▶ noun
predicament

مخمل

/makhmal/ ▶ adjective
velvet

مخملی

/makhmali/ ▶ adjective
velvet

مخملی کردن

/makhmali kardan/ ▶ verb
velvet

مخوف

/makhuf/ ▶ adjective
gruesome - ghastly - ugsome - horrible - hideous

مد

/mod/ ▶ noun
mode - highwater - vogue - chic

مداحی

/madâhi/ ▶ noun
eulogy

مداحی کردن

/madâhi kardan/ ▶ verb
adulate - eulogize

مداخله

/modâkhele/ ▶ noun
intervention - intermediation

مداخله گر

/modâkhelegar/ ▶ adjective
pryer - meddlesome

مداد

/medâd/ ▶ noun
pencil

مدار

/madâr/ ▶ noun
zone - theme - circuit - orbit - pivot

مدارا

/modârâ/ ▶ adjective
tolerance - reserve - affability

مدافع

/modâfe'/ ▶ adjective
apologist - defender - contestant

مدافعه
/modâfe'e/ ► noun
plea - apology - advocacy

مدال
/medâl/ ► noun
medal

مدام
/modâvem/ ► noun
unremitting - perpetual

مداوا
/modâvâ/ ► noun
therapy - medicament

مداوا کردن
/modâvâ kardan/ ► verb
medicate

مداوم
/modâvem/ ► adjective
steady - stable - continuous - ongoing -
unremitting

مداومت
/modâvemat/ ► noun
perseverance - assiduity

مدتی
/modati/ ► noun
a while

مدح
/madh/ ► noun
eulogy

مدح کردن
/madh kardan/ ► verb
laud - eulogize

مدخل
/madkhal/ ► noun
gateway - gate - estuary - entry - entree -
entrance - portal - access

مدد
/madad/ ► noun
reinforcement - help

مدد رساندن
/madad resândan/ ► verb
help

مدرج
/modarej/ ► noun
gaduate - gradient - scaled

مدرس
/modares/ ► noun
teacher - lecturer

مدرسه
/madrese/ ► noun
school - academy

مدرسه ابتدایی
/madreseye ebtedâyi/ ► noun
elementary school

مدرک
/madrak/ ► noun
testimony - proof - voucher - document

مدیحه

/madihe/ ► noun
panegyric

مدرن

/modern/ ► adjective
modern

مدیر

/modir/ ► noun
director - padrone - master - manager -
helmsman

مدعی

/moda'i/ ► adjective
complainant - claimant - attorney -
adversary - actor - plaintiff - suitor

مدیریت

/modiriyat/ ► noun
management

مدعی بودن

/moda'i budan/ ► verb
maintain

مدیون

/madyun/ ► noun
debtor - indebted

مدعی علیه

/moda'i alayh/ ► noun
defendant

مدیون بودن

/madyun budan/ ► verb
owe

مدفوع

/madfu'/ ► noun
stool - excretion - excrement

مذاکره

/mozâkere/ ► noun
interview - discussion - conference - talk

مدفون ساختن

/madfun sâkhtan/ ► verb
inter

مذاکره کردن

/mozâkere kardan/ ► verb
negotiate - converse - parley

مدل

/model/ ► noun
reconstruction - model

مذاکره کننده

/mozâkere konande/ ► adjective
negotiator

مدنی

/madani/ ► adjective
civil - civic - urban

مذبور

/mazbur/ ► noun
aforesaid

مدور

/modavar/ ► adjective
circular - round

مذكر

/mozakar/ ► noun
masculine - male

مذكور

/mazkur/ ► noun
said

مذهب

/mazhab/ ► noun
religion

مذهبى

/mazhabi/ ► adjective
devout - religious

مراجعت كردن

/morâje'at kardan/ ► verb
return

مراجعه

/morâje'e/ ► noun
respect - referral - reference - recourse

مراجعه كردن

/moraje'e kardan/ ► verb
confer - refer

مراد

/morâd/ ► noun
gist - wish - aim

مراسله

/morâsele/ ► noun
letter

مراسم

/marâsem/ ► noun
ceremony - rite

مراعات

/morâ'ât/ ► noun
heed - consideration - regard -
ovservation

مرافعه

/morâfe'e/ ► noun
lawsuit - cross - case - suit - spat

مرافعه كردن

/morâfe'e kardan/ ► verb
litigate

مراقب

/morâgheb/ ► adjective
observer - observant - watchman -
watchful - watcher - lookout - vigilant

مراقب بودن

/morâgheb budan/ ► verb
mind

مراقبت

/morâghebat/ ► noun
surveillance - ovservation - watchful -
lookout - vigilance

مرام

/marâm/ ► noun
tenet - intent

مراوده

/morâvede/ ▶ noun
intercourse

مربا

/morabâ/ ▶ noun
jam - preserve - confection

مربع

/moraba'/ ▶ noun
quadrangular - quadrangle - square

مربوط

/marbut/ ▶ noun
proper - material - pertinenet - apposite -
affiliate - dependent - coordinate -
coherent - relevant

مربوط بودن

/marbut budan/ ▶ verb
depend - pertain

مربوطه

/marbute/ ▶ noun
respective

مربی

/morabi/ ▶ noun
preceptor - mentor - corrector - teacher

مرتاض

/mortâz/ ▶ adjective
ascetic

مرتب

/moratab/ ▶ adjective
neat - regular - intrinsic - methodic -
prissy - shipshape - straight - tidy - trim

مرتب کردن

/moratab kardan/ ▶ verb
arrange - address - regularize - redd -
range - tidy - straighten - serialize

مرتبا

/morataban/ ▶ adverb
away

مرتبط

/mortabet/ ▶ adjective
correlate

مرتبط کردن

/mortabet kardan/ ▶ verb
correlate

مرتبه

/martabe/ ▶ noun
stair - sphere - place - order

مرتد

/mortad/ ▶ noun
apostate - heterodox - heretic - pervert -
renegade - relapse

مرتد شدن

/mortad shodan/ ▶ verb
defect

مرتع
/marta'/ ▶ noun
tore - pasture - park

مرحبا
/marhabâ/ ▶ noun
hurrah

مرتعش
/mortaesh/ ▶ noun
vibrant - quaker - seismic - tremulous

مرحله
/marhale/ ▶ noun
stage - stadium - scene - grade - order - rung - process - point - phase

مرتعش ساختن
/mortaesh sâkhtan/ ▶ verb
tremble

مرحمت
/marhamat/ ▶ noun
grace - mercy

مرتعش کردن
/mortaesh kardan/ ▶ verb
strum

مرحوم
/marhum/ ▶ noun
late - decedent

مرتفع
/mortafa'/ ▶ noun
high

مرخصی
/morkhasi/ ▶ noun
permission - vacation - leave

مرتفع کردن
/mortafa' kardan/ ▶ verb
obviate

مرخصی گرفتن
/morkhasi gereftan/ ▶ verb
recess - vacation

مرثیه
/marsiye/ ▶ noun
jeremiad - elegy

مرداب
/mordâb/ ▶ noun
swampland - swamp - quagmire

مرجان
/marjân/ ▶ noun
coral

مردابی
/mordâbi/ ▶ adjective
paludal

مرجح
/marjah/ ▶ noun
preferable

مردار
/mordâr/ ▶ noun
carrion

مردانه

/mardâne/ ► adjective
virile - masculine - mannish - manly -
male

مردنی

/mordani/ ► adjective
goner - dying - mortal

مرده

/morde/ ► adjective
vapid - defunct - dead - extinct -
exanimate

مردد

/moradad/ ► adjective
suspense - unready - uncertain - hesitant

مردد بودن

/moradad budan/ ► verb
oscillate - wobble - vacillate - linger -
hesitate - scotch

مردود

/mardud/ ► adjective
reprobate - castaway - washout

مردود شدن

/mardud shodan/ ► verb
runout

مردم

/mardom/ ► noun
population - people

مرز

/marz/ ► noun
outskirt - ridge - rand - mark - precinct -
boundary - bound - border - balk

مردمان

/mardomân/ ► noun
people

مرزیابی کردن

/marzyâbi kardan/ ► verb
delimit

مردمک چشم

/mardomake cheshm/ ► noun
apple - pearl - pupil

مرسوله

/marsule/ ► noun
consignment

مردمی

/mardomi/ ► adjective
humanity

مردن

/mordan/ ► verb
dying - perish - quail - passaway

مرسوم

/marsum/ ► noun
standard - usual - prevalent - vogue -
customary

مرسوم کردن
/marsum kardan/ ▶ verb
introduce - standardize

مرغابی
/morghâbi/ ▶ noun
duck

مرشد
/morshed/ ▶ noun
mentor - master - preceptor

مرغان
/morghân/ ▶ noun
bird

مرض
/maraz/ ▶ noun
malady - disease

مرغداری
/morghdâri/ ▶ noun
aviculture

مرطوب
/martub/ ▶ adjective
muggy - moist - humid - wet

مرغزار
/marghzâr/ ▶ noun
turf - lawn - meadow - prairie

مرطوب ساختن
/martub sâkhtan/ ▶ verb
damp - humidify

مرغوب
/marghub/ ▶ adjective
desirable

مرطوب شدن
/martub shodan/ ▶ verb
moisten

مرقد
/marghad/ ▶ noun
tabernacle

مرغ
/morgh/ ▶ noun
hen - bird

مرکب
/morakab/ ▶ noun
composite - roadster - ink

مرغ عشق
/morghe eshgh/ ▶ noun
lovebird

مرکبدان
/morakabdân/ ▶ noun
inkwell - inkstand

مرغ ماهیخوار
/morghe mâhikhâr/ ▶ noun
pelican - kingfisher

مرکز
/markaz/ ▶ noun
seat - station - centennial - meddle - hub
- heart

مرکزی
/markazi/ ► adjective
central - umbilical

مرگ
/marg/ ► noun
departure - decease - death - dying

مرگ آور
/magâvar/ ► adjective
lethal - mortal

مرگبار
/margbâr/ ► adjective
mortal

مرمت
/maremat/ ► noun
repair - upkeep

مرمری
/marmari/ ► adjective
jet - marble

مرموز
/marmuz/ ► adjective
recondite - inscrutable - mysterious - shady

مرهم
/marham/ ► noun
balm - unguent - unction - ointment - oil - chrism - salve

مرهون
/marhun/ ► noun
indebted

مرهون بودن
/marhun budan/ ► verb
owe

مروارید
/morvârid/ ► noun
pearl

مروت
/morovat/ ► adjective
humanity

مرور
/morur/ ► noun
tract - revision - revisal - glance - perusal - lapse

مرور کردن
/morur kardan/ ► verb
turnover

مری
/meri/ ► noun
swallow - gullet

مرید
/morid/ ► noun
devotee - disciple

مریزاد
/marizâd/ ► noun
bravo

مریض
/mariz/ ► noun
sick - morbid - patient

مریض شدن

/mariz shodan/ ▶ verb
sick

مریض کردن

/mariz kardan/ ▶ verb
indispose

مریی

/morabi/ ▶ adjective
visible - obvious

مزاج

/mezâj/ ▶ noun
temperament - temper - kidney - blood -
health

مزاجی

/mezâji/ ▶ adjective
quirk

مزاح

/mezâh/ ▶ noun
prank - humor - wit

مزاح کردن

/mezâh kardan/ ▶ verb
jest

مزاحم

/mozâhem/ ▶ adjective
troublous - troublemaker

مزاحم شدن

/mozâhem shodan/ ▶ verb
perturb - annoy - buttonhole - disturb -
obtrude

مزاحمت

/mozâhemat/ ▶ noun
trouble - trade

مزار

/mazâr/ ▶ noun
sepulcher - bier

مزایا

/mazâyâ/ ▶ noun
premium

مزایده

/mozâyede/ ▶ noun
outcry - auction - bid

مزخرف

/mozakhraf/ ▶ adjective
trashy - tawdry - ludicrous - baloney -
absurd - nonsensical - nonsense

مزد

/mozd/ ▶ noun
wage - hire - pension

مزدور

/mozdur/ ▶ adjective
grub - grub - barrator - hireling - help

مزرعه

/mazra'e/ ▶ noun
farm - stead

مزمزه
/mazmaze/ ▶ noun
sip - gust - assay

مزین
/mozayan/ ▶ adjective
clad - ornate

مزمزه کردن
/mazmaze kardan/ ▶ verb
sip

مزین کردن
/mozayan kardan/ ▶ verb
emboss - dress - furnish - beset

مزمن
/mozmen/ ▶ adjective
chronic

مژگان
/mozhgân/ ▶ noun
eyelash - lash

مزه
/maze/ ▶ noun
flavor - smack - savor - zest - taste

مژه
/mozhe/ ▶ noun
eyelash

مزه تند
/mazeye tond/ ▶ noun
tang

مس
/mes/ ▶ noun
copper

مسئله
/mas'ale/ ▶ noun
theorem - question - problem - example

مزه دار کردن
/mazedâr kardan/ ▶ verb
flavor

مسابقات المپیک
/mosâbeghate olampik/ ▶ noun
olympiad

مزیت
/maziyat/ ▶ noun
vantage - profit - privilege - prepayment
- preference - ascendency - advantage

مسابقه
/mosâbeghe/ ▶ noun
match - contest - competition - chase-
chace - race - game

مزیت دادن
/maziyat dâdan/ ▶ verb
advantage

مسابقه دادن
/mosâbeghe dâdan/ ▶ verb
race - compete

مساحت
/masâhat/ ▶ noun
area - space

مساعد
/mosâ'ede/ ▶ adjective
auspicious - adjutant - propitious

مساعدت
/mosâ'edat/ ▶ noun
help

مساعده
/mosâ'ede/ ▶ noun
advance

مسافت
/masâfat/ ▶ noun
distance

مسافر
/mosâfer/ ▶ noun
pilgrim - passenger - roomer - traveler

مسافرت
/mosâferat/ ▶ noun
journey - tour

مسافرخانه
/mosâferkhâne/ ▶ noun
inn

مسالمت آمیز
/mosâlematâmiz/ ▶ adjective
peaceful

مسامحه
/mosâmehe/ ▶ noun
neglect

مسامحه کردن
/mosâmehe kardan/ ▶ verb
connive

مساوات
/mosâvât/ ▶ noun
equality

مساوی
/mosâvi/ ▶ noun
adequate - even - equal

مساوی بودن
/mosâvi budan/ ▶ verb
equal

مسبب
/mosabeb/ ▶ adjective
inducement

مست
/mast/ ▶ adjective
drunken - drunk

مست کردن
/mast kardan/ ▶ verb
sot - tipple - intoxicate - inebriate - lush
- booze - befuddle - fuzz

مستاجر
/mosta'jer/ ▶ noun
tenant - lodger - lessee - roomer

مستراح

/mostarâh/ ▶ noun
toilet - restroom

مستشار

/mostashâr/ ▶ noun
counselor

مستطیل

/mostatil/ ▶ noun
rectangular - oblong

مستعد

/mosta'ed/ ▶ adjective
susceptible - prone - apt - capable

مستعفی شدن

/mostafi shodan/ ▶ verb
resign

مستعمره

/mosta'mere/ ▶ noun
colony

مستغلات

/mostaghelât/ ▶ noun
tenement

مستقبل

/mostaghbal/ ▶ noun
future

مستقر

/mostaghar/ ▶ noun
put - deepseated

مستبد

/mostabed/ ▶ adjective
opinionated

مستبدانه

/mostabedâne/ ▶ adverb
arbitrary - despotic

مستتر کردن

/mostater kardan/ ▶ verb
occult

مستثنی

/mostasnâ/ ▶ noun
exempt

مستثنی کردن

/mostasnâ kardan/ ▶ verb
exclude

مستحق

/mostahagh/ ▶ adjective
just - worthy - meritorious

مستحکم

/mostahkam/ ▶ adjective
tenacious - redoubtable

مستخدم

/mostakhdem/ ▶ noun
man - employee - retainer

مستدل

/mostadal/ ▶ adjective
arguable - reasonable - rational

مستقر شدن
/mostaghar shodan/ ▶ verb
set - fix

مستهجن
/mostahjan/ ▶ adjective
lurid

مستقل
/mostaghel/ ▶ noun
independent - maverick

مستهلک شدن
/mostahlak shodan/ ▶ verb
merge

مستقیم
/mostaghim/ ▶ noun
straight - stiff - upstanding - right

مستور
/mastur/ ▶ adjective
covered

مستقیما
/mostaghiman/ ▶ adverb
sheer - straight - bolt - perse

مستولی شدن
/mostoli/ ▶ verb
prevail

مستمر
/mostamer/ ▶ adjective
continuum

مستی
/masti/ ▶ noun
spree - rut - drunk - languor - inebriety

مستمسک
/mostamsak/ ▶ adjective
pretext

مسجد
/masjed/ ▶ noun
mosque

مستمع
/mostame'/ ▶ adjective
auditor - listener

مسحور
/mas'hur/ ▶ adjective
spellbound - rapt

مستمند
/mostamand/ ▶ adjective
poor

مسحور کردن
/mas'hur kardan/ ▶ verb
bewitch - bedevil - charm - ravish

مستند کردن
/mostanad kardan/ ▶ verb
predicate

مسخرگی
/maskharegi/ ▶ noun
tomfoolery

مسخره

/maskhare/ ▶ adjective
fool - clown - rustic

مسکن

/maskan/ ▶ noun
settlement - dwelling - roof- abode

مسخره آمیز

/maskhareâmiz/ ▶ adjective
ridiculous - droll - burlesque

مسکوکات

/maskukât/ ▶ noun
coinage

مسخره کردن

/maskhare kardan/ ▶ verb
clown - buffoon - mimic

مسکونی

/maskuni/ ▶ adjective
residential

مسکین

/meskin/ ▶ adjective
poor

مسدود

/masdud/ ▶ adjective
shut - barred

مسلح کردن

/mosalah kardan/ ▶ verb
equip - weapon - force

مسدود ساختن

/masdud sâkhtan/ ▶ verb
stockade

مسلخ

/maslakh/ ▶ noun
slaughterhouse

مسرور

/masrur/ ▶ adjective
glad - vivacious

مسلسل

/mosalsal/ ▶ noun
uninterrupted - unceasing - unbroken -
unbroke - reel - serial

مسطح

/mosatah/ ▶ adjective
flat - even - plane - planar - plain

مسلط

/mosalat/ ▶ adjective
dominant - preponderant - predominant

مسقط

/masghat/ ▶ noun
abortive

مسلط بودن

/mosalat budan/ ▶ verb
predominate

مسلک
/moslek/ ▶ noun
sect

مسن
/mosen/ ▶ adjective
elderly - old

مسلم
/mosalam/ ▶ noun
sure - cretain - natural - given -
undoubted - moslem - incontrovertible

مسند
/masnad/ ▶ noun
seat - substance - predicate

مسلم دانستن
/mosalam dânestan/ ▶ verb
presume

مسواک زدن
/mesvâk zadan/ ▶ verb
brush

مسلما
/mosalaman/ ▶ adverb
indisputable

مسی
/mesi/ ▶ adjective
cuprous

مسلمان
/mosalmân/ ▶ noun
moslem - moor

مسیح
/masih/ ▶ noun
christ

مسموع
/masmu'/ ▶ noun
audible

مسیحا
/masihan/ ▶ noun
messiah

مسموم شدن
/masmum shodan/ ▶ verb
venom - loco

مسیحی
/masihi/ ▶ adjective
christian

مسموم کردن
/masmum kardan/ ▶ verb
poison - venom

مسیحیت
/masihiyat/ ▶ noun
christianity - christendom

مسیر
/masir/ ▶ noun
path - point - vector - course - orbit -
race - career - run

مسکن

/mosaken/ ▶ adjective
narcotic - calmative - palliative

مشابه

/moshâbeh/ ▶ adjective
homogeneous - equivalent - similar

مشابهت

/moshâbehat/ ▶ noun
similarity - parallelism

مشاجره

/moshâjere/ ▶ noun
dispute - plea - pique - scuffle

مشارکت

/moshârekat/ ▶ noun
communion - partnership

مشارکت کردن

/moshârekat kardan/ ▶ verb
common

مشاهده

/moshâhede/ ▶ noun
seeing - ovservation

مشاهده کردن

/moshâhede kardan/ ▶ verb
see - observe - behold - perceive

مشاور

/moshâver/ ▶ noun
adviser - counselor - consultant

مشاوره

/moshâvere/ ▶ noun
council - conference

مشبک کردن

/moshabak kardan/ ▶ verb
interweave - interlace

مشت

/mosht/ ▶ noun
punch - yerk - fist - clump - knock -
wisp - buffet - pounce - handful

مشت خوردن

/mosht khordan/ ▶ verb
scuff

مشت زن

/moshtzan/ ▶ noun
boxer - pugilist

مشتاق

/moshtâgh/ ▶ adjective
enthusiastic - earnest - eager - wistful -
keen - raring - fond - avid - hungry -
perfervid

مشتاق بودن

/moshtâgh budan/ ▶ verb
yearn

مشتاقانه

/moshtâghâne/ ▶ adverb
intensive - intense

مشترک

/moshtarak/ ▶ noun
joint - joint - common

مشتری
/moshtari/ ► noun
patron - habitue - customer - client -
chap

مشتق
/moshtagh/ ► noun
derivative - offshoot

مشخص
/moshakhas/ ► noun
signal - ditinct - antiseptic

مشخص کردن
/moshakhas kardan/ ► adverb
characterize - denote - delineate -
specify

مشخصات
/moshakhasât/ ► noun
specs - specification - characteristic

مشرب
/moshreb/ ► noun
grain - mood - habit

مشرف
/mosharaf/ ► adjective
dominant - verge

مشرق
/mashregh/ ► noun
sunrise

مشرقی
/maghreghi/ ► adjective
oriental

مشرک
/moshrek/ ► adjective
pagan - heathen

مشروب
/mashrub/ ► noun
drink - liquor - beverage

مشروبات
/mashrubât/ ► noun
moonlight

مشروح
/mashruh/ ► adjective
punctual - unabridged - elaborative

مشروط
/mashrut/ ► adjective
eventual - provisional - provided

مشروطه
/mashrute/ ► noun
conditional

مشروع
/mashru'/ ► adjective
loyal - legitimate - legal - lawful -
rightful

مشروعیت
/mashru'iyat/ ► noun
legitimation

مشعل

/mash'al/ ► noun
torch

مشکی

/meshki/ ► adjective
black - raven - sable

مشعوف ساختن

/mash'uf sâkhtan/ ► verb
grace

مشمول

/mashmul/ ► noun
inclusive - liable

مشغول

/mashghul/ ► noun
at - busy - engross

مشمولیت

/mashmuliyat/ ► noun
incurrence - incidence

مشغول کردن

/mashghul kardan/ ► verb
busy - amuse - employ

مشهود

/mashhud/ ► adjective
sensible - obvious - evident

مشغولیت

/mashghuliyat/ ► noun
engagement - avocation

مشهور

/mashhur/ ► adjective
reputable - name - grand - famous -
putative

مشق

/mashgh/ ► noun
homework - exercise

مشورت

/mashverat/ ► noun
advice - rede - counsel - consult

مشقت

/masheghat/ ► noun
travail - hardship - pressure

مشورت کردن

/mashverat kardan/ ► verb
consult - confer

مشکل

/moshkel/ ► noun
difficult - uphill - problem - ill - hard

مشورتی

/mashverati/ ► adjective
advisory

مشکوک

/mashkuk/ ► noun
skeptic - suspicious - dubious - doubtful
- questionable - uncertain - precarious

مشوش کردن

/moshavash kardan/ ► verb
disconcert

مصادف شدن

/mosâdef shodan/ ► verb
hurtle

مشوق

/moshavegh/ ► adjective
incentive

مصادم

/mosâdem/ ► noun
afoul

مشی

/mash'y/ ► noun
tack - gang - demarche

مصالح

/mosâleh/ ► noun
stuff

مشیت

/mashiyat/ ► noun
ordinance

مصالحه

/mosâlehe/ ► noun
accord - reconciliation - compromise

مشیت الهی

/mashiyate elâhi/ ► noun
providence

مصالحه کردن

/mosâlehe kardan/ ► verb
compromise

مصاحب

/mosâheb/ ► noun
consort - fere

مصدر

/masdar/ ► noun
orderly

مصاحبت

/mosâhebat/ ► noun
companionship

مصدع

/mosade'/ ► noun
troublesome

مصاحبت کردن

/mosâhebat kardan/ ► verb
accompany

مصر

/mesr/ ► noun
Egypt

مصادره کردن

/mosâdere kardan/ ► verb
sequester - confiscate

مصر

/moser/ ► adjective
demanding - precarious - insistent -
shrill - strenuous - stickler

مصری
/mesri/ ▶ adjective
Egyptian

مصرانه
/moserâne/ ▶ adverb
shrill - importune

مصرف
/masraf/ ▶ noun
expenditure - consumption - waster -
wasteful - utilization - utilizable - use

مصرف کردن
/masraf kardan/ ▶ verb
consume - expend - eat - useup - use

مصطلح
/mostalah/ ▶ noun
yclept - ycleped - colloquial

مصلح
/mosleh/ ▶ noun
righter - reformer - peacemaker

مصلحت
/maslehat/ ▶ noun
advice - interest - expedient - rede

مصلحتی
/maslehati/ ▶ adjective
advisable

مصلوب شدن
/maslub shodan/ ▶ verb
hang

مصمم
/mosamam/ ▶ adjective
stalwart - unflinching - undeviating -
intent - resolute

مصنف
/mosnef/ ▶ noun
writer - composer

مصنوع
/masnu'/ ▶ noun
manufacture - made - artifact - ornate

مصنوعی
/masnu'i/ ▶ adjective
dummy - false - postiche - sophisticated

مصور
/mosavar/ ▶ adjective
pictorial

مصون
/masun/ ▶ adjective
immune

مصون ساختن
/masun sâkhatan/ ▶ verb
frank

مصونیت
/masuniyat/ ▶ noun
security - immunity

مصيبت
/mosibat/ ▶ noun
tragedy - sorrow - curse - disaster -
catastrophe - calamity - bale

مصيبت بار
/mosibatbâr/ ▶ adjective
calamitous

مضاعف
/mozâ'af/ ▶ noun
multiple - binary

مضاف
/mozâf/ ▶ noun
addend

مضايقه
/mozâyeghe/ ▶ noun
spare

مضحک
/mozhek/ ▶ adjective
comic - ridiculous - grotesque -
laughable - hilarious - preposterous -
ludicrous - absurd - burlesque

مضر
/mozer/ ▶ adjective
pernicious - inadvisable - harmful -
insanitary - injurious - inimical -
obnoxious - noxious - nocuous

مضرب
/mazrab/ ▶ noun
multiple

مضروب
/mazrub/ ▶ noun
multiple

مضطرب
/moztareb/ ▶ adjective
panicky - unruly - uneasy - vexatious

مضيقه
/mazighe/ ▶ noun
pinch - extremity - stress

مطابق
/motâbegh/ ▶ noun
to - pursuant - similar - respondent -
relevant - within - after

مطابق بودن
/motâbegh budan/ ▶ verb
tally

مطابقت
/motâbeghat/ ▶ noun
accordance - compatibility -
correspondence - concord

مطالبه
/motâlebe/ ▶ noun
claim - demand

مطالبه کردن
/motâlebe kardan/ ▶ verb
demand

مطالعات

/motâle'ât/ ▶ noun
ovservation

مطلع

/moti'/ ▶ adjective
understanding - hep

مطالعه

/motâle'e/ ▶ noun
study - perusal - reading

مطلق

/motlagh/ ▶ adjective
absolute - total - stark - slick - sheer -
downright

مطالعه کردن

/motâle'e kardan/ ▶ verb
study - conciliate

مطلقا

/motlaghan/ ▶ adverb
utterly

مطب

/matab/ ▶ noun
clinic - policlinic

مطلوب

/matlub/ ▶ adjective
desirable - favorite - nice - lief -
idealistic

مطبوع

/matbu'/ ▶ adjective
sweet - scrumptious - toothsome -
proper - exquisite - douce - dainty -
graceful

مطمئن

/motma'en/ ▶ adjective
secure - sure - confident

مطبوعات

/matbu'ât/ ▶ noun
press - literature

مطمئنا

/motma'enan/ ▶ adverb
certainly

مطرود

/matrud/ ▶ adjective
abject - castaway - rejcet - outcast -
despicable

مطمح نظر

/matma'e nazar/ ▶ adjective
scope

مطیع

/moti'/ ▶ adjective
obedient - able - limber

مطلب

/matlab/ ▶ noun
subject - thought - theme

معاشر
/moâsher/ ▶ noun
socialite - sociable

مظفر
/mozafar/ ▶ adjective
victorious

معاشرت
/moâsherat/ ▶ noun
commerce - society

مظنون
/maznun/ ▶ adjective
suspect - defiant

معاشقه
/moâsheghe/ ▶ noun
courtship

مظنون بودن
/maznun budan/ ▶ verb
suspicion - suspect

معاصر
/maâser/ ▶ noun
current - contemporary -
contemporaneous

مظهر
/mazhar/ ▶ adjective
showing

معاف
/moâf/ ▶ noun
exempt

معادل
/mo'âdel/ ▶ noun
tantamount - equivalent

معاف کردن
/moâf kardan/ ▶ verb
remit - frank - exempt - excuse -
dispense - dismiss

معادله
/mo'âdele/ ▶ noun
equation

معارض
/mo'ârez/ ▶ adjective
opponent

معافیت
/moâfiyat/ ▶ noun
immunity - freedom - exemption

معارفه
/mo'ârefe/ ▶ noun
introduction

معالج
/moâlej/ ▶ noun
therapeutic

معاش
/ma'âsh/ ▶ noun
sustenance - livelihood

معالجه
/moâleje/ ▶ noun
treatment - therapy

معبر

/ma'bar/ ▶ noun
pathway - road - crossover - conduit -
traverse - thoroughfare

معبود

/ma'bud/ ▶ noun
idol

معتاد

/mo'tâd/ ▶ noun
addict - inveterate - habitue - habitual

معتاد ساختن

/mo'tâd sâkhtan/ ▶ verb
accustom

معتاد شدن

/mo'tâd shodan/ ▶ verb
won - accustom

معتاد کردن

/mo'tad kardan/ ▶ verb
habit - inure - customize

معتبر

/mo'tabar/ ▶ adjective
trusty - reliable - credible - authoritative
- authentic - valid

معتبر بودن

/mo'tabar budan/ ▶ verb
dow

معامله

/moâmele/ ▶ noun
bargain - intercourse - treatment -
transaction

معامله کردن

/moâmele kardan/ ▶ verb
transact - truck - chap - deal

معاند

/moâned/ ▶ adjective
dissident - dissenter - defiant -
nonconformist - spiteful

معاهده

/moâhede/ ▶ noun
treaty - compact - pact - bond

معاوضه

/moâveze/ ▶ noun
swap - exchange

معاون

/moâven/ ▶ noun
secondbest - assistant - adjunct -
accessory - helpmeet - vicar

معاینه

/moâyene/ ▶ noun
examination

معبد

/ma'bad/ ▶ noun
shrine

معجون

/ma'jun/ ▶ noun
confection

معتدل

/mo'tadel/ ▶ adjective
modest - moderate - mild - middleman -
medium

معدل

/mo'adel/ ▶ noun
average - norm

معترض

/mo'tarez/ ▶ noun
demonstrator

معدن

/ma'dan/ ▶ noun
mineral - mine

معترف

/mo'taref/ ▶ adjective
confessor

معدنی

/ma'dani/ ▶ adjective
inorganic - mineral

معتقد

/mo'taghed/ ▶ adjective
believer

معده

/me'de/ ▶ noun
stomach - tummy - breadbasket - kyte

معتقدات

/mo'taghedât/ ▶ noun
belief

معدود

/ma'dud/ ▶ noun
scant - paucity - poor - little

معتمد

/mo'tamed/ ▶ adjective
trustworthy

معدوم کردن

/ma'dum kardan/ ▶ verb
ruinate - obliterate

معجزه

/mo'jeze/ ▶ noun
miracle

معذرت خواستن

/ma'zerat khâstan/ ▶ verb
pardon - apologize - excuse

معجزه آسا

/mo'jeze âsâ/ ▶ adjective
miraculous

معذورداشتن

/ma'zur dâshtan/ ▶ verb
excuse

معراج
/me'râj/ ▶ noun
ascension

معرض
/ma'raz/ ▶ noun
open

معرفت
/ma'refat/ ▶ noun
wisdom - cognizance - cognition

معرفی
/moarefi/ ▶ noun
presentation - introduction

معرفی کردن
/moarefi kardan/ ▶ verb
recommend - nominate - introduce -
inset - present

معروف
/ma'ruf/ ▶ adjective
famous - grand

معروفیت
/ma'rufiyat/ ▶ noun
renown - popularity

معزول کردن
/ma'zul/ ▶ verb
deprive - depose - eject - recall

معشوق
/ma'shugh/ ▶ noun
lover

معشوقه
/ma'shughe/ ▶ noun
sweetheart - stallion - girl - paramour -
love

معصوم
/ma'sum/ ▶ adjective
immaculate - innocent

معصیت
/ma'siyat/ ▶ noun
sin

معصیت کردن
/ma'siyat kardan/ ▶ verb
sin

معطر
/moatar/ ▶ adjective
redolent - nutty - aromatic - scented -
spicy

معطل شدن
/moatal shodan/ ▶ verb
wait

معطل کردن
/moatal kardan/ ▶ verb
loiter - detain

معقول
/ma'ghul/ ▶ adjective
sensible - wise - reasonable - rational -
conscionable

معکوس
/ma'kus/ ► noun
contrary - reverse - obverse -
upsidedown - inverse - setback

معلق
/moalagh/ ► adjective
headlong - handstand - pendant

معلق کردن
/moalagh kardan/ ► verb
suspend

معلم
/moalem/ ► noun
teacher

معلول
/ma'lul/ ► noun
effect

معلوم
/ma'lum/ ► noun
apparent - active - intelligible - overt -
obvious - cretain - definite

معلومات
/ma'lumât/ ► noun
information - wives - witting

معما
/moama/ ► noun
crux - conundrum - enigma - problem -
mystery - quandary - puzzle

معمار
/me'mâr/ ► noun
architect

معماری کردن
/me'mâri kardan/ ► verb
architect

معمولا
/ma'mulan/ ► adverb
usually

معمولی
/ma'muli/ ► adjective
commonplace - common - ornery -
ordinary - general - banal

معنوی
/ma'navi/ ► noun
spiritual - virtual - moral - incorporate -
immaterial - abstract

معنویت
/ma'naviyat/ ► noun
idealism

معنی
/ma'ni/ ► noun
purporst - significance - sense - effect -
drift - definition - connotation - abstract
- moral - intent

معنی دار
/ma'nidâr/ ► adjective
punctual - meaningful

معنی کردن
/ma'ni kardan/ ► verb
define - translate

مغالطه
/moghâlete/ ► noun
sophistry - sophism - chicanery

مغایر
/moghâyer/ ► noun
variant - anomalous - discordant

مغایر بودن
/moghâyer budan/ ► verb
jar - disagree

مغایرت
/moghâyerat/ ► noun
aversion - variance - repugnance - odds -
contrast

مغتنم
/moghtanam/ ► noun
pleasurable

مغتنم شمردن
/moghtanam shemordan/ ► verb
prize

مغرب
/maghreb/ ► noun
sunset - occident - west

مغرض
/moghrez/ ► noun
partial

مغرور
/maghrur/ ► adjective
proud - jaunty - snobbish - snob -
swagger - supercilious

معوق کردن
/moavagh/ ► verb
retard

معونت
/ma'naviyat/ ► noun
emolument

معیشت
/ma'ishat/ ► noun
livelihood

معین
/moayan/ ► adjective
specific - punctual - definite - regular

معیوب
/ma'yub/ ► adjective
incorrect - incomplete

معیوب ساختن
/ma'yub sâkhtan/ ► verb
defect - vitiate

معیوب شدن
/ma'yub shodan/ ► verb
maim

معیوب کردن
/ma'yub kardan/ ► verb
damage - impair - mar

مغازه
/maghâze/ ► noun
store - shootinggallery

مغرورانه
/maghrurâne/ ▶ adverb
contemptuous - vain - lofty

مفاصا
/mofasalan/ ▶ adverb
quits

مغز
/maghz/ ▶ noun
kernel - nucleus - brain - pate - mind - marrow

مفت
/moft/ ▶ adjective
gratuitous - gratis

مغزی
/maghzi/ ▶ adjective
braid - mental - cerebral - cacuminal - welt - nuclear

مفتاح
/meftâh/ ▶ noun
passkey - clef - opener - keyword

مفتخر
/moftakhar/ ▶ adjective
proud

مغشوش
/maghshush/ ▶ adjective
haywire

مفتضح
/moftazeh/ ▶ adjective
ignominious - infamous

مغفرت
/maghferat/ ▶ noun
pardon

مفتوح
/maftuh/ ▶ adjective
open - patent

مغلوب ساختن
/maghlub sâkhtan/ ▶ verb
overcome - defeat - vanquish

مفتوح شدن
/maftuh shodan/ ▶ verb
open

مغناطیس
/meghnatis/ ▶ noun
magnet

مفتول
/maftul/ ▶ noun
wire

مفاد
/mafâd/ ▶ noun
significance - sense - substance - text - tenor - purporst - scope - context - content - intent

مفر
/mafar/ ▶ noun
exhaust - loophole

مفقود

/mafghud/ ▶ adjective
lost - absent

مفرح

/mofarah/ ▶ adjective
fun

مفرد

/mofrad/ ▶ noun
singular

مفهوم

/mafhum/ ▶ noun
context - concept - moral - intention -
intelligible - implicit - implication

مفرط

/mofrat/ ▶ adjective
intensive - inordinate - extreme -
extravagant - boisterous - excessive

مفید

/mofid/ ▶ adjective
profitable - beneficial - useful -
instrumental - effect - remedial

مفروض

/mafruz/ ▶ noun
putative - given

مفیدبودن

/mofid budan/ ▶ verb
advantage - benefit - stead

مفروضات

/mafruzât/ ▶ noun
information

مقابل

/moghâbel/ ▶ noun
opposite - contrary - inverse

مفسر

/mofaser/ ▶ noun
commentator - interpreter

مقابله

/moghâbele/ ▶ noun
contrast - collation - opposition

مفصل

/mofasal/ ▶ noun
spacious - joint - juncture - joint - ample
- hinge - voluminous - copula - copious

مقابله کردن

/moghâbele kardan/ ▶ verb
beard - repel - check

مفعول

/maf'ul/ ▶ noun
object - passive

مقاربت

/moghârebat/ ▶ noun
intercourse - coition

مقاربت جنسی

/moghârebate jensi/ ▶ noun
gash - coitus

مقاربتی

/moghârebati/ ▶ adjective
copulative - venereal

مقارن

/moghâren/ ▶ noun
toward - against - into

مقاطعه

/moghâte'e/ ▶ noun
contract - jobbery

مقاطعه کار

/moghâte'ekâr/ ▶ noun
contractor

مقاله

/maghâle/ ▶ noun
article - paper - essay - dissertation -
disquisition - tract - theme

مقام

/maghâm/ ▶ noun
status - station - title - post - portfolio -
pew - order - office - rank - function -
capacity - dignity

مقاوم

/moghâvem/ ▶ adjective
adamant - resister - resister - resistant -
refractory

مقاومت

/moghâvemat/ ▶ noun
defiance - resistance - opposition

مقاومت کردن

/moghâvemat kardan/ ▶ verb
pulloff

مقایسه

/moghâyese/ ▶ noun
analogy - comparison - collation -
resemblance

مقایسه کردن

/moghâyese kardan/ ▶ verb
compare

مقبره

/maghbare/ ▶ noun
sepulcher - tomb - monument -
mausoleum - bier - kil

مقبول

/maghbul/ ▶ adjective
acceptable

مقتدر

/moghtader/ ▶ adjective
dominant - mighty - authoritative

مقتضی

/moteghâzi/ ▶ noun
appropriate - advisable - meet - material
- expedient - due - suitable - just

مقتول
/maghtul/ ▶ noun
slain

مقدار
/meghdâr/ ▶ noun
content - extent - percentage - value -
quantity - proportion - size

مقدر
/moghadar/ ▶ adjective
tacit - fey

مقدر شدن
/moghadar shodan/ ▶ verb
fate

مقدس
/moghadas/ ▶ adjective
innocent - holy - numinous -
sanctimonious - saint - sacrosanct -
sacred

مقدس کردن
/moghadas kardan/ ▶ verb
hallow

مقدس نما
/moghadasnâma/ ▶ adjective
sanctimonious

مقدم
/moghadam/ ▶ adjective
first - antecedent - prior - previous -
premier - preferential

مقدم بودن
/moghadam budan/ ▶ verb
precede

مقدمات
/moghadamât/ ▶ noun
preliminary

مقدماتی
/moghadamâti/ ▶ noun
primary - preparatory - preliminary -
elementary - first

مقدمه
/moghadame/ ▶ noun
introduction - prelude - preface - start -
snap - prologue - prolegomenon

مقدور
/maghdur/ ▶ adjective
possible

مقر
/maghar/ ▶ noun
seat - stead - domicile - chair

مقرر
/mogharar/ ▶ noun
regular - statutory - standard

مقررات
/moghararât/ ▶ noun
institute - manual - precept

مقلب

/moghaleb/ ► noun
yclept - ycleped

مقرری

/mogharari/ ► noun
pension - emolument

مقلوب

/maghlub/ ► adjective
anagram

مقسوم

/maghsum/ ► noun
part

مقهور ساختن

/maghhur sâkhtan/ ► verb
subdue

مقصد

/maghsad/ ► noun
aim - goal - destination

مقوا

/moghavâ/ ► noun
carton - cardboard - card

مقصر

/moghaser/ ► noun
culprit - culpable - guilty - hangdog

مقوله

/maghule/ ► noun
category

مقصود

/maghsud/ ► noun
purpose - proposition - significance -
sentiment - innuendo - idea - design -
drift

مقوی

/moghavi/ ► adjective
tonic - hearty - cordial

مقطع

/maghta'/ ► noun
segment - section - cutting

مقیاس

/meghyâs/ ► noun
gauge - criterion - meter - measure -
indicator - scale - yardstick

مقعد

/magh'ad/ ► noun
anus - rectum - croup

مقید

/moghayad/ ► adjective
pent - modal - bound - conditional

مقعر

/magh'ar/ ► noun
dished - concave - cave

مقیم
/moghim/ ▶ noun
resident - denizen - inmate - inhabitant

مکانیزم
/mekânizm/ ▶ noun
mechanism

مک
/mek/ ▶ noun
intake - suck

مک زدن
/mek zadan/ ▶ verb
suck

مکانیزه کردن
/mekânize/ ▶ verb
mechanize - mechanization

مکار
/makâr/ ▶ adjective
cunning - pawky

مکانیک
/mekânik/ ▶ noun
machanist - mechanics - mechanic

مکاشفه
/mokâshefe/ ▶ noun
apocalypse

مکانیکی
/mekâniki/ ▶ adjective
gadget - mechanic

مکالمه
/mokâleme/ ▶ noun
conversation

مکتب
/maktab/ ▶ noun
school - academy - ism

مکالمه کردن
/mokâleme kardan/ ▶ verb
parley

مکث
/maks/ ▶ noun
halt - period - pause

مکان
/makân/ ▶ noun
stead - spot - locus - location - locality -
place - part

مکث کردن
/maks kardan/ ▶ verb
pause - halt - letup

مکدر
/mokader/ ▶ adjective
eerie

مکان شناسی
/makânshenâsi/ ▶ noun
topology

مکر
/makr/ ▶ noun
ruse - guile - wile

مگر
/magar/ ▶ adverb
except - but - unless

مکرر
/mokarar/ ▶ adjective
bis - continual - eternity - eternal -
repetitious

مگراینکه
/magar inke/ ▶ adverb
unless

مکررا
/mokararan/ ▶ adverb
freuqently

ملا
/molâ/ ▶ noun
mullah

مکروه
/makruh/ ▶ noun
execrable - detestable

ملاحظه
/molâheze/ ▶ noun
consideration - respect - regard - heed -
tact - prudence

مکزیکی
/mekziki/ ▶ adjective
Mexican

ملاحظه کاری
/molâhezekâri/ ▶ noun
canniness

مکش
/makesh/ ▶ noun
suction

ملاحظه کردن
/molâheze kardan/ ▶ verb
perceive - heed - consider - note -
observe - remark - regard

مکعب
/moka'ab/ ▶ noun
cube

ملازم
/molâzem/ ▶ noun
retainer - concomitant - attendant -
adjunct - valet

مکمل
/mokamel/ ▶ noun
supplementary - supplement -
complementary - complement

ملازمت
/molâzemat/ ▶ noun
attendance

مکیدن
/mekidan/ ▶ verb
suck - intake

ملافه
/malâfe/ ▶ noun
slip - sheet - bedsheet

ملافه کردن
/malâfe kardan/ ▶ verb
sheet

ملامت کردن
/malâmat kardan/ ▶ verb
upbraid - blame - calldown - reprove -
rebuke

ملاقات
/molâghat/ ▶ noun
visit

ملایم
/molâyem/ ▶ adjective
soft - smooth - gentle - clement -
moderate - mild

ملاک
/melâk/ ▶ noun
criterion - evidence - document - lord -
landowner - landlord - proprietor

ملایمت
/molâyemat/ ▶ noun
suavity - equanimity - calmness -
warmth - amenity - leniency

ملالت
/malâlat/ ▶ noun
humdrum - boredom - gloom - ennui -
tedium

ملبس کردن
/mobalas kardan/ ▶ verb
dight

ملالت آور
/malâlatavar/ ▶ adjective
tedious

ملبوس
/malbus/ ▶ noun
clothes

ملالت انگیز
/malâlatangiz/ ▶ adjective
dismal

ملت
/melat/ ▶ noun
state - people - nation

ملامت
/molâyemat/ ▶ noun
reproof - rebuke - snuff - tax

ملتزم
/moltazem/ ▶ noun
sponsor

ملامت آمیز
/molâyematâmiz/ ▶ adjective
reproachful

ملتفت
/moltafet/ ▶ adjective
aware - attentive - conscious

ملتفت بودن
/moltafet budan/ ▶ verb
mind - beware

ملکی
/melki/ ▶ noun
possessive - agrarian

ملوان
/malavân/ ▶ noun
shipman - seaman - sailor

ملتمس
/moltames/ ▶ adjective
supplicant - suppliant - wishful

ملوکانه
/molukâne/ ▶ adverb
royal

ملحد
/molhed/ ▶ adjective
atheist

ملول
/malul/ ▶ adjective
lukewarm - heartsick - glum

ملحفه
/malhafe/ ▶ noun
bedsheet

ملی
/meli/ ▶ noun
public - national - popular

ملخ
/malakh/ ▶ noun
quaker - grasshopper

ملی شدن
/meli shodan/ ▶ verb
nationalize

ملعون
/mal'un/ ▶ adjective
unblest - unblessed - execrable - cussed
- cursed - foul

ملیت
/meliyat/ ▶ noun
nationality

ملغی
/molghâ/ ▶ noun
null - abrogate

ممارست
/momâresat/ ▶ noun
practice

ملکه
/malake/ ▶ noun
rial - empress - queen - monarch

مماس
/momâs/ ▶ noun
tangent

ممانعت

/momâne'at/ ▶ noun
prohibition - rein - blockage -
annoyance

ممانعت کردن

/momâne'at/ ▶ verb
impede - prevent - check - stall

ممتاز

/momtâz/ ▶ adjective
superior - excellent - elite - ditinct -
knockout - good - prize - preferential

ممتحن

/momtahen/ ▶ noun
proctor - examiner - examinant - tester

ممتنع

/momtane'/ ▶ noun
recusant

ممر

/mamar/ ▶ noun
resource

ممکن

/momken/ ▶ noun
possible

مملکت

/mamlekat/ ▶ noun
realm

مملو

/mamlov/ ▶ noun
laden - rife

ممنوع

/mamnu'/ ▶ noun
barred - illicit

ممنوع کردن

/mamnu' kardan/ ▶ verb
bar - debar - countermand - prohibit

ممنوعیت

/mamnu'iyat/ ▶ noun
embargo - interdict

ممنون

/mamnun/ ▶ adjective
thankful - indebted

ممه

/mame/ ▶ noun
tit - teat - pap

ممیزی

/momayezi/ ▶ noun
survey - audit

ممیزی کردن

/momayezi kardan/ ▶ verb
verify - survey

من من

/men men/ ▶ noun
mutter

منابع طبیعی
/manâbe'e tabi'i/ ► noun
natural resources

مناجات
/monâjât/ ► noun
chant - cant

منادی
/monâdi/ ► adjective
front - precursor - herald - harbinger

مناره
/manâre/ ► noun
minaret - pharos

منازعه
/monâze'e/ ► noun
disputation - debate - plea - struggle -
tilt

مناسب
/monâseb/ ► adjective
proper - suitable - appropriate - relevant
- fit - convenient - expedient

مناسبت
/monâsebat/ ► noun
decorum - felicity - rapport - attune -
adequacy - pertinence

مناظره
/monâzere/ ► noun
disputation - discussion - parlance -
agument

مناظره کردن
/monâzere kardan/ ► verb
debate

منافع
/manâfe'/ ► noun
revenue - rent

منبت کار
/monabatkâr/ ► noun
woodcutter - woodcarver

منبت کاری کردن
/monabatkâri kardan/ ► verb
splay

منبر
/menbar/ ► noun
rostrum - pulpit - tribune

منبسط
/monbaset/ ► adjective
trig

منبسط کردن
/monbaset kardan/ ► verb
extend - explode - expand - rarefy -
stretch

منبع
/man'ba'/ ► noun
source - mine - original - cistern -
resource - fountain

منتخب

/montakhab/ ▶ adjective
chosen - choice

منتسب

/montasab/ ▶ adjective
germane

منتسب کردن

/montasab kardan/ ▶ verb
relegate - refer

منتشر شدن

/montasher shodan/ ▶ verb
spread - circulate

منتشر کردن

/montasher kardan/ ▶ verb
publish - propagate - disseminate -
broaden - broadcast - print

منتشرساختن

/montasher sâkhtan/ ▶ verb
release

منتظر

/montazer/ ▶ adjective
wistful - anticipator - anticipant

منتظر بودن

/montazer budan/ ▶ verb
await - antedate - expect

منتقل کردن

/montaghel kardan/ ▶ verb
transmigrate - transfer - render - wend -
abalienate

منتهی

/montahi/ ▶ noun
supreme

منجر شدن

/monjar shodan/ ▶ verb
redound

منجم

/monajem/ ▶ noun
astronomer - astrologer

منجمد

/monjamed/ ▶ noun
rimy

منجمد شدن

/monjamed shodan/ ▶ verb
ice - congeal - freeze

منجمد کردن

/monjamed kardan/ ▶ verb
jell - curdle - ice

منجنیق

/manjanigh/ ▶ noun
catapult

منحرف
/monharef/ ▶ adjective
devious - deviant - oblique - pervert -
perverse - hellbent

منحوس
/manhus/ ▶ adjective
disastrous

منحرف شدن
/monharef shodan/ ▶ verb
wander - digress - swerve - stray

مندرجات
/mondarajât/ ▶ noun
content

منحصر
/monhaser/ ▶ noun
limited

مندرس
/mondares/ ▶ adjective
seedy - threadbare - rundown

منحصر کردن
/monhaser kardan/ ▶ verb
confine - limit

منزجر بودن
/monzajer budan/ ▶ verb
loathe

منحصرا
/monhaseran/ ▶ adverb
only

منزل
/manzel/ ▶ noun
home - house

منحصربفرد
/monhaser befard/ ▶ adjective
sole - particular - individual - exclusive

منزلت
/manzelat/ ▶ noun
altitude

منحط
/monhat/ ▶ adjective
amiss - degenerate - decadent

منزلگاه
/manzelgâh/ ▶ noun
dome

منحل کردن
/monhal kardan/ ▶ verb
dissolve - disband

منزه
/monazah/ ▶ adjective
sacrosanct - sublimate

منحنی
/monhani/ ▶ noun
round - cycloid - crump - bent

منزوی
/monzavi/ ▶ adjective
insular - hermit - recluse - solitudinarian
- solitary - secluded

منشى

/monshi/ ▶ noun
secretary - scribe - clerk - characteristic
- actuary

منسوب

/monsub/ ▶ adjective
sib - relative

منصب

/mansab/ ▶ noun
position - appointment

منسوخ

/mansukh/ ▶ adjective
abrogate - dead - outdated - obsolete -
obsolescent

منصف

/monsef/ ▶ adjective
square - just - unprejudiced - author

منسوخ شدن

/mansukh shodan/ ▶ verb
outmode - obsolesce

منصفانه

/monsefâne/ ▶ adverb
just - candid

منصوب

/mansub/ ▶ noun
nominee

منسوخ کردن

/monsukh kardan/ ▶ verb
abrogate - abolish

منصوب کردن

/mansub kardan/ ▶ verb
invest - appoint

منش

/manesh/ ▶ noun
character

منصور

/mansur/ ▶ adjective
triumphant

منشا

/mansha'/ ▶ noun
offspring

منطق

/mantegh/ ▶ noun
logic - frame

منشعب شدن

/monsha'eb shodan/ ▶ verb
ramify - fork - branch

منطقه

/mantaghe/ ▶ noun
zone - locale

منشور

/manshur/ ▶ noun
charter - prism

منطقی
/manteghi/ ▶ adjective
logical - dialectician - dialectical -
rational

منظر
/manzar/ ▶ noun
spectrum - aspect - appearance - visage -
image - face

منظره
/manzare/ ▶ noun
perspective - vision - prospect - scenery
- scene - sight - spectacle

منظم
/monazam/ ▶ adjective
square - regular - orderly - ordered

منظومه
/manzume/ ▶ noun
epopee - poem - system

منع
/man'/ ▶ noun
prohibition - snub - stoppage - stop -
interdict - veto - obstruction - restriction
- restraint

منعقد شدن
/mon'aghed shodan/ ▶ verb
coalesce

منعکس شدن
/mon'akes shodan/ ▶ verb
rebound

منعکس کردن
/mon'akes kardan/ ▶ verb
resound

منفجر شدن
/monfajer shodan/ ▶ verb
explode - erupt - detonate - blowout -
puff

منفجر کردن
/monfajer kardan/ ▶ verb
burst - blowup - dynamite

منفرجه
/monfajere/ ▶ noun
obtuse

منفرد
/monfared/ ▶ noun
solitaire - single

منفصل
/monfasel/ ▶ noun
disjoin - discontinuous - free

منفعت
/manfe'at/ ▶ noun
benefit - profit - payoff - gain

منفعت بردن
/manfe'at bordan/ ▶ verb
profit

منفور
/manfur/ ▶ adjective
unpopular - ungracious - hateful

منفی

/manfi/ ▶ noun
negative

منقار

/menghâr/ ▶ noun
bill - beak - rostrum - gouge

منقبض شدن

/monghabez shodan/ ▶ verb
twitch

منقبض کردن

/monghabez kardan/ ▶ verb
contract - constrict - condense - retract -
shrug - scrunch

منقرض

/mongharez/ ▶ noun
extinct

منقضی کردن

/monghazi kardan/ ▶ verb
terminate

منقطع

/monghate'/ ▶ adjective
discontinuous

منقوش کردن

/manghush kardan/ ▶ verb
characterize - engrave - imprint - stamp

منکر

/monker/ ▶ adjective
dissenter

منکر شدن

/monker shodan/ ▶ verb
repudiate - controvert

منکرخدا

/monkere khodâ/ ▶ noun
atheist

منگنه

/mangene/ ▶ noun
compressor - nip

منگوله

/mangule/ ▶ noun
tuft - tassel - bob

مننژیت

/manenzhit/ ▶ noun
meningitis

منها

/menhâ/ ▶ noun
minus

منهدم کردن

/monhadem kardan/ ▶ verb
ruinate - exterminate

منوال

/menvâl/ ▶ noun
rate

منور

/monavar/ ▶ adjective
illuminate

منوط بودن

/manut budan/ ▶ verb
depend

منی

/meni/ ▶ noun
semen - sperm

منیع

/mani'/ ▶ noun
inaccessible

مه

/meh/ ▶ noun
vapor - mist - fog

مه آلود

/mehâlud/ ▶ adjective
turbid - caliginous

مه آلود بودن

/mehâlud budan/ ▶ verb
fog

مه گرفتن

/meh gereftan/ ▶ verb
fog - mist

مهاجر

/mohâjer/ ▶ noun
immigrant - pilgrim - migrant - evacuee
- emigrant - refugee

مهاجرت

/mohâjerat/ ▶ noun
exodus - migration

مهاجرت کردن

/mohâjerat kardan/ ▶ verb
migrate

مهاجم

/mohâjem/ ▶ noun
aggressor - aggressive - invader -
offensive - raider

مهار

/mahâr/ ▶ noun
stay - halter

مهار کردن

/mahâr kardan/ ▶ verb
restrain

مهارت

/mahârat/ ▶ noun
craft - proficiency - versatility -
ingenuity - tact - sophistication - skill

مهبل

/mohbal/ ▶ noun
cunt

مهتاب

/mahtâb/ ▶ noun
moonlight - moon

مهتر

/mehtar/ ▶ adjective
senior - groomsman - groom

مهر

/mehr/ ▶ noun
signet - love

مهر

/mohr/ ▶ noun
seal- cachet

مهر زدن

/mohr zadan/ ▶ verb
stamp - frank - imprint - impress

مهربان

/mehrabân/ ▶ adjective
kind - gentle - amiable - affable

مهربانی

/mehrabâni/ ▶ noun
amiability - affability - blithe - kindness

مهره

/mohre/ ▶ noun
die - nut - glaze - vertebrate - vertebra -
bead

مهریه

/mehriye/ ▶ noun
dowry

مهلت

/mohlat/ ▶ noun
break - vacation

مهلک

/mohlek/ ▶ noun
noxious - fatal - dire - deadly - lethal -
pernicious - mortal

مهم

/mohem/ ▶ adjective
significant - serious - substantial -
material - main - principal - important

مهمات

/mohemât/ ▶ noun
ordnance - ammo - munition

مهمان

/mehmân/ ▶ noun
guest - visitor

مهمان سرا

/mehmânsarâ/ ▶ adjective
resthouse

مهمان کردن

/mehmân kardan/ ▶ verb
treat - banquet - invite - guest

مهمانخانه

/mehmânkhâne/ ▶ noun
lobby - inn

مهماندار

/mehmândâr/ ▶ noun
lodger

مهمانی

/mehmâni/ ▶ noun
party

مهمتر
/mohemtar/ ► adjective
premier (re)

مهمل
/mohmel/ ► noun
trashy - trash - preposterous - nonsense

مهندس
/mohandes/ ► noun
bachelor - engineer

مهیا
/mohayâ/ ► noun
prone - present - bound

مهیا ساختن
/mohayâ sâkhtan/ ► verb
prepare

مهیا شدن
/mohayâ shodan/ ► verb
unlimber

مهیا کردن
/mohayâ kardan/ ► verb
ready

مهیب
/mahib/ ► adjective
horrible - horrendous - hideous

مهیج
/mohayej/ ► adjective
sensational - stimulant - dramatic - racy
- unco

مو
/mu/ ► noun
hair

مواج
/mavâj/ ► adjective
undulatory - billowy

مواجب
/mavâjeb/ ► noun
salary - stipend - emolument

مواجه شدن
/movâjeh shodan/ ► verb
face

مواجهه
/movâjehe/ ► noun
affront - encounter

موازات
/movâzât/ ► noun
parallelism

موازنه
/movâzene/ ► noun
equilibrium - balance

موازی
/movâzi/ ► noun
parallel

مواظب
/movâzeb/ ► adjective
cautious - careful - aware - attendant

موثر
/moaser/ ▶ adjective
effective - drastic - pathetic - impressive

مواظب بودن
/movâzeb budan/ ▶ verb
tend - watch

موثق
/movasagh/ ▶ adjective
trustworthy - authentic - credible -
reliant - reliable

مواظبت
/movâzebat/ ▶ noun
attention - assistance - vigilance

موج
/môj/ ▶ noun
cockle - wave

مواظبت کردن
/movâzebat kardan/ ▶ verb
mind - attend - assist

موج دار
/môjdâr/ ▶ adjective
undulant - lumpy

موافق
/movâfegh/ ▶ adjective
compliant - sympathetic - congruent -
concurrent - respondent

موج زدن
/môj zadan/ ▶ verb
shimmer - surge - wave

موافق بودن
/movâfegh budan/ ▶ verb
agree - adapt

موج شکن
/môjshekan/ ▶ noun
pile - pier - bulwark - breakwater

موافقت
/movâfeghat/ ▶ noun
approval - approbation - agreement -
adhesion - accordance - accord - consent

موجب
/môjeb/ ▶ noun
cause - inducement - incentive

موتلف
/mo'talef/ ▶ noun
confederate

موجدار
/môjdâr/ ▶ adjective
storied - rippler

موتور
/motor/ ▶ noun
motor - engine

موجدار بودن
/môjdâr budan/ ▶ verb
undulate - surge

موجر
/mujer/ ▶ noun
renter - lessor - landlord

موجز
/mujez/ ▶ adjective
summary - succinct - terse - laconic -
concise - compendious

موجود
/môjud/ ▶ noun
real - extant - existent - bound -
available - present - handy - life - thing

موجودات
/môjudât/ ▶ noun
life

موجودی
/môjudi/ ▶ noun
supply - store

موجودیت
/môjudiyat/ ▶ noun
existence

موجی
/môji/ ▶ adjective
sinuous - undulatory

موچین
/muchin/ ▶ noun
tweezer

موحد
/movahed/ ▶ adjective
theist

موحش
/movahesh/ ▶ adjective
redoubtable - horrible - lurid

موخر
/movakher/ ▶ adjective
junior

مودار
/mudâr/ ▶ noun
whisker

مودب
/moadab/ ▶ adjective
courteous - respectful - nice

مودبانه
/moadabâne/ ▶ adverb
courteous - urbane

مودت
/mavadat/ ▶ adjective
amity

موذی
/muzi/ ▶ adjective
insidious - mischievous - baneful - arch
- sly - shrewd

مور
/mur/ ▶ noun
ant

موزون
/môzun/ ▶ adjective
symphonic - level

مورب
/movarab/ ▶ noun
diagonal - crisscross

موزیک
/muzik/ ▶ noun
music

مورچه
/murche/ ▶ noun
ant

موزیکال
/mizikâl/ ▶ noun
musical

مورخ
/movarekh/ ▶ noun
historian

موسس
/moases/ ▶ noun
father - originator - author

مورد
/mored/ ▶ noun
occasion - instance

موسسه
/moasese/ ▶ noun
institution - institute

مورد اطمینان
/morede etminân/ ▶ adjective
trusty

موسوم
/môsum/ ▶ noun
yclept - ycleped

مورد اعتماد
/morede etminân/ ▶ adjective
dependable

موسیقی
/musighi/ ▶ noun
music

مورمور
/mur mur/ ▶ noun
horror

موسیقی دان
/musighidân/ ▶ noun
musician

مورمور شدن
/murmur shodan/ ▶ verb
creep

موش
/mush/ ▶ noun
mouse

موروثی
/môrusi/ ▶ adjective
inborn - congenital

موطن
/muten/ ▶ noun
home

(Idiom: موش زبان کسی را خورده
Cat got someone's tongue)

موظف
/movazaf/ ▶ adjective
bound

موشک
/mushak/ ▶ noun
projectile - rocket - missile

موعظه
/mô'eze/ ▶ noun
sermon

موشکافی
/mushekâfi/ ▶ adjective
subtlety - splithair - scrutiny

موفق
/movafagh/ ▶ adjective
prosperous - upbeat - lucrative

موشکافی کردن
/mushekâfi kardan/ ▶ verb
analyze - scrutinize

موفق شدن
/movafagh shodan/ ▶ verb
wow - attain - arrive - succeed - prosper

موصوف
/môsuf/ ▶ noun
noun

موضع
/môze'/ ▶ noun
locality - position

موفقیت
/movafaghiyat/ ▶ noun
prosperity - success

موضوع
/môzu'/ ▶ noun
topic - theme - text - proposition -
subject - object - question

موقت
/movaghat/ ▶ adjective
interim - provisional

موقتی
/movaghati/ ▶ noun
temporary - provisional - interim

موضوعات
/môzu'ât/ ▶ noun
index

موقر
/movaghar/ ▶ adjective
demure - grave - solemn - sober - sedate
- staid

موضوعی
/môzu'i/ ▶ noun
thematic

موقرانه
/movagharâne/ ▶ adverb
solemn

موکل
/movakel/ ▶ noun
client - constituent

موقع
/moghe'/ ▶ noun
term - situation - period - occasion -
room

موکول
/môkul/ ▶ noun
conditional

موقع شناس
/mughe' shenâs/ ▶ adjective
tactful

موکول کردن
/môkul kardan/ ▶ verb
relegate - postpone

موقعی که
/moghe'ike/ ▶ preposition
when

مولد
/movaled/ ▶ adjective
reproductive - productive - birthplace -
active

موقعیت
/moghe'iyat/ ▶ noun
situation - occasion - berth - position -
plot - pertinence - location

مولف
/moalef/ ▶ noun
writer - author

موقعیت اجتماعی
/moghe'iyate ejtemâ'i/ ▶ noun
social status

مولود
/môlud/ ▶ noun
son

موقوف
/môghuf/ ▶ noun
sacred

موم
/mum/ ▶ noun
wax - beeswax

مومی شکل
/mumi shekl/ ▶ adjective
wax

موکد
/mo'akad/ ▶ noun
emphatic - accentual

مونث
/moanas/ ▶ noun
feminine - woman

موهبت
/muhebat/ ▶ noun
gift - endowment

میان
/miyan/ ▶ noun
among - between - middling - meddle

موهن
/muhen/ ▶ adjective
derogatory

میان بر
/miyânbor/ ▶ noun
crosscut

موهوم
/môhum/ ▶ noun
superstitious - superstition

میانجی
/miyânji/ ▶ noun
conciliator - gobetween - intermediate -
intermediary - midway - medium -
mediator

موهومات
/môhumât/ ▶ noun
superstition

میانجی شدن
/miyânji shodan/ ▶ verb
interpose

موی سر
/muye sar/ ▶ noun
head - hair

میانجی گری
/miyânjigari/ ▶ noun
intermediation - intercession

موید
/mo'ayed/ ▶ noun
subsidiary

میانگین
/miyângin/ ▶ noun
median - mean - average

مویرگ
/muyrag/ ▶ noun
capillary

میانه
/miyâne/ ▶ noun
normal - intermediate - median - medial
- average

مویز
/maviz/ ▶ noun
currant

میانه رو
/miyânerô/ ▶ adjective
sober - moderate

می
/mei/ ▶ noun
wine

میخواره
/meikhâre/ ► adjective
drunkard

میانه روی
/miyâneravi/ ► noun
mean

میدان
/meidân/ ► noun
place - ring - ground - scope - purview -
square

میانی
/miyâni/ ► noun
centric - innermost - inmost - meddle -
mid - median - medial

میدان نبرد
/meidâne nabard/ ► noun
battlefield

میثاق
/misâgh/ ► noun
pact - covenant - convention

میراث
/mirâs/ ► noun
patrimony - bequest - heritage - legacy -
inheritance

میثاق بستن
/misâgh bastan/ ► verb
stipulate - covenant

میراث بر
/mirâsbar/ ► adjective
heritage

میخ
/mikh/ ► noun
peg - nail - spike

میراث بری
/mirâsbari/ ► noun
inheritance

میخانه
/meikhâne/ ► noun
tavern - cabaret

میز
/miz/ ► noun
table

میخچه
/mikhche/ ► noun
picket - corn - spile

میز تحریر
/mize tahrir/ ► noun
writingdesk - desk

میخکوب کردن
/mikhkub kardan/ ► verb
transfix - spike

میزان
/mizân/ ► noun
scale - yardstick - adjustment - balance -
unit - meter - measure - criterion

میخوارگی
/meikhâregi/ ► noun
spree

میزان کردن

/mizân kardan/ ▶ verb
orient - regulate - range - modulate -
adjust - temper

میزبان

/mizbân/ ▶ noun
host - landlady

میسر

/moyasar/ ▶ noun
possible

میسر ساختن

/moyasar sâkhtan/ ▶ verb
provide

میعاد

/mi'âd/ ▶ noun
rendezvous

میعادگاه

/mi'âdgâh/ ▶ noun
tryst - hangout - recourse

میکده

/meikade/ ▶ noun
cabaret - bar

میکرب

/mikrob/ ▶ noun
microbe - germ

میکروسکپ

/mikroskop/ ▶ noun
microscope

میکروفن

/mikrofon/ ▶ noun
microphone

میگسار

/meigosâr/ ▶ adjective
bibulous

میگساری

/meigosâri/ ▶ noun
rouse - orgiastic - binge

میل

/meil/ ▶ noun
zest - turquoise - tendency - desire -
delight - will

میلاد

/milâd/ ▶ noun
birthday

میله

/mile/ ▶ noun
bar - slat - shaft - style - stilt - stem -
spike - rod - filament - gad - lever

میلیمتر

/milimetr/ ▶ noun
millimeter

میلیون

/miliyun/ ▶ noun
million

میلیونر

/miliyuner/ ▶ adjective
millionaire

میمون

/meimun/ ▶ noun
simian - pygmy - propitious - ape -
monkey

مین

/min/ ▶ noun
verily

مینا

/minâ/ ▶ noun
aster

مینیاتور

/miniyâtor/ ▶ noun
miniature

میهن

/mihan/ ▶ noun
home - motherland

میهن پرست

/mihanparast/ ▶ adjective
patiot

میومیو

/miyomiyo/ ▶ noun
miaow

میوه

/mive/ ▶ noun
fruit - blossom

ن – نـ

nun /ne/ ▶ twenty-ninth letter of the Persian alphabet

ناآرامی

/nâ ârâmi/ ▶ noun
disquiet - unrest

ناآزمودگی

/nâ âzmudegi/ ▶ noun
inexperience

ناآزموده

/nâ âzmude/ ▶ adjective
simple - clumsy - chicken - fresh -
untried - ungainly

ناآشنایی

/nâ âshenâyi/ ▶ noun
unfamiliarity - unfamiliar

ناآگاه

/nâ âgâh/ ▶ adjective
unwary

ناامن

/nâ'amn/ ▶ adjective
insecure

ناامنی

/nâ'amni/ ▶ noun
insecurity

نامید

/nâomid/ ▶ adjective
gray - chill

ناب

/nâb/ ▶ adjective
pure - unalloyed - limpid

ناباب

/nâyâb/ ▶ noun
unsuitable - unfit

نابالغ

/nâbâlegh/ ▶ adjective
immature - unripe - unfledged -
underage

نابجا

/nâbejâ/ ▶ adjective
aberrant - malapropos

نابخرد

/nâbekhrad/ ▶ adjective
unreasonable - brassy

نابرابر

/nâbarâbar/ ▶ adjective
disparate - unequal

نابسامان

/nâbesâmân/ ▶ adjective
unorganized

نابغه
/nâbeghe/ ▶ adjective
genius - wizard

نابکار
/nâbekâr/ ▶ adjective
wicked - nefarious

نابود شدن
/nâbud shodan/ ▶ verb
go

نابودی
/nâbudi/ ▶ noun
ruin - naught

نابینا
/nâbinâ/ ▶ noun
sightless - blind

ناپاکی
/nâpâki/ ▶ adjective
impurity - pollution

ناپایدار
/nâpâidâr/ ▶ adjective
transitory - transient - changeable -
ramshackle - impermanent

ناپدید
/nâpadid/ ▶ adjective
invisible

ناپسری
/nâpesari/ ▶ noun
stepson

ناپسند
/nâpasand/ ▶ adjective
chilish - absurd - unappealing -
incommensurate

ناتمام
/nâtamâm/ ▶ adjective
inconclusive - incomplete - imperfect -
partial - unfinished

ناتوان
/nâtavân/ ▶ adjective
invalid - infirm - incapable - impotent -
unable

ناتوان ساختن
/nâtavân sâkhtan/ ▶ verb
incapacitate

ناتوانی
/nâtavâni/ ▶ adjective
inability - impotence - intolerance -
insufficiency - insufficience - infirmity

ناجور
/nâjur/ ▶ adjective
dissonant - dissimilar - disparate -
inapplicable - heterogeneous

ناجی
/nâji/ ▶ noun
savior

ناچار
/nâchâr/ ▶ noun
inevitable

ناچیز

/nâchiz/ ► noun
teeny - trivial - trifle - nugatory -
negligible - runty - poor -little

ناحیه

/nâhiye/ ► noun
sector - terrain - zone - region - realm -
district - area

ناخدا

/nâkhodâ/ ► noun
shipmaster - commodore - captain

ناخن

/nâkhon/ ► noun
talon - nail - claw - ungual

ناخواسته

/nâkhâste/ ► adjective
officious - unwelcome - unsought -
undesirable - uncalledfor

ناخوانا

/nâkhânâ/ ► adjective
illegible

ناخوانده

/nâkhânde/ ► adjective
uninvited - uncalledfor

ناخودآگاه

/nâkhodâgâh/ ► noun
unconscious - unaware - unawares -
subconscious

ناخوش

/nâkhosh/ ► adjective
sick - unwell - unsound - unhealthy -
morbid - ill

ناخوشایند

/nâkhoshâyand/ ► adjective
unsightly - uncomplimentary -
uncomfortable - unbecoming

ناخوشی

/nâkhoshi/ ► noun
disease - metastasis - malady

نادان

/nâdân/ ► adjective
silly - fool - inept - ignorant - unwise -
untaught - unlettered - asinine

نادانی

/nâdâni/ ► noun
puerility - ignorance - ineptitude

نادر

/nâder/ ► adjective
curious - rare - uncommon - infrequent -
scarce

نادرست

/nâdorost/ ► adjective
incorrect - untrue - unsound - unfair -
false - erroneous - dishonest

نادم

/nâdem/ ► adjective
penitent - repent – remorseful

ناراحت

/nârâhat/ ▶ adjective
tense - fidgety - distraught - upset -
unhandy - uneasy - uncomfortable

ناراحت کردن

/nârâhat kardan/ ▶ verb
distemper - disquiet - discomfort -
discomfit

ناراحتی

/nârâhati/ ▶ noun
turmoil - irritation - inconvenience -
ailment

ناراضی

/nârâzi/ ▶ adjective
tedious - peevish - malcontent

نارس

/nâres/ ▶ adjective
jejune - unripe - immature - premature -
raw - green

نارسا

/nâresâ/ ▶ adjective
insufficient - incommensurate -
inaudible - highland - unfledged -
unexpressive

نارسایی

/nâresâyi/ ▶ noun
incompetence - inadequacy

نارنج

/nârenj/ ▶ noun
orange

نارنجک

/nâranjak/ ▶ noun
bomb - canister - grenade

نارنجی

/nârenji/ ▶ adjective
orange

نارو

/nârô/ ▶ adjective
treachery

ناروا

/nâravâ/ ▶ adjective
inadvisable - inadmissible - illegitimate
- unjust - unduly - undue

ناز

/nâz/ ▶ adjective
demur

نازا

/nâzâ/ ▶ adjective
sterile - barren

نازایی

/nâzâyi/ ▶ noun
sterility

نازک

/nâzok/ ▶ adjective
tenuous - soft - slim - spare - ethereal -
eggshell - gossamer - frail - fine -
attenuate

نازنین

/nâzanin/ ► adjective
nice

ناسازگار

/nâsâzegâri/ ► adjective
discordant - irreconcilable - alien -
adverse

ناسازگار بودن

/nâsâzegâr budan/ ► verb
alien - conflict - discord - disagree

ناسازگاری

/nâsâzegâri/ ► noun
inconvenience - inconsistency -
inconsistency - incongruity -
incoherence

ناسالم

/nâsâlem/ ► adjective
unsound - unhealthy - insanitary -
morbid

ناسزا

/nâsezâ/ ► noun
swearword - swear - profanity

ناشایست

/nâshâyest/ ► adjective
unrighteous

ناشایسته

/nâshâyeste/ ► adjective
objcetionable

ناشر

/nâsher/ ► noun
publisher - publicist

ناشناخته

/nâshenâkhte/ ► adjective
unknown - unfamiliarity - unfamiliar

ناشناس

/nâshenâs/ ► adjective
strange - incognito - unknown - unco

ناشنوا

/nâshenavâ/ ► adjective
indistinct

ناشی

/nâshi/ ► adjective
maladroit - laity - awkward - unperfect

ناشیگری

/nâshigari/ ► noun
bunlge

ناصح

/nâseh/ ► adjective
mentor

ناطق

/nâtegh/ ► adjective
talker - spokesman - speaker - orator

ناقل

/nâghel/ ▶ noun
vehicle

ناظر

/nâzer/ ▶ adjective
viewer - warden - supervisor - steward -
spectator

ناقلا

/nâgholâ/ ▶ adjective
sly - shrewd - clever - rogue - astute -
arch

ناف

/nâf/ ▶ noun
bellybutton - navel

ناقوس

/nâghus/ ▶ noun
bell - gong - ring

نافذ

/nâfez/ ▶ adjective
trenchant - dominant - incisive -
predominant - pervasive

ناکار

/nâkâr/ ▶ adjective
inert

نافرمان

/nâfarmân/ ▶ adjective
insubordinate - disobedient - wayward -
naughty

ناکارآیی

/nâkârâyi/ ▶ noun
deficiency

نافرمانی

/nâfarmâni/ ▶ noun
disobedience

ناکام

/nâkâm/ ▶ adjective
unhappy

نافع

/nâfe'/ ▶ adjective
beneficial - lucrative

ناکس

/nâkes/ ▶ adjective
villain - ignoble

نافی

/nâfi/ ▶ noun
umbilical

ناگاه

/nâgâh/ ▶ adjective
unexpected

ناقص

/nâghes/ ▶ adjective
unperfect - mutilate - malformed -
incorrect - incomplete – imperfect

ناگزیر

/nâgozir/ ▶ adjective
needful - perforce - inevitable

ناگزیر بودن

/nâgozir budan/ ▶ verb
have

ناگفتنی

/nâgoftani/ ▶ noun
unspeakable - inexpressible

ناگفته

/nâgofte/ ▶ adjective
untold - unsaid

ناگهان

/nâgahân/ ▶ adverb
sudden - slapdash - abrupt - aback - bolt
- unaware - unawares

ناگهانی

/nâgahâni/ ▶ adverb
abrupt - precipitate - snap - sudden

ناگوار

/nâgovâr/ ▶ adjective
horrible - harsh - burdensome -
unsavory - unpleasant

ناگوارا

/nâgovârâ/ ▶ adjective
unwholesome

نالان

/nâlân/ ▶ adjective
weepy

نالایق

/nâlâyegh/ ▶ adjective
infelicitous - incompetent - incapable -
villainous - unworthy

ناله

/nâle/ ▶ noun
croon - dolor - grumble - groan - whine -
whimper - wail - moan

نالیدن

/nâlidan/ ▶ verb
complain - grunt - groan - whine -
whimper

نام

/nâm/ ▶ noun
title - fame - noun - nomenclature -
name - renown

نام بردن

/nâm bordan/ ▶ verb
mention

نام خانوادگی

/nâme khânevâdegi/ ▶ noun
surname - patronymic

نام نهادن

/nâm nahâdan/ ▶ verb
title - entitle

نام نویسی

/nam nevisi/ ▶ noun
levy - registration

نامریی

/nâmar'i/ ▶ noun
sightless - inconspicuous

نامبارک

/nâmobârak/ ▶ adjective
inauspicious - unblest

نامریی بودن

/nâmar'i budan/ ▶ verb
invisibility

نامتجانس

/nâmotejânes/ ▶ adjective
incongruous

نامزد

/nâmzad/ ▶ noun
nominee - candidate

نامجو

/nâmju/ ▶ adjective
ambitious

نامزد کردن

/nâmzad kardan/ ▶ verb
espouse - engage - designate - nominate
- betroth

نامحدود

/nâmahdud/ ▶ adjective
infinite - indeterminable - indefinite -
unrestrained - unqualified - unlimited

نامساعد

/nâmosâed/ ▶ adjective
inimical - unfavorable - bad

نامدار

/nâmdâr/ ▶ adjective
name

نامساوی

/nâmosâvi/ ▶ noun
disparate - unequal

نامربوط

/nâmarbut/ ▶ adjective
inconsequential - irrelevant - uncouth

نامشخص

/nâmoshakhas/ ▶ noun
indeterminate - unlimited

نامرد

/nâmard/ ▶ adjective
coward - effeminate - caitiff

نامشروع

/nâmashru'/ ▶ adjective
illicit - illegal - unlawful

نامردی

/mâmardi/ ▶ noun
cowardice

نامطلوب

/nâmatlub/ ▶ adjective
unfavorable - undesirable - uncalledfor

نامرغوب

/nâmarghub/ ▶ adjective
poor - inferior - raunchy

نامعلوم

/nâma'lum/ ▶ adjective
unknown - inconspicuous - incalculable
- indistinct - indescribable - pendant -
unlimited

ناملایم

/nâmolâyem/ ▶ adjective
harsh

نامناسب

/nâmonâseb/ ▶ adjective
unsuitable - unrighteous - unmeet -
incompetent - incommensurate - inapt -
inappropriate - improper

نامنظم

/nâmonazam/ ▶ adjective
erratic - acrostic

نامه

/nâme/ ▶ noun
epistle - manifest - letter

نامهیا

/nâmohayâ/ ▶ adjective
unready

ناموزن

/nâmôzun/ ▶ adjective
unequal

ناموس

/nâmus/ ▶ noun
honor

ناموفق

/nâmovafagh/ ▶ adjective
unsuccess (ful)

نامی

/nâmi/ ▶ adjective
famous - illustrious

نامیدن

/nâmidan/ ▶ verb
style - term - entitle - call - nominate -
name

نان

/nân/ ▶ noun
bread

نانوا

/nânvâ/ ▶ noun
baker

ناهار

/nâhâr/ ▶ noun
lunch - meat

ناهار خوردن

/nâhâr khordan/ ▶ verb
lunch - dine

ناهماهنگ

/nâhamâhang/ ▶ adjective
disharmonic

ناهمگن

/nâhamgen/ ▶ adjective
heterogeneous

ناهموار
/nâhamvâr/ ▶ adjective
scaly - jagged - rugged - rude - rough -
ragged - bumpy - unfair - uneven

نبات
/nabât/ ▶ noun
plant - vegetable - candy - rockcandy

ناهنجار
/nâhanjâr/ ▶ adjective
dissonant - nefarious - gruff - raucous

نبش
/nabsh/ ▶ noun
edge

ناو
/nâv/ ▶ noun
ship

نبض
/nabz/ ▶ noun
pulse

ناودان
/nâvdân/ ▶ noun
spout - sike - tube - cullis

نبوت
/nabovat/ ▶ noun
prophecy

ناوگان
/nâvgân/ ▶ noun
navy

نبوغ
/nobugh/ ▶ noun
genius - ingenuity

نایاب
/nâyâb/ ▶ adjective
extinct

نبی
/nabi/ ▶ noun
prophet

نایب
/nâyeb/ ▶ noun
deputy - lieutenant - proctor

نت
/not/ ▶ noun
theme

نایل شدن
/nâyel shodan/ ▶ verb
gain - attain - agree - accede

نتیجه
/natije/ ▶ noun
consequence - result - resolution -
growth - outgrwth - outcome

نایلون
/nâylon/ ▶ noun
nylon

نتیجه بخش
/natijebakhsh/ ▶ adjective
consequent

نثر
/nasr/ ▶ noun
prose

نجابت
/nejâbat/ ▶ noun
chastity - nobility - decency - honor

نجات
/nejât/ ▶ noun
salvation

نجات دادن
/nejât dâdan/ ▶ verb
deliver - reclaim

نجار
/najâr/ ▶ noun
carpenter

نجاری
/najâri/ ▶ noun
woodcraft - carpentry

نجاری کردن
/najâri kardan/ ▶ verb
carpenter

نجاست
/nejâsat/ ▶ noun
excrement

نجس
/najes/ ▶ adjective
unclean

نجم
/najm/ ▶ noun
star

نجوا
/najvâ/ ▶ noun
whisper

نجومی
/nojumi/ ▶ noun
planetary

نجیب
/najib/ ▶ adjective
decent - noble - nice - gentle - genteel -
bland - meek

نجیب زاده
/najibzâde/ ▶ adjective
magnate - patrician - aristocrat -
wellborn - nobleman - knight

نحس
/nahs/ ▶ adjective
infelicitous - inauspicious

نحیف
/nahif/ ▶ adjective
slight - skimpy - skimp - spare - scrimp -
scant - frail - gaunt - haggard - lean -
meager

نخ

/nakh/ ▶ noun
cotton - fiber-fibre - string

نخاله

/noghâle/ ▶ adjective
odd - grit - misfit - bran

نخست

/nokhost/ ▶ adjective
first

نخستین

/nokhostin/ ▶ adjective
first - prime - primary - premier - incipient

نخل

/nakhl/ ▶ noun
date - palm

نخوت

/nekhvat/ ▶ noun
arrogance

ندا

/nedâ/ ▶ noun
calling - call

ندامت

/nedâmat/ ▶ noun
contrition - repentance - remorse - compunction - penitence

ندامتگاه

/medâmatgâh/ ▶ noun
penitentiary

ندیم

/nadim/ ▶ noun
courtier

نذر

/nazr/ ▶ noun
bet - avow - vow

نذر کردن

/nazr kardan/ ▶ verb
avow

نذری

/nazri/ ▶ adjective
votive

نر

/nar/ ▶ noun
bull - masculine - husband

نرخ

/nerkh/ ▶ noun
rate

نرد

/nard/ ▶ noun
backgammon

نردبان

/nardebân/ ▶ noun
stairwell - stair - ladder

نرده
/narde/ ▶ noun
rail - parapet - pale - balustrade - list

نرسیده
/nareside/ ▶ adjective
unripe

نرگس
/narges/ ▶ noun
narcissus

نرم
/narm/ ▶ adjective
soft - smooth - slick - sleek - silky

نرم شدن
/narm shodan/ ▶ verb
supple - soften - relent

نرم کردن
/narm kardan/ ▶ verb
soften - loosen - humanize - levigate -
modulate

نرم و ملایم
/narmo molâyem/ ▶ adjective
blithe

نرمی
/narmi/ ▶ adjective
suavity - pash - unction - amenity -
plasticity - leniency - gloss

نروژ
/norvezh/ ▶ noun
Norway

نروژی
/norvezhi/ ▶ adjective
Norwegian

نزاع
/nezâ'/ ▶ noun
battle - affray - scuffle - strife - squeal

نزاع طلبی
/nezâ' talabi/ ▶ noun
militancy

نزاع کردن
/nezâ' kardan/ ▶ verb
jar - tussle - wrangle - quarrel

نزاکت
/nezâkat/ ▶ noun
suavity - tact - propriety - comity -
civility

نزد
/nazd/ ▶ noun
about - to

نزدیک
/nazdik/ ▶ adjective
proximate - neighbor - near - close - in -
hailfellow - upcoming - besides -
adjacent

نزدیک بودن
/nazdik budan/ ► verb
being close

نژادپرستی
/nezhâdparasti/ ► noun
ethnography - racism - racialism

نزدیک ترین
/nazdiktarin/ ► adjective
closest

نژادی
/nezhâdi/ ► noun
ethnic - racial

نزدیک کردن
/nazdik kardan/ ► verb
approximate

نساجی
/nasâji/ ► noun
loom

نزدیکی
/nazdiki/ ► noun
proximity - propinquity - contiguity -
rapprochement - vicinity - verge -
approximation - affinity - adjacency

نسب
/nasab/ ► noun
parentage - genealogy - descent

نسبت
/nesbat/ ► noun
proportion - scale - cognation - respect -
relationship - relation - ratio

نزول
/nozul/ ► noun
discount - descent - fall

نزول کردن
/nozul kardan/ ► verb
sink - comedown - descend

نسبتا
/nesbatan/ ► adverb
somedeal - enough - rather - partly

نژاد
/nezhâd/ ► noun
strain - descent - race - blood

نسبی
/nesbi/ ► adjective
comparative - respective - relative

نژادپرست
/nezhâdparast/ ► adjective
racist - ethnocentric

نسبیت
/nesbiyat/ ► noun
relativity - ratio

نشان دهنده
/neshândahande/ ► adjective
demonstrator - poniter

نشان گذار
/neshângozâr/ ► noun
marker

نشان گذاردن
/neshângozârdan/ ► verb
check - impress

نشان گذاری
/neshângozari/ ► noun
punctuation - impression

نشان ویژه
/neshâne vizhe/ ► noun
trait - characteristic

نشاندن
/neshândan/ ► verb
stud - set - seat - infix - imprint - enchase - embed

نشانه
/neshâne/ ► noun
sign - symptom - proof - mark - portent - allegory

نشانه رفتن
/neshâne raftan/ ► verb
train

نسل
/nasl/ ► noun
slip - race - foster

نسنجیده
/nasanjide/ ► adjective
unconsidered

نسوز
/nasuz/ ► adjective
incombustible

نسیان
/nosyân/ ► noun
oblivion - amnesia - lapse

نسیم
/nasim/ ► noun
breeze - breath - air - guff

نسیه
/nasiye/ ► noun
credit

نشاسته
/neshâste/ ► noun
starch

نشاط
/neshât/ ► noun
vivacity - mirth - merriment - hilarity - alacrity - esprit - spree - jazz

نشان
/neshân/ ► noun
medal - mark - brand - sign

نشانی

/neshâni/ ▶ noun
address

نصب

/nasb/ ▶ noun
installation - pitch

نشت

/nasht/ ▶ noun
leakage - leak

نصرت

/nosrat/ ▶ noun
victory

نشت کردن

/nasht kardan/ ▶ verb
permeate

نصف

/nesf/ ▶ noun
half

نشخوار

/noshkhâr/ ▶ noun
cud - champ - quid

نصفه

/nesfe/ ▶ noun
half

نشر

/nashr/ ▶ noun
emission

نصیب

/nasib/ ▶ noun
portion

نشر کردن

/nashr kardan/ ▶ verb
transpire - infiltrate - edit

نصیحت

/nasihat/ ▶ noun
advice

نطفه

/notfe/ ▶ noun
sperm - semen

نشریه

/nashriye/ ▶ noun
journal

نطق

/notgh/ ▶ noun
speech - utterance - address - locution -
peroration - oration

نشست

/nasht/ ▶ noun
session - seance - meet

نظارت

/nezârat/ ▶ noun
supervision - stewardship - proctorship

نشستن

/neshastan/ ▶ verb
sit - perch

نظریه
/nazariye/ ► noun
theory - viewpoint

نظارت کردن
/nezârat kardan/ ► verb
control - administer - address - proctor -
supervise

نظریه دادن
/nazariye dâdan/ ► verb
counsel - opine

نظاره کردن
/nezâre kardan/ ► verb
behold

نظم
/nazm/ ► noun
rhyme - rank - order - discipline - array -
verse - meter - poetry - poem

نظام
/nezâm/ ► noun
system - military

نظم دادن
/nazm dâdan/ ► verb
regularize

نظام اجتماعی
/nezâme ejtemâ'i/ ► noun
society

نظیر
/nazir/ ► noun
analogue - like - match - make

نظامنامه
/nezâmnâme/ ► noun
bylaw - precept - manual - workbook

نظیف
/nazif/ ► noun
clean

نظامی
/nezâmi/ ► noun
trooper - soldier - military - martial

نعره
/na're/ ► noun
slogan - yell

نظر
/nazar/ ► noun
sight - shim - esteem - discretion -
regard - opinion - look - advice -
viewpoint - view

نعره کشیدن
/na're keshidan/ ► verb
yell

نظری
/nazari/ ► noun
visionary

نعش
/na'shodan/ ► noun
corpse

نعش کش

/na'shkesh/ ▶ noun
hearse

نفخ

/nafkh/ ▶ noun
bloat - emphysema - wind

نعل زدن

/na'l zadan/ ▶ verb
calk

نفر

/nafar/ ▶ noun
person - unit

نعلبکی

/nalbeki/ ▶ noun
saucer

نفرت

/nefrat/ ▶ noun
enmity - disgust - odium - aversion -
hatred - hate

نعلبند

/na'lband/ ▶ noun
blacksmith - shoelace

نفرت آور

/nefratâvar/ ▶ adjective
dispiteous

نعمت

/ne'mat/ ▶ noun
gift - luxury

نفرت انگیز

/nefratangiz/ ▶ adjective
odious - obnoxious - execrable

نغمه

/naghme/ ▶ noun
tune - song

نفرت داشتن

/nefrat dâshtan/ ▶ verb
despise

نفاق

/nefâgh/ ▶ noun
dissension - discord - split

نفرین

/nefrin/ ▶ noun
gaff - curse - imprecation

نفاق انداختن

/nefâgh andâkhtan/ ▶ verb
disunite

نفس

/nafas/ ▶ noun
snuff - self - air - breath - oneself - wind
- ego

نفت

/naft/ ▶ noun
petroleum - oil

نفس کشیدن

/nafas keshidan/ ▶ verb
respire - breathe

نفی

/naf'y/ ▶ noun
disavow - nope

نفسانی

/nafsâni/ ▶ noun
sensual - carnal

نفیس

/nafis/ ▶ adjective
precious - valuable - exquisite

نفع

/naf'/ ▶ noun
gain

نق زدن

/negh zadan/ ▶ verb
nag

نفقه

/nafaghe/ ▶ noun
alimony

نقاب

/neghâb/ ▶ noun
veil - mask

نفهم

/nafahm/ ▶ adjective
stupid - incapable - hick

نقاد

/naghâd/ ▶ noun
critic

نفوذ

/nofuz/ ▶ noun
influence - importance - prestige

نقاش

/naghâsh/ ▶ noun
painter - drawer

نفوذپذیر

/nofuzpazir/ ▶ adjective
permeable - penetrable - sensitive

نقاشی

/naghâshi/ ▶ noun
skip - portrait

نفوذناپذیر

/nofuznâpazir/ ▶ adjective
inscrutable

نقاشی کردن

/naghâshi kardan/ ▶ verb
crayon - contour - picture - brush - paint

نفوس

/nofus/ ▶ noun
population

نقال

/naghâl/ ▶ noun
scop - storyteller

نقالی کردن

/naghâli kardan/ ▶ verb
narrate

نقب

/naghab/ ▶ noun
tunnel - burrow - hole - mine

نقب زدن

/naghab zadan/ ▶ verb
undermine - burrow - bore - tunnel

نقدی

/naghdi/ ▶ noun
pocket - pecuniary

نقرس

/neghres/ ▶ noun
gout

نقره

/noghre/ ▶ adjective
silver

نقره کار

/noghrekâr/ ▶ adjective
silversmith

نقش

/naghsh/ ▶ noun
stamp - figure - impress - legend -
inscription - infraction

نقشه

/naghshe/ ▶ noun
scheme - project - program - chart -
design - model - map

نقشه بردار

/naghshebardâr/ ▶ noun
surveyor

نقشه برداری

/naghshebardâri/ ▶ noun
topography - survey

نقشه کش

/naghshekesh/ ▶ noun
tracer - draftsman - plotter

نقشه کشیدن

/naghshe keshidan/ ▶ verb
project - compass - engine - map - plot -
plat - plan

نقص

/naghs/ ▶ noun
deficiency - defect - incompetence -
handicap - blemish

نقصان

/noghsân/ ▶ noun
want - depletion

نقض

/naghz/ ▶ noun
reversal

نقطه

/notfe/ ▶ noun
point - plot - mark - iota - dot

نکوهش

/nekuhesh/ ▶ noun
reproof - remonstrance - criticism

نقل

/naghl/ ▶ noun
drop - confetti - story - transfer

نکوهش کردن

/nekuhesh kardan/ ▶ verb
reprove - criticize

نقل کردن

/naghl kardan/ ▶ verb
transcribe - tell - convey - relate

نگارش

/negâresh/ ▶ noun
record

نکاح

/nekâh/ ▶ noun
matrimony - wedlock

نگاره

/negâre/ ▶ noun
chart

نکبت

/nekbat/ ▶ noun
lousy - misery

نگاشتن

/negâshtan/ ▶ verb
write - register

نکته

/nokte/ ▶ noun
poniter - point

نگاه

/negâh/ ▶ noun
look - glance - regard

نکته بین

/noktebin/ ▶ adjective
particular

نگاه داشتن

/negâh dâshtan/ ▶ verb
save - retain - refrain - keep - guard - hold

نکته سنج

/noktesanj/ ▶ adjective
punctilious

نگاه کردن

/negâh kardan/ ▶ verb
see - regard - look - eye

نکره

/nakare/ ▶ noun
theorem - indefinite

نگاهدارنده

/negâhdâr/ ▶ adjective
preservative

نگران

/negarân/ ▶ adjective
solicitous - agog - agaze

نگرانی

/negarâni/ ▶ noun
stew - solicitude - pine - umbrage -
anxiety - worry

نگرش

/negaresh/ ▶ noun
attitude

نگریستن

/negaristan/ ▶ verb
regard - look

نگهبان

/negahbân/ ▶ noun
lifeguard - escort - keeper - guardian -
watchman - watchdog

نگهبانی

/negahbâni/ ▶ noun
sentry

نگهبانی کردن

/negahbâni kardan/ ▶ verb
sentinel - guard

نگهدار

/negahdâr/ ▶ adjective
buttress - backer - patron - looker -
keeper - tenter - protector - prop -
stanchion

نگهداری

/negahdari/ ▶ noun
sustenance - maintenance - preservation
- upkeep - conservation - retinue -
retention - restraint

نگهداری کردن

/negahdari kardan/ ▶ verb
ward - keep - conserve - patronize -
upkeep - maintain - protect

نگهداشتن

/negahdâshtan/ ▶ verb
imprison - hold - restrain - sustain - prop

نم

/nam/ ▶ noun
damp - moisture - humidity - humid

نم زدن

/nam zadan/ ▶ verb
sauce - baste - dabble - dabber

نم نم باران

/namname bârân/ ▶ noun
drizzle

نما

/namâ/ ▶ noun
surface - index - hue - visage - louver -
air - front - diagram

نماد

/nemâd/ ▶ noun
symbolism - symbol

نمادین
/nemâdin/ ▶ noun
symbolic

نماز
/namâz/ ▶ noun
prayer

نماز خواندن
/namâz khândan/ ▶ verb
pray

نمایان
/namâyân/ ▶ noun
seeming - egregious - dominant -
ostensible - visible

نمایاندن
/namâyândan/ ▶ verb
represent

نمایش
/namâyesh/ ▶ noun
spectacle - showing - show - parade -
appearance - histrionics - presentation -
portrayal - play - performance -
exposure - exhibition

نمایشگاه
/namâyeshgâh/ ▶ noun
exposition - exhibition - playhouse

نمایشگر
/namâyeshgar/ ▶ noun
showman

نمایشنامه
/namâyeshnâme/ ▶ noun
drama - play

نمایشی
/namâyeshi/ ▶ noun
expository - dramatic - scenic

نماینده
/namâyande/ ▶ noun
indicator - agent - delegate -
representative - representation

نمایه
/namâye/ ▶ noun
index

نمد
/namad/ ▶ noun
wad - muffler

نمدار
/namdâr/ ▶ noun
humid - moist

نمره
/nomre/ ▶ noun
score - number - mark

نمک زدن
/namak zadan/ ▶ verb
corn

نمکدان

/namakdân/ ▶ noun
saltshaker - saltcellar - salt

نمکزار

/namakzâr/ ▶ noun
salt

نمکین

/namakin/ ▶ adjective
briny - salty - saline

نمناک

/namnâk/ ▶ adjective
dank - moist - humid

نمود

/nemud/ ▶ noun
appearance - phenomenon - growth

نمودار

/nemudâr/ ▶ noun
schema - diagram - conspectus - chart -
graph

نمودار شدن

/nemudâr shodan/ ▶ verb
outcrop - rear

نمونه

/nemune/ ▶ noun
sample - specimen - paradigm - parable
- instance - model - example

نمونه بودن

/nemune budan/ ▶ verb
typify

ننگ

/nang/ ▶ noun
stain - shame - scandal - opprobrium -
reproach - dishonor (ur) - infamy

ننگ آور

/nangâvar/ ▶ adjective
ignominious - opprobrious

ننه

/nane/ ▶ noun
mother

ننوشته

/naneveshte/ ▶ noun
unwritten

نه

/na/ ▶ noun
no

نه

/noh/ ▶ noun
nine

نهاد

/nahâd/ ▶ noun
institution - inclination

نهادن

/nahâdan/ ▶ verb
set - invest

نهال
/nahâl/ ► noun
plant - slip - scion - sapling

نهان
/nahân/ ► noun
stealth - secret - ulterior - covert - recondite

نهانکاری
/nahânkâri/ ► noun
secrecy

نهانی
/nahâni/ ► adjective
surreptitious - suberranean - secret - occult - underhand - undercover - potential - last

نهایت
/nahayat/ ► noun
extremity - outrance

نهایی
/nahayi/ ► adjective
terminal - ultimatum - ultimate - conclusive

نهر
/nahr/ ► noun
slough - stream - dike - creek - kil

نهفتن
/nahoftan/ ► verb
hide - conceal - closet

نهمین
/nohomin/ ► adjective
ninth

نهنگ
/nahang/ ► noun
alligator - whale

نهی
/nahy/ ► noun
prohibition - prohibit - interdict - injunction

نهی کردن
/nahy kardan/ ► verb
interdict - proscribe

نو
/nô/ ► adjective
scion - mint - novel - new

نو کردن
/nô kardan/ ► verb
renovate - renew

نوآموز
/nô'âmuz/ ► adjective
novice

نوآور
/nô'âvar/ ► adjective
innovator

نوا
/navâ/ ► noun
tone - tune

نواختن

/navâkhtan/ ► verb
sound - execute

نوار

/navâr/ ► noun
tape - strip - ribbon - band - ligature - lace

نوارچسب

/navâre chasb/ ► noun
tape

نوازش

/navâzesh/ ► noun
pat - caress

نوازش کردن

/navâzesh kardan/ ► verb
stroke - cuddle - coddle - coax

نوازنده

/navâzande/ ► adjective
musician - player

نوامبر

/novâmbr/ ► noun
november

نوبت

/nôbat/ ► noun
period - inning - heat - tour - turquoise - shift

نوبتی

/nôbati/ ► noun
tyupical - shift - serial - periodic - intermittent

نوبه

/nôbe/ ► noun
malaria

نوجوان

/nôjavân/ ► noun
younker - juvenile - juvenescent - adolescent

نوجوانی

/nôjavâni/ ► noun
adolescence

نوحه

/nôhe/ ► noun
dirge

نوحه سرایی

/nôhe sarâyi/ ► noun
jeremiad - dirge

نود

/navad/ ► adjective
ninety

نور

/nur/ ► noun
light - glory

نور افشاندن

/nurafshândan/ ▶ verb
shine

نور افکندن

/nurafkan/ ▶ verb
beam - irradiate

نورافشانی

/nurafshâni/ ▶ adjective
refulgence

نورافکن

/nurafkandan/ ▶ noun
spotlight - searchlight

نورانی

/nurâni/ ▶ adjective
luminous

نورمهتاب

/nuremahtâb/ ▶ noun
moonlight

نوزاد

/nôzâd/ ▶ noun
chick - newborn - grub - bambino - baby
- babe

نوسازی

/nôsâzi/ ▶ noun
renovation - rehabilitation -
reconstruction

نوسازی کردن

/nôsâzi kardan/ ▶ verb
reconstruct

نوسان

/navasân/ ▶ noun
swing - sway - undulation - lurch -
pendulum - vibration

نوسان داشتن

/navasân dâshtan/ ▶ verb
undulate

نوش

/nush/ ▶ noun
nectar - hobnob - pledge

نوشتن

/neveshtan/ ▶ verb
write - pen - inscribe

نوشته

/neveshte/ ▶ adjective
scrip - paperwork - manuscript -
inscription - deposition - epigraph

نوشدارو

/nushdâru/ ▶ adjective
panacea

نوشیدنی

/nushidan/ ▶ noun
potable

نوشین

/nushin/ ▶ adjective
sweet

نوید
/navid/ ▶ noun
promise

نویسنده
/nevisande/ ▶ noun
scrivener - craftsman - composer -
writer - author

نوین
/novin/ ▶ adjective
modern - new - young

نی
/nei/ ▶ noun
straw - sprit - junk - tube - cane

نیاز
/niyâz/ ▶ noun
need - necessity - want - requirement

نیاز داشتن
/niyâz dâshtan/ ▶ verb
require - need

نیازمند
/niyâzmand/ ▶ adjective
destitute - needy - needful

نیازمند بودن
/niyâzmand budan/ ▶ verb
need

نیام
/niyâm/ ▶ noun
scabbard - tunic - legume - pod - vagina

نوظهور
/nôzohur/ ▶ adjective
mewfangled

نوع
/nô'/ ▶ noun
type - class - order - navigate - nature -
kind - kidney - genus - gender

نوعی
/nô'i/ ▶ noun
generic

نوک
/nok/ ▶ noun
top - tip - jag - summit - point - peak -
vertex - horn - head - ascendant - apex

نوکدار
/nokdâr/ ▶ adjective
pointy

نوکر
/nôkar/ ▶ noun
server - servant - henchman

نومیدی
/nômidi/ ▶ noun
despair

نوه
/nave/ ▶ noun
grandson - granddaughter - grandchild

نیایش

/niyâyesh/ ▶ noun
benediction - adoration - veneration -
praise - invocation

نیت

/niyat/ ▶ noun
purpose - sentiment - will - resolution -
effect - animus

نیرنگ

/neirang/ ▶ noun
trap - trickery - trick - artifice - art -
deception - craft - witchcraft

نیرو

/niru/ ▶ noun
force - energy - might - power - strength

نیروبخش

/nirubakhsh/ ▶ adjective
tonic

نیروگاه

/nirugâh/ ▶ noun
powerhouse

نیرومند

/nirumand/ ▶ adjective
strong - stout - prolific - vigorous -
valiant - mighty - main - potent

نیرومندی

/nirumandi/ ▶ noun
virility - vigor - potency - intensity

نیز

/niz/ ▶ noun
too - also - again - both - likewise

نیزه

/neize/ ▶ noun
dart - gig - gaff - gad - harpoon - lance -
shaft - spear

نیستی

/nisti/ ▶ noun
nothing - naught

نیش

/nish/ ▶ noun
sting - tooth - tang - twinge - bite - prick
- nip

نیش زدن

/nish zâdan/ ▶ verb
sting - bite

نیشخند

/nishkhand/ ▶ noun
sneer

نیشدار

/nishdâr/ ▶ adjective
poignant - sarcastic - punctual

نیشکر

/neishekar/ ▶ noun
cane

نیشگون

/nishgun/ ► noun
pinch

نیلی

/nili/ ► adjective
indigo - blue

نیک

/nik/ ► adjective
good

نیم

/nim/ ► noun
half

نیکل

/nikel/ ► noun
nickel

نیم پز کردن

/nimpaz kardan/ ► verb
coddle - underdo

نیکو

/niku/ ► noun
good

نیمروز

/nimruz/ ► noun
noontime - noontide - noon - midday

(Idiom: کار نیکو کردن از پر کردن است
Practice makes perfect)

نیمکت

/nimkat/ ► noun
squab - sofa - settee - seat - bench -
couch

نیکوکار

/nikukâr/ ► adjective
samaritan - upright - beneficent -
benefactor - righteous

نیمه

/nime/ ► noun
mid

نیکوکاری

/nikukâri/ ► noun
charity - beneficence

نیمه تمام

/nimetamâm/ ► adjective
inchoate

نیمه شب

نیکی

/niki/ ► adjective
beneficence

/nimeshab/ ► noun
midnight

نیل

/neil/ ► noun
indigo

و

vâv /ve/ ▶ thirtieth letter of the Persian alphabet

و
/va/ ▶ preposition
and

وا داشتن
/vâdâshtan/ ▶ verb
stand - cause - wrest - appoint

وا ماندن
/vâmândan/ ▶ verb
overweary

وابستگی
/vâbastegi/ ▶ noun
relationship - coherency - dependence - contiguity

وات
/vânet/ ▶ noun
watt

واجب
/vâjeb/ ▶ adjective
essential - fundametal - necessitous - vital - momentous

واجبی
/vâjebi/ ▶ noun
depilatory

واجدشرایط
/vâjedesharâyet/ ▶ adjective
eligible

واحد
/vâhed/ ▶ noun
single - one - unity - unit

وادی
/vâdi/ ▶ noun
valley

وارث
/vâres/ ▶ adjective
heir

وارد شدن
/vâred shodan/ ▶ verb
enter - arrive

وارسته
/vâraste/ ▶ adjective
pious - light

وارسی کردن
/vârasi kardan/ ▶ verb
sift - investigate

وارونه
/vârune/ ▶ adjective
reverse - opposite - upsidedown

واژگونی
/vâzheguni/ ► noun
overturn - reversal - upset

وارونه شدن
/vârune shodan/ ► verb
keel

واژه
/vâzhe/ ► noun
word

واریز
/vâriz/ ► noun
settlement - settle

واژه نگاری
/vâzhenegâri/ ► noun
lexicography

واریز کردن
/vâriz kardan/ ► verb
square - settle - even

واسطه
/vâsete/ ► noun
intermediate - gobetween

واژگان
/vâzhegân/ ► noun
terminology - vocabulary

واشر
/vâsher/ ► noun
washer

واژگون
/vâzhegun/ ► noun
converse - upsidedown - subversive

واضح
/vâzeh/ ► adjective
obvious - vivid - plain - perspicuous -
palpable - lucid - explicit - ditinct -
crystalline - clear - overt

واژگون ساختن
/vâzhegun sâkhtan/ ► verb
subvert

واژگون سازی
/vâzhegunsâzi/ ► noun
reversal

واعظ
/vâ'ez/ ► noun
preacher

واژگون شدن
/vâzhegun shodan/ ► verb
capsize - purl

واغ واغ
/vâghvâgh/ ► noun
yip - yelp

واژگون کردن
/vâzhegun kardan/ ► verb
topple - upset - overturn - reverse

واغ واغ کردن
/vâghvâgh kardan/ ► verb
yelp

واکس
/vâks/ ► noun
shiner

واقع بودن
/vâghe' budan/ ► verb
stand

واکس زدن
/vâks zadan/ ► verb
polish

واقع بین
/vâghe'bin/ ► adjective
pragmatic

واکسن
/vâksan/ ► noun
vaccine

واقع گرایی
/vâghe'garâyi/ ► noun
realism

واکنش
/vâkonesh/ ► noun
response - repercussion - reflex -
rebound

واقعا
/vâghean/ ► adverb
quite - really

واگذار کردن
/vâgozâr kardan/ ► verb
transfer - yield - surrender - assign -
admit - abdicate - abandon

واقعه
/vâghe'e/ ► noun
event - rede - occurrence - incident

واگذاردن
/vâgozârdan/ ► verb
devolve - betake

واقعه ناگوار
/vâghe'ye nâgovâr/ ► noun
accident

واگذاری
/vâgozari/ ► noun
submission - bail - assignment -
abandonment - abandon

واقعی
/vâghe'i/ ► adjective
true - real - essential - literal - lifelike -
actual

واگن
/vâgon/ ► noun
wagon - car

واقف
/vâghef/ ► adjective
benefactor

واگیر

/vâgir/ ► noun
contagious - epidemic - infectious

واگیردار

/vâgirdâr/ ► adjective
zymotic - contagious

وال

/vâl/ ► noun
voile - whale

والا

/vâlâ/ ► adjective
sublime - prominent - grand - otherwise
- haughty

والامقام

/vâlâmaghâm/ ► adjective
eminent

والد

/vâled/ ► noun
father

والدین

/vâledein/ ► noun
parent

وام

/vâm/ ► noun
debt - loan

وام دادن

/vâm dâdan/ ► verb
lend

واماندگی

/vâmândegi/ ► noun
lag

وان

/vân/ ► noun
tub - bath

وانمود

/vânemud/ ► noun
pretension

واهی

/vâhi/ ► noun
airy - unsubstantial - unrealistic - unreal
- romantic

وبا

/vabâ/ ► noun
cholera

وتر

/vatar/ ► noun
hypotenuse

وثیقه

/vasighe/ ► noun
guaranty - guarantee - surety - security

وجب

/vajab/ ► noun
span - palm

وجب کردن
/vajab kardan/ ► verb
span

وجه
/vajh/ ► noun
payment

وجهه
/vejhe/ ► noun
phase

وجوب
/vojub/ ► noun
incumbency

وجود داشتن
/vojud dâshtan/ ► verb
be - exist

وحدت
/vahdat/ ► noun
unity - unification - oneness

وحشت
/vahshat/ ► noun
dread - fright - fray - horror - abhorrence
- awe - panic

وحشت آور
/vahshatâvar/ ► adjective
awesome - morbid - gruesome - terrible

وحشت زدگی
/vahshatzadegi/ ► noun
startle - dismay

وحشت زده
/vahshatzade/ ► adjective
aghast

وحشتناک
/vahshatnâk/ ► adjective
grisly - dreadful - bloodcurdling -
terrible

وحشی
/vahshi/ ► adjective
uncivilized - brutal - wild

وحشیانه
/vahshiyâne/ ► adverb
barbaric

وحشیگری
/vahshigari/ ► noun
savagery - vulgarity - brutality -
barbarism

وحی
/vah'y/ ► noun
vision - inspiration - oracle - revelation

وخیمتر
/vakhim/ ► adjective
worse

ودیعه
/vadi'e/ ► noun
trust

ورزیدگی
/varzidegi/ ► noun
experience - skill

ورشکست
/varshekast/ ► noun
broke

ورشکست شدن
/varshekast shodan/ ► verb
smash - bust

ورشکسته
/varshekaste/ ► adjective
broke - bankrupt

ورشو
/varshô/ ► noun
nickel

ورق
/varagh/ ► noun
sheet - leaf - card

ورق زدن
/varagh zadan/ ► verb
leaf - turnover

ورقه
/varaghe/ ► noun
layer - brede - paper

ورم
/varam/ ► noun
tumor - welt - dropsy - bunny - bulge - botch

وراثت
/verâsat/ ► noun
heredity - inheritance

وراج
/verâj/ ► adjective
talkative - chatty - loudmouthed - loquacious - blabbermouth - blabber

وراجی
/verâji/ ► noun
palaver - cackle - yack - jaw

وراجی کردن
/verâji kardan/ ► verb
rattle - verbalize - blab - yawp

ورد
/verd/ ► noun
abracadabra - jaber - slogan

ورزش
/varzesh/ ► noun
sport - practice - ploy - exercise

ورزشکار
/varzeshkâr/ ► adjective
gymnast - athletic - athlete - sportsman

ورزشی
/varzeshi/ ► noun
sporty - athletic

ورود

/vorud/ ▶ noun
entry - entree - entrance - arrival

وزیر

/vazir/ ▶ noun
queen

وریدی

/varidi/ ▶ noun
venous

وزین

/vazin/ ▶ adjective
weighty - heavy - ponderous

وزارت

/vezârat/ ▶ noun
ministry

وساطت

/vesâtat/ ▶ noun
agency - intermediary - intercession

وزارتخانه

/vezâratkhâne/ ▶ noun
ministry

وسایل

/vasâyel/ ▶ noun
utensil

وزش

/varzesh/ ▶ noun
blast - plunk - guff - whop - whiff

وسط

/vasat/ ▶ noun
amidst - amid - middling - meddle -
mediocre

وزغ

/vazagh/ ▶ noun
toad - frog

وسطی

/vasati/ ▶ noun
meddle - mid - median - medial - mean -
centric

وزن

/vazn/ ▶ noun
weight - scale

وسعت

/vos'at/ ▶ noun
extent - width - gamut - latitude

وزنه

/vazne/ ▶ noun
sinker

وسواس

/vasvâs/ ▶ noun
scape - scrupulosity - obsession -
whimsy - whim - maggot

وزیدن

/vazidan/ ▶ verb
puff - whiff - blow

وسوسه

/vasvase/ ▶ noun
temptation

وصلت

/vaslat/ ▶ noun
union

وسیع

/vasi'/ ▶ adjective
spacious - comprehensive - wide -
extensive - immense - vast

وصله

/vasle/ ▶ noun
splotch - patch - imp - inset - vamp

وسیع کردن

/vasi' kardan/ ▶ verb
broaden - enlarge - gum

وصول

/vosul/ ▶ noun
recovery

وسیله

/vasile/ ▶ noun
resource - instrument - handle -
appliance

وصی

/vasi/ ▶ noun
executor - administer

وصیت

/vasiyat/ ▶ noun
will

وسیله نقلیه

/vasileye naghliye/ ▶ noun
transport - steed - conveyance - vehicle

وصیت کردن

/vasiyat kardan/ ▶ verb
will

وصال

/vesâl/ ▶ noun
joiner

وصیت نامه

/vasiyatnâme/ ▶ noun
testament - devise - will

وصف

/vasf/ ▶ noun
description - picture

وضع

/vaz'/ ▶ noun
situation - setup - self - stick - status -
station

وصفی

/vasfi/ ▶ adjective
ordinal - descriptive - apposition -
adjective - adjectival

وضعیت

/vaz'iyat/ ▶ noun
status - situation - condition - position

وضوح
/vozuh/ ▶ noun
speciosity - lucidity - light - clarity

وفا
/vafâ/ ▶ noun
troth

وطن
/vatan/ ▶ noun
home - fatherland

وفا کردن
/vafâ kardan/ ▶ verb
adhere - abide

وظیفه
/vazife/ ▶ noun
duty - function - role - office -
obligation - work - assignment

وفات کردن
/vafâ kardan/ ▶ verb
pass

وفات نامه
/vafatnvafatnâme/ ▶ noun
epitaph

وظیفه داشتن
/vazife dâshtan/ ▶ verb
function

وفادار
/vafâdâr/ ▶ adjective
loyal - constant

وظیفه شناس
/vazifeshenâs/ ▶ adjective
loyal - conscientious - dutiful

وفاداری
/vafâdâri/ ▶ noun
troth - constancy - camaraderie - loyalty
- allegiance

وعده
/va'de/ ▶ noun
promise

وفاق
/vefâgh/ ▶ noun
consensus

وعده دادن
/va'de dâdan/ ▶ verb
invite

وفق
/vefgh/ ▶ noun
accordance

وعظ
/va'z/ ▶ noun
sermon

وعظ کردن
/va'z kardan/ ▶ verb
preach - admonish

وفق دادن
/vefgh dâdan/ ► verb
suit - reconcile - conform - attune -
assimilate - adjust - adapt - accord

وفور
/vofur/ ► adjective
opulence - wealth - bounty - affluence -
abundance

وقاحت
/veghâhat/ ► noun
obscenity

وقار
/vaghâr/ ► adjective
solemnity - serenity - poise - elegance -
dignity - gravity

وقت
/vaght/ ► noun
period - hour - time

وقت شناس
/vaghtshenâs/ ► adjective
punctual

وقتیکه
/vaghtike/ ► preposition
when

وقف
/vaghf/ ► noun
devotion

وقف کردن
/vaghf kardan/ ► verb
endow - devote - dedicate - amortize -
bequeath - avow

وقفه
/vaghfe/ ► noun
suspension - pause

وقوع
/voghu'/ ► noun
incidence - outbreak - occurrence - rede

وقوف
/voghuf/ ► noun
knowledge

وقیح
/vaghih/ ► adjective
hideous

وکالت
/vekâlat/ ► noun
deputation - attorney - agency -
advocacy - bar - proctorship

وکالت دادن
/vekâlat dâdan/ ► verb
empower - delegate

وکالتنامه
/vekâlatnâme/ ► noun
proxy

وکیل

/vakil/ ► noun
deputy - attorney - agent - lieutenant - proxy

وگرنه

/vagarna/ ► noun
otherwise

ول

/vel/ ► adjective
licentious - irresoluble - loose - baggy

ولایت

/velâyat/ ► noun
province

ولتاژ

/voltâzh/ ► noun
voltage

ولخرج

/velkharj/ ► adjective
spendthrift - profligate - wasteful

ولد

/valad/ ► noun
son

ولرم

/velarm/ ► adjective
lukewarm - tepid

ولگرد

/velgard/ ► adjective
swinger - stray - tramp - vagabond

ولی

/vali/ ► preposition
but

ولیعهد

/valiahd/ ► noun
prince

وهله

/vahle/ ► noun
stage - place - instance - heat - onset - occasion

وهم

/vahm/ ► noun
delusion - fiction - fancy - whim

ویترین

/vitrin/ ► noun
showcase - window

ویتنامی

/vietnâmi/ ► adjective
vietnamese

ویراستن

/virâstan/ ► verb
edit

ویران

/virân/ ► noun
subversive - ruinous - desolate

ویران کردن

/virân kardan/ ► verb
devastate - destroy - - ravage - ruinate

ویرانگر

/virângar/ ▶ adjective
ruinous - destroyer

ویلا

/vilâ/ ▶ noun
villa

ویرانه

/virâne/ ▶ adjective
ruin

ویرانی

/virâni/ ▶ noun
destruction - demolition - ravage -
ruination

ویرایش

/virâyesh/ ▶ noun
edition

ویروس

/virus/ ▶ noun
virus

ویزا

/vizâ/ ▶ noun
visa

ویزیتور

/vizitor/ ▶ noun
salesman

ویژگی

/vizhegi/ ▶ noun
trait

ویژه

/vizhe/ ▶ adjective
particular - peculiar - specific

ه ـه ـ ه

he /he/ ▶ thirty first letter of the Persian alphabet

هافبک

/hâfbak/ ▶ noun
halfback

هاگ

/hâg/ ▶ noun
spore

هاله

/hâle/ ▶ noun
corona - halo

ها

/hâ/ ▶ preposition
plural sign

هالو

/hâlu/ ▶ adjective
hallo

هادی

/hâdi/ ▶ adjective
polestar - ductile - guide

هامون

/hâmun/ ▶ noun
plain

هار

/hâr/ ▶ adjective
rabid

های

/hây/ ▶ preposition
hey

هارمونی

/hârmuni/ ▶ noun
harmony

هتاک

/hatâk/ ▶ adjective
irreverent

هاشور زدن

/hâshur zadan/ ▶ verb
hatch

هتاکی

/hatâki/ ▶ noun
affront

هاضمه

/hâzeme/ ▶ noun
digestive

هتل

/hotel/ ▶ noun
hostel

هجونامه
/hajv nâme/ ▶ noun
satire

هجی
/heji/ ▶ noun
spelling

هجی کردن
/heji kardan/ ▶ verb
spell

هدایت
/hedâyat/ ▶ noun
guidance - lead - steerage

هدایت کردن
/hedâyt kardan/ ▶ verb
steer - rede - direct - conduct - lead

هدف
/hadaf/ ▶ noun
target - purpose - goal - aim - parrot

هدف گیری
/hadafgiri/ ▶ noun
level

هدیه
/hediye/ ▶ noun
present - gift

هدیه دادن
/hediye dâdan/ ▶ verb
donate – gift

هجده
/hejdah/ ▶ noun
eighteen

هجدهم
/hejdahom/ ▶ adjective
eighteenth

هجدهمین
/hejdahomin/ ▶ adjective
eighteenth

هجو
/hajv/ ▶ noun
libel - lampoon

هجو کردن
/hajv kardan/ ▶ verb
satirize - lampoon

هجوآمیز
/hajv âmiz/ ▶ adjective
caustic

هجوم
/hojum/ ▶ noun
offense - invasion - inroad - influx - throng

هجوم آوردن
/hojum âvardan/ ▶ verb
swarm - scrouge - raid

هجوم بردن
/hojum bordan/ ▶ verb
rush

هذیان
/hazyân/ ▶ noun
delirium - maze

هراسیدن
/harâsidan/ ▶ preposition
apprehend

هر
/har/ ▶ preposition
any - every - each

هرجا
/harjâ/ ▶ adverb
anywhere - anyplace

هر آنکس
/harânkas/ ▶ adverb
whoever

هرجاکه
/harjâyike/ ▶ adverb
wherever

هر آنکه
/harânke/ ▶ adverb
whoever

هرچند
/harchand/ ▶ preposition
however

هر شب
/har shab/ ▶ adjective
nightly

هرچه
/harche/ ▶ adverb
whatsoever - whatever - whatever - what

هراس
/harâs/ ▶ noun
fright - feeze - panic - alarm

هرچیز
/harchiz/ ▶ adverb
apiece - anything - anyone

هراسان
/harâsân/ ▶ adjective
afraid

هردو
/hardo/ ▶ adjective
both

هراسانیدن
/harâsânidan/ ▶ verb
feeze - fray - affray

هرز
/harz/ ▶ adjective
weedy

هراسناک
/harâsnâk/ ▶ adjective
panicky

هرز دادن
/harz dâdan/ ▶ verb
waste

هرزگی

/harzegi/ ► noun
profligacy - incontinence - lechery -
depravity - debauchery - debauch

هرزه

/harze/ ► adjective
licentious - libertine - lewd - lascivious

هرس

/haras/ ► noun
recision

هرس کردن

/haras kardan/ ► verb
prune - lop - rogue

هرقدر

/har ghadr/ ► noun
whatsoever - whatever

هرقدرهم

/har ghadr ham/ ► preposition
however

هرکجا

/har kojâ/ ► adverb
where - anywhere

هرکجاکه

/har kojâke/ ► adverb
wherever

هرکدام

/har kodâm/ ► adverb
apiece

هرکدام که

/harkodâmke/ ► adverb
whichever

هرکس

/harkas/ ► adverb
anyone - everybody

هرکسی

/harkasi/ ► adverb
everybody

هرکسی که

/harkasike/ ► adverb
whoever

هرکه

/harke/ ► adverb
every - whoever

هرگز

/hargez/ ► adverb
ever - never

هرگونه

/hargune/ ► adverb
all

هروقت

/harvaght/ ► adverb
when

هروقت که

/harvaght ke/ ► adverb
whenever

هرويين
/hero'in/ ▶ noun
heroin

هستی
/hasti/ ▶ noun
existence - essence - reality - objectivity

هریک
/haryek/ ▶ adverb
each - apiece

هشت پا
/hashtpâ/ ▶ noun
octopus - devilfish

هزار
/hezâr/ ▶ noun
thousand

هشتاد
/hashtâd/ ▶ noun
eighty

هزل
/hazl/ ▶ noun
smut

هشتادم
/hashtâdom/ ▶ adjective
eightieth

هزیمت
/hazimat/ ▶ noun
defeat

هشتادمین
/hashtâdomin/ ▶ adjective
eightieth

هزینه
/mazine/ ▶ noun
expense - expenditure - disbursement -
cost

هشدار
/hoshdâr/ ▶ noun
alarm

هشدار دادن
/hoshdâr dâdan/ ▶ verb
warn

هژیر
/hazhir/ ▶ noun
praiseworthy

هست
/hast/ ▶ noun
existent

هشیار
/hoshyâr/ ▶ adjective
wary - wakeful

هسته
/haste/ ▶ noun
stone - kernel - nucleus - atom

هشیاری
/hoshyâri/ ▶ noun
watchful

هضم
/hazm/ ▶ noun
digestion

هفتمین
/haftomin/ ▶ adjective
seventh

هضم شدن
/hazm shodan/ ▶ verb
digest

هفته
/hafte/ ▶ noun
week

هضم کردن
/hazm kardan/ ▶ verb
digest

هکتار
/hektâr/ ▶ noun
hectare

هفت
/haft/ ▶ noun
seven

هل
/hol/ ▶ noun
jostle - push - shove - cardamom

هفتاد
/haftâd/ ▶ adjective
seventy - septuagenarian

هل دادن
/hol dâdan/ ▶ verb
poke - poach - hustle - hitch - haul -
shove - shoulder - push - yerk - jog

هفتادم
/haftâdom/ ▶ adjective
seventieth

هلالی
/helâli/ ▶ noun
embowed

هفتادمین
/haftâdomin/ ▶ adjective
seventieth - septuagenarian

هلند
/holand/ ▶ noun
Netherlands

هلندی
/holandi/ ▶ adjective
Holland

هفتگی
/haftegi/ ▶ noun
weekly

هلهله
/helhele/ ▶ noun
yell - jubilation

هفتم
/haftom/ ▶ adjective
seventh - seven

هلیکوپتر
/helikupter/ ▶ noun
helicopter

هم
/ham/ ▶ preposition
too - both - likewise - even

هم آورد
/hamâvard/ ▶ adjective
supplement - antagonist - adversary -
rival

هم پیمان
/hampeimân/ ▶ adjective
confederate - ally

هم تراز
/mantarâz/ ▶ adjective
yokefellow - justified - level

هم تراز کردن
/hamtarâz kardan/ ▶ verb
equal

هم چشمی
/hamcheshmi/ ▶ noun
competition - rival

هم دوره
/hamdore/ ▶ adjective
contemporary

هم قطار
/hamghatâr/ ▶ adjective
colleague

هم معنی
/ham mani/ ▶ adjective
synonymous - synonym - equivalent

هم میهن
/ham mihan/ ▶ adjective
patiot

هم نوا
/hamnavâ/ ▶ adjective
symphony - symphonic - unisonous

هم نوایی
/hamnavâyi/ ▶ noun
symphony

همان
/hamân/ ▶ adjective
same - very

همانا
/hamânâ/ ▶ adverb
certainly - indeed

همانند
/hamânand/ ▶ noun
similar - alike - like - equal

هماوایی
/hamâvâyi/ ▶ noun
unison

همایش
/hamâyesh/ ▶ noun
congress

همدردی

/hamdardi/ ▶ noun
pity - condolence - sympathy

همایون

/homâyun/ ▶ noun
imperial - august

همدست

/hamdast/ ▶ adjective
complier - cooperator - associate - aid -
accomplice - partner - pal

همبازی

/hambâzi/ ▶ noun
playmate

همدستی

/hamdasti/ ▶ noun
cooperation - pally - assistance

همبستگی

/hambastegi/ ▶ noun
adhesion - correlation - solidarity

همدم

/hamdam/ ▶ adjective
jo - comate - cahoot - mate - billy

همتا

/hamtâ/ ▶ noun
counterpart - match

همدم شدن

/hamdam shodan/ ▶ verb
associate

همچنان

/hamchenân/ ▶ adverb
so - likewise - like

همراه

/hamrâh/ ▶ noun
participant - attendant - along - escort

همچنانکه

/hamchenânke/ ▶ adverb
as

همراهان

/hamrâhân/ ▶ noun
suite - attendance - entourage - retinue

همچنین

/hamchenin/ ▶ adverb
too - also - eke

همراهی

/hamrâhi/ ▶ noun
companionship - camaraderie

همچون

/hamchon/ ▶ adverb
like

همراهی کردن

/hamrâhi kardan/ ▶ verb
squire - accompany - accompany –
companion

همدرد

/hamdard/ ▶ adjective
sympathetic

همصدا

/hamsedâ/ ▶ adjective
homophone

همرتبه

/ham martabe/ ▶ adjective
equal

همصدایی

/hamsedâyi/ ▶ noun
consonance - assonance - unison

همزاد

/hamzâd/ ▶ noun
double

همفکری

/hamfekri/ ▶ noun
sympathy

همزمان

/hamzamân/ ▶ adjective
simultaneous - simultaneity - synchronic

همکار

/hamkâr/ ▶ noun
colleague

همزمانی

/mahzamâni/ ▶ noun
simultaneity

همکاری

/hamkâri/ ▶ noun
solidarity - assist - cooperation

همساز

/hamsâz/ ▶ adjective
accommodate

همکلاس

/hamkelâs/ ▶ noun
classmate

همسان

/hamsân/ ▶ adjective
isotope

همگان

/hamegân/ ▶ noun
public - general

همسر

/hamsar/ ▶ noun
partner - associate - consort - fere -
spouse

همگانی

/hamegâni/ ▶ noun
universal - communal - general - public

همسفر

/hamsafar/ ▶ noun
outfit

همگن

/hamgen/ ▶ adjective
equal

همشهری

/hamshahri/ ▶ noun
townsman

همگی

/hamegi/ ► noun
altogether - all

همنام

/hamnâm/ ► adjective
namesake

همنوایی

/hamnavâyi/ ► noun
conformity

همنوایی کردن

/hamnavâyi kardan/ ► verb
conform

همه

/hame/ ► adjective
all - every - whole

همه پرسی

/hameporsi/ ► noun
referendum - plebiscite

همه جا

/hamejâ/ ► adjective
overall

همه چیز

/hamechiz/ ► adjective
all - everything

همه ساله

/hamesâle/ ► adjective
perennial

همه کاره

/hamekâre/ ► adjective
jack of all trades

همهمه

/hamhame/ ► noun
tumult - ruckus - uproar - buzz

همهمه کردن

/hamhame kardan/ ► verb
hum

هموار

/hamvâr/ ► adjective
smooth - flat - even - plane - plain -
level

هموار کردن

/hamvâr kardan/ ► verb
even - grade - shim

همیشه

/hamishe/ ► adverb
always

همینطور

/hamintor/ ► adverb
also - so

همینقدر

/haminghadr/ ► adverb
so

هنجار

/hanjâr/ ► noun
norm

هندبال

/handbâl/ ▶ noun
handball

هندسی

/hendesi/ ▶ noun
numeral

هندل

/hendel/ ▶ noun
winch

هندوانه

/hendevâne/ ▶ noun
melon - watermelon

(با یک دست دو هندوانه برداشتن :Idiom
Bite off more than you can chew)

هندوستان

/hendustân/ ▶ noun
India

هندی

/hendi/ ▶ adjective
Indian

هنر

/honar/ ▶ noun
artifice - art - accomplishment - mystery
- craft

هنرپیشه

/honarpishe/ ▶ noun
player - artist - actor – craftsman

هنرستانی

/honarestâni/ ▶ noun
vocation

هنرشناس

/honarshenâs/ ▶ noun
virtuoso

هنرکده

/honarkade/ ▶ noun
studio

هنرمند

/honarmand/ ▶ adjective
handicraft - virtuoso - artist - craftsman

هنرور

/honarvar/ ▶ adjective
artist - mechanic

هنگ

/hang/ ▶ noun
legion

هنگام

/hengâm/ ▶ noun
term - season - moment - during

هنگامه

/hengâme/ ▶ noun
scrimmage - tumult - uproar - rumpus

هنگامیکه

/hengâmike/ ▶ preposition
while - whenever

هواسنج

/havâsanj/ ▶ noun
barometer

هنگفت

/hengoft/ ▶ noun
large - enormous - great

هواشناس

/havâshenâs/ ▶ noun
weatherman

هنوز

/hanuz/ ▶ noun
still - yet - never&eless - however

هوانوردی

/havânavardi/ ▶ noun
aviation

هو کردن

/hô kardan/ ▶ verb
jeer - hoot

هوایی

/havâyi/ ▶ noun
pneumatic - atmospheric - airy - aerial

هوا

/havâ/ ▶ noun
weather - air

هوس

/havas/ ▶ noun
fancy - whimsy - whim - libido -
heartthrob

هوابرد

/havâbord/ ▶ noun
airborne

هواپیما

/havâpeimâ/ ▶ noun
plane - airplane - aircraft - aeroplane

هوس آمیز

/havasâmiz/ ▶ adjective
chimerical

هواخواه

/havâkhâh/ ▶ adjective
zealous - devotee - enthusiast - disciple -
votary

هوسباز

/havasbâz/ ▶ adjective
capricious

هواخواهی

/havâkhâhi/ ▶ noun
zealotry - devotion - adherence

هوسران

/havasrân/ ▶ adjective
swinger

هوادار

/havâdâr/ ▶ adjective
pneumatic

هوشمند

/hushmand/ ▶ adjective
sagacious - intelligent

هوشمندی
/hushmandi/ ► noun
sagacity

هیبت
/heibat/ ► noun
solemnity - awe

هوشیار
/hushyâr/ ► adjective
sober - cautious - observant - conscious
- astute - alert - vigilant

هیجان
/hayejân/ ► noun
tornado - thrill - fit - dither - unco - boil
- lather - ignition

هوشیار بودن
/hushyâr budan/ ► verb
sober

هیجان انگیز
/hayejânangiz/ ► adjective
rapturous

هولناک
/hôlnâk/ ► adjective
ghastly - terrific - terrible

هیجانی
/hayejâni/ ► adjective
emotion

هوی و هوس
/havâ va havas/ ► noun
vagary - whim

هیجده
/hijdah/ ► noun
eighteen

هویت
/hoviyat/ ► noun
identity - personality

هیچ
/hich/ ► adverb
zero - nothing - none

هویدا
/hoveidâ/ ► noun
eminent - eidetic - obvious

هی
/hei/ ► preposition
hey - hallo - gee

هیچ چیز
/hich chiz/ ► adverb
anything

هیچکدام
/hichkodâm/ ► adverb
none

هیاهو
/hayâhu/ ► noun
hubbub - explosion - commotion –
ruckus

هیچکس

/hichkas/ ▶ adverb
nobody

هیچگاه

/hichgâh/ ▶ adverb
never

هیچگونه

/hichgune/ ▶ adverb
any - whatsoever

هیچیک

/hichyek/ ▶ adverb
none - neither- nor

هیزم

/hizom/ ▶ noun
wood

هیزم شکن

/hizomshekan/ ▶ noun
woodman - woodcutter - woodchopper

هیس

/his/ ▶ noun
shush - goose

هیکل

/heikal/ ▶ noun
physique - person - statue

هیولا

/hayulâ/ ▶ noun
monstrous - monstrosity - monster

ی - يـ

ye /ye/ ▶ thirty second letter of the Persian alphabet

یا

/yâ/ ▶ preposition
or

یاالله

/yâ al'lâh/ ▶ noun
hallo

یابو

/yâbu/ ▶ noun
tit - nag - workhorse

یاخته

/yâkhte/ ▶ noun
cell

یاد

/yâd/ ▶ noun
memory

یاد آوردن

/yâd âvardan/ ▶ verb
remember

یاد کردن

/yâd kardan/ ▶ verb
reminisce

یاد گرفتن

/yâd gereftan/ ▶ verb
learn

یادآور

/yâdâvar/ ▶ adjective
memento - reminiscent - reminder

یادآوری

/yâdâvari/ ▶ noun
mention - reminiscence - reminder -
remembrance

یادبود

/vâdbud/ ▶ noun
souvenir - token - memory - memorial -
reminiscent - reminiscence

یادداشت

/yâdâsht/ ▶ noun
notation - reminiscence - record - chit -
minute - memorandum - memoir

یادداشت کردن

/yâdâsht kardan/ ▶ verb
note

یادگار

/yâdegâr/ ▶ noun
souvenir - token - memory - memorial -
relic

یادگاری

/yâdegâri/ ▶ noun
remembrance - memento - token

یار

/yâr/ ▶ noun
friend - partner - helpmate - helper

یاغی گری

/yâghigari/ ▶ noun
muitiny

یارو

/yâru/ ▶ noun
party - guy - skate

یاغی گری کردن

/yâghigari kardan/ ▶ verb
rebel

یاری

/yâri/ ▶ noun
help - aid - companionship

یافتن

/yâftan/ ▶ verb
discover - meet

یاری کردن

/yâri kardan/ ▶ verb
aid - help - succor

یاقوت

/yâghut/ ▶ noun
ruby

یاری نمودن

/yâri nemudan/ ▶ verb
help

یاور

/bâvar/ ▶ adjective
assistant - assist - aid - adjutant - helper

یازده

/yâzdah/ ▶ noun
eleven

یاوه

/yâve/ ▶ noun
tattle - nonsense - babble - absurd

یاس

/yâs/ ▶ noun
letdown - despair

یاوه سرایی

/yâvesarâyi/ ▶ noun
rant

یاسمن

/yâsaman/ ▶ noun
gardenia

یاوه گفتن

/yâve goftan/ ▶ verb
babble

یاغی

/yâghi/ ▶ adjective
turbulent - rebel - mutinous - malcontent

یایسگی

/yâ'isegi/ ▶ noun
menopause

یدکی
/yadaki/ ▶ adjective
extra - reserve - refill - spare

یبوست
/yobusat/ ▶ noun
irregularity

یراق
/yarâgh/ ▶ noun
trapping - stripe

یتیم
/yatim/ ▶ adjective
orphan

یرقان
/yaraghân/ ▶ noun
jaundice

یتیم خانه
/yatimkhâne/ ▶ noun
asylum - orphanage

یزدان
/yazdân/ ▶ noun
god

یخ
/yakh/ ▶ noun
ice

یشمی
/yashmi/ ▶ adjective
jaspery

یخ بستن
/yakh bastan/ ▶ verb
ice - congeal - freeze

یعنی
/ya'ni/ ▶ noun
nee - namely - innuendo

یخ زدگی
/yakhzadegi/ ▶ noun
rime - freeze

یفما
/yaghmâ/ ▶ noun
spoil - sack - booty - plunder - pillage -
despoliation - ravage

یخچال
/yakhchâl/ ▶ noun
icebox - refrigerator

یخدان
/yakhdân/ ▶ noun
chest

یفماگر
/yaghmâgar/ ▶ adjective
predatory

یدک
/yadak/ ▶ noun
trailer

یقه
/yaghe/ ▶ noun
collar

یقین

/yaghin/ ► noun
sure - positive - certitude - certainty

یک

/yek/ ► noun
one - an

یک جا

/yekjâ/ ► noun
together

یک جانبه

/yekjânebe/ ► noun
unilateral

یک درمیان

/yekdarmiyân/ ► noun
alternate

یک دنده

/yekdande/ ► adjective
strict

(Idiom: یک دنده و کله شق بودن
Be a hard nut to crack)

یک صدا

/yeksedâ/ ► noun
univocal

یک صدایی

/yeksedâyi/ ► noun
unison

یک طرفه

/yektarafe/ ► adjective
sideway

یک لا

/yeklâ/ ► adjective
unifilar

یک نواخت

/yeknavâkht/ ► adjective
singsong - level

یک وری

/yekvari/ ► noun
lopsided - sidle

یکباردیگر

/yekbâre digar/ ► noun
again - once

یکپا

/yekpâ/ ► noun
unipod

یکتا

/yektâ/ ► adjective
alone - unique

یکتاپرست

/yektâparast/ ► adjective
unitary - unitarian

یکجور

/yekjur/ ► noun
homogeneous - alike

یکنوا
/yeknavâ/ ► adjective
univocal

یکدنده
/yekdande/ ► adjective
adamant - dogged

یکنواخت کردن
/yeknavâkht kardan/ ► verb
uniform

یکسان
/yeksân/ ► noun
equal - alike - akin - similar - same

یکنواختی
/yeknavâkhti/ ► noun
tedium - humdrum - monotony -
uniformity

یکسره
/yeksare/ ► noun
indiscriminate - hipandthigh - altogether
- all - nonstop

یکه تاز
/yeketâz/ ► adjective
totalitarian

یکسو
/yeksu/ ► adjective
away

یکه خوردن
/yeke khordan/ ► verb
upstart

یکشنبه
/yekshanbe/ ► noun
sabbath - sunday

یکی
/yeki/ ► verb
one

یکطرفه
/yektarafe/ ► adjective
overhand - unilateral

یگان
/yegân/ ► noun
unitage - unit

یکم
/yekom/ ► adjective
first

یگانگی
/yegânegi/ ► noun
oneness - marriage - unity - unification

یکماهه
/yekmâhe/ ► adjective
monthly

یگانه
/yegâne/ ► adjective
sole - only - one - unique

یکمرتبه
/yekmartabe/ ► adjective
short - ensemble - once

يهودی
/yahudi/ ► adjective
hebrew - jewish - jew

يواش
/yavâsh/ ► adjective
slow

يواشکی
/yavâshaki/ ► noun
stealthy

يورتمه
/yurtme/ ► noun
trot

يورتمه رفتن
/yurtme raftan/ ► verb
trot

يورش
/yuresh/ ► noun
pash - attack - assault - pounce - rush -
raid - onslaught - onrush - offensive

يورش بردن
/yuresh bordan/ ► verb
push

يوزپلنگ
/yuzpalang/ ► noun
panther

يوغ
/yugh/ ► noun
yoke

يوم
/yôm/ ► noun
day

يونان
/yunân/ ► noun
Greece

يونانی
/yunâni/ ► adjective
Greek

يونجه
/yonje/ ► noun
alfalfa

يويو
/yôyô/ ► noun
yoyo

ييلاق
/yeilâgh/ ► noun
country – summer

Other Books

of Interest

Learn Farsi in 100 Days

The Ultimate Crash Course to Learning Farsi Fast

The goal of this book is simple. It will help you incorporate the best method and the right strategies to learn Farsi FAST and EFFECTIVELY.

Learn Farsi in 100 days helps you learn speak Farsi faster than you ever thought possible. You only need to spend about 90-120 minutes daily in your 100-day period in order to learn Farsi language at advanced level. Whether you are just starting to get in touch the Farsi language, or even if you have already learned the basics of the language, this book can help you accelerate the learning process and put you on the right track.

Learn Farsi in 100 days is for Farsi learners from the beginning to the advanced level. It is a breakthrough in Farsi language learning — offering a winning formula and the most powerful methods for learning to speak Farsi fluently and confidently. Each contains 4 pages covering a comprehensive range of topics. Each day includes vocabulary, grammar, reading and writing lessons. It gives learners easy access to the Farsi vocabulary and grammar as it is actually used in a comprehensive range of everyday life situations and it teaches students to use Farsi for situations related to work, social life, and leisure. Topics such as greetings, family, weather, sports, food, customs, etc. are presented in interesting unique ways using real-life information.

Purchase on Amazon website:

https://goo.gl/eG2n11

Published By:

LearnPersianOnline.com

Farsi Conversations
Learn the Most Common Words
and Phrases Farsi Speakers use Every Day

Learning about a new culture is always an exciting prospect and one of the best ways to get to know about another country, its people and their customs, is to learn the language.

Now, with Farsi Conversations: Learn the Most Common Words and Phrases Farsi Speakers use Every Day you can learn how to communicate in Farsi and learn more about Persian culture at the same time.

In this unique guide, you will be able to practice your spoken Farsi with FREE YouTube videos. It is an ideal tool for learners of Farsi at all levels, whether at school, in evening classes or at home, and is a 'must have' for business or leisure.

Farsi students can learn;

- How to use the right language structures and idioms in the right context
- Practice Farsi vocabulary and phrases needed in everyday situations
- Gain proficiency in written and spoken Farsi
- New ways of mastering Farsi phrases

By the end of the book you will have learned more than 2500 Farsi words, have mastered more than 300 commonly used Farsi verbs, key expressions and phrases and be able to pose more than 800 questions.

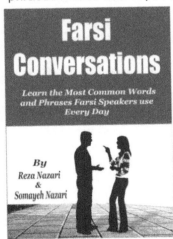

Purchase on Amazon website:

https://goo.gl/bGpVNZ

Published By:
LearnPersianOnline.com

Learn to Speak Persian Fast: For Beginners

Learn to Speak Persian Fast is a multi-level series for Persian learners from the beginning to the advanced level. It is a breakthrough in Persian language learning — offering a winning formula and the most powerful methods for learning to speak Persian fluently and confidently. Each book provides 10 chapters covering a comprehensive range of topics. Each chapter includes vocabulary, grammar, reading and writing lessons. There is a series of exercises that gives you extra practice in using new concepts and inspires you to construct personalized conversations.

Book 1 of *Learn to Speak Persian Fast* series is designed for beginning students needing a comprehensive, slow-paced arrangement of basic pronunciation, grammar structures, and vocabulary. It gives learners easy access to the Persian vocabulary and grammar as it is actually used in a comprehensive range of everyday life situations and it teaches students to use Persian for situations related to work, social life, and leisure. Topics such as greetings, family, weather, sports, food, customs, etc. are presented in interesting unique ways using real-life information. Beautiful illustrations enable students learn vocabulary and grammar lessons effectively.

The Only Book to Master Persian Language!

Purchase on Amazon website:

https://goo.gl/XQJ37D

Published By:

LearnPersianOnline.com

Learn to Speak Persian Fast: For Intermediate

Learn to Speak Persian Fast is a multi-level series for Persian learners from the beginning to the advanced level. It is a breakthrough in Persian language learning — offering a winning formula and the most powerful methods for learning to speak Persian fluently and confidently. Each book provides 10 chapters covering a comprehensive range of topics. Each chapter includes vocabulary, grammar, reading and writing lessons. There is a series of exercises that gives you extra practice in using new concepts and inspires you to construct personalized conversations.

Book 2 of *Learn to Speak Persian Fast* series builds on the foundations established in the book one for smooth and accurate communication in Persian. It is designed for intermediate students needing a comprehensive approach to learn grammar structures and vocabulary. It gives learners easy access to the Persian vocabulary and grammar as it is actually used in a comprehensive range of everyday life situations and it teaches students to use Persian for situations related to work, social life, and leisure. Topics such as weather, sports, transportation, customs, etc. are presented in interesting unique ways using real-life information. Beautiful illustrations enable students learn vocabulary and grammar lessons effectively.

The Only Book to Master Persian Language!

Purchase on Amazon website:

https://goo.gl/68p476

Published By:

LearnPersianOnline.com

Farsi Grammar in Use

For Beginners
An Easy-to-Use Guide with Clear Rules and Real-World Examples

Farsi Grammar in Use is an entertaining guide to Farsi grammar and usage. This user-friendly resource includes simple explanations of grammar and useful examples to help students of all ages improve their Farsi.

Farsi Grammar in Use is written for students who find the subjects unusually difficult and confusing -or in many cases, just plain boring. It doesn't take a lifetime to master Farsi grammar. All it takes is Farsi Grammar in Use. Filled with clear examples and self-assessment quizzes, this is one of the most highly trusted Farsi language resources available.

Farsi Grammar in Use is the only grammar Book You'll ever need! It can be used as a self-study course - you do not need to work with a teacher. (It can also be used with a teacher). You don't even need to know a little Farsi before starting.

Purchase on Amazon website:

https://goo.gl/0fFyll

Published By:
Learn**Persian**Online.com

Top 1,500 Persian Words

Essential Words for Communicating in Persian

Designed as a quick reference and study guide, this reference book provides easy-to-learn lists of the most relevant Persian vocabulary. Arranged by 36 categories, these word lists furnish the reader with an invaluable knowledge of fundamental vocabulary to comprehend, read, write and speak Persian.

Top 1,500 Persian Words is intended to teach the essentials of Persian quickly and effectively. The common words are organized to enable the reader to handle day-to-day situations. Words are arranged by topic, such as Family, Jobs, weather, numbers, countries, sports, common verbs, etc. A phonetic pronunciation accompanies each word.

With daily practice, you can soon have a working vocabulary in Persian!

The book "*Top 1,500 Persian Words*" is incredibly useful for those who want to learn Persian language **quickly** and **efficiently.**

Top 1,500
Persian Words

Essential Words for
Communicating
in Persian

Reza Nazari

Learn Most Common Persian Words FAST!

Purchase on Amazon website:

https://goo.gl/YvhpKe

Published By:

LearnPersianOnline.com

200 Absolutely Essential Persian Verbs

200 Essential Persian Verbs is the only reference you need to master Persian most common verbs. This book will help you learn verb conjugating, usage, phrasal verbs, and even the roots of verbs, both present and past.

This book is not just another reference list of verbs. It shows the depth of variation and irregularity among Persian verbs, and it groups similar verbs together to make the patterns behind them easier to learn. Verbs in this book are arranged from least popular to most.

Inside you'll find:

- 200 most common Persian verbs, their meanings and pronunciation guide.
- Synonyms and Antonyms listed for each of the model Persian verbs.
- Hundreds of example sentences showing verbs in action.
- An easy-to-use format for both quick reference and in-depth study.

Purchase on Amazon website:

https://goo.gl/9IqS6J

Published By:

LearnPersianOnline.com

Persia Club Dictionary Farsi - English (Persian Edition)

Designed for people interested in learning standard Farsi, this comprehensive dictionary of the Farsi-English languages contains more than 12,000 entries and definitions as well as pronunciation guides, word types, Current phrases, slang, idioms, scientific terms and other features.

The Dictionary is fully updated with the latest lexical content. It's a unique database that offers the fullest, most accurate picture of the Farsi language today. Hundreds of new words cover technology, computing, ecology, and many other subjects.

• A comprehensive Farsi - English dictionary
• Fully updated with the latest lexical content
• Offers more than 12,000 Farsi entries
• A unique database that offers the fullest, most accurate picture of the Farsi language today
• Contains pronunciation guides, word types, slangs, idioms, scientific terms and other features
• Hundreds of new words cover technology, computing, ecology, and many other subjects.

An excellent reference resource for Persian learners to have on-hand!

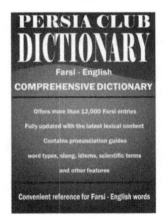

The Best Persian - English Dictionary!

Purchase on Amazon website:

 https://goo.gl/ofHCF8

Published By:

LearnPersianOnline.com

Easy Persian Phrasebook

Essential Expressions for Communicating in Persian

Designed as a quick reference and study guide, this comprehensive phrasebook offers guidance for situations including traveling, accommodations, healthcare, emergencies and other common circumstances. A phonetic pronunciation accompanies each phrase and word.

Easy Persian Phrasebook is designed to teach the essentials of Persian quickly and effectively. The common words and phrases are organized to enable the reader to handle day to day situations. The book should suit anyone who needs to get to grips quickly with Persian, such as tourists and business travelers.

The book "*Easy Persian Phrasebook*" is incredibly useful for those who want to learn Persian language quickly and efficiently.

You'll be surprised how fast you master the first steps in learning Persian, this beautiful language!

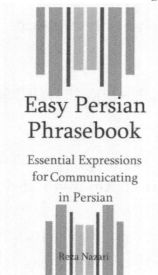

Purchase on Amazon website:

 https://goo.gl/d21Ivg

Published By:

LearnPersianOnline.com

Persian for Travel

English - Persian Travel Phrases:
Start Speaking Persian Today!

This Book is for people who need to be able to communicate confidently and effectively when travelling. Typical situations covered are: at an airport, checking into a hotel, seeing a doctor, booking tickets and changing arrangements.

The emphasis is on understanding authentic Persian; on practicing the structures necessary to ask questions and check information and on extracting information from brochures, regulations and instructions. Vocabulary is clearly illustrated in context, and American English variants are provided.

"*Persian for Travel*" effortlessly teaches all the essential phrases you'll need to know before your trip. This book can be used as a self-study course - you do not need to work with a teacher. (It can also be used with a teacher). You don't even need to know a little Farsi before starting.

Purchase on Amazon website:

https://goo.gl/PMfdPL

Published By:

Learn**Persian** Online.com

   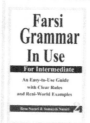 

"learn Persian Online" Publications

Learn Persian Online authors' team strives to prepare and publish the best quality Persian Language learning resources to make learning Persian easier for all. We hope that our publications help you learn this lovely language in an effective way.

Please let us know how your studies turn out. We would like to know what part of our books worked for you and how we can make these books better for others. You can reach us via email at info@learnpersianonline.com

We all in Learn Persian Online wish you good luck and successful studies!

Learn Persian Online Authors

Best Persian Learning Books

Published By:
LearnPersianOnline.com

Learn to Speak Persian Online

Enjoy interactive Persian lessons on Skype with the best native speaking Persian teachers

Online Persian Learning that's Effective, Affordable, Flexible, and Fun.

Learn Persian wherever you want; when you want

Ultimate flexibility. You can now learn Persian online via Skype, enjoy high quality engaging lessons no matter where in the world you are. It's affordable too.

Learn Persian With One-on-One Classes

We provide one-on-one Persian language tutoring online, via Skype. We believe that one-to-one tutoring is the most effective way to learn Persian.

Qualified Native Persian Tutors

Working with the best Persian tutors in the world is the key to success! Our Persian tutors give you the support & motivation you need to succeed with a personal touch.

It's easy! Here's how it works

Request a FREE introductory session
Meet a Persian tutor online via Skype
Start speaking Real Persian in Minutes

Send Email to: info@LearnPersianOnline.com

Or Call: + 1-469-230-3605

Made in the USA
Las Vegas, NV
29 September 2024

95979613R00398